A GENETIC HISTORY OF THE NEW ENGLAND THEOLOGY

A Genetic History of the New England Theology

By

FRANK HUGH FOSTER

NEW YORK

RUSSELL & RUSSELL · INC

1963

FIRST PUBLISHED IN 1907
REISSUED, 1963, BY RUSSELL & RUSSELL, INC.
L. C. CATALOG CARD NO: 63—12564
PRINTED IN THE UNITED STATES OF AMERICA

PREFACE

The following work—suggested by the professional obligations of a professor of church history; continued and at last completed under a sense of pious duty toward the great men who toiled to hand down to their posterity an undiminished and perfected system of doctrinal truth; necessarily the fruit of long labors, interrupted by other engagements, but resumed and completed when opportunity has offered—is now presented to the public. It has been written directly from the sources. The selection of material has been determined by the purpose to write a genetic history, and not a mere record of opinions, however interesting they might be in themselves. By the aid of great libraries, above all that of Harvard University, from which I have received hundreds of tracts for examination, but also of that in the Congregational House, of the Massachusetts Historical Society, the Athenaeum, the Boston Public Library, and the libraries in Union Theological Seminary, New York, in Oberlin and Olivet Colleges, and in Andover and Pacific Theological Seminaries, it has been possible to examine all the important sources. Acknowledgments are hereby made to the publishers of the *American Journal of Theology* and of the *Bibliotheca Sacra* for permission to use matter which had already appeared in their pages. There have been no predecessors in this particular line of study of our theology from whom I could draw; but I take the opportunity to acknowledge my indebtedness to the late Professors Gottfried Thomasius, of Erlangen, for my conception of historical method, and Edwards A. Park, of Andover, for much help of a historical character, both personal and through his historical writings, as well as for

v

the dogmatic point of view of the whole period. Professor
George P. Fisher has afforded a splendid example of
scientific treatment of our theology in his historical articles,
by which he became the pioneer and unsurpassed chief of
American dogmatic history. And to ease and success in
discovering and handling the vast apparatus which has
passed under my eye, the marvelous bibliography of the
great historian of Congregational polity, Dr. Henry M.
Dexter, has contributed indispensable aid. Some considerable additions to Dr. Dexter's lists will be found in the
notes to the following text.

Descendant of Puritan and Pilgrim as I am, born and
baptized in one of our most ancient Massachusetts churches,
trained at our oldest university, and taught my profession
at the center of intensest interest in "the New England
theology," it would be strange if I had not begun this history
with a feeling of the warmest appreciation of our New England Fathers and a conviction that they had originated a
school destined, under whatever changes, to the exercise of
a long-extended influence. These sentiments are reflected
upon the earlier pages of the book in many a phrase which
I have left standing. With the progress of the work my
point of view and my feeling have changed together. The
final historical review of the whole period has made me
a critic of the school and its work, and led me to the perception of a fact that was long hidden from me—that it
was not without reason that a strong reaction set in against
this theology about the year 1880. I find myself no longer
reckonable to its adherents. But all the more does it seem
to me important to learn from this great movement the
lessons it has to teach the present time and all the future, to
appropriate its good and to avoid its evil. And, certainly,
no American theological scholar can claim to understand
the course of religious thought among us, who has not

made himself familiar with this greatest indigenous school of American theology.

The chief peculiarity of the style of the book is the large use made of quotation from the authors discussed. My object has been, not merely to secure thereby the true objectivity of the report I have given, but also, in the certainty that very few of my readers will have access to the originals, to give them an acquaintance at first hand, though brief, with these pioneers and fathers of our theology.

So I send out the book; and to the historian's commendation I add the dogmatician's exhortation: Prove all things; hold fast that which is true.

F. H. F.

TABLE OF CONTENTS

THE DEVELOPING SCHOOL

THE GREAT CONTROVERSIES

THE RIPENED PRODUCT

THE HISTORICAL BACKGROUND

INTRODUCTION

Among the great events of the eighteenth century was the rise, in an obscure corner of the civilized world, of a new school of theology. The place was southwestern New England, the region fed intellectually and spiritually by the recently founded Yale College. The leaders were natives of New England, of the pure English stock, educated for the most part at Yale—parish ministers in small villages and hamlets, and occasionally missionaries upon the near frontier, practical religious leaders who were stimulated to constructive thought by definite religious necessities in their own charges. One might have thought that a movement so originating and in such a place, far from the great centers of thought and the great accumulations of scholarly material, led by men indifferently trained, could never be of interest to the Christian world beyond. But New England was destined in the divine providence to become the principal element in the development of a great nation; and the theological movement begun by Jonathan Edwards when he preached his sermons upon "Justification by Faith" in Northampton, in 1734, acquired an importance for the whole Christian civilization when it became the molding force of a great part of the constructive religious work done in the United States of America. For this was its future. It became the dominating school of thought in New England Congregationalism, and this denomination took the initiative in the greatest forward movements of American Christianity in all its formative years. In foreign missions, in home missions, in the founding and equipping of theological seminaries, in the planting of colleges, in revivals, in denominational co-operation, Congregationalism, during the period of the supremacy in

3

its midst of the Edwardean theology, took the unquestioned lead among American churches. Its practical labors grew directly out of its theology, just as its theology grew directly out of its practical problems. Thus the obscure fountain widened into the mighty stream.

In its wider relations and its deepest sources this movement is not to be fully comprehended unless it is put in its place among the religious movements of the whole Protestant world. However prominent it may be in American thought, it is but one of the movements which have begun here. American history is in many respects unique. For the first time since the church passed out from the freedom which its obscurity and weakness had given it into the light of publicity and under the yoke of the state, in the time of Constantine, it has found in America an opportunity on a large scale to develop its thought and to form its life under the unconstrained operation of its own inherent forces. At the same time a multitude of problems of the most weighty kind have been presented to it. It has not only had a new country to subdue, repeating thus in some respects the problem which Rome had to attempt after the beginning of the German migrations, but it has had conditions to meet which have sprung from the rise of a new civilization largely made by itself and then brought into conflict with the older civilizations of Europe as maintained by myriads of immigrants. While its problems have been chiefly practical, their solution has reacted upon the formation of doctrine. Far from hindering the modification of theology or the attainment of new views of truth, this attention to the practical has favored change and progress. Indeed, such has always been the case. It was the vigorous life of the early church that made its doctrinal productivity so great. The rise of the missionary orders and the development of Scholasticism in the Middle Ages were two phases of the same vital growth. The Reformation, which was first of all a movement in the sphere of life, was also productive of the greatest development of systematic thought which the church has seen in any one age. It has therefore been in perfect conformity to the law operating elsewhere that multitudes of speculations have arisen in America, resulting sometimes in the creation of new ecclesiastical communions, sometimes in the development of heresies, sometimes merely in the formation of distinct theological schools. Some have perpetuated themselves to the present day; many have perished after having contributed their portion to the influences, good or bad, which are forming the religious life of the nation. And such is doubtless to be the course of things through a long period, the end of which is far beyond the limits of vision.

But the relations of New England theology are not exclusively, or even principally, to other currents of thought in America. The Reformation united the great nations of the Teutonic family which it took out of the fold of Rome by a community of interests, not only political and religious, but also theological. The same currents of thought flow successively through them all. The same cycle of intellectual events recurs in each. Even the periods are remarkably coterminous. Internal forces of similar character in some cases, in others the direct influence of thought communicated by all the methods by which men exert influence upon one another, lead to similar results. Differences of language and customs are not able to prevent this. Remoteness and rarity of communication do not destroy it. Ties of blood and intimate political relations serve only to facilitate it. The channels of communication, like subterranean streams, it may sometimes be impossible to trace. The whole phenomenon depends upon and illustrates the fundamental unity of Protestantism amid all its superficial diversity.

Thus, the Reformation in Germany as a constructive period may be said to have been brought to a close by the compilation of the "Formula of Concord" in 1577. Upon construction always follows systematization, and the next period was that of the scholastic Lutheran orthodoxy, the natural course of which was interrupted by the Thirty Years' War, which brought in its train great religious demoralization and theological deadness. Pietism, which began with Spener's *Collegia Pietatis* in 1670, was an unsuccessful attempt to revive the national spiritual life, and resulted in scarcely anything more than helping to introduce the rationalistic movement, which began about 1750 and terminated about the time of Schleiermacher's death in 1834. The restored Lutheran orthodoxy has since that time been seeking to deepen its insight into the Christian system, and, amid the distractions of a peculiarly unfavorable position, to develop the life of the church. Construction, systematization, corruption, restoration—such are the cycles through which Lutheran theology ran.

The same cycles reappear in Calvinism. It had its constructive period in Switzerland, France, and Holland, ending formally in the Synod of Dort in 1618. In this period was embraced its first great conflict, that with Arminianism. Thereupon follow side by side the development of scholastic orthodoxy and that of Arminianism, till both end in theological decay. The principal arena of conflict transferred to England, where for more than a century the reformed theology had been constructing its system, and had constantly grown more Calvinistic and more Puritan, we have for a time, after the Synod of Dort, the theological struggle merged in the political, till Calvinism, triumphant with the triumph of Parliament, could formulate its theology in the Westminster Confession in 1646. This was the period of the great systematic divines. It is overwhelmed with reverse when in 1660 Charles II brings in the monarchy again, and with it the period of Latitudinarianism (1680–1700). The Latitudinarians were Arminian in their tendencies, and this form of theology may be said to have had control in England largely during the eighteenth century in connection with an Arian movement, both constituting a real corruption of the evangelical theology of Westminster. But in the same century an evangelical Arminianism under the lead of John Wesley (1738 ff.) began the movement of restoration, as a result of which a mild Calvinism prevailed very largely in the churches of England, established and dissenting, from about 1800 to 1832.

The fundamental connection of New England with all this international ferment and development is seen in the remarkable fact that, in spite of its apparent and real isolation, the same great periods of theological history are repeated here with almost identical dates. The Puritans and Pilgrims had shared in the constructive period of English Protestantism at home. They planted New England just as Puritanism was on the eve of triumph in the mother-country, though they were far from perceiving this. They shared in its victory, and appropriated its results when in 1648 they adopted the Westminster standards as their own. They had their period of theological corruption, arising from indigenous causes, but also originated and promoted in part by influences communicated from the debased England of the Restoration after the year 1660. From 1720 to 1750 the Arminian tendencies of the mother-country powerfully affect the life of the colonies. In 1750 these begin to give place to Arianism, which continues to be a threatening force within the New England churches till the year 1833. But in New England there is a more immediate reaction against theological corruption than in either Germany or England. The Arminian movement is met almost at its beginning by the youthful Jonathan Edwards in his sermons on justification in 1734, and by his *Freedom of the Will* in 1754. With the earlier of these dates New England theology as a distinct school begins. It thus long antedates the labors of the German Schleiermacher, and coincides closely with the conversion of Wesley (1738). It soon develops the disposition to meet the new conditions with a new presentation of the truth, which is the principal merit of Schleiermacher, and it displays the same devotion to evangelical truth and to the practical work of saving souls which appear in Methodism. Its restoration is a restoration of the historic Calvinism, which it modifies, but to the spirit of which it remains true to the end.

These facts show how fully New England theology is a world-phenomenon. Beginning in the first half of the eighteenth century, it continued till late in the nineteenth. Within these limits it was always in motion. It struggled with great forces. It produced great treatises. It developed great truths. It inspired great activities. But it was singularly homogeneous, since it derived its motive forces from a single source. The materials with which the New England writers wrought, and the later impulses which they received from various quarters, were English, Puritan, Calvinistic exclusively. Universalism, which like a flint struck out the ablest thoughts which New England set forth upon the atonement, was an English distortion of Calvinism. Unitarianism, which furnished the occasion for the perfection of many of the characteristic New England doctrines in anthropology, was transplanted from England to America, and developed in the isolation of a country which knew no source of fruitful ideas but the mother-land. If Moses Stuart dealt with German writers, translated German grammars, and referred copiously to German authorities in his doctrinal discussions, it is doubtful whether he ever received a single dogmatic idea from any source outside of the line of English Puritan thought, orthodox and unorthodox. Nathaniel W. Taylor was a purely American product. Edwards A. Park, who had studied in Germany and was familiar with the German language and literature, introduces no materials from such quarters into his theological lectures. Nevertheless, New England theology was a world-phenomenon. It was borne upon the same currents as carried the theology of other lands through similar rounds of degeneration and restoration. The English sources upon which it depended were themselves replenished from the universal Protestant thought. Unknown modes of communication brought ideas upon invisible wings to this remote corner of the world from many another. The life which pulsates in all its veins is the one life of all Protestant Christendom.

This double interest, therefore, belongs to the study of New England theology: that of a restricted subject of investigation, where the phenomena can be all brought into the field of vision, and their causal connections determined, and that of a significant and representative movement, in which as in a mirror the great movements in the onward march of the world are reflected. Even the microscopic can be microcosmic. In many respects New England theology is a microcosm.

These considerations increase our sense of the importance of its study; but they also prescribe the method of that study. It is a growth, a development, which we have before us. An adequate history cannot, therefore, be mere annals, a "chronicle," an unconnected heap of opinions. A history of doctrine is not the same thing as a register of discordant and meaningless theories. Ideas grow. One writer is dependent upon another. A thought is found in one man as a seed, it germinates in another, it comes to form and fruitfulness in others. The stages of this growth should be marked, the connections of these men noted. The action and reaction of mind upon mind, of idea upon idea, is the interesting thing in the history. A true history must therefore be genetic. Ideas in their genesis, their growth, and their fruit are its theme. Not all of the opinions of every writer need to be considered by it, but what has had an influence, contributed to growth, or in some way carried on the work of the school of thought.

The object of this book is, therefore, to construct a truly genetic history of New England theology, a history which shall perform the service, not merely of recording the various distinguishing views of the several writers, but of setting forth their productive work in the circumstances under which they developed, in comparison with the errors which they were designed to meet, in their consistency with other views which the writers held, and in their connection with the theology which has sprung out of them as productive intellectual causes.

The story begins with the first landing of immigrants upon the New England shores, and traces the history of the first century as the background upon which the growth of the New England theology proper is to be depicted, a century in which the natural results of the defective theories of the original Calvinism of England and New England united with the universal tendencies of frontier life to produce degeneration and decay. The influence of theological degeneration in the mother-country, with its Deism and Arminianism, contributed to accelerate the downward movement. The protagonist of the theological revival was Jonathan Edwards, who, dying in 1758, left to his two friends, Hopkins and Bellamy, the task of extending and developing the new views of truth which he had more suggested than formulated. Before Hopkins left the stage, the controversy with the original Universalists, in which the younger Jonathan Edwards was the leader, was in full course. Then came with the beginning of the last century the Unitarian controversy, with its attendant development of anthropology. The school of Taylor, its antagonism against Tylerism, the rupture with Presbyterianism, the foundation of Oberlin, till we have at last the Andover of Park and the Oberlin of Fairchild, crowd the scene with a various and brilliant succession of figures of the highest interest and importance. Such is the theme of this work in briefest outline, and to its development the history may now turn without further delay.

CHAPTER I

THE FIRST CENTURY IN NEW ENGLAND, 1620-1720

The first immigrants to New England were the Pilgrim Fathers, who landed at Plymouth in 1620. Though the church collected at Scrooby was the direct result of the Puritan movement in the English universities, the Pilgrims were for the most part themselves of humble origin, and were little fitted to contribute much to the theological development of the new state. There is but one figure among them of sufficient intellectual eminence to engage the attention of subsequent generations, that of John Robinson,[1] the pastor of the little flock at Leyden, who was member of two universities, and a foremost disputant in the ranks of the defenders of Congregationalism. His heroic devotion to principle, the picturesque vicissitudes of his career, his intellectual power and breadth, his prophetic vision, and above all his sincere and deep piety, made him a constant subject of quotation and an acknowledged authority among all the New England churches.

The writings of Robinson which have come down to us [2] are chiefly occupied with those matters which lay nearest to his heart as a Separatist. We have thus a long and elaborate discussion of ecclesiastical polity, treating nearly all the topics in controversy between the Independents and the Church of England. There is, however, one considerable treatise upon doctrinal theology, the *Defence of the*

[1] Born 1575; died in Leyden, 1625; graduated at Cambridge; became a fellow in 1598-99; minister in Norfolk in the English church; suspended for scruples about vestments, etc.; ministered some time secretly to the congregation at Scrooby; emigrated with them to Holland in 1608; member of the University of Leyden, 1615. Discussed Arminianism publicly with Episcopius. See the "Life" in the edition of his works. (This chapter originally appeared in the *American Journal of Theology*.)

[2] Collected in an edition entitled *The Works of John Robinson*, etc., *with Memoir*, etc., by Robert Ashton, 3 vols. (London, 1851).

Doctrine Propounded by the Synod at Dort, which serves to show the harmony of doctrinal view between the Separatists and the Puritan movement in general, and later exerted a positive influence in prolonging that harmony throughout New England. It is what it purports to be, strictly a "defence," and in no respect goes beyond the common Calvinism of the day, or rises above its level. It is completely deficient in the philosophical element; but this is less to be wondered at in an age when Descartes had not yet introduced the methods, and called forth the spirit, of modern philosophy. It is, therefore, scarcely necessary to dwell upon this, the first in the long series of doctrinal treatises produced by the Congregational leaders. It may be dismissed with the following brief extracts, which will be sufficient to exhibit its flavor and distinguishing characteristics.

Robinson's reticence upon one of the great perplexities of theology is indicated in the following passage:

If any demand how this can be, that God who forbiddeth and hateth sin, yet should so order persons and things, by his providence, and so from eternity purpose to order them, as that the same cannot but be? I answer, by free acknowledgment, that the manner of God's working herein is to me, and to all men, inconceivable; and withal avouch, that he, who will not confess, that God can, and could in Adam's sin, by his infinite wisdom and power, most effectually, and infallibly, in regard of such event, order and dispose of things, without violation to his holiness, or violence to the creature's will, as no mortal man is able to conceive the manner thereof, is himself in a high degree guilty of that pride which was Adam's ruin, by which he desired to be as God in knowledge. Gen., chap. 3. Who is able to understand the manner of God's working, in giving the Holy Ghost to man, and in directing the tongues and pens of the prophets infallibly, and so as they could not err? Much less discernible is God's manner of working in, and about the creature's sinful actions. And because many take great offense at this doctrine of truth and work of God, I will, the Lord assisting me, plainly and briefly as I can, prove that all events, even those most sinful, in regard of the creature's work in, and of them, come to pass necessarily, after a sort, in respect of God's providence, as being a hand steady and which swerveth not, in ordering the creature in and unto the same.[3]

He thinks that the alleged inconsistency of God's commanding Adam not to sin, and yet decreeing that he should sin, is sufficiently removed by the following distinctions:

For us, we do not hold, that God decreed Adam's sin, as they conceive, that is, either to approve it or command it or compel unto it, nothing less; but we affirm that God decreed to leave Adam to himself, in the temptation and not to assist him with that strength of grace, by which he could, if he would, have upheld him; and so to order both him and all things about him, in that his temptation, as that he, by the notion and sway of his own free will following his natural appetite to the pleasant but forbidden fruit and that false persuasion wherewith his understanding was by Satan overclouded, should both choose and eat the forbidden fruit.[4]

There is an evident struggle in his mind to maintain a certain freedom of the will of man from compulsion,[5] and in general to hold to that more generous type of theology characteristic of English Puritanism in distinction from continental.[6] Thus he is distinctly sublapsarian,[7] though he holds firmly to a limited atonement.[8] But when all credit for the influence upon his system of clearer intuitions of truth, or of the plain common-sense of which he had a considerable share, has been given, the general accord of the whole with that extreme application of the doctrine of divine sovereignty and of the helplessness of man which was to spread a deadly paralysis through all the spiritual life of New England, is apparent from such passages as the following:

They [Calvinists] believe, as the Scriptures teach, that all men in Adam have sinned, Rom. 5:12-15; and by sin lost the image of God

[3] Robinson, *Works*, Vol. I, pp. 274, 275.
[4] *Ibid.*, pp. 280, 281.
[5] *Ibid.*, pp. 274 *et al.*
[6] Compare the Westminster Confession, chaps. iii, ix, and x.
[7] *Works*, Vol. I, p. 289.
[8] *Ibid.*, p. 329.

in which they were made; so as the law is impossible, Rom. 8:3; unto them by reason of the flesh, and so cannot possibly but sin, by reason of the same flesh reigning in the unregenerate, and dwelling in all: which these light persons, expressly confess . . . . : and that this so comes to pass by God's holy decree, and work of providence answerable, not forcing evil upon any, but ordering all persons in all actions, as the supreme Governor of all: and that the wicked, being left of God, some, destitute of the outward means, the gospel; all of them, of the effectual work of the Spirit, from that weak flesh, and natural corruption, daily increased in them, sin both necessarily as unable to keep the law, and willingly, as having in themselves the beginning and cause thereof, the blindness of their own minds, and perverseness of their will and affections; and so are inexcusable in God's sight.[9]

The founding of the Massachusetts colony, about ten years later than the Plymouth, brought a different class to New England. There were many men of education and wealth among the laymen of Boston, and its clergymen were largely university men, well read in divinity, and intense in their attachment to the Calvinistic system. The overthrow of the monarchy in England resulted in 1646 in the formation of the Westminster standards. They were hardly issued when they were adopted in Massachusetts (1648) as the general standard of doctrine among the churches, and were later (1708) welcomed in Connecticut with equal cordiality. Old Calvinism, shaped by the prevailing acceptance of the Westminster Confession, continued to be the dominant and well-nigh unchallenged system in the New England churches even after Arminianism had begun to make serious inroads at the beginning of the eighteenth century.

For a while there could, of course, be little theological production amid the labors of subduing the wilderness. The standard writers of the old countries were enough for the time. Among these Wollebius,[10] a sublapsarian, free

[9] *Ibid.*, pp. 398 f.

[10] *Compendium theologiae christianae*, etc., published in many editions, 1633 and subsequently. In 1650 it was translated.

from the deformities of scholasticism, and Ames,[11] whose *Medulla* was employed as a textbook in the colleges, were the principal favorites. Indigenous production was called forth by a cause of a somewhat startling and unpleasant nature. This was the appearance of a book entitled *The Meritorious Price of Our Redemption,*[12] by a layman, a man of considerable prominence as the founder of Springfield, William Pynchon,[13] which contained sentiments too much at variance with the current system to be received with equanimity. It was the first outbreak of the independent spirit of Congregationalism, and it was sternly suppressed. The book was first burned, and then refuted by order of the General Court, and Mr. Pynchon found it convenient to return to England, where he died.

Pynchon's work was the protest of plain common-sense against the current representations of the atonement which taught that Christ suffered the very torments of the lost, and against the theory of imputation upon which such representations depended. He objected most strongly to these ideas because they involved the thought that Christ bore the wrath of God, whereas in fact his sufferings were inflicted upon him by the rage and enmity of "the old serpent."[14] His argument is principally scriptural, and is derived both from the silence of Scripture, which relieves us from the necessity of believing that Christ suffered the infinite wrath of God, and from its positive affirmations, which he often discusses at great length. It is, further, not necessary that Christ should bear the punishment of our

[11] *Medulla theologica,* etc. (Amsterdam, 1623); many editions subsequently.

[12] Published in London, 1650. The refutation by John Norton was entitled: *A Discussion of That Great Point in Divinity, The Sufferings of Christ,* etc. (London, 1653).

[13] An incorporator of the Massachusetts Company; came to America in 1630; first settled at Dorchester, then at Roxbury; was soon treasurer of the colony; emigrated to Springfield in 1636; returned to England in 1652; died October 29, 1662.

[14] "Preface to the Reader."

sins, since his obedience is enough to satisfy for the sins of the elect. We see thus that Pynchon did not abandon the idea of a limited atonement.[15] And then Christ could not suffer the pains of hell, for they consist either in the "pain of loss," or separation from God, which he did not suffer, or in the "pain of sense," which consists in eternal sufferings, which also he did not suffer. He gives utterance to an axiomatic truth, afterwards to play a considerable part in New England: "The rule of God's justice doth require that soul only to die which sins . . . . Ezek., chap., 18. By this rule of justice God cannot inflict the torments of hell upon an innocent, to redeem a guilty person." [16] He also suggests the word "chastisement" as a suitable one to describe the nature of Christ's sufferings. Against imputation, he urges its injustice, for God's imputation is always connected with guiltiness; and also the fact that imputation would destroy the possibility of Christ's being a redeemer, for the redemption consists in the mediatorial obedience, and Christ would then have been a disobedient sinner.

Pynchon then goes on to say:

That which Christ did to redeem us from the curse of the law was not by bearing the said curse really in our stead (as the common doctrine of imputation doth teach), but by procuring his Father's atonement by the invaluable price or performance of his own mediatorial obedience, whereof his mediatorial sacrifice of the atonement was the finishing masterpiece. This kind of obedience was that rich thing of price which the Father required and accepted as satisfactory for the procuring of his atonement for our full redemption, justification, and adoption.[17]

And then he adds, with an idea closely akin to that of Anselm, if not actually a filtration down through the ages from that first great writer upon this theme:

God the Father was more highly pleased with the obedience of the Mediator than he was displeased with the disobedience of Adam.

[15] *Op. cit.,* p. 2; cf. pp. 87, 88.
[16] *Ibid.,* p. 81.
[17] *Ibid.,* pp. 83, 84.

If so, then there is no need that our blessed Mediator should pay both the price of his mediatorial obedience and also bear the curse of the law really for our redemption. I never heard that ever any Turkish tyrant did require such a double satisfaction of any redeemer for the redemption of galley slaves . . . . to pay both the full price which they demanded for this redemption of their galley slaves and to bear the punishment of their curse and slavery also in their stead. . . . . Why then doth the doctrine of imputation make God the Father to be a harder creditor in the point of satisfaction than ever any rigid creditor was among men? . . . . The gross substance of that blood that was shed . . . . is not to be taken by itself alone considered for that precious price. . . . . We must take the blood of Christ . . . , for his mediatorial obedience.[18]

Pynchon consistently rejected the imputation of Christ's obedience to the believer, which he thinks inconsistent with justice as well as useless, for "the law binds every singular person to perform exact obedience by his own natural power, without any help from any surety whatsoever, or without any supernatural help of faith." Besides, the active obedience of Christ cannot be imputed to us for a variety of reasons. He did not perform all the acts required of us, since he did not enter all the conditions of life. Then, he was bound to obey for himself, and the acts of his legal obedience were not mediatorial. Pynchon also explains the true nature of justification as consisting simply in "the Father's merciful atonement, pardon, and forgiveness. It is a gracious acquittal, as when a father forgives his son and receives him into favor."

Norton in his refutation of Pynchon thus expressed his own doctrine.

The Lord Jesus Christ, as God-man mediator according to the will of the Father and his own voluntary consent, fully obeyed the law, doing the command in a way of works and suffering the essential punishment of the curse [note the word "essential"] in a way of obedient satisfaction unto divine justice, thereby explicitly fulfilling the first covenant; which active and passive obedience of his, together with his original righteousness as a surety, God of his rich

[18] *Loc. cit.,* pp. 84, 85.

grace actually imputeth unto believers, whom upon the receipt thereof by the grace of faith, he declareth and accounteth as perfectly righteous, and acknowledgeth them to have right unto eternal life.

The reply was keen and able, but it was simply a defense of the old theology according to the command of the General Court, and added nothing to the common understanding of the theme. In a personal interview with him, Norton seems to have made more impression upon Pynchon, for in a communication to the General Court [19] he stated that he was now "inclined to think that his [Christ's] sufferings were appointed by God for a further end, namely, as the due punishment of our sins by way of satisfaction to the divine justice." After his return to England he recurred to the theme, publishing in 1655 *A Further Discussion of That Great Point in Divinity, The Sufferings of Christ*, etc., in which he reaffirmed his old positions. He tried to do something in the way of a development of the doctrine, bringing out with more distinctness the fact that Christ's sufferings were not substitutionary, since they do not fulfil the covenant made with Adam, but a new one "made by the persons of the Trinity from eternity." And he finally expresses his own theory somewhat more fully in the following language. Referring to his former treatise, he says:

The dialogue doth . . . . oppose the way of vindicative justice; but yet it makes all Christ's sufferings to be performed in a way of justice according to the order of justice in the voluntary cause and covenant. . . . . The dialogue . . . . shows from God's declaration in Gen. 3:15, that the devil must combat against the seed of the deceived woman, and that Christ in his human nature must combat against him and break his head plot by continuing obedient to the death, and that, therefore, his sufferings and death were meritorious because it was all performed in a way of justice, namely, in exact obedience to all the articles of the voluntary covenant.[20]

Thus Pynchon's work was one-sided, incomplete, and

[19] *Massachusetts Records*, Vol. IV, Part I, p. 48.
[20] *Further Discussion*, p. 176.

immature. It was essentially a protest, not in any way a constructive effort. It had no immediate effect in producing modification of theory in New England, for most of the following writers pass over all he said as if they had never heard of him, or at least never read him;[21] and doubtless few had. No trace of positive influence exerted upon the later New England writers has yet been discovered. The book seems to have exhaled its life in the flames in which it was burned upon Boston market place. But the same sturdy protest against scholastic deformations of Christian doctrine was at a later day to receive a more cordial hearing.

If Pynchon thus exerted little positive influence, it seems to have been due to the stimulus afforded by such a phenomenon as heresy in New England that there soon began to be a series of systematic treatises upon divinity, John Norton,[22] who had refuted Pynchon in 1653, appearing with his *Orthodox Evangelist* in 1654. This book, though small—for it comprises but 355 quarto pages—possesses a high degree of minuteness, accuracy, and technicality. Its epistle dedicatory expresses confidence in the progress of the truth. "Even fundamental truths . . . . have been and shall be transmitted more clear from age to age in the times of reformation." The body of the work begins with chapters upon the divine essence and the Trin-

[21] Charles Chauncy, in a volume of sermons (1659) entitled in Hebrew *The Lord Our Righteousness*, says (pp. 52, 53): "Christ by way of satisfaction for sinners suffered the full and utmost punishment due to the sins of the elect . . . . the punishment of the second death." John Eliot, in *The Harmony of the Gospels in the Holy History of the Humiliation and Sufferings of Jesus Christ* (1678), teaches that Christ suffered the pains of hell, using the distinction which Norton had employed between a "penal" and a "local" hell (p. 119).

[22] Born in Stortford, England, May 6, 1606; educated at Cambridge; came in 1635 to Plymouth, Mass., but soon became the minister of Ipswich; in 1652 became associate minister in Boston; sent to England after the restoration to assure the king of the loyalty of Massachusetts; returning, died at Boston, April 5, 1663.

ity, and closes with a treatment of the state of the blessed; but it is chiefly occupied with the discussion of the way of salvation, thus foreshadowing the interest in anthropological themes characteristic of New England divinity. On the order of the decrees it is predominantly supralapsarian. On the will it teaches that "the liberty of man, though subordinate to God's decree, freely willeth the very same thing and no other than that which it would have willed if (upon a supposition of impossibility) there had been no decree."[23] Again: "Man acts as freely as if there were no decree; yet as infallibly as if there were no liberty." There is no theory of the will, properly speaking, though Norton finds some help in the idea that the will is a second cause. He rejects the "indifferency of the will to act or not to act independent of the decree," but has no positive theory to offer, and upon the allied subject of conversion is led by his desire to meet the Arminians to lay so much stress upon divine sovereignty as to emphasize passivity in conversion overmuch.

Isaac Chauncy [24] published in 1694 *The Doctrine Which is according to Godliness,* etc., which was a system of divinity in the form of question and answer, upon the basis of the Westminster Catechism. It was a vigorous and independent work, in complete conformity to the Westminster standards in every important point. On the will Chauncy says that God's decree "maintains the liberty of the creature's will, that all free agents act as freely according to the decree as agents by necessity do act necessarily." For the sake of maintaining the true deity of Christ, he even ventured to contradict the Nicene Creed. "The Father doth not communicate Godhead in begetting, but Sonship only. It is very improper to say Christ is God of God [the

---

[23] *Evangelist,* pp. 74–76.

[24] Son of Charles, president of Harvard College.

Nicene phrase], but every person is essentially absolutely first, having the whole Godhead in it."

There exists in manuscript in the library of the Massachusetts Historical Society *A Whole Body of Divinity in a Catechetical Way* by Samuel Stone,[25] of Hartford, copied by Samuel Willard,[26] marked by the same originality of expression and the same agreement with Westminster. It serves to continue the line of systematic writers to Willard himself, who from 1688 to 1707 delivered a course of expository lectures upon the Shorter Catechism which was published in 1726 in a folio of 914 pages, under the title of *A Complete Body of Divinity.* It is a big, but not a great, work. In the treatment of the Scriptures he reverses the order of the proof as given in the Confession, putting the character of the Bible, such as its contents, work in the soul, majesty, etc., first, and coming to the testimony of the Spirit last, and that under the head of "Testimony," which is subdivided into two heads, the human and the divine. Under the subject of the fall he has the remarkable statement that God "gave not to Adam those influences of confirming and assisting grace that were needful to his standing; and yet providence is not to blame, because Adam did not want any of those influences till he was willing to want them."[27]   Thus sin comes from lack of grace, and lack of grace comes from sin! There is a blind effort here to place the responsibility of the existence of sin upon the free will of man, as Willard says elsewhere: "Adam sinned voluntarily or by consent, in that he abused his own free will."[28]   As to the order of the decrees, Willard was a

[25] Born in Hertford, England, about 1602; emigrated to Cambridge, New England, in 1633; pastor there; removed to Hartford, Conn., 1636, with the founders of that town; pastor there till his death, in 1663.

[26] Born in Concord, Mass., 1640; graduated at Harvard, 1659; pastor of the Old South Church, Boston, 1676 (?) to his death, 1707.

[27] *Op. cit.*, pp. 178, 179.

[28] *Ibid.*, p. 186.

supralapsarian. The means of grace, preaching, etc., "have no efficiency in the production of this habit [of faith] by moral suasion;" [29] i. e., preaching has no efficiency in regeneration.

Thus to all appearance the ancient Calvinism had fully maintained itself down to the close of the century. There was still found in 1707 a minister in one of the chief churches of Boston who was regularly lecturing upon divinity with the minuteness only to be expected in a theological school, and adhering with absolute faithfulness to the Westminster system. And yet beneath the surface there was widespread departure and alienation from that system. Another side of the history of the first century needs now to be reviewed.

There is an analogy between ideas and material bodies in the particular of their gravity; and the first century of New England history was to show how the Puritan divinity, in the proportion and with the emphasis with which it was held, by a natural gravitation tended downward.

It was the beginning of a chapter of misfortunes when Mrs. Anne Hutchinson [30] arrived in Boston in 1635. She was a woman of talent, of a deeply religious nature, very much attached to her pastor, Rev. John Cotton, [31] who had left her home, Boston, England, to become the minister of the New England Boston. Much prayer had brought her to the conviction that she had been "trusting in a covenant

[29] *Ibid.*, p. 434.

[30] The best general view of this episode is found in Punchard, *History of Congregationalism*, Vol. IV, pp. 196 ff. Original authorities are: Welde, *A Short Story of the Rise, Reign, and Ruine of the Antinomians*, etc. (1644); E. Johnson, *The Wonderworking Province of Sions Saviour* (1654; reprinted, Andover, 1867); Cotton Mather, *Magnalia* (1702; Hartford ed., 1853, always cited in the following pages, Vol. II, p. 508), gives an account of no great value; C. Chauncy, *Seasonable Thoughts* (1743), reproduces something from Welde.

[31] Born in Derby, England, 1585; fellow of Emanuel College, Cambridge, subsequently dean; settled at Boston, England, in 1612; emigrated to Boston, New England, in 1632, and died there in 1652.

of works," and in connection with the higher spiritual experiences which she had gained in her effort to throw her-
self more fully upon the mercy of God, she had become
visionary and fanatical. So she conceived that it was "revealed" to her that she must go to New England and "be
persecuted and suffer much trouble." Arrived here, she
began soon to assemble the women in her house for religious meetings, repeating the sermons of Mr. Cotton with
comments of her own, and before long had become the
head of a considerable party, who were charged with An-
tinomian errors, and thus stirred up a controversy which
divided the church and town, and excited so much feeling
as to become the cause of a serious crisis in the life of the
young community. A synod was called against her errors
in 1637, and they were condemned. Subsequently she was
banished, and died at the hands of the Indians upon Long
Island.

It is exceedingly difficult, if not impossible, to arrive at
this late day at an exact and reliable estimate of the nature
and tendency of Mrs. Hutchinson's views. No one can
read the various contemporary accounts without the feeling that misunderstanding played a great part in creating
the conviction that she had seriously departed from the
orthodoxy of the day. The most valuable source of information, Welde's *Short Story,* is of no great historical
worth. It is marred by superstition,[32] its common honesty
is somewhat doubtful,[33] and it must hence be employed
with the greatest caution. As commonly understood, her
peculiar views gathered about two points: the doctrine of
the indwelling of the Spirit and the assurance of justifica-

[32] It contains a most incredible account of the birth of a monster to the
wife of a certain William Dyer.

[33] See references under Dexter, *Congregationalism as Seen in Its Literature*
(New York, 1880), bibliography, title No. 972. This invaluable work has been a
constant dependence.

tion. The Holy Spirit dwelt in a justified person personally. "Gifts and graces" were of no value in evidencing Christian character, but the witness of the Spirit was the only evidence. Hence the assurance of justification was immediately given to the soul by the Spirit. It was not evidenced by the sanctification of the believer, but was totally independent of this. Hence works were of no value, and hence the Christian might live in sin. Justification was entirely separated from faith. A man was justified before he believed. A further distinction was drawn between the covenant of works and that of grace. All who rested their evidence upon the fruits of the Spirit were said to be trusting in a covenant of works. The covenant of grace was restricted to those who experienced the inward witness of the Spirit.

It is at least probable that these expressions were only individual methods of emphasizing the dominant ideas of the Calvinistic system as then commonly preached, and especially as presented in the ordinary ministrations of Mr. Cotton, Mrs. Hutchinson's favorite minister. The second error which Welde mentions, "that a man is united to Christ and justified without faith; yea, from all eternity," seems nothing but an extreme formulation of the doctrine of election. In fact, Rev. John Wheelwright, in defending himself against Welde's charges, says [34] of this very charge: The writer holds it to be true "if it be meant respecting God's decree," but in no other sense. Many of the expressions quoted seem also to be of the same nature as that extreme application of the doctrine of union with Christ which was to appear subsequently in Rellyanism, itself only an exaggerated Calvinism. Such, for example are these: "Christ is the new creature;" "All graces are in Christ as the subject and none in us, so that Christ

[34] *Mercurius Americanus* (1645; reprinted by the Prince Society, 1876), p. 9.

believes, Christ loves," etc.[35]   And Mr. Wheelwright's denials that he held that sanctification was no evidence of justification are repeated and explicit.

The mere unraveling of a snarl of insignificant temporary aberrations from truth is of no interest or importance in the present history. But besides the evident tendency to overemphasize the divine sovereignty and allied truths which already appears, there is one further phenomenon, exhibited in connection with the synod, which is of the greatest significance. This is the substantial ignorance of the nature of saving faith brought to light by the discussions upon justification. Mr. Cotton seems, at first sight, to have been farther from the truth than his colleagues, and was brought with some difficulty to a partial agreement with them. He held that our "union with Christ" is complete before and without the work or act of faith though not before or without the "habit" or gift of faith. It is evident from his own subsequent expressions[36] that he was after all in substantial agreement with the rest, for he says, "I looked at union with Christ as equivalent to regeneration." This as the divine part in conversion does at least logically precede the act of faith. But, however they might be divided upon this point, Mr. Cotton and all the rest were united in viewing man as passive in faith. For the sake of securing the honor of God as the author of regeneration, they held views of divine sovereignty, inability, and regeneration which in effect rendered man totally passive till the indispensable condition was· fulfilled, upon which faith followed, as a spontaneous act, it is true, but still as necessary.

In this confusion the New England fathers were not alone. It was generally true that but little light was to be

---

[35] *Short Story*, errors 17, 16.
[36] *The Way of Congregational Churches Cleared*, etc. (1648), pp. 41 ff.

found upon the nature of the action of the human mind in religious matters in any of the standard writers of the day. The will was still linked inseparably with the emotions in the common psychology, and its office and operation hence much obscured. The Westminster Confession confounds saving faith with historical faith in the expression: "By this faith a Christian believeth to be true whatsoever is revealed in the Word." [37] Even Calvin had said: "Faith . . . . is a certain and steady knowledge of the divine benevolence towards us." [38] And though in case of both of these authorities there can be found other expressions calculated to give a good practical impression to the popular mind, yet when the emphasis was laid upon man's inability to repent which was laid in those days, the activity of man was brought into so great darkness and doubt that paralysis of the spiritual forces of the soul often followed, and the work of repentance which man "could not do" remained largely undone.

The consequences of this confused and paralyzing theology soon became apparent. Cotton Mather may tell the piteous story:

When our churches were come to between twenty and thirty years of age, a numerous posterity was advanced so far into the world, that the first planters began apace in their several families to be distinguished by the name of grandfathers; but among the immediate parents of the grandchildren, there were multitudes of well-disposed persons, who, partly through their own doubts and fears, and partly through other culpable neglects, had not actually come up to the covenanting state of communicants at the table of the Lord. The good old generation could not, without many uncomfortable apprehensions, behold their offspring excluded from the baptism of Christianity, and from the ecclesiastical inspection which is to accompany that baptism; indeed, it was to leave their offspring under the shepherdly government of our Lord Jesus Christ in his ordinances, that they had brought their lambs into this wilderness. When the apostle bids churches to

[37] Chap. xiv.
[38] *Institutes*, III, ii, 7.

"look diligently, lest any man fail of the grace of God," there is an ecclesiastical word used for that "looking diligently;" intimating that God will ordinarily bless a regular church-watch, to maintain the interests of grace among his people; and it was therefore the study of those prudent men, who might be called our seers, that the children of the faithful may be kept, as far as may be, under a church-watch, in expectation that they might be in the fairer way to receive the grace of God; thus they were "looking diligently," that the prosperous and prevailing condition of religion in our churches might not be *res unius aetatis*—"a matter of one age alone." Moreover, among the next sons or daughters descending from that generation, there was a numerous appearance of sober persons, who professed themselves desirous to renew their baptismal-covenant and submit unto the church-discipline, and so have their houses also 'marked for the Lord's; but yet they could not come to that experimental account of their own regeneration, which would sufficiently embolden their access to the other sacrament. Wherefore, for our churches now to make no ecclesiastical difference between these hopeful candidates and competents for those our further mysteries; and pagans, who might happen to hear the word of God in our assemblies, was judged a most unwarrantable strictness, which would quickly abandon the biggest part of our country unto heathenism. And, on the other side, it was feared that, if all such as had not yet exposed themselves by censurable scandals found upon them should be admitted unto all the privileges in our churches, a worldly part of mankind might, before we are aware, carry all things into such a course of proceeding, as would be very disagreeable unto the kingdom of heaven.[39]

No one can fail to perceive the surprise with which Mather, and doubtless all the rest of the New England leaders, looked upon this state of things. There were, no doubt, many elements entering into the production of the result,[40] some of which cannot now be fully understood. The early plan of requiring of candidates for church membership a long and detailed account of gracious exercises, however appropriate when the first little companies had

[39] *Magnalia*, Vol. II, pp. 277 ff.

[40] It has been common to ascribe the movement for the "Half-Way Covenant" to the desire to enlarge the franchise, which was at first restricted in Massachusetts to church members. But there is no evidence that this consideration had any influence. See Dexter, *Congregationalism as Seen in Its Literature*, p. 468; also *New England and Yale Review*, February, 1892, article by Professor W. Walker.

gathered together under the stress of persecution in England, and when all their religious exercises must of necessity have been marked, could only serve as an unfortunate and embarrassing condition among a later generation, born and brought up in the perfect freedom of the New World, and without the thrilling experiences of their fathers to give point to their views and depth to their experience. But with all the rest, there was a theological root to the trouble, and this was that doctrine of inability, one application of which we have already seen. The doctrine of the sovereignty of God is one which affects the church differently at different times. The first Puritans, sure in their own hearts that they were the elect of God, found the doctrine necessary to sustain them in the tremendous struggles through which they passed. As the waves of the storm rose higher about them, they looked more and more to God, who was yet ruler above all the commotion of the elements, and would save his people. Hence the doctrine nerved to greater activity; and it produced a similar effect, during the first period of the promulgation of Calvinism, among every nation which accepted the system. The Calvinists were the great active forces of an advancing Protestantism. But when such mighty stimulus was removed, when inability was preached to men who were not conscious that they were the elect, when passive waiting for the gracious deliverance of God was inculcated upon men whom the tide of events no longer forced to activity in spite of themselves and of their theories, it produced sluggishness, apathy, self-distrust, despair. It has never been a good way to induce men to repent to tell them that they cannot. Thus, in part, it was the theology of the period which wrought the paralysis which Mather sketches, and which continued in spite of all the ecclesiastical nostrums of the Half-Way Covenant, and sunk the churches lower and lower.

An inspection of the preaching of the early ministers of New England would show how predominantly depressing and discouraging their ministrations were. There were not lacking many appeals which were adapted to stir the conscience, produce repentance, and call out faith; for, when men are moved by the great forces of the soul, and the truths of the gospel are presented to them, they will respond in the natural manner, regardless of the theories which they may be taught and which at other times may paralyze their action. But when every allowance has been made for the brighter and better side of the early preaching, it still remains that the general impression of the pulpit was that the sinner is "dead," helpless, cannot be interested in divine things, and has nothing to do but to wait for God. Innumerable quotations might be made to illustrate this statement; [41] but unless counterbalanced by

[41] For example: John Higginson, minister of Salem, 1659–1708 (*Our Dying Saviour's Legacy of Peace,* 1868), was a rather cheerful preacher, bringing out man's activity in faith. Jonathan Mitchell, minister of Cambridge, 1650–68 (*A Discourse of the Glory to Which God Hath Called Believers by Jesus Christ,* 1721), is like the average. Thomas Cobbett, minister in Lynn from 1637 to (?) 1657 (*A Practical Discourse of Prayer,* 1654), cannot deny the duty of the unregenerate to pray, and yet spends his time in finding reasons for their prayer though they are entirely wicked in praying; Solomon Stoddard, minister of Northampton, 1669–1729, takes up so much time, even by his *Guide to Christ* (1714), in getting around the difficulties of inability, that he has no time left for directions actually to exercise faith (compare also his *The Safety of Appearing at the Day of Judgment in the Righteousness of Christ,* etc., 1687, and his *The Nature of Saving Conversion,* 1719). To the same effect are: Charles Chauncy, *The Lord Our Righteousness* (1659); John Cotton, *The Church's Resurrection* (1642), *The Way of Life* (1641; rather helpful, but upon p. 187 hopelessly lost in reconciling election with the heinousness of sin upon the basis of inability), *The Covenant of God's Free Grace* (1645), *Christ the Fountain of Life* (1651; see p. 173; the grace of Christ "conveys such a spirit of grace into us as gives us power to receive Christ"); Thomas Hooker, minister in Hartford, 1636–47, *The Soul's Humiliation* (1638), *The Unbeliever's Preparing for Christ* (1638), *The Soul's Vocation* (1638), and *The Poor Dying Christian Drawn to Christ* (1643)—all very gloomy; John Davenport minister in New Haven, 1638–68, then in Boston till he died in 1670 (see quotations in Cotton's *Covenant of Free Grace,* pp. 34–40). Of Mather it is enough to quote the titles of two collections of sermons, *The Greatest Sinners Exhorted and En-*

others which space forbids, the impression they would give
would be even too gloomy and hopeless. Suffice it to say
that to the time of Increase Mather there was scarcely a
single preacher who seemed to possess the evangelistic instinct and who could wield the evangelistic methods. In
Mather's case hard common-sense and practical tact out-
weighed theory. He flung the doctrine of inability into the
depths and preached sermons which live and breathe today.
But he only serves to show by contrast how unfavorable
the general style was in its effect upon the majority of
hearers.

Thus out of the undue and unseasonable emphasis which
the Puritan theology laid upon the divine sovereignty and
man's inability there had sprung a blighting influence which
had reduced the number of conversions greatly, and was
beginning to deplete the churches of members. The Half-
Way Covenant was the method hit upon to remedy the
difficulty. It allowed parents, themselves baptized, of correct life, who would "own the covenant"—that is, would
acknowledge the rightfulness of God's claims upon them,
and promise to submit to the discipline of the church,
though not professing conversion—to have their children
baptized. The arguments for this arrangement were
strange. Though much drawn out, in substance they were
all one. The infants in question were first proved members of the church (the position of the Episcopal church
in England, but repudiated hitherto in New England), and
from this their right to baptism was inferred. Thus, in
effect, the character of the church was changed. The old
Congregational idea had been that the church was the fellowship of believers, and that only they had a right to its
privileges, including the baptism of their children. Thus,

couraged to Come to Christ and that Now, without Delaying (1686), and Now
or Never (1713).

while the church had an educational function and was to train up men to be Christians, it was viewed, in its strictly ecclesiastical character, not as a school, but as a fellowship of persons already thus trained and already converted. Now it was to perform the function of a school, and within its fold train up men to religion. The full scope of the change was not at first seen, but it was consummated when in 1707 Solomon Stoddard, of Northampton, proposed to admit the unregenerate to the Lord's Supper as a means of grace—that is, of conversion. Thus ultimately the doctrine of inability broke down the theory of the new birth in its relation to the church, as it early discouraged the actual exercise of repentance.

The precise causes leading to this remarkable result are somewhat difficult to trace. There was much dispute upon the subject, and the churches were brought to adopt the new method only with great reluctance. Increase Mather wrote in connection with John Davenport, of New Haven, strongly against it, but years afterward took the other side.[42] His treatises upon the side of the new scheme throw some light upon the previous history of the idea. He naturally attempts to gain some support for the plan from the earlier writers, and entitles his first book (of the year 1675): *The First Principles of New England concerning the Subject of Baptism*. In this he quotes John Cotton [43] as being in favor of the plan. The passages quoted pronounce, indeed, in favor of the baptism of the children of the unregenerate "children," but only upon condition

---

[42] Against the synod, *An Apologetical Preface* to John Davenport's *Another Essay;* for it, besides the book above mentioned, *A Discourse concerning the Subject of Baptism,* etc. (1675).

[43] See pp. 2 ff. He quotes Cotton's *Book of the Way of the Churches,* pp. 87, 88, 106, 115, and his *Keyes*. The former quotations contain nothing decisive and in the *Keyes* of 1644 (reprinted, Boston 1843), and the *Vindiciae clavium* (1645), there is nothing to the point. He quotes also Hooker, *Survey of Church Discipline,* pp. 8, 48; but he is discussing another point there.

that their "grandparents" assume the training of them. This was Cotton's position in public utterances of the year 1645. But the increasing pressure of the condition of things seems to have led him to waver, and at last, in a letter dated November 8, 1648, and quoted by Mather,[44] we have the following passage, which looks somewhat doubtfully in the direction of the Half-Way Covenant:

It is not necessary that they [upon a reformation of the church] should take carnal members of the parish into the fellowship of this renewed election of their ministers, and yet it is not improper but the ministers may perform some ministerial acts to them, as not only to preach the word to them, but happily [i. e., haply] also to baptize their children. For such members are like the church members with us baptized in their infancy yet not received to the Lord's Supper when they come to age, nor admitted to fellowship of voting in admissions, elections, censures, till they come to profess their faith and repentance, and lay hold of the covenant of their parents before the church. And yet, they being not cast out of the church nor the covenant thereof, their children may be capable of the first seal of the covenant, so in this case till the parents themselves grow scandalous and thereby cast out of the covenant of the church.

Other evidences of a tendency to change the early practice before the synod had actually recommended it are adduced by Mather, but most of them are derived from unpublished manuscripts. His father, Richard Mather, who had published a catechism in 1650 which was supposed to bear against the Half-Way Covenant, left a manuscript in which he said that he was in favor of the Covenant, and that the catechism was to be interpreted in consistency with this. Other less famous men are quoted by Mather, and among them is the utterance of John Norton upon his dying-bed (1663), who, when asked what the sins of New England were for which God was displeased with the country, said, among other things, "and for the neglect of baptizing the children of the church, those that some call grandchildren, I think God is provoked by it."

[44] *First Principles*, p. 5.

Thus it is evident that it was the pressure of an unexpected state of things which led these fathers reluctantly to a change in their methods. But the particular change made was determined by a peculiarity of their view of the Scriptures, by which the Old and New Testaments were brought upon pretty much the same level as doctrinal authorities, and the distinction between the systems and the dispensations of the two almost obliterated. A very prominent idea with them was that of the "covenant," derived, no doubt, from the Federal School of Holland. God stands in a covenant with believers and their households. Now, as he stood in a covenant with Israel also, the style of interpretation common in New England led to an identification of these covenants in all possible respects; and as an uncircumcised person was outside of the ancient covenant, and excluded from all share in the privileges of the people of God, and in the condition of a pagan; so it was thought that a child brought up in the Christian community and remaining unbaptized would also be outside of the covenant, the recipient of none of the special blessings of grace, and to a considerable degree in a hopeless state. If unbaptized children were indeed outside of the covenant, and thus in a condition but little better than "pagans," as the piteous phrase ran, the thing to be done was to get them into covenant relations that they might be saved. The fact that their parents did not seem to be saved, though in the covenant, escaped the fathers.[45]

It was therefore no superstitious regard for sacraments, no thought of baptismal regeneration, and no conscious lapse from the doctrine of the regenerate church to the view that the church is a school for the gradual training of Christians by the sacraments and Christian teaching,

[45] The full arguments of the synod are given in Mather's *Magnalia*, Vol. II, pp. 276 ff.

which created the Half-Way Covenant, but simply the passive theology of the times, which waited for God in the matter of conversion as for a sovereign whose gifts of grace were in his own inscrutable disposal, and without whom man was absolutely unable to do anything. To be sure, to baptize children was in the power of man, and this must be done. But repentance was the gift of God, and therefore not the act of man.[46]

But the remedy had no curative effect. The Half-Way Covenant was introduced very largely into the churches and ·remained sometimes till into the last century,[47] but the course of things was downward. The Indian war broke out (1675–76), agriculture suffered from drought and blight, commerce suffered at sea, pestilences and epidemics arose, and the consciences of the people, educated under the Jewish ideas of which we have already seen an

[46] The following extract is from Mitchell and Mather's *Defense of the Answer and Arguments of the Synod* (1664) p. 45: "It is the Lord's cwn way and his institutions only, which he will bless, not man's invention, though never so plausible. Neither hath God in his wisdom so instituted the frame of his covenant, and the constitution of the church thereby, as to make a perfect separation between good and bad, or to make the work of conversion and initial instruction needless in the churches. Conversion is to the children of the covenant a fruit of the covenant, saith Mr. Cotton. *If we do not keep in the way of a converting, grace-giving covenant, and keep persons under those church dispensations wherein grace is given, the church will die of a lingering though not of a violent death.* The Lord hath not set up churches only that a few old Christians may keep one another warm while they live, and then carry away the church into the cold grave with them when they die: No, but that they might with all the care and with all the obligations and advantages to that care that may be, nurse up still successively another generation of subjects to Christ, that may stand up in his kingdom when they are gone, that so he might have a people and kingdom successively continued to him from one generation to another."

Increase Mather, in his *Discourse Concerning the Subject of Baptism* (1675), pp. 7 and 8, says: "The persons in question are either belonging to the visible church, or of the world only. The Scripture speaketh of those two terms, church and the world, etc. But to say that the persons in question and their children are of the world only, is in effect to say that they are visibly the devil's and none of the Lord's children."

[47] For example, in the First Church in Cambridge (Mitchell's church) till 1828. See *Manual*, 1872. Still the lists of those received in this particular church under the scheme show that it could have had little influence on the vital religion of the church.

example in the discussions upon the covenant, saw in these calamities the visitations of God for their sins. A "reforming synod" was accordingly called, and met in Boston in 1679. The document put forth by the synod mentions a great many particulars in which the churches had fallen away from their duty and stood in need of a reformation. The reader must make considerable allowance for the phraseology of the day, and for the over-strict views upon many topics which prevailed in New England at the time. Cotton Mather in his account of the matter seems to have an inkling that the terms of the document would be likely to give posterity an unduly unfavorable view of the condition of things, for he says:

Indeed, the people of God in this land were not gone so far in degeneracy but that there were further degrees of disorder and corruption to be found, I must freely speak it, in other, yea in *all* other places where the protestant religion is professed: and the most impartial observers must have acknowledged that there was proportionably still more of true religion, and a larger number of the stricter saints in this country, than in any other on the face of the earth.[48]

Still, with all allowances, it is evident that there was decline in the community. The positive sins mentioned— the increase of profanity, intemperance, and licentiousness —show that there was rising a community about the church which deserved the name of "the world," and that the church was not subduing it. Though the synod recommended vigorous measures, and though many churches held special meetings of reconsecration, the evil was not stayed. The Half-Way Covenant had a strong influence in this direction. Those who had come forward and owned the covenant and had their children baptized seemed satisfied with this, and, as Mr. Stoddard said, there was a "general neglect" of the Lord's Supper. "About forty years past," he says in his sermon of the year 1707, "there were multi-

[48] *Magnalia,* Vol. II, p. 317.

tudes in the country unbaptized: but that neglect was taken into examination, and now there is an alteration in that particular. But to this day there are four to one that do neglect the Lord's Supper, as if it did not belong to them to magnify God on account of the work of redemption." The organized churches were, therefore, in danger of extinction, since the body of communicants, who were the members in full standing, and could alone perpetuate the organizations, was decreasing.[49] The evil began probably in connection with the difficulties which had led to the Half-Way Covenant; and we find that to meet it there had already been practiced some laxness in admitting members to the communion without a personal confession of faith. One of the remedies for the prevailing evils proposed by the "reforming synod" gives more than a hint of this. The synod said:

It is requisite that persons be not admitted unto communion in the Lord's Supper without making a personal and public profession of their faith and repentance, either orally or in some other way, so as shall be to the just satisfaction of the church; and that, therefore, both elders and churches be duly watchful and circumspect in this matter.[50]

The careful phraseology shows that in some instances, at least, all proper confession of personal faith had been omitted.

But it was left to Rev. Solomon Stoddard, of Northampton, Mass.,[51] to make an open proposal to adopt this lax practice as the regular method of the churches. In 1707 he preached the sermon from which a quotation has already

[49] Trumbull, in his *History of Connecticut*, Vol. I, p. 472, says that in the year 1696 "the practice of making a relation of Christian experiences, and of admitting none to full communion but such as appeared to be Christians indeed, yet prevailed; and the number of church members, in full communion, was generally small. In those churches where the owning of the covenant was not practiced, great numbers of children were unbaptized."

[50] *Magnalia*, Vol. II, p. 326.

[51] Born 1643; died 1729; pastor at Northampton, 1669–1729.

been made, and which bore this title: "The Inexcusable-
ness of Neglecting the Worship of God under a Pretence
of Being in an Unconverted Condition." The occasion was
a somewhat public one, as the "Inferior Court" was then
sitting. It was thus, no doubt, intended to have a general
application, and to introduce a practice at least in some
respects new. Yet it seems to have grown out of Mr. Stoddard's own experiences as a parish minister. In seeking to
restore the Lord's Supper to its proper place in the public
observance, he had apparently tried to persuade certain
persons to come to the Lord's table, who had met him with
the excuse that they were unregenerate, and so had no
right to the privilege he urged upon them. So he explains
the object of his sermon, when it had been attacked by Increase Mather,[52] as being "to answer a case of conscience
and direct those that might have scruples about participat-
ing in the Lord's Supper because they have not a work of
saving conversion, and not at all to direct the churches to
admit any that were not to rational charity true believers." [53]   The doctrine he propounded to this end he expresses thus: "That sanctifying grace is not necessary
unto the lawful attending of any duty of worship." The
general argument is characteristic of New England, though
now applied in a new way. It acquires all its strength from
the identification of the Jewish system with the Christian at
a multitude of points in which they are in fact widely separated. The Lord's Supper ought as much to be observed
as any other act of worship, and unconverted persons are
just as inexcusable for not attending it as any others; and
this all the more, since the Passover in the Old Testament
was kept by all the people without regard to their holy
estate.

[52] In *A Dissertation,* etc. (Boston, 1708).
[53] *Appeal to the Learned* (1799), pp. 2, 3.

The most startling view proposed in the sermon was that the unconverted should be urged to come to the sacrament as a converting ordinance. At first sight this looks like a return to the sacramentarianism of the Roman church, but it was not such in fact. On the contrary, Stoddard seems to have held a view of the Lord's Supper too low rather than too high. Among the reasons he gives for his doctrine are that "it is needful that others [than the regenerate] should attend duties of worship that the worship of God *may be carried on.*" And again, "This is very useful that men may obtain sanctifying grace. . . . . God in the Lord's Supper invites us to come to Christ, makes an affecting representation of his sufferings for our sins," etc.[54] He styles it a "seal of the covenant," but he says in his later treatise "that the sacraments do not seal up pardon and salvation to all that receive them, but they are seals to the truth of the covenant."[55] Now, if Stoddard meant by the first clause of this last sentence that the seals did not seal simply as outward elements, no one in New England would have disagreed with him; but he probably intended to deny that the sacraments had *any* personal application as seals of forgiveness to the believing recipient, and to limit their sealing efficacy to the covenant in general, that is, to make them mere monuments—a view far from the Scriptures, the Confessions, and the consensus of teaching in New England at the time. Thus the main thing about them was the affecting representation they made; their efficiency was that of a sermon, or a prayer, and hence they should be attended by the unregenerate, as these should be.[56]

[54] *Sermon* of the year 1707, pp. 15, 16.

[55] *Appeal*, pp. 22, 23.

[56] Stoddard was, however, not a man to use theological terms with accuracy, and there are many contradictions in his forms of presenting his ideas which cannot be fully cleared up. He said, for example, that "those that are saints by

This sermon was, however, not only a factor in the decline of the New England churches, but also incidentally a witness that the decline had already proceeded to quite an alarming point. Upon nothing had the earliest Congregationalists insisted with greater or juster emphasis than upon the necessity of a godly ministry. The Cambridge Platform made the divine calling an indispensable prerequisite of the office.[57] The minute pains taken to secure a regenerate church membership would have had no significance, had not even greater been taken to secure a ministry who could impress the truths of the gospel with power because they had a deep experience of the divine word themselves. But a declining church had now produced a declining ministry, and we find Mr. Stoddard gravely arguing for his new position that sanctifying grace was not necessary unto attending any duty of worship, from the further position, which is stated as an acknowledged principle, that "sanctifying grace is not necessary unto . . . . preaching of the word!" He says:

It is upon all accounts most desirable that preachers should be godly men, and, *ceteris paribus,* they that are converted themselves are most likely to be instruments of the conversion of sinners and the edification of saints. Yet it is lawful for men in a natural condition to preach the word. Jesus Christ sent out Judas to preach the gospel as well as the other disciples.[58]

And later he says again:

If a man do know himself to be unregenerate, yet it is lawful for him to administer baptism and the Lord's Supper. The blessing

calling are to be accepted by the church, whether they be converted or not" (*Sermon,* p. 23). But "called saints" are converted, calling being the divine side, and conversion the human side of the same thing. Again, the whole contention of his sermon was that persons that knew themselves to be unconverted should come to the Lord's table, and yet he said that it was not his object, to "direct the churches to admit any that were not to *rational charity* true believers." But how could "rational charity" call a man a true believer who knew and said himself that he was not? That would seem to be very *irrational* charity.

[57] Chap. viii, § 1.

[58] *Sermon,* p. 6.

of this ordinance doth not depend upon the piety of him that doth administer it. . . . . Men that are destitute of grace are not prohibited in the word of God to administer the ordinances of God.[59]

Now this, we are to note, is by no means the position that the unworthiness of the ministrant does not affect the validity of the sacrament administered, to him who receives it, though this acknowledged principle is used as an argument in its favor; but it is the position that an unconverted man may, so far as he is himself concerned, go on lawfully to administer the ordinances, or, in other words, that a man who knows himself to be in God's eye out of the church may do those things which belong alone to the members of the church to do!

How, now, could such a position be for an instant maintained, had there not already been discussion among the churches upon this topic, which was called out by some patent and strange fact? How, unless there were already ministers who could not in honesty claim to be converted, and for whom some way of justification had been anxiously sought? The later complaint of Whitefield about "unconverted ministers," whom, to his own mind, he found in many places in New England, points in the same direction, and gives too much reason to fear that the decay in the churches had now confessedly reached even the ministers themselves.[60]

[59] *Ibid.,* p. 14.

[60] Mr. Stoddard claimed that the direction of the synod of 1679, cited above, was not contrary to his position in the *Sermon* of 1707, for the words, as they ran in the synod's result ("that persons be not admitted unto communion in the Lord's Supper without making a personal and public profession of their faith and repentance"), were substituted at his request for the more precise and searching formula at first reported, in which the phrase was found, "without making a relation of the work of God's Spirit" (*Appeal,* p. 94). But this was scarcely so. That he made the proposal to change the wording, and that it was done upon his request, we must accept upon his assertion; but that the change had, in the mind of the synod at large, any such significance is impossible. Indeed, an anonymous writer, in reply to Mr. Stoddard (*An Appeal of Some of the Unlearned,* 1709), said (p. 17): "The story told as to the blotting of a passage in the result of the synod, we are upon good information from the

The main object of Mr. Stoddard, in his sermon, was accomplished, and though Increase Mather opposed him with strong logic of the reason, that stronger logic of events was with the innovator, and the practice became general in the valley of the Connecticut at least to admit persons to the communion who did not profess to be converted.[61]   Rev. Benjamin Colman, of Boston, also favored the idea,[62] and doubtless many others, though there was also always a large number who repudiated both the Half-Way Covenant and its daughter, lax communion.   The spiritual dearth increased, revivals were uncommon, immorality grew apace, and the state of religion went lower and lower.[63]   Theological modifications naturally entered with lax practice, and the Arminian writings of Tillotson, Whitby, Taylor, and Clarke, and subsequently the Socinian treatises of Emlyn (reprinted in America in 1756, and no doubt read long before that) and others were read and had a large influence.   How far the Congregational clergy became Arminian at this time (about 1720) it is impossible to say.   The impression was abroad that many, both in the ministry and the churches, were in greater or less sympathy with this style of thought.   Proofs and traces of it will be found at a later point in this history; but it is now enough to note that so keen an observer as Jonathan Edwards thought Arminianism "prevailing" and was led to devote his principal writing to opposing it, and, indeed, began the great revival work of his life with a repreaching

moderator himself, who drew that result, assured it is a mistake, and a gross one."

[61] Trumbull, *History*, Vol. II, p. 146: "A great proportion of the clergy at that time were of opinion that unregenerate men, if externally moral, ought to be admitted to all the ordinances." Cf. *ibid.*, p. 178.

[62] *Sermon*, 1727, title: "Parents and Grown Children should be together at the Lord's Table."

[63] Cf. Trumbull, *History*, Vol. II, p. 137, with Edwards' *Works*, edition of 1830, Vol. IV, p. 19.

of the fundamental doctrines of Calvinism, the effects of which went far to show that his diagnosis of the disease was correct.

The course of this review has brought the reader to the lowest point of religious decline reached in New England, whether it be considered from a practical or a doctrinal point of view. Before he begins to trace the upward course of things, and to view the influences under which that took place, he should pause long enough to perceive that the progress downward has its fruitful cause in the one fact of an alarming absence of vital piety in the New England communities. There was not regenerate material for the regenerate church. It was sought to remedy the difficulty in various ways, but they did not touch this underlying cause. The children of the unregenerate were baptized, but that did not secure their conversion, and the church continued to grow fewer and fewer in number. Then the unregenerate were invited to the Lord's table, but though a greater number of communicants was thus secured, the general condition of the community did not improve, and all that New England was founded for, or her pious sons still cared for, went slowly to ruin. And, doctrinally considered, the cause of all was the doctrine of inability, so preached as to deplete the churches, by discouraging repentance and faith.

The influence of the style of thought becoming largely prevalent in England has been hinted at. The complete understanding of this thought, of importance not only for its direct, but for many indirect, influences upon subsequent New England thinking, demands that a still fuller consideration be given to it in the following pages.

JONATHAN EDWARDS

JONATHAN EDWARD

CHAPTER II

EDWARDS' EARLIER LABORS

The New England churches have now evidently come to a crisis. They have been established in America for a full century. The forces embraced in the perfected system of Calvinism, both good and evil, have been at work a hundred years upon a field singularly favorable to their normal development, protected by its isolation from the most demoralizing tendencies, but not wholly excluded from the general influences, of the age. The course of events has been against the better of them and has tended to emphasize the worse. Political and social degeneration resulting from the trials of the frontier has operated to assist. And, at the end, it seems that the whole theological system is about to give way to another, and with this change the great principles of the Protestant Reformation seem about to fall. But much of the old was evidently good, and cannot be surrendered, and much of the new is bad, and must be resisted. Evidently a great work is waiting to be done, and one demanding a man. What man is there who can do it?

The answer was providentially given in the birth and career of Jonathan Edwards.[1] Born and trained in a par-

[1] Born at East Windsor, Conn., October 5, 1703, the son of Rev. Timothy Edwards, who was of Welsh descent; died at Princeton, N. J., March 22, 1758. Very precocious; his notes made in childhood upon the habits of the spider show great talent in the study of nature. He graduated from Yale at the age of seventeen (1720), and was installed at Northampton, after having served his college as tutor, in 1727. The revival began in 1734, and broke out again in 1740. The *Distinguishing Marks of a Work of the Spirit of God* appeared in 1741, *Thoughts on the Revival* in 1742, the *Religious Affections* in 1746, and *Qualifications for Full Communion* in 1749. In 1750 he was dismissed, went as a missionary to the Indians to Stockbridge, where he wrote his *Freedom of the Will* (1754), *Nature of Virtue* (1755), and *Original Sin* (1758). He became president of Princeton college in 1758. Life by Dwight in his edition of Edwards' *Works;* another by Professor A. V. G. Allen (Boston, 1889); another still expected, of a very elaborate character, by the late Professor E. A. Park.

47

sonage, it was but natural that his early religious experiences should be marked. For a time they were overshadowed by the intellectual interests which engaged his opening mind. At ten years of age he was able to refute with cogency and wit the doctrine that the soul is material and sleeps with the body till the resurrection. At thirteen he was ready for college, and at fourteen he was reading Locke's *Essay upon Human Understanding* and enjoying a far higher pleasure in the perusal of its pages "than the most greedy miser finds when gathering up handfuls of silver and gold from some newly discovered treasure." With the sensational philosophy of this great thinker he became entirely familiar, but the spiritual and mystical tendences of his own mind, combined no doubt with the influence of that strain of thought which, first put by Augustine into the words, *Omne bonum aut Deus aut ex Deo,* had become the determining element in Calvinism, led him to conclusions substantially identical with those of Bishop Berkeley, with whose writings he may have been familiar.[2] The great thoughts of Leibnitz and of Malebranche, of Cumberland and of Hutcheson, became familiar to him, probably through the personal reading of their works. And by his own independent study he had already arrived, while a mere boy, at those great leading principles which formed the staple of his later thinking and constitute his chief contribution to the thought of his age.[3]

[2] See Allen's *Edwards,* pp. 14–17, 309. Both Professor G. P. Fisher, and Professor Fraser, the editor of Berkeley, doubt whether he read Berkeley (Fisher, *Unpublished Essay of Edwards,* p. 18).

[3] There is a tendency among writers to assume that the New England divines cannot have been acquainted very largely with the literature of their times. But this is a great mistake. Professor Park has given lists of the books known to have been read by Hopkins (*Memoir,* p. 53) and Emmons (*Memoir,* pp. 68 ff.). Yale College library was well supplied with books. Cumberland's *De Legibus Naturae,* 3d ed., 1694, was early put there, the English translation of 1727 shortly after publication, and both editions appear in the first catalogue of 1743. Leibnitz' correspondence with Clarke was a common book.

Thus Edwards became intellectually equipped for the task of a theologian above any of his contemporaries. He brought from his studies competent learning, the matured fruits of original thinking, marked independence and entire candor of mind, exceptional acuteness and thoroughness, and chief of all the unquenched fire of native genius of a high order. But he possessed higher qualifications for the work that was to fall to him than even these. That early spiritual experience of divine truth, which had suffered a partial eclipse in later childhood, had been renewed and deepened with his increasing maturity of mind. It is significant, and to a large degree determinative of the whole development of New England theology, that it was about the doctrine of the divine sovereignty that his thoughts principally centered, and that this doctrine, the central idea of Calvinism as distinguished from the Arminianism which was just then entering New England and creating the problem which Edwards was providentially set to solve, though it once "used to appear like a horrible doctrine" to him, became "not only a conviction, but a delightful conviction." [4] His mind possessed the power of spiritual intuition, characteristic of his Welsh ancestry, in a large degree. He seemed to behold spiritual truths by direct vision. And he was eminently a man of prayer, of intimate communion with God as his Father and Friend.

It is comparatively easy for us who live at this later day to formulate the problem which lay before Edwards. It was not to make all things new. The fruits of a historical development were not to be rashly or carelessly relinquished. What was good in the old formulations of doctrine was to be preserved. But at the same time the old could not be reintroduced without modification. Theological opposition and innovation is never properly met by

---

[4] Dwight's *Life*, p. 60.

simple reaffirmation of old positions in the old language.
The reason for the objection must be perceived and appreciated by him who would give it a due and conclusive
answer. What is true in it must be acknowledged and
given proper weight. He who will teach must himself
learn. Hence what has justly offended the newly awakened mind of an inquiring age must be set aside, and out
of all the materials afforded by the times, new and old, the
theologian must go on to introduce, with his better formulations of the old principles, other principles which may
be absolutely new.

It cannot be said that Edwards placed the problem before himself in any such form. He was profoundly attached to the Calvinistic system, and his first instinct was
to restore it to its high place of influence. This was so
far well, and he was hereby preserved from the first great
danger of a leader at such a time, that of disloyalty to the
past. But, though he may have had no thought of doctrinal
change, his mind was too original and his studies too
exact to permit him to remain where his fathers had been.
He was, possibly, somewhat deficient at first in respect for
the positions of his adversaries, though not for the influence which they were exerting. But his perfect candor,
his clear perception of truth, and his personal humility
combined to open to him many new vistas as he studied,
and what truth he saw he acknowledged and made his
own. Thus he made a reply to the departures of the day
which was capable of meeting the situation and of advancing the interests of theology. If his natural intensity of
conviction and expression as to what he was led to adopt,
which seems to make all his writings pulsate with life, be
added, the fitness of Edwards to solve the theological problem of his day, largely unconscious as it was, will have
been made clear.

Edwards' ministry began in a place where the full force of the theological situation could be felt, in Northampton, as the colleague of Solomon Stoddard, to whom he sustained the relation of grandson. In that parish, where the most extreme application of the Half-Way Covenant had been made, the subtle influences of Arminianism were most likely to attract the attention and excite the opposition of such a man as Edwards. For a time no sign of this appears. His grandfather survived his ordination two years, and for two more nothing occurs to mark his work as in any sense peculiar. But in the year 1731 he was invited to preach the "public lecture" in Boston, and selected as his theme "God Glorified in Man's Dependence."[5] He set forth the absolute and universal dependence of the redeemed upon God as the cause, and only proper cause, of all their good. The grace, the power, the direct agency of God are emphasized, and he is presented as the "objective" and "inherent" good of his saints. The doctrine of the sermon was in no respect remarkable, but something in its tone attracted great attention. Its secret is revealed in the following passage from the "use." Says Edwards:

Hence those doctrines and schemes of divinity that are in any respect opposite to such an absolute and universal dependence on God, derogate from his glory and thwart the design of our redemption. And such are those schemes that . . . . own an entire dependence upon God for *some* things, but not for others; they own that we depend on God for the gift and acceptance of a Redeemer, but deny so absolute a dependence on him for the obtaining of an *interest* in the Redeemer. They own an absolute dependence on the Father for giving his Son, and on the Son for working out redemption, but not so entire a dependence upon the Holy Ghost for *conversion*, and a being in Christ, and so coming to a title to his benefits. They own a dependence on God for *means* of grace, but not absolutely for the benefit and success of those means, etc.

It is unquestionable that the preacher, in this reference

[5] *Works*, Dwight's edition in ten volumes (hereafter always quoted, unless otherwise specified), Vol. VII, p. 149.

to undue emphasis upon human independence and initiative, had in mind that "prevailing" Arminianism against which the principal contests of his life were to be waged.

Three years later the silence was again broken by a sermon,[6] preached in his own church, upon the doctrine of a "Divine and Supernatural Light Immediately Imparted to the Soul by the Spirit of God," which was defined as consisting not in our natural convictions of sin and misery, nor in any impression made upon the imagination, nor in any new truths not contained in the word of God, but in a "*sense* of the divine and superlative excellency of the things of religion," and "a conviction of the truth and reality of them." If in the former sermon the logical and doctrinal theologian was foreshadowed, here we find the spiritual seer.

These sermons were like the first booming of a solitary gun upon the opening of a great battle. The more special work of Edwards began when in 1734 he preached a sermon, afterwards expanded into a treatise and published, which initiated his first revival, and began a new epoch in American religious life. It was entitled *Justification by Faith,* and was a direct attack upon Arminianism.[7] It is a strong and original presentation of the common doctrine of the Reformed churches upon this subject. Positions are maintained which Edwards' successors, following out principles which he had given them, were led to reject, although we easily trace at such points a certain conventionality of treatment,[8] which indicates the controlling influence of theological tradition. But at other points the investigating mind which was always asking the reason for every accepted doctrine, and the spiritual trend of the writer's

[6] *Works,* Vol. VI, p. 171.

[7] *Ibid.,* Vol. V, p. 345.

[8] Cf. *ibid.,* pp. 400, 402.

thought, come prominently to view. Justification is defined as consisting, not merely in the forgiveness of our sins, but in the imputation of Christ's righteousness to us whereby we have that which is the ground of our being rewarded with eternal life. The defense of imputation is conventional.[9] But the definition of faith and of repentance marks a distinct advance upon the tone of the previous century,[10] and the explanation of the reason why faith should be made the condition of justification departs widely from the mechanical methods of Calvinistic scholasticism and reproduces the true spiritual atmosphere of the better days. Every idea of merit in faith is excluded—here is the evangelical element; but faith is said to be the condition of forgiveness, because it unites the soul to Christ so that there is a *fitness* in bestowing such a favor in consequence of it. Justification is thus a "manifestation of God's regard to the beauty of that order that there is in uniting those things that have a natural agreement and congruity and unition of the one with the other." [11]

One can scarcely refrain, as he thus passes over the first great influential work of the originator of a new school in theology, from asking how far the future master was seen in his first attempt; nor from considering more seriously whether Edwards really showed himself the man fully to cope with the New England situation. We have already traced the condition of the churches at this time to the lack of conversions, and this lack to the constant preaching of the divine sovereignty in the form of the inability of man. The mind of the age, as well as the experience of the churches, had come to the point where the old doctrine of sovereignty needed modification. More

[9] See particularly p. 395.
[10] *Ibid.*, p. 430.
[11] *Ibid.*, p. 369.

room was demanded for the activity of man. It was at this point that the new leader was to be tested. Could he perceive the real difficulty? Had he any sufficient remedy to offer?

In reply to these questions, a somewhat ambiguous answer must be made. Edwards saw what all saw—Arminians, Half-Way men like Stoddard, and Calvinists alike— that the great necessity of the times was conversions. He saw, what many did not see, that the conversion required was a deep and pervading, a divinely wrought work in the soul. He saw also that the tendency among the Arminians to confuse a "good, moral life" with the Christian life, and to depend for salvation upon the striking at the day of judgment of a kind of moral balance-sheet between good and bad deeds, was a fundamental abandonment of the gospel. The new emphasis upon the worth and place of man in the scheme of things had forgotten for the time that he had misused his freedom radically, and was guilty and ruined. What was wanted, therefore, was just the old doctrine of salvation by faith, by spiritual union with God, and by justification, by the free forgiveness of the sinner in the infinite grace of God in Jesus Christ;[12] and this Edwards enforced with great power. The result was the renewal of what had almost ceased, of conversions, and the revival by the logic of facts in the thinking of the churches of the doctrine of the new birth.[13] There was no new truth brought forward at this point, but a new impression of the truth was made which was almost equivalent to the impression which a new truth is adapted to make. The doctrine of regeneration acquired practical effectiveness, for men were actually born again in great numbers in the revivals of the years 1735 and 1740, and thus the old paralysis of New England was broken up.

[12] See Edwards' own testimony, *Works*, Vol. IV, p. 37.
[13] Cf. Tracy, *Great Awakening*, pp. ix ff.

But Edwards did not at this time see the source of that old paralysis in the doctrine of inability. His influence was that of a great preacher, not yet that of a great thinker. He was not yet at the point where the arguments of his opponents could begin to have a large effect upon his own convictions. He held too strong views as to the divine sovereignty, and had found the doctrine too "delightful" to be much inclined to learn where it had gradually obscured other truths by its too rank development. Hence the doctrine of inability, the source of the whole difficulty which he so clearly saw, did not appear to him in its unfavorable aspects. Indeed, it somewhat obscured his own view of the freeness of God's grace and of the divine readiness to forgive. His preaching was still too much as if men were to give themselves *completely* to God, to surrender themselves *wholly,* to fulfil *every* condition prescribed by the gospel, and then to remain in entire uncertainty whether, after all, God would bless them or not. He even says, quite in the line of the earlier thought, that fixedness of resolution sufficient to obtain salvation is "not in our power." [14] Certainly, such a strain of remark as the following was not eminently calculated to encourage the hearer to action:

You must not think much of your pains, and of the length of time; you must press towards the kingdom of God, and do your utmost, and hold out to the end, and learn to make no account of it when you have done. You must undertake the business of seeking salvation upon these terms, and with no other expectation than this, that *if ever God bestows mercy,* it will be in his own time; and not only so, but also that when you have done all, God *will not hold himself obliged* to show you mercy at last.[15]

Not encouraging, certainly, in its outcome is this passage; and yet there is an appeal to "press" and "do" and "hold out," which has a ring anticipatory of later and bet-

[14] *Works,* p. 462.
[15] *Ibid.,* p. 467.

ter preaching; and this tone of exhortation to action which sounded through all Edward's preaching—the thrilling, intense activity of his ardent soul—this it was which moved men to repentance and conversion, and this first actually broke down the doctrine of inability. That doctrine has never played any actual part in the thinking of men in times of real revival.

Evidently, then, the thinker and reformer has not yet come to his full strength. There is a promise, but still little present exercise, of the powers of a great intellectual leader. It is the instinctive working of a great mind which we see here, rather than the well-planned efforts of one who had surveyed the field and fully comprehended his task.

The external history of the revival does not concern us here. Its vicissitudes, the interruption which it suffered until renewed under the agency of Whitefield, the abundant labors of Edwards at home and abroad, the abnormal phenomena attending it, however interesting, are all matters aside from our present purpose. It called out intense opposition from many moderate men among the New England clergy, of whom the most prominent was Charles Chauncy, minister of the First Church in Boston, who wrote several tracts against it, among them his *Seasonable Thoughts on the State of Religion in New England* (1743).[16] The divine character and the religious worth of the revival were denied, and hence Edwards felt called upon to come to its defense. In a large measure he became the historian of the great spiritual upheaval. He was also led to the production of a work which was designed to lay the foundation for more solid and successful labor in the field of practical religion by removing the obscurity which overhung the nature of true religion, and by setting forth

---

[16] See Dexter's bibliography for 1740 and following years, in his *Congregationalism as Seen in Its Literature*.

the distinguishing notes of that virtue which is acceptable in the sight of God. It was entitled *A Treatise Concerning Religious Affections*,[17] and was an exceedingly thorough affair. In a sense it may be regarded as the full presentation of the ideas which had formed the substance of the sermon upon illumination of 1734. It rests upon the conception of the nature of virtue which was elaborated in the treatise of 1755, and it is involved in some of the confusion which marked the first principles of the treatise upon the will. It will therefore require some attention at a later point in the study of the history of Edwards' ideas, but is of the first importance in immediate connection with the review of his services in the period now under consideration, since it is the chief illustration of his entire accord with the spiritual side of the Westminster theology to which notice has already been drawn.

"True religion, in great part," says Edwards, "consists in holy affections." What the affections are he does not clearly define, for though distinguishing between what are called in the better phraseology of modern days, volitions, and the emotions proper, he blurs the distinction and refuses to acknowledge that there are two distinct faculties of the mind here concerned. His thought, stated in modern language, is, however, clearly this, that religion consists in the holy choice of the will accompanied by the lively play of the appropriate emotions. Having established this point, he goes on to discuss most searchingly some supposed signs of true religion which are no certain evidences of its existence. It is, for example, no sign that religious affections are "truly gracious" that they are "very great," or that they have "great effects upon the body," or that they cause fluency or fervor, or that they are "not excited by us," or "come with texts of Scripture," or that their sub-

[17] *Works,* Vol. V, pp. 1–344.

jects have great confidence; etc., etc. And then he passes to the positive treatment of the theme, in which he follows the lines of his former sermon. Truly spiritual affections arise from supernatural operations on the heart; their object is the excellency of divine things "as they are in themselves;" they are founded on the moral excellency of divine things; they arise from divine illumination; they are attended with a conviction of the reality and certainty of divine things; and their fruit are tempers of heart and courses of life that are manifestly truly Christian.

In the course of the treatise many incidental definitions are thrown out which add much to the clearness of the general thought above that of the former discussion. The sense of divine things which the true Christian has, is unfolded at some length, and is condensed in the following definition: "A new foundation laid in the nature of the soul for a new kind of exercises of the same [i. e., the original] faculty of the understanding." But when Edwards comes to the peculiar certainty which the Christian has of the truth of divine things, he is particularly clear and valuable. He says:

> It is evident that there is a spiritual conviction of the truth, or a belief peculiar to those who are spiritual, who are regenerated, and who have the Spirit of God, in his holy communications, dwelling in them as a vital principle. . . . . A view of the divine glory directly convinces the mind of the divinity of these things. . . . . They therefore that see the stamp of this glory in divine things, they see divinity in them, they see God in them, and so see them to be divine; because they see that in them wherein the truest idea of divinity consists. Thus a soul may have a kind of intuitive knowledge of the divinity of the things exhibited in the gospel; not that he judges the doctrines of the gospel to be from God without any argument or deduction at all; but it is without any long chain of arguments; the argument is but one and the evidence direct; the mind ascends to the truth of the gospel but one step, and that is its divine glory. . . . . The gospel of the blessed God does not go abroad a begging for its evidence so much as some think: it has its highest and most proper evidence in itself.[18]

[18] *Loc. cit.,* pp. 176 ff.

And he further adds, with reference to the importance of this argument:

Unless men may come to a reasonable solid persuasion and conviction of the truth of the gospel by internal evidences in the way that has been spoken, viz., by a sight of its glory, it is impossible that those who are illiterate and unacquainted with history should have any thorough and effectual conviction of it at all. . . . . After all that learned men have said to them, there will remain innumerable doubts on their minds; they will be ready, when pinched with some great trial of their faith, to say, "How do I know this or that? How do I know when these histories were written? Learned men tell me these histories were so and so attested in their day; but how do I know that there were such attestations then?" . . . . But the gospel was not given only for learned men. . . . . It is unreasonable to suppose that God has provided for his people no more than probable evidences of the truth of the gospel. . . . . And if we come to fact and experience, there is not the least reason to suppose that one in a hundred of those who have been sincere Christians and have had a heart to sell all for Christ, have come by their conviction of the truth of the gospel this way [viz. by external arguments]. . . . . And indeed, it is but very lately that these arguments have been set in a clear and convincing light even by learned men themselves: and since it has been done, there never were fewer thorough believers among those who have been educated in the true religion. Infidelity never prevailed so much in any age as in this wherein these arguments are handled to the greatest advantage.[19]

Edwards did not neglect the external arguments,[20] as Calvin had not; but we see here clearly that he placed the weight of argument where it should be, in the inner certainty of the specific Christian experience. This was the trend of the Westminster confession; and under Edwards' influence it maintained itself for a generation longer in New England. Under what influences it gave place to the purely external treatment of the subject which was characteristic of the middle of the present century, the history of the Unitarian controversy will clearly reveal.

[19] *Ibid.*, pp. 182 ff.

[20] He says: "They may be in some respects subservient *to the begetting of a saving faith in men*" (Vol. V, p. 186), and he pays attention to them in his "Observations," Vol. VII, pp. 244 ff.

The last important work owing its origin immediately
to the results of the revival was the *Qualifications for Communion*. Edwards had at first followed unquestionably in
the path marked out by his grandfather Stoddard, and admitted to the communion without special examination as
to evidences of conversion upon the part of the communi-
cant. But he discovered a bad moral condition in the community affecting its younger members, some of whom
were communicants; and the resistance which was made
by prominent families to necessary discipline led him to
examine the subject with care, and he soon adopted the
original position of the New England churches and determined to admit none to communion who were not "osten-
sible" Christians. His attempts to carry out his new views
in practice led to his dismissal from his pastorate, and to the
preparation of this treatise in defense of himself before his
people. He thereby laid the foundation for the general
practice of Congregationalists for more than a century.

His proposition, carefully guarded, is that none should
be admitted to the Lord's Supper but "such as are in profession and in the eye of the church's Christian judgment
godly or gracious persons." He does not seek to secure infallibly the actual possession of saving grace in every com-
municant, for that would involve on the part of the church
the power of reading men's hearts; but there should be
what is now phrased a "credible profession." The arguments he employed are these:

None ought to be admitted as members of the visible church of
Christ but visible and professing saints. . . . . All who are capable
of it are bound to make an explicit and open profession of the true
religion. . . . . The profession should be of real piety [against the
idea of professing a belief in Christianity in general without a profession of personal faith in Christ]. . . . . There is no good reason
why the people of God should not profess a proper respect to Christ
in their hearts as well as a true notion of him in their heads. . . . .

The teachings of Christ. the practice of the primitive church, and the Scriptures in general, require it.

He modestly but strongly refutes the position of Mr. Stoddard, saying that the natural tendency of the Lord's Supper to move the heart and lead to conversion is no proof that this was its designed object, and finally strikes at the root of the whole Half-Way system by saying, in effect, that the things which baptism and the Lord's Supper signify do not exist in the case of the unregenerate, and hence to bestow the badges of repentance and forgiveness upon such persons is an empty and dishonoring honor.

The importance of the practical service rendered by the *Qualifications for Communion* can scarcely be overestimated. It is too evident to need long discussion here. Its influence in the doctrinal sphere, though indirect, was permanent and broad. Wherever there were "Edwardeans," after there came to be a distinctively Edwardean school, evidences of regeneration were scrutinized with care, and a consequent emphasis was laid upon the doctrine of regeneration, and upon the allied doctrines of the will, and of virtue, and of sin, which form the great staple of New England discussion. It is probable that Edwards' practical work as a revivalist and a faithful and scrupulous pastor had as great an influence upon the future of his native province as that which he did in his study by the methods of the philosophic divine. Yet in the providence of God he was to do both works; and the separation from Northampton, which was so unjust, and which cost him so much anguish, was the divine means of transplanting him to the desolate and distant Stockbridge, where his mind, released from most of the interruptions of active life, was at leisure to bring forth out of its treasure-house things new and old. To this period, the loftier and greater in its results for American religious thought, the history now turns.

CHAPTER III

THE TREATISE ON THE FREEDOM OF THE WILL

If the great characteristic of Edward's mind was acuteness, next, if not upon an equality with this, are to be placed his depth and thoroughness. He had met Arminianism upon the side of its practical opposition to evangelical religion, of its coldness, its self-righteousness, its antagonism to the practical measures by which a pure Christian church could alone be sustained. But he was content with no superficial consideration of what were mere symptoms. These outward phenomena were traceable to some definite cause, and that some particular idea. Edwards conceived this to be the philosophy of the will which had become prevalent, and as early as 1747 he had sketched the plan of a work upon this theme, which the disturbances leading up to his dismissal had rendered it impossible for him to carry out.[1] In Stockbridge he took up the thread, and in 1754 printed his *Careful and Strict Inquiry into the Modern Prevailing Notions of That Freedom of the Will Which is Supposed to be Essential to Moral Agency,* etc.[2] Its importance is evident not only from the universal plaudits with which it was received, and from the position among the great men of the world which it secured to its author, but by the permanence of its influence as a classic of the New England theology. In actual fact, it was but the first of a considerable series of treatises in New England in which the theory of the will was discussed, and by which it was essentially modified and improved; but in the imagination of the different leaders of the school, down to the latest, it was the unsurpassed ideal with which they all sought to prove their entire agreement.

[1] Dwight's *Life,* p. 250.   [2] *Works,* Vol. II, pp. 1–300.

The *Freedom of the Will* cannot be correctly understood without a clear view of Edwards' starting-point. Two particulars are to be carefully observed, of which the first is his conception of the idea of cause. There are evidences in those remarkable *Notes on the Mind,* written while he was a youth in college, that Edwards early busied himself with this problem; and it is noteworthy that the treatise written in mature manhood went no farther than the notes of the youth. The *Notes* say succinctly: "Cause is that after or upon the existence of which, or the existence of it after such a manner, the existence of another thing follows." [3] And in the treatise the definition runs:

Therefore I sometimes use the word *cause,* in this enquiry, to signify any *antecedent,* either natural or moral, positive or negative, on which an event, either a thing, or the manner and circumstance of a thing, so depends, that it is the ground and reason, either in whole or in part, why it is, rather than not; or why it is as it is, rather than otherwise; or, in other words, any antecedent with which a consequent event is so connected that it truly belongs to the reason why the proposition which affirms that event, is true; whether it has any positive influence, or not. And agreeably to this, I sometimes use the word *effect* for the consequence of another thing which is *perhaps rather an occasion than a cause,* most properly speaking.[4]

Upon the idea of cause as thus defined the whole treatise rests, for an event in the realm of mind without a cause is as inconceivable to Edwards as such a one in the realm of matter. This is the great positive argument of the discussion, though rather an assumed axiom than the subject of prolonged elaboration. And thus it comes to pass that into the very foundation of the whole argument there is inserted an ambiguity which doubtless deceived Edwards himself, and has given rise to two distinct interpretations of the

[3] *Ibid.,* Vol. I, p. 668.

[4] *Ibid.,* p. 50. Cf. the language of J. S. Mill, *Logic* (Harper's ed., p. 236): "To certain facts, certain facts always do, and, as we believe, will continue to, succeed. The invariable antecedent is termed the cause; the invariable consequent, the effect."

work. Motives are "causes" determining the will. Is the motive an occasion upon which the efficient will acts, or itself an efficient cause operating upon the will? Edwards' definition gives no answer to this question, for he has wrapped up in one term both efficient and occasional causes. It was doubtless true that his idealism had much to do with this. If God was the only agent, if, according to the occasionalism of Malebranche, God does everything upon occasion of certain events in the mundane sphere, then there is no essential difference between the occasional, and what seems to us to be the efficient cause. But, however the ambiguity was introduced into his thinking, there it was, at the very foundation of the edifice he was about to rear, and destined to make its whole structure insecure to the highest pinnacle.[5]

The second particular calling for attention is the division of the mind into faculties, understanding, and will, which Edwards, following Calvin,[6] and deserting at this redeeming point his master, Locke,[7] unfortunately adopted. Thus he confounded the emotions, the action of which is necessary, with the will, the action of which is free, and attributed to the latter, as a matter of self-evidence, all the necessity of the former. The confusion resulted in the entire ambiguity of the word "inclination,"[8] which is sometimes used to denote an emotion and often in the same sentence, and in the process of a vital argument, used immediately thereafter, and as if no change of meaning had been made, to denote a volition.[9] Hence as an argument the whole treatise splits upon the rock of this ambiguous mid-

[5] The whole reply to Chubb (p. 96, 1) is vitiated by this confusion. The idea of *power* was, in like manner, eviscerated (Vol. I, p. 681).

[6] *Institute,* Book I, chap. xv, §§ 6–8; cf. Book II, chap. ii, § 2.

[7] *Works,* Vol. II, p. 17; cf. Vol. V, p. 10; Vol. I, p. 693.

[8] And similar words, such as "preferring" (pp. 22, 24, etc.).

[9] For example, pp. 20, 35, 70, 166. P. 24, bottom, verges perilously near it. Examples, more or less forcible, can, however, be found on nearly every page.

dle. It is one of the curiosities of literature that in our own
day there should be found some, who accept the threefold
division of the mind and the true efficiency of second causes,
to declare that they agree with Edwards on the doctrine of
the will!

With such fundamental conceptions long since incorporated in his whole style of thinking, Edwards came into
contact with the Arminian writers of his day. Among these
the chief was Daniel Whitby,[10] who in his work entitled
Six Discourses[11] discussed, not only the will, but also all the
so-called "Five Points" of controversy between the Calvinists and the Arminians. Thus he taught a "conditional election to be made sure by good works," as well as the doctrine
of general atonement, and combated the Calvinistic views
upon irresistible grace, bondage of the will, and the perseverance of the saints.

Such a setting to the doctrine of free will did not help
it with Edwards. But in its details this doctrine impinged
upon his established methods of thought. The will, according to Whitby, is free not only in the sense of being the
faculty of choice, but as having no determination either to
evil or good. Its liberty he thus defines: "a power of acting
from ourselves, or doing what we will."[12] Thus it is free,
not only from "co-action," but from what, in distinction
from that, was called "necessity." In a quotation from a
certain Mr. Thorndike the word "indifference" is used to
describe this freedom.[13]

Upon this free will motives, such as promises and threats,
operate and exercise influence; but when the motives are
presented, the decision still lies with the will. It may choose
in the one way equally with the other; and it chooses as it

[10] Church of England, rector of St. Edmund's, Salisbury; born 1638, died
1726.

[11] Edition at hand is the American reprint (Worcester, 1801).

[12] *Op. cit.*, p. 249.   [13] *Ibid.*, p. 231.

does by "self-determination." True, Whitby does not, so far as noted, employ this precise word, upon which Edwards rings so many changes; but the thought is his, and he does once at least say that the will "determines itself."[14] If, now, it determines itself, says Whitby, there is evidently no rational ground for knowing beforehand what the action of the will in a given case may be, even when all the operating motives are supposed to be known. The omniscience of God, which embraces his foreknowledge, is therefore an attribute entirely mysterious. It also follows that man in conversion is not passive and that the grace of God is not irresistible.

The arguments by which Whitby sustained his positions were not novel, and moved in the plain sphere of common-sense. He first sought to show that it was as essential that the will should be free from "necessity" as from "co-action," and then directed his easy task toward showing that there could be, in consistence with the condition in which man is (a state of probation), and with the treatment which he receives as an object of praise or blame, of commands, and of promises, no "co-action" of the will.

To this treatise, and to others like it, as, for example, that of Mr. Chubb,[15] Edwards gave minute attention. It doubtless seemed to him that the answer was easy. The philosophical world had before it in the work of Locke the complete materials for the refutation. He had only to sit down, as he thought, and with sufficient thoroughness explain and enforce what Locke had already said in brief, and then show at length how inconsequent and illogical in the comparison each several position of the antagonists was,

---

[14] *Loc. cit.*, 240.

[15] Edwards quotes in this treatise: Whitby, *Discourses;* Hobbes; Samuel Clarke, *Demonstration;* Turnbull, *Christian Philosophy;* Chubb, *Collection of Tracts;* Stebbing, *Treatise on the Operations of the Spirit;* Taylor, *Original Sin;* Lord Kames, *Essays;* and others.

and the work would be done. It is therefore necessary briefly to review Locke's theory of the will in preparation for the consideration of Edwards himself.

It has already been noted that Edwards early read Locke's *Essay on Human Understanding*. That early reading seems to have made the strongest impression upon his mind, and, as we shall see, the improvements which Locke introduced in his second edition were generally rejected by Edwards in the preparation of his great treatise.

Locke begins his treatment of the will[16] by defining the idea of liberty as "the idea of a power in any agent to do or forbear any particular action according to the determination or thought of the mind whereby either of them is preferred to the other." It will be seen that some stress was laid by him in the development of his thought upon the word "forbear" in this definition; but apart from this modification, liberty is always external liberty, the power to do as one wills. He even says that it is an "unreasonable because unintelligible question whether man's will be free or no."

> Liberty, which is but a power, belongs only to agents, and cannot be an attribute or modification of the will which is also but a power. . . . . To ask whether the will has freedom is to ask whether one power has another power, one ability another ability. . . . . We can scarce tell how to imagine any being freer than to be able to do what he wills.

In developing this thought, he touches the question "whether a man be at liberty to will which of the two he pleases, motion or rest?" Which he answers thus:

> This question carries the absurdity of it so manifestly in itself that one might thereby sufficiently be convinced that liberty concerns not the will. For to ask, whether a man be at liberty to will either motion or rest, speaking or silence, which he please, is to ask whether a man can will what he wills, or be pleased with what he is pleased

[16] *Human Understanding*, Book II, chap. xxi, "Of Power." The edition used is the "ninth" (really the second), (London: Churchill, 1726). Edwards quotes the "seventh," which was also properly the second. A thorough critical edition of Locke is still lacking, and would clear up many obscure points.

with. A question which I think needs no answer; and they who can make a question of it must suppose one will to determine the acts of another, and another to determine that; and so on *in infinitum*.

This argument, it should be noted, is the famous *reductio ad absurdum* which formed the staple of Edwards' reply to his adversaries.

Locke now takes up the central topic of the theme, and asks the question: "What determines the will?" At this point the important difference between the first and second editions of the *Human Understanding* comes into view. Locke says:

> It seems so established and settled a maxim by the general consent of all mankind that good, the greater good, determines the will, that I do not at all wonder that, when I first published my thoughts on this subject, I took it for granted; and I imagine that by a great many I shall be thought more excusable for having then done so than that now I have ventured to recede from so received an opinion. But yet upon a stricter enquiry I am forced to conclude that good, the greater good, though apprehended and acknowledged to be so, does not determine the will until our desire, raised proportionably to it, makes us *uneasy* in the want of it.

The answer to the question propounded—"What determines the will?"—is, then, in both editions: "The motive before it;" but in the first edition, where the will had not been sharply distinguished from the desire, it was the objective motive, the good, whereas now it is the subjective motive, or the desire excited by the good presented to the mind. This distinction depended upon the new conception Locke had gained of the "perfect distinction" of the will from the desire, which, he says, "must not be confounded."

But, now, what moves desire? Locke replies, "Happiness." "What has an aptness to produce pleasure in us, is that we call good." But a good must be so situated as to stir desire, or it will never influence action. An absent good, for example, is less effective than some present uneasiness.

The drift of all this discussion has evidently been to place the will completely under the causative control of the desires. But at just this point Locke introduces the saving element for which he has previously opened the way. It is natural, he says, that the greatest and most pressing uneasiness—

should determine the will to the next action; and so it does for the most part, but not always. For the mind having in most cases, as is evident in experience, a power to suspend the execution and satisfaction of any of its desires, and so all, one after another, is at liberty to consider the objects of them, examine them on all sides, and weigh them with others. *In this lies the liberty man has,* and from the not using of it right, comes all that variety of mistakes, errors, and faults which we run into in the conduct of our lives, and our endeavors after happiness, whilst we precipitate the determination of our wills and engage too soon before due examination.

But when deliberation has taken place, the action not only follows according to the "most pressing uneasiness," but it should do this, for "'tis not a fault but a perfection of our nature to desire, will, and act according to the last result of a fair examination."

Upon this basis, as already said, the reply of Edwards to Whitby and his associates was prepared. In substance, it was as follows:

Every act of the will is an act of choice and involves alternatives. Placed between two eligible things, the question in discussion is: "What determines the will to choose the one rather than the other?" The Arminians said that the will determined itself. Edwards says that the will is determined by the motive which it actually follows.

To motives are therefore ascribed a positive power. They are causes, and, so far as a tendency to the occasionalism of Malebranche which is evident in his writings allowed, Edwards ascribed to them efficient causation. They could be calculated, and upon a perfect knowledge of their nature and potency the future action of a being influenced by them could be predicted. In this the subjective conditions which determine the influence of motives were not neglected, but still positive power was left to the objective motive.

Thus the prevailing motive both determines that the action of the will shall take place and also how it shall take place. It does this because it possesses a certain attractive power, or because it is an apparent good. And, inasmuch as it acts as a cause, it is evident that the greatest apparent good in any group of conflicting apparent goods will determine the will. Hence the maxim: "The will is as the greatest apparent good."

Hence the choices of the will are as necessary as the events of the physical world. They are caused by motives in the same sense as these are caused by the forces of objects and events in nature. Yet this does not infringe upon the liberty of man, because it leaves him so far entirely able *to do* what he wills; and this is the meaning of liberty and the only meaning it can have. To suppose that freedom means that a man can will as he wills, is to involve oneself in self-contradiction. The only conceivable liberty is external liberty.

Virtue or vice consists in the nature of the choice made in any case irrespective of its origin. Commands and threats are motives which may be employed, but whatever the motives, as a man chooses, so is he.

Such is a summary view of the theory brought forward in answer to Whitby.[17] Its importance demands that it be presented in the very words of its author. After some pre-

[17] There is another and quite different interpretation of Edwards. It is founded upon the ambiguity of the word "cause" in his philosophy. It makes motives merely the occasion of the action of the will, which here follows, not a "law," but a "usage"—to employ the favorite phrase of Professor Park. But, when every allowance has been made, this cannot be said to be an objective interpretation of Edwards. It was first brought forward by the younger Edwards as an expedient to meet the objections of Samuel West, and is essentially, however excusably or unconsciously, a partisan interpretation. A full discussion will be found in the appropriate place below.

liminary definitions, which have been already noted, Edwards begins the development of his theme by defining the determination of the will. He says: "By determining the will, if the phrase be used with any meaning, must be intended *causing* that the act of the will should be thus and not otherwise," etc.[18]

Now, evidently Edwards' meaning in the further development of his theme will be dependent upon the meaning attached by him to the word "causing." This he elsewhere explains in the following words:

Sometimes by moral necessity is meant that necessity of connection and consequence which arises from such moral causes as the strength of inclination or motives, and the connection which there is in many cases between these and such certain volitions and actions. . . . . By natural necessity as applied to men I mean such necessity as men are under through the force of natural causes as distinguished from what are called moral causes. . . . . *This difference, however, does not lie so much in the nature of the connection as in the two terms connected.*[19]

The causes are *motives,* which are thus defined:

By motive I mean the whole of that which moves, excites, or invites the mind to volition, whether that be one thing singly, or many things conjunctly. Many particular things may concur and unite their strength to induce the mind; and when it is so, all together are as one complex motive. And when I speak of the strongest motive, I have respect to the strength of the whole that operates to induce a particular act of volition whether that be the strength of one thing alone or many together.[20]

The law of the action of motives is thus expressed:

Things that exist in the view of the mind have their strength, tendency, or advantage to move, or excite its will, from many things appertaining to the nature and circumstances of the thing viewed, the nature and circumstances of the mind that views, and the degree and manner of its view; of which it would perhaps be hard to make a perfect enumeration. But so much I think may be determined in general, without room for controversy, that whatever is

[18] "Freedom of the Will," *Works*, Vol. II, p. 18.
[19] *Ibid.,* pp. 32 f.
[20] *Ibid.,* p. 19.

perceived or apprehended by an intelligent and voluntary agent, which has the nature and influence of a motive to volition or choice, is considered or viewed *as good;* nor has it any tendency to engage the election of the soul in any further degree than it appears such. For to say otherwise, would be to say, that things that appear good have a tendency, by the appearance they make, to engage the mind to elect them, some other way than by their appearing eligible to it; which is absurd. And therefore it must be true, in some sense, that *the will always is, as the greatest apparent good is.*[21]

Edwards' system is thus a system of necessity, and avowedly so. But it is not a system of physical necessity, and he is at considerable pains to make this plain, futile as the distinction will prove to be under his management of the theory. He expresses himself variously. At one time he says:

Metaphysical or philosophical necessity is nothing different from . . . . certainty. I speak not now of the certainty of knowledge, but the certainty that is in things themselves, which is the foundation of the certainty of the knowledge.[22]

At another time:

Philosophical necessity is really nothing else than the full and fixed connection between the things signified by the subject and predicate of the proposition which affirms something to be true . . . . And in this sense I use the word necessity in the following discourse when I endeavor to prove that necessity is not inconsistent with liberty.[23]

Broad and free as this may sound, it is to be read in connection with what appears upon the next following page:

The only way that anything that is to come to pass hereafter is or can be necessary, is by a *connection* with something that is necessary in its own nature, or something that already is or has been; so that, the one being supposed, the other certainly follows.

[21] *Loc. cit.,* p. 20. At another place Edwards says: "An appearing most agreeable to the mind or pleasing to the mind and the mind's preferring and choosing seem hardly to be distinct." Of this passage Henry B. Smith observes (*System of Christian Theology,* p. 246): "In our view this is the least satisfactory passage in Edwards' treatise on the Will. In this view the motive would be the efficient and not merely the occasional cause of volition."

[22] *Ibid.,* p. 28.

[23] *Ibid.,* p. 29.

Now, it is to be remembered that this "connection" is by *causation.*

Equally careful is Edwards to define the phrase "moral inability." He says:

> Moral inability consists . . . . either in the want of inclination; or the strength of a contrary inclination [meaning here, probably, an affection of the sensibility]; or the want of sufficient motives in view, to induce and excite the act of the will, or the strength of apparent motives to the contrary. Or both these may be resolved into one; and it may be said in one word, that moral inability consists in the opposition or want of inclination [meaning here, probably, a choice of the will].[24]

The decisive passage upon the meaning of the word "liberty" in Edwards' scheme is the following:

> The plain and obvious meaning of the words freedom and liberty in common speech is *the power, opportunity, or advantage that any one has, to do as he pleases.* Or in other words, his being free from hindrance or impediment in the way of doing or conducting in any respect as he wills.[25]

In this he confessedly follows Locke, and refers to him for further amplification of the point.[26]   And, quite in Locke's vein, he goes on to say, a little farther down: "To talk of liberty or the contrary as belonging to the very will itself, is *not to speak good sense.*"

These may suffice for quotations from the first part of the work, which is taken up with definitions. The second part considers "whether there is or can be any such sort of freedom of the will as that wherein Arminians place the essence of the liberty of all moral agents; *and whether any such thing ever was or can be conceived of!*" The answer is, of course, "No," and is arrived at by the most acute, minute, and elaborate reasoning, discussion, refutation, and (supposed) annihilation of the enemies' position; for Ed-

24 *Ibid.,* p. 35.
25 *Ibid.,* p. 38.
26 *Ibid.,* p. 39.

wards did not intend to leave the least possibility of an
answer.

Discussing the "self-determining power of the will," he
says:

Therefore, if the will determines all its own free acts, the *soul*
determines them in the exercise of a power of willing and choosing;
or, which is the same thing, it determines them of choice; it *determines* its own acts by *choosing* its own acts. If the will determines
the will, then choice orders and determines the choice; and acts of
choice are subject to the decision and follow the conduct of *other*
acts of choice. And, therefore, if the will determines all its own free
acts, then every free act of choice is determined by a preceding act
of choice, choosing that act. And if that preceding act of the will
be also a free act, then, by these principles, in this act, too, the will
is self-determined: that is, this, in like manner, is an act that the soul
voluntarily chooses; or, which is the same thing, it is an act determined still by a preceding act of the will choosing that. Which
brings us directly to a contradiction: for it supposes an act of the
will preceding the first act in the whole train, directing and determining the rest; or a free act of the will before the first free act
of the will. Or else we must come at last to an act of the will determining the consequent acts, wherein the will is not self-determined
and so is not a free act, in this notion of freedom: but if the first
act in the train, determining and fixing the rest, be not free, none
of them all can be fr ee, as is manifest at first view, but [a "first view"
not being enough for a man like Edwards] shall be demonstrated pres-
ently.[27]

The following page and a half are an elaborate restate-
ment of this argument, and it is substantially repeated, in
varying forms, on a moderate estimate, a hundred times in
this treatise. At one time it appears thus:

Still the questi on returns, wherein lies man's liberty in that anti-
cedent act of will which chose the consequent act. The answer according to the same principles must be, that his liberty in this also
lies in his willing as he would, or as he chose, or agreeable to another act of choice preceding that. And so the question returns *in
infinitum,* and the like answer must be made *in infinitum.* In order
to support their opinion, there must be no beginning, but free acts
of will must have been chosen by foregoing free acts of will in the
soul of every man, without beginning.[28]

[27] *Loc. cit.,* p. 43.   [28] *Ibid.,* p. 62.

This argument, with the other argument that there is no event without a cause, form the only positive arguments of this part of the work, which goes on to consider the possibility of choosing things absolutely indifferent, to explore still further the idea of liberty, and to discuss the connection of volition with motives. The foreknowledge of God comes into the sweep of the theme, and an elaborate biblical argument exhibits the minuteness of the divine foreknowledge of men's volitions, and then Edwards infers necessity, which, as inferred, is "certainty" and, as used, is a causative connection. The third part of the treatise discusses the supposed necessity of the Arminian idea of liberty to moral agency, etc.; and the last part, the chief grounds of the reasoning of the Arminians, without, however, introducing anything essentially new, and with innumerable repetitions of what had already been exhaustively said.

The impression produced by the work was enormous. The new doctrine of a free will had so much to commend itself to the ordinary reason of man that, when a champion of necessarianism again ventured to come forth, and when he succeeded in defending the old positions with such acuteness, and with such an air of invincibleness, the whole world wondered, and the defenders of the old doctrines went back to the old theories with the feeling that now they were forever safe. And yet the work, judged simply upon its merits as an intellectual creation, must be styled a logical failure on a great scale. The ambiguities involved in its fundamental positions have been already pointed out. The application of the law of causality to the operations of the mind is in contravention of the simplest facts of consciousness. The fallacy of the infinite series may be forced upon every argument touching the domain where God and man unite and the spheres of the finite and infinite intersect. If Edwards overthrew freedom by his argument, he also virtually overthrew the existence of God; for if God is required as a cause of the world, then a cause is required for God, and a cause for this cause, and so on *ad infinitum.* Nor was the work original except in the fulness of its treatment of its theme, and in its minuteness and acuteness. Substantially, as has now been made fully evident, it is a reproduction of Locke's theory. The idea of liberty is the same; of determination by motive; of the different weight of different motives; of the causative relation between motive and action. The argument from causation is in Locke, though obscured by his sensational philosophy; the general conception of the inconceivability of the Arminian position is Locke's; and even the argument of the *reductio ad absurdum.*

But these defects did not essentially interfere with the service which the treatise was capable of rendering to the progress of New England theology. As a permanent answer to the Arminians, it was a philosophical failure; but, as the case against the Arminians was not purely philosophical, it was capable of meeting them successfully in the more purely theological sphere, and this it did. In maintaining freedom, some of them maintained a "liberty of indifference," or that "equilibrium whereby the will is without antecedent bias." This was not true of Whitby, though he might at times be construed so; but it was true of others. Thus they would destroy, not only the controlling power, but the real influence of motives, and fall back into the old Pelagian view which destroyed the universal depravity of man, and the certainty that without grace he will never repent and turn to God. Now, the real answer to this theory upon its philosophical side is man's consciousness of the influence of motives, and if Edwards proved too much by ascribing to motives causative power, the sound residuum of his argument, when his extrava-

gances were corrected, was effective in giving a basis for
the theological doctrines, which were too evidently scriptural to be denied by any who would listen to a biblical
argument.

Edwards' discussion of foreknowledge is also noteworthy. His two propositions are: first, God foreknows
our volitions; second, foreknowledge infers necessity. His
proof of the first proposition is derived from prophecy
which has foretold events, even minute ones, depending
upon the volitions of men. The argument for the second
point is concisely that nothing can be known or foreknown
without evidence, and that the only evidence establishing
the certainty of future events is the will of God. From
this argument he draws the corollary that the decrees of
God are no more inconsistent with human liberty than the
foreknowledge of God, thus connecting his theme immediately with the subject of election. This was clearly superior to the Arminian reference of the whole subject to
the realm of mystery, however unsatisfactory as a rationale
of the theme.

However defective, then, the treatise on the will was,
its effect was to bring the theology of New England back
to Calvinism, and this was a great service. The Arminianism which threatened it was not an Arminianism depending upon better views of the will, though at some
points it had them. It was a Pelagianizing Arminianism
which denied the essential doctrines of grace. It needed
rebuttal. It emphasized the manward side of theology too
much, just as the extreme Calvinism of the early day had
emphasized the godward side too much. The future lay
with neither extreme. New England theology was finally
to attempt a better adjustment of these two elements to one
another; but it was indispensable that it should not first

forget the divine side. This Edwards prevented, and thus made all the following sound development possible.

But Edwards' service was not exhausted in the conservative force of his treatise, or in its negative results. He had propounded a distinction which was not correct or successful as he presented it, but which proved, with a better understanding, of great use to his successors—that between natural and moral ability and inability. In a word, natural ability and inability arise from natural or physical causes; moral ability and inability, from motives, or states of the will which are resolvable, in the last analysis, into motives.

Now, inasmuch as Edwards' "motives" are true causes, moral inability does not really differ in essence from natural; for both are effects. Hence the distinction is sophistical as presented in Edwards. But in Edwards' followers it became correct and valuable, and was of use in distinguishing between what were described as the "can't" of lack of power, and the "can't" which is really "won't." Thus much light was shed at several points upon difficult doctrines. The old Calvinism had had no place for any ability to good, and this had been the paralyzing influence of the early days. Edwards introduced *an* ability, which in process of time became a *true* ability, under which revival preaching arose; and good practice in converting men and good theology went together.

Another distinct service rendered by this treatise was the introduction into New England thought of a topic upon which subsequent writers were largely to busy themselves with advantage to the prevailing methods of defending the Christian faith. This topic was the origin of evil. It arose in consequence of the argument urged by the Arminians that necessity made God the author of sin. In attempting to meet them, Edwards simply carried out the system which he had already laid down in the earlier por-

tions of the treatise.   It is another example of his thoroughness that he did not adopt the scheme of the Westminster Confession, by which the fall of Adam was referred to his own free will, which acted "contingently."
Edwards believed in no contingence.   The fall was like
every other event in the world proceeding from the will—
a volition caused by motives.   These motives were in the
last analysis presented by God, and in this sense God willed
the fall.   This is High Calvinism, and substantially supralapsarianism—a theory to which Edwards was in another place to give a death-blow.   But Edwards does not
prefer the phrase, "God willed the fall;" he rather teaches
that God ordered the system in which sin would infallibly
come to pass.   He draws the line of agency, and so of the
authorship of sin, at the action—that is, at the sin—making this man's, upon the testimony of consciousness, to use
a modern equivalent for his expressions.   For his doctrine
as to the divine government he depended upon the Scripture.   Thus God is the author of the system, man of the sin.

The immediate outcome of the treatise on the will, in
spite of all the drawbacks which we have noted, is to be
estimated as an essential service to both theology and religion.   It determined that the new school of thought whose
foundations Edwards was unconsciously laying should be
evangelical, effective, and thorough.   But there are larger
questions which remain still unanswered.   Was the work,
ideally considered, such a work as a theologian, bent on
really forwarding the cause of theology, ought to write?
Was it, in particular, characterized by the disposition to
learn from the adversary?   Such a question can only be
answered in the negative.   It was absolute reaction.   To
Edwards Arminianism and all its works were evil and
nothing but evil.   Calvinism is essentially determinism.
Without a theory of determinism it cannot stand; given a

theory of determinism, and the resulting theology must be Calvinistic. Therefore Edwards simply reaffirmed Calvinism, and did it by reaffirming determinism.

In this reply the answer to another question which we must ask is not obscurely hinted. Given such an answer to the spirit of the day, what was likely to be the effect upon the future development of the school, since the labors of Edwards did actually result in a school? Calvinism was essentially a system of abstract logic, deriving the whole framework of the system from the sole causality of God by logical deductions, without much, if any, appeal to consciousness. Considered as a new philosophical proposal, the Arminianism of Whitby was an appeal to consciousness. Had Edwards been disposed to learn from Whitby, he would have asked what the true meaning and value of this proposal was. When, now, this question had been brushed aside without consideration, and determinism strenuously reaffirmed, and especially when this had been done in a treatise of such power as was the *Freedom of the Will,* what would be the effect upon the future? Could this appeal be permanently ignored? If it could be for a time at least, what would be the tendency of thought under its suppression? Would it be to an ever more reckless disregard of consciousness? Would the divine sovereignty be ever more emphasized with increasing disregard of human agency? Or would the tendency be to recoil from the Edwardean position toward a real freedom? If such a recoil took place, would it be successful? Would men be able to get away from the influence of Edwards to whom they were so deeply indebted; or would their allegiance to him substantially block the way of their progress? Would they recognize the fact when they had fundamentally abandoned him; or would they fail to bring their views into a consistent form because of their allegiance to their great founder? Would the school come at last to a satisfactory position upon this great theme, and formulate a system comprehensive, consistent, and successful; or would it be foredoomed by the very greatness of the treatise which laid its foundation, to an inextricable confusion which, when at last discovered, should lead to a speedy and lamentable downfall?

Such questions a historian, thoroughly penetrated with the historical spirit, would be constrained to ask, as he paused over this remarkable work. Their answer could be gained only by continued studies in the history of the Edwardean school.

CHAPTER IV

EDWARDS' REMAINING METAPHYSICAL TREATISES

The conflict with the Arminians could not remain in the more exclusively metaphysical sphere in which it had hitherto been waged since Edwards retired to Stockbridge. A work was soon put into his hands which attacked the doctrine of original sin and which seemed to call for his careful attention. This was the book entitled *The Scriptural Doctrine of Original Sin Proposed to Free and Candid Examination,* by Dr. John Taylor, of Norwich, England, a Unitarian, which appeared in the year 1740. With it he received two other works by the same author, his *Key to the Apostolical Writings* and his *Paraphrase to the Epistle to the Romans.*

These works were characterized by some excellent features. The same recoil from artificial and false modes of statement which was to lead to some of the most important modifications of the current Calvinism by the New England school had led Taylor to take positions and make definitions which must command the assent of the candid mind. Sin is with him a strictly personal matter. Punishment must be as personal as guilt. He rejects the doctrine of the imputation of sin, and even enunciates the great principle that ability and obligation are commensurate. This better side of Taylor is evident in the following extract from his *Original Sin:*

A representative of moral action is what I can by no means digest. A representative, the guilt of whose conduct shall be imputed to us, and whose sins shall corrupt and debauch our nature, is one of the greatest absurdities in all the system of corrupt religion. That the conduct of ancestors should effect the external circumstances of posterity, is a constitution just and wise, and may answer good purposes; and that representatives of civil societies, or any other persons intrusted with the management of affairs, may injure those who employ them, is agreeable' to a state of trial and imperfection; but that any man without my knowledge and consent, should so represent me, that when he is guilty I am to be reputed guilty, and when he transgresses I shall be accountable and punishable for his transgression, and thereby subjected to the wrath and curse of God, nay, further, that his wickedness shall give me a sinful nature, and all this before I am born, and consequently while I am in no capacity of knowing, helping or hindering what he doth; surely anyone who dares use his understanding, must clearly see this is unreasonable, and altogether inconsistent with the truth, and goodness of God.[1]

But these merits of the work did not help it with Edwards, though they drove him to some modifications of old theories, as will be seen. They were too intimately associated with another side of Taylor's theology—with his superficial view of sin and his feeble religious experience. He holds that Adam's sin resulted subjectively in guilt, shame, and fear and that he fell thereby under subjection to sorrow, labor, and death. This death, however, is to be understood simply of physical death. The ruin of man did not seem to him to be very great, as will be evident from the following extract:

We are born as void of actual knowledge as the brutes themselves. We are born with many sensual appetites, and consequently liable to temptation and sin. But this is not the fault of our nature, but the will of God, wise and good. For every one of our natural passions and appetites are in themselves good; of great use and advantage in our present circumstances; and our nature would be defective, sluggish or unarmed without them. Nor is there any one of them we can at present spare. Our passions and appetites are in themselves, wisely, and kindly implanted in our nature. They are good, and become evil only by unnatural excess, or wicked abuse. The possibility of which excess and abuse is also well and wisely permitted for our trial. For without some such appetite, our reason would have nothing to struggle with, and consequently our virtue could not be duly exercised and proved in order to its being rewarded. And the appetites we have, God hath judged most proper, both for our use and trial. . . . .

[1] Edition employed, the reprint of the fourth edition (London, 1845), pp. 177, 178.

This idea then we ought to have of our being; that everything in
it is formed and appointed just as it should be; that it is a noble and
invaluable gift bestowed upon us by the bounty of God, with which
we should be greatly pleased, and for which we should be continually
and heartily thankful; that it is a perishable thing, which needeth to
be diligently guarded and cultivated; that our sensual inclinations are
to be duly restrained and disciplined, and our rational powers faith-
fully applied to their proper uses; that God hath given us those rational powers attended with those sensual inclinations, as for other
good purposes, so in particular to try us, whether we will carefully
guard and look after this most invaluable gift of his goodness; and
that if we do not, he will in justice punish our wicked contempt of
his love; but if we do, he will graciously reward our wisdom and
virtue. And all, and every one of these considerations should be a
spur to our diligence, and animate our endeavors to answer these
most high and most excellent purposes of his wisdom and goodness.[2]

Thus it is true that Taylor perceived, long before the
school of Edwards, the excrescences of the doctrine of
original sin, but it is also true that he let fall at the same
time the invaluable truth contained in that doctrine. It
was the perception of this, and the consciousness of an
undercurrent of unevangelical thought and feeling, which
principally moved Edwards to write against the book.[3]
It led Wesley to do the same thing, though he had no
objection to Arminianism as such. No doubt, Taylor's
views upon the atonement increased the suspicion against
him. He taught that the whole work of Christ was comprised in his obedience; his example powerfully attracted
men; and he was thereby rendered worthy that for his
sake the great good of forgiveness should be bestowed
upon men. The doctrine of satisfaction to justice in every
form, whether the justice be taken as distributive or public, is entirely left out.[4]

The reply of Edwards fills a large volume, but must

[2] *Op. Cit.*, pp. 103, 104.

[3] Edwards was anticipated one year by Samuel Niles, of Braintree, in *The
True Scripture Doctrine of Original Sin Stated and Defended*, etc. (318 pages;
Boston, 1757). Chiefly exegetical, it discusses Taylor very thoroughly.

[4] *Key*, etc., pp. 44 ff.

be dismissed in the briefest possible space.[5]   There are
two elements of the doctrine, he says, which are so united
in thought that they are either both accepted or both rejected.   These are the depravity of our nature and the imputation of Adam's sin.   The proof of the first involving
that of the other, Edwards' attention is chiefly directed
to the question of depravity.   The argument is strong and
is marked by the characteristic effort to reduce doctrines
to their elements and to urge the most fundamental proofs
which can be given.   Universal sinfulness is first proved.
This, as "universal, constant, infallible," is employed as a
proof of a "tendency or propensity."   Should it be said
that the evil proved is not a "tendency" in man, but has
its location rather in external nature, in the circumstances
by which man is surrounded, still the difficulty is not removed.   Man is then born into the world, as it is, in such
a condition as to lead universally to sin; and such a condition is itself a nature unfitted, as things are, to lead to
holiness, and hence it is essentially a depraved nature.

Advancing to the positive argument, Edwards derives
this principally from the Scriptures.   But he also revives
an argument at least as old as Anselm,[6] drawn from the
infinity of sin, which is to forestall the reply that the tendencies of man toward good are greater than those toward
evil.   Sin is infinite, since it is the rupture of an obligation which is infinite in being an obligation toward an
infinite being.   Other arguments are brought to prove
the greatness of man's sin, such as his propensity to sin
as soon as he is capable of it, to sin continually and pro-
gressively, and also the remains of sin in the best men.

---

[5] "The Great Christian Doctrine of Original Sin Defended," etc., *Works*,
Vol. II, pp. 301–583 (1758).   The same year came out Peter Clark's *The Scrip-
ture-Doctrine of Original Sin*, which formed the orthodox part of quite a little
controversy.   See Dexter's bibliography nos. 3354, 3365, 3366, 3367, 3368, 3371.

[6] *Cur Deus homo*, Book I., chap. xxi.

And then objections are answered: that Adam was not depraved and yet sinned, and so may we; that free will is a sufficient reason for the existence of sin; that the corruption of man may be owing to bad example, which, Edwards says, is explaining the thing by itself; that the senses grow up first, and thus the animal passions get the start of the reason, which is in substance original sin; and the propriety that virtue should meet with trials. Thus thorough was the discussion.

Up to this point Edwards has contributed nothing specially original to the defense or explanation of the doctrine. But he never handled a subject without impressing upon it at some point the force of his own independent thought, and he soon began to let fall hints and advance positions which were to be fruitful in later days. The theory of the current Calvinism required the supposition that there rested upon the descendants of Adam a double guilt —that of Adam's first sin, imputed to them, and that of a corrupted nature which was truly and properly sin. The order of thought is: first, Adam made a federal head; second, his sin imputed; third, corruption of nature visited upon mankind; finally, actual sin in consequence. This is the so-called "immediate imputation." Upon this theory there are two kinds of sin, voluntary and involuntary.

Edwards had already taught that sin was voluntary. It remained to decide whether he would teach that such sin was the only sin, or that all sin was voluntary. The present discussion led him to contemplate this problem, and to adopt this further position. He had already avoided any expression which should make him teach that depravity was properly sin. He accepted the federal headship of Adam, and, as he viewed death as the penalty of the sin of Adam, he was obliged to suppose that all who die are guilty of that sin, or that its guilt lies upon all men.[7]   Yet he cannot accept the common view that men are charged with something which they have not done, any more than Taylor.   Sin is imputed, he therefore says, but not in order to make it the sin of all men.   It is imputed because it is the sin of all men, for they have committed it in Adam. Thus he extends his doctrine, excludes every sin but voluntary sin, and so gives fully to New England theology its first great distinguishing doctrine, that all sin consists in choice.   Thus he completes at this point the work begun in the treatise on the will.[8]

To maintain this connection of the race with Adam, Edwards proposes a theory somewhat new.   He had already rejected the idea that original sin consisted in a positive taint, which had been the view of original sin opposed by Taylor.   He says simply that the Holy Spirit must and did withdraw from man after his sin.   The immediate result of this was that man set himself up as his own standard and fell into further sin.   Hereupon, in consequence of the established course of nature, or of a special divine constitution, the descendants of Adam were born, as he was, after his sin, destitute of holiness, thus negatively evil or depraved, out of communion with God and certain to pursue the course of their fleshly affections; that is, to fall into sin.   So, "all are looked upon as sinning in and with their common root; and God righteously withholds special influences and special communications from all for this sin."   In consequence of this act of God's, men consent to Adam's sin as soon as they begin to act.   Imputation follows this consent.   Edwards says: "The first depravity of heart, and that imputation of that sin are both the consequences of that established union;

[7] This is the fallacy of Augustine, perpetuated by Calvin.
[8] *Works,* Vol. II, pp. 542 ff.

but yet in such order that the evil disposition is first and the charge of guilt consequent, as it was in the case of Adam himself." Edwards' order is, then: first, the "constitution;" second, birth of men without the Spirit; third, positive evil disposition or sin, which is consent to Adam's sin; fourth, the charge of guilt.

But it is now an interesting question: How did Edwards justify this constitution to himself? The answer comes out in his reply to a supposed objection that things cannot be "viewed and treated as one which are not one but totally distinct." The objection, he says, is founded upon a false idea of identity. Some things entirely distinct and very diverse are yet united by the constitution of the creator so that they are in a sense one, as for instance the oak, a hundred years old, and the acorn. Even the identity of created intelligences depends upon the constitution of God. Continuance of the same consciousness, or memory, is essential to continued personal identity; and yet this continued memory is the constitution of God and not the work of the man himself. Indeed, the continued existence of every created entity, whether person or thing, is nothing but the continued creation of God. It is altogether equivalent to an immediate production out of nothing at every moment. The continued identity of anything is therefore only the consistency with which God produces now what he produced a moment since; or it is the divine constitution. By the same constitution, Adam and the race may be the same person, and so the loss of Adam be the loss of his posterity.

If, now, it is necessary to sum up in one glance the features of progress for the developing thought of New England contributed by this treatise passed in so brief review, they may be summarized (1) in the extension of the proposition that sin is voluntary action to the explicit

principle that all sin is voluntary action; (2) in the removal from the theology of the idea that man's corruption
consists in a positive taint imparted to his nature (for the
whole matter is explained in strict conformity with the
moral instincts when it is taught that the Holy Spirit is
withdrawn from sinning Adam, and corruption is traced
to this root); and (3) in an idea introduced—one which reappears upon many a page of later writers—the maintenance of the doctrine of the actuality of depravity in man
by the supposition of an established order of nature, or
divine constitution. If the doctrine of natural depravity
be accepted, there is need of some explanation of the connection of Adam with this result. Heredity may serve
as a partial explanation, and yet only a partial one. The
corruption of man is not all of the body. Unless we believe in traducianism (a theory now coming into favor in
certain quarters), it will be difficult to explain the disharmony of soul, as it is in psychology to explain the trans-
mittance of traits of character from father to son. But
the thought of a continued creation with the added idea of
a divine constitution would throw light upon the subject.
In the case of every new-born person, God is again operative, and that in accordance with a plan of his own. As
the nature of the oak is determined by the nature of the
acorn, and that by its parent oak, so with the child. And
thus, according to an intelligible method, God can determine to treat men according as Adam, their constituted
head, shall remain holy, or fall.

If we were to ask at this point again those questions
which we have previously asked as to Edwards' adaptation to further the cause of theology in a time of controversy, we should have to reply that now at last he has
come to perceive more accurately his proper task. This
treatise is no mere piece of reaction. He learns as he

reads.   He innovates as he writes.   There is movement, change, life, in this work as in no preceding one.   It is most significant that some things he says nothing about. There is no refutation of such a sound principle as that ability and obligation are commensurate.   What he opposes are the real errors of Taylor, not the great illuminating suggestions which were later to form a large part of the working materials of New England theology.   And there is here already that emphasis of the ethical element of theology which was to be more and more characteristic of the school as it advanced to the very end.   Our corruption, even, is an ethical corruption, since it consists principally in the deprivation of the Holy Spirit under which we suffer—nothing physical, nothing merely mysterious. Hence Edwards now understands how to conserve the old, how to learn from even erroneous proposals, how to study the spirit of his age, how to change old forms as new light breaks upon him.   He has arrived at last at the true position of a leader.[9]

The remaining principal treatise of Edwards is in many respects the most remarkable of the series.   The others had been prepared with immediate reference to the demands of the contest against the Arminians, and all suffered from the defects, as well as partook of the vigor and interest, incidental to such an origin.   The *Dissertation Concerning the Nature of True Virtue* [10] was more largely the spontaneous fruit of early and later meditations.   The Arminians are not mentioned in it.   It breathes the calm spirit of quiet studies.   In these respects it stands comparatively isolated among Edwards' writings; and it is isolated in

[9] Dr. Charles Chauncy, pastor of the First Church, Boston, wrote a series of *Five Dissertations on the Scripture Account of the Fall and its Consequences* in 1785, in which he controverted Edwards at some length.   Like his *Salvation of all Men,* it was the product of a gradual and lifelong departure from the standard Calvinism.

[10] *Works,* Vol. III, pp. 91–157.

another respect, in that its great ideas, though early formed, and put down in writing with great clearness in the manly notes of the youthful student at college, seem never to have influenced the general course of his speculations upon other themes, fruitful in the extreme as they were to be under the hand of his successors. He defines justice as virtuous only when governed by benevolence, with perfect clearness in the "Notes," [11] but in after years he discusses the justice of God in its application to future punishment and to the atonement exactly as if no such distinction had ever entered his mind. To this extent the work which he had performed in the formulation of the principle of all virtue remained unappreciated by its author; but so far-reaching and revolutionary were to be its effects upon succeeding systems that it merits the designation of Edwards' principal contribution to religious thought. It may be said to have given the determining principle to the whole school of thinking which was to bear the name of Edwardean.

The *Nature of Virtue* cannot be fully understood, either in its own greatness as a philosophical achievement or in the peculiarities which mark the progress of its discussions, without a glance at the previous history of ethical theory.[12] Edwards himself goes back to Hobbes, when noticing antagonistic views, and it is to Hobbes that the rise of independent and valuable discussion upon ethics in the English-speaking world is to be attributed. He was the first to bring in the idea of the good as something to be sought, though he was unfortunate in the form of his discussion, since he identified it too largely with pleasure. Any further usefulness which he might have served was destroyed by the common understanding that he taught

[11] See *ibid.*, Vol. I, p. 700.

[12] See Sidgwick's excellent review in *Encyclopaedia Britannica*, article "Ethics."

that the only foundation of social morality was the law of the state, and thus denied that it had any ground in the objective nature of things. The Cambridge Platonists opposed him at this point, and emphasized the eternal distinctions between good and evil; but they rendered comparatively little service in promoting the growth of ethical doctrine, since they produced only an ill-arranged collection of aphorisms upon morals, and substantially went over to Hobbes's ground as to the pursuit of pleasure. Richard Cumberland, however, published in 1672 a treatise entitled *De legibus naturae disquisitio philosophica,* which has been worthily styled a fountain-head of English ethics,[13] and which did much to build upon the foundation which Hobbes had suggested and to point the way, at least, to the elimination of the errors into which he had fallen. Like Hobbes, he began with the idea of the good, but he defined it more comprehensively, since he embraced in it even moral acts, though always considering it too much under the category of the natural good—that, namely, which, preserves or renders created beings "more perfect or happy." He introduces an idea which was entirely lacking in Hobbes, the "common good" as an object of effort, under which he almost unconsciously included a much wider definition of good than his more formal statements made place for. But his chief service was that he reduced all the maxims of morality to one general principle, "regard for the common good." Three separate sentences may serve to afford a comprehensive view of his thought. "I judge it requisite to the natural perfection of the human will that it follow the most perfect reason." "Those acts of the will which are enjoined by the same law may all be comprehended in the general name of the most extensive and operative benevolence." "The greatest benevolence

[13] See Dr. G. F. Magoun's excellent account, *Bibliotheca Sacra,* Vol. XLIII, pp. 528 ff.; Vol. XLIV, pp. 91 ff.

does consist in a constant volition of the greatest good towards all." Hence an action is "morally good" which contributes to this end. Cumberland anticipated the objection, which has been voiced in our own day, that benevolence cannot be said to include all virtue, since it cannot include the proper attitude of man toward God except by such torsion as shall evacuate it of all meaning, and laid down the proposition that "to promote the common good of the whole system of rationals" "includes our love of God and of all mankind, as parts of this system." But he could not have defended himself successfully against the charge of utilitarianism, for utilitarian he undoubtedly was. His most conspicuous failure as a moralist was in his definition of conscience, in reference to which, says Dr. Magoun,

It is difficult to decide whether our author regarded conscience as anything more than the discernment of our acts as means to ends, or of the results of acts, pleasant or painful. . . . . One will look in vain through this . . . . treatise . . . . for any discussion of the relations of right or conscience to obligation, either as an idea or as feeling.[14]

Locke, while agreeing with Hobbes as to the egoistic basis of conduct and the definition of good, yet does something to suggest a higher style of treating the subject when he supposes that ethics might be put among the demonstrative sciences, like mathematics, if the idea of the Supreme Being and that of ourselves in relation to him were properly carried out. He thus substantially makes ethics to rest upon intuitive principles. Shaftesbury forwarded the theme by showing that the social affections are natural, and that they are in harmony with the self-regarding. Of all this series of writers Hutcheson was the greatest. Upon the basis of Shaftesbury's work he erected, by the help of Cumberland's principles, the most complete edifice

[14] Articles cited, Vol. XLIII, pp. 539, 540.

of moral philosophy which Britain had seen till that time. He brought out the fact that there is a special power in the human soul to discern moral ideas and relations, for among the "senses" he enumerated one of beauty, a "public sense," "a determination to be pleased with the happiness of others," and a "Moral Sense" "by which we perceive virtue and vice." [15]   True, his treatment of the moral sense is too loose and vague to throw much light upon the real nature of this faculty.   He is also completely utilitarian, at least in the criterion by which the virtue of a proposed action is to be tested.   "That action is best which procures the greatest happiness for the greatest numbers, and that worst which, in like manner, occasions misery."   The most distinctive feature of his work is the consistency with which he carries out Cumberland's principle of benevolence.   In opposition to Hobbes's account of the origin of moral actions, Hutcheson maintains that benevolence is the only ground upon which man approves of any action.   He thus makes it the sole constituent of virtue.   Actions flowing purely from self-love and yet evidencing no lack of benevolence are morally indifferent.   In respect to many personal actions which men generally morally approve, such as industry, man is virtuous in them because he is to exercise benevolence toward himself.   If Hutcheson is not wholly successful in his discussion of this portion of the theme, he contributes something, at any rate, in incorporating the moral subject himself in the scheme of beings toward whom moral relations are to be sustained.

It is at this point that the work of Edwards is to be introduced into the history.   He had early gained the elevated plane upon which his whole consideration of the subject is conducted.   Though he followed his predeces-

[15] See Professor Fowler's article, "Hutcheson," *Encyc. Brit.*

sors in viewing some things as "goods," he did not begin his development of his theme with this topic. He had found, as it seemed to him, the reason both of the nature of the good and of the source of obligation in the fundamental idea that the universe was a "system" and that its ideal harmony was the goal of all individual existence, and hence the reasonable and obligatory object of moral choice. When considered in this light, the whole nature of virtue and its binding obligation are immediately evident, being written in the very nature of man. And hence, while the theory is, like that of Cumberland and Hutcheson, a theory of benevolence, it avoids the utilitarianism into which they had fallen, and replaces their defective analyses of conscience, self-love, etc., with better.

So evident, in fact, was the truth of his theory to the intuitive gaze of Edwards that he scarcely stops to give formal proof of it. The body of his short treatise is occupied with explanations which shall unfold its meaning and free it from various objections. What there is of proof may be summarized thus:[16]

Virtue is something beautiful, or some kind of beauty, yet not every kind of beauty, but a beauty of a moral nature—that is, one belonging to the disposition and will. Nor is it any "particular" beauty, or beauty in a limited sphere, but it is one which still appears beautiful when viewed "most perfectly, comprehensively, and universally, with regard to all its tendencies and its connections with everything to which it stands related." After these definitions, the author is ready to answer the question "wherein this true and general beauty of the heart does most essentially consist;" and the reply is: "Benevolence in general. Or perhaps, to speak more accurately, it is that consent, propensity, and union of heart to being in general, which is

[16] See *Works,* Vol. III, pp. 93–95.

immediately exercised in a general good will." And he goes on to say—thus giving all the proof he has to offer:

The things before observed respecting the nature of true virtue naturally lead us to such a notion of it. If it has its seat in the heart, and is the general goodness and beauty of the disposition and its exercise, in the most comprehensive view, considered with regard to its universal tendency, and as related to everything with which it stands connected; what can it consist in but a consent and good will to being in general? Beauty does not consist in discord and dissent, but in consent and agreement. And if every intelligent being is in some way related to being in general, and is a part of the universal system of existence, and so stands in connection with the whole; what can its general and true beauty be, but its union and consent with the great whole.

Edwards supposed himself to be in accord in this position, not only with the Scriptures and "Christian divines," but with the "more considerable deists" and "the most considerable writers" upon such topics. He could therefore dispense the more properly with lengthened proofs, and could proceed to those definitions by which he hoped to clear up some prevalent "confusion in discourses upon this subject." He explains therefore, first, that such benevolence to being in general may be exercised in a benevolent affection toward a particular person, and that such a particular act of benevolence is virtuous when it arises "from a generally benevolent temper, or from that habit or frame of mind wherein consists a disposition to love being in general." In other words, the great motive of universal love must underlie every volition which is to be virtuous. He also defines in passing the "being" had in mind as "intelligent being," though he had better said *sentient* being.

The love which constitutes virtue is thus the love of benevolence, that which seeks the well-being or happiness of being considered simply as such. It is thus not the love of complacence, which presupposes beauty, or virtue, in which complacence can be felt, nor, for the same reason, is it gratitude. But—

> The first object of a virtuous benevolence is being, simply considered; and if being, simply considered, be its object, then *being in general* is its object; and what it has an ultimate propensity to, is the *highest good* of being in general. And it will seek the good of every *individual* being unless it be conceived as not consistent with the highest good of being in general. In which case the good of a particular being, or some beings, may be given up for the sake of the highest good of being in general. And particularly, if there be any being irreclaimably opposite, and an enemy to being in general, then consent and adherence to being in general will induce the truly virtuous heart to forsake that enemy and to oppose it.[17]

One more quotation is needed to prepare the reader for the highest reach of the Edwardean conception:

> Further, if being, simply considered, be the first object of a truly virtuous benevolence, then that object who has *most* of being, or has the greatest share of existence, *other things being equal,* so far as such a being is exhibited to our faculties, will have the *greatest* share of the propensity and benevolent affections of the heart.[18]

Hence, since God is the being who has "most of being," he is the supreme object of choice; and men, since they are in general of the same importance, will have equal shares in the choices of virtuous beings. Hence this theory of virtue is summarized in the biblical rule that we are to love God with all our heart, and our neighbor as ourselves.

Edwards also felt the force of that objection to this theory of virtue which Cumberland had anticipated, which denies the possibility of including God within the scope of the creature's "benevolence." He set at work vigorously to remove it. He reinforced the reasoning just sketched by a further discussion. He distinguishes first between the primary ground of love, which is simply being, and a secondary, which is the moral excellence which may exist

[17] *Ibid.,* p. 97.
[18] *Ibid.,* p. 97.

in any being. This is fitted to call forth complacence, but it is also fitted to call forth the love of benevolence, by which he means the choice to seek to promote the virtue in which it delights. Toward God, the most holy of all beings, such a love is most eminently fit; and yet in his case it will consist largely in the love of complacence. Has it, indeed, any true benevolent element? It has, replies Edwards; for benevolence consists not only in seeking to promote, but also in rejoicing in, the happiness of the being toward whom benevolence is exercised. But more than this, benevolence can be directly exercised toward God, since men can be instrumental in promoting his glory, in which he delights.

Edwards insists the more strenuously upon this point because upon it turns the chief purpose of his treatise, which was to put morality in a new relation to religion. Previous moralists had been too exclusively occupied in considering their theme with simple reference to the relations of man toward man. Edwards would show, on the contrary, that true virtue must include a virtuous attitude toward God himself, which is, however, the essence of religion, and would thus advance to the lofty position that there can be no true virtue in the narrower sphere of what is ordinarily called morality, which is not, at the same time, religious. Religion and morality are essentially one. He that is truly moral is implicitly already religious; and he who is religious must also be moral. In his own words:

Whatever other benevolence or generosity towards mankind, and other virtues or moral qualifications which go by that name, any are possessed of, that are not attended with a love to God which is altogether above them and to which they are subordinate and on which they are dependent, there is nothing of the nature of true virtue or religion in them. And it may be asserted in general that nothing is of the nature of true virtue in which God is not the first and the last; or which, with regard to their exercises in general have not their first foundation and source in apprehensions of God's supreme dignity and glory, and in answerable esteem and love of him, and have not respect to God as the supreme end.[19]

But against this view the objection would be raised that there are many things which do not spring from such a benevolence as this which are commonly thought to partake of the character of the moral, and which receive the commendation of men. How can they have this seeming, without having a true, morality? This is the vital question between Edwards and most of his predecessors, and to the answer of it he devotes the remainder of his treatise, nearly two-thirds of its entire compass. The motive of the work here comes to light. It was to root out thoroughly from the minds of men that confidence which they are so prone to feel in the value of a morality which is confessedly not religious. These actions commonly approved have says Edwards in substance, a certain beauty about them, but it is not the true beauty which virtue has. It is an inferior beauty, analogous only to that consisting in the fitness of the act in its relations, and comparable to the beauty of a chess-board, or of a piece of chintz or brocade, or of a square, an equilateral triangle, or a regular polygon. To employ his own words:

There is a beauty of order in society besides what consists in benevolence or can be referred to it, which is of a secondary kind; as when the different members of society have all their appointed office, place,, and station, according to their several capacities and talents, and every one keeps his place and continues in his proper business. In this there is a beauty, not of a different kind from the regularity of a beautiful building, or piece of skillful architecture, where the strong pillars are set in their proper place, the pilasters in a place fit for them, the square pieces of marble in the pavement, the panels, partitions, and cornices, etc., in places proper for them.[20]

And among other virtues he specially instances justice as consisting in the agreement, or fitness which there is

[19] *Ibid.*, p. 109.
[20] *Ibid.*, p. 114.

between the doing of evil, for example, and the receiving of pain.

Thus these so-called virtues have a beauty, but it is not the beauty of true virtue consisting in love to being in general and to God, the being of beings.

The same argumentative necessity leads Edwards now to take up the discussion of self-love which Hutcheson had dropped. Defining it as having meaning only when it signifies regard for one's "confined private self," he discusses here in the main the question whether certain so-called virtues, such as love to friends, gratitude, etc., may not arise from mere self-love, or to use the modern term, from selfishness. He shows that, since kind actions toward us gratify our selfishness, it may be nothing but our perception of this which calls forth our gratitude for them. Far from being virtuous, or having any character of "public benevolence," such affections will be purely selfish. They may possibly at times spring from a feeling of desert, but then they are to be referred to the sense of justice previously spoken of, and are nothing but a delight in the "secondary" beauty, which gives no foundation for true virtue.

With the same general purpose in mind, Edwards next passes to the discussion of the "natural conscience," by which he means the conscience of the natural man. It consists in two things: (1) in a "disposition to approve or disapprove the moral treatment which passes between us and others from a determination of the mind to be easy or uneasy in a consciousness of our being consistent or inconsistent with ourselves;" and (2) in a "sense of desert" as previously explained. It is, in other words, a perception of moral relations, and perceives even the beauty of true benevolence, though it may not itself "taste its primary and essential beauty;" and it covers in the range of its utter-

ances the same subjects as are covered by a true spiritual
sense—that is, by a conscience spiritually enlightened. But
it does not imply, as some have taught, "a disposition to
true virtue, consisting in a benevolent temper naturally implanted in the hearts of all men;" for then, the clearer the
perceptions of conscience, the stronger the virtuous principle—which experience shows frequently not to be the
case. Even the wicked at the last day will approve their
sentence; but, under this perception of conscience, they
will not manifest a disposition to repent of their wickedness.

In the same way Edwards discusses natural instincts
leading to natural affections which have no real virtue in
them; and then passes to consider the reason why all these
things are often mistaken for true virtue. And he closes
the whole with the investigation whether virtue is founded
in sentiment, and whether this is given to men by God arbitrarily, or whether it is founded in the very nature of
things. The considerations presented here are in substance
the same as those upon which the whole theory was first
established.

This is the substance of the great ethical treatise which
Edwards wrote in his closing years and which was published after his death. The far-reaching consequences involved in it for theology, his successors were only slowly
to appreciate and develop; but it finally created an independent school of ethics, as well as of theology.

The review of the most important services of Edwards
to theology is now complete. Were it the present object
to discuss his entire career and influence as a historical
character, much more would need to be said. The present
problem is a narrower one. Not what he was, but what
he did; and not what he did upon the broader field even of
theology, but what he contributed to the improvement of

the system which he received from his teachers, is the subject of the present study. He performed many lesser services not fitted to rank with these prime labors. Professor
Park, in the introduction which he prefixed to his collection
of *Essays* from various New England writers upon the
atonement, has shown how independent the mind of Edwards everywhere was, and how many fruitful suggestions he let fall in passing, as it were, upon the greatest
themes. His preaching of future punishment was valuable for the refutation of numerous dangerous errors.[21]
Perhaps the temper of mind which he bequeathed to his
spiritual followers was his greatest gift—that perfect independence combined with entire loyalty to the truth, that
living sense of the possibility of progress, that keen vision
of the necessities of the present hour and that unquestion-
ing subordination of every merely theoretical interest to
the practical interests of the Redeemer's kingdom, which
have largely distinguished the New England school among
thinkers to this day. But it were enough to substantiate
his claim to a high position among the theologians of the
Christian ages to have begun, as he did, those discussions
of the will, of the nature of sin, and of the principle of
virtue which resulted finally in the large inheritance into
which his children have entered. If his daring and keen
speculations gave to the theology something of a rationalistic turn, which his own deep spirituality could not neu-

[21] But a portion of the manuscripts of Edwards was published. The remaining portions have been repeatedly re-examined to see if they threw further
light upon his opinions, but without leading to any essential enlargement of publication. Two little tracts upon the Trinity have been published, in answer to
an open demand made by Oliver Wendell Holmes in connection with the assertion
that Edwards became substantially a Unitarian in his later thinking; but they
have not sustained the charge. They have, however, shown how he subjected all
theological topics to original and searching investigation, and how the scope of
his own independent thought was continually enlarging. See the tracts: E. C.
Smyth, *Observations concerning the Scripture Economy of the Trinity*, etc., and
G. P. Fisher, *An Unpublished Essay of Edwards' upon the Trinity* (1903). See
also Professor Park's valuable remarks upon Edwards' intellectual habits in the
Bibliotheca Sacra, Vol. XXXVIII.

tralize, it was because the age succeeding the advocacy of Deism must be a rationalizing one; and if the evil effects of this strain of thought are to be detected even to the present, it is because the forces which have from time to time arrayed themselves against evangelical theology have been the direct descendants of the ancient Deistic movement. For himself, Edwards as powerfully promoted the spiritual life of the churches as he did their theology.

EDWARDS' CONTEMPORARIES AND
COLABORERS

CHAPTER V

JOSEPH BELLAMY

The impetus given by Edwards to New England theology began to exhibit itself before he himself passed off the scene. A figure so unique as his, and one of so great eminence as a practical worker, could not fail to attract attention and, in the paucity of teachers in New England, draw pupils for longer or shorter instruction in the ministerial calling. It was in this way that he gained for the new principles which he was presenting two adherents who were to prove during his lifetime efficient colaborers with him in his practical efforts, and after his death successors and leaders in his school. These were Bellamy[1] and Hopkins.

The particular course which Bellamy's theological labors took was determined by his position as a pastor and by the number of important controversies which were carried on during his time. At the very beginning of his ministry he took part in the great revival of 1741–43, preaching widely, and observing necessarily the widespread harm done by certain theological errors. It was the direct consequence of this that, in 1750, first among the ministers of his state, he came out against the Half-Way Covenant. He noted and refuted the errors of "Antinomians," "Sandemeans," etc. But there was an inner force in his mind, which had been communicated to him by Edwards, which impelled him to more fundamental work than the

---

[1] Joseph Bellamy, born in Cheshire, Conn., February 20, 1719; graduated at Yale College in 1735, at the early age of sixteen; studied with Edwards at Northampton in 1736; settled at Bethlehem (next south of Litchfield) April 2, 1740, when a little more than twenty-one years old; remained pastor here, having declined many calls, among others one to New York, till his death in 1790. He was created Doctor of Divinity by Aberdeen in 1768.

mere refutation of errors, and made him a constructive theologian. While thus we find treatises from his pen upon *The Half Way Covenant, There is but One Covenant,* etc., and *Theron, Paulinus, and Aspasio* (on justification), his great works are his *True Religion Delineated* and *The Wisdom of God in the Permission of Sin,* etc., which are lifted by their themes upon the high plane of constructive discussion, although not without constant reference to the immediate religious needs of men.[2]

The *True Religion Delineated* discusses the nature of religion, and gives two answers, apparently different, but in the end coalescing in one; viz., that it consists in a conformity to the law of God, and a compliance with the gospel of Christ. These two answers determine the two parts of the treatise. The first treats the law, which it finds perfectly fulfilled in the one exercise of love. The second then considers the gospel, and is thus led to the successive topics of the ruin of man, the atonement, and the application of that atonement through faith, together with the reward of everlasting life promised to the believer.

As might be gathered from the definition given of conformity to the law of God, the leading idea of this whole treatise is that of the Edwardean theory of virtue. We have here accordingly the first application of this theory to New England theology. As might be expected, it is a partial application. The greater and more profound effects of this theory upon the doctrine of sin and of the atonement escaped, at first, the eye of theologians. But at least the theory was definitely held by Bellamy and beautifully applied to his definition of religion.

This agreement between Edwards and Bellamy has sometimes been denied. It has been said that Bellamy did not follow Edwards "in this single exceptional case wherein

---

[2] Best edition of his works is that of the Doctrinal Tract and Book Society (Boston, 1853), from which the citations in the following pages are made.

he was eccentric to his main orbit." [3]   But careful study of
Bellamy will show a minute, as well as a general, acceptance of the theory of virtue.   In a letter dated 1766 he refers to Edwards' treatise by name.[4]   In explaining love
toward our neighbor he coincides with his teacher in
phraseology as well as thought.   He speaks of the "esteem"
which is due to our neighbor for the valuable qualities
which he possesses; [5] then of his "happiness as to soul and
body" toward which we are to exercise a benevolent regard; this to be excited by his "capacities;" then of the
delight and complacence which we are to feel in his holiness; all of which are strikingly Edwardean.   The same
idea of obligation is held by him as by Edwards.   The obligation to love God arises from the "infinite excellence of
the divine nature antecedent to all selfish consideration,"
and is infinitely, unchangeably, and eternally binding.
Love to our neighbor is "right and fit in itself."   Like Edwards he opposes utilitarianism, only with a power of sarcasm and a keenness of wit [6] which Edwards, with all his
excellences, did not possess.

Bellamy was, then, a thoroughgoing Edwardean as far
as the theory of virtue is concerned.   Like Edwards, he
was also in general upon the plane of the old Calvinism.
In many things his positions will be found to be identical
with those of Edwards, sometimes, however, with a quiet
suppression of Edwards' more daring flights of speculation, as, for example, his attempt to explain the constitutional connection of Adam with his posterity.   At the same
time, many of his forms of statement and many suggestions proved fruitful in developing among his pupils and
successors the new divinity.

[3] *Bibliotheca Sacra,* Vol. X, p. 706.

[4] *Works* (Memoir), Vol. I, pp. xxix, xxx.

[5] See *Works,* Vol. I, pp. 119 ff.

[6] *Ibid.,* pp. 188 ff.

These statements and suggestions, found in the *True Religion,* may be grouped under the following heads:

1. *Ability.*—Here he follows exactly in the path suggested by Edwards upon the will. The Arminians and Antinomians who surrounded him sought in various ways to evade the searching demands of the gospel. He answers them in pungent terms, and we begin at once to see the power of the New England preaching, stimulated and directed by Edwards' leading ideas, to lay hold of the hearts and consciences of men. Something of his style, as well as his contribution to thought, will be seen in the following extracts:

"But to love God, or to have any disposition to love him, is a thing supernatural, clean beyond the powers of nature, improved to the utmost: how can I, therefore, be wholly to blame?"—It is a thing supernatural, you say; that is, in other words, you have no heart to it, nor the least inclination that way; nor is there anything in your temper to work upon by motives to bring you to it; and now, because you are so very bad a creature, therefore you are not at all to blame. This is your argument. But can you think that there is any force in it? What! are moral agents the less to blame the worse they grow? And are God's laws no longer binding than while his subjects are disposed to obey them? [7]

And again:—

Thus we see, that, as to a natural capacity, all mankind are capable of a perfect conformity to God's law, which requires us only to love God with all our hearts: and that all our inability arises merely from the bad temper of our hearts, and our want of a good disposition, and that, therefore, we are wholly to blame and altogether inexcusable. Our impotency, in one word, is not natural, but moral, and, therefore, instead of extenuating, does magnify and enhance our fault. *The more unable to love God we are, the more are we to blame.* Even as it was with the Jews; the greater contrariety there was in their hearts to their prophets, to Christ and his Apostles, the more vile and blame worthy were they. And in this light do the Scriptures constantly view the case. There is not one title in the Old Testament, or in the New, in the law or in the gospel, that gives the least intimation of any deficiency in our natural faculties. The law

[7] *Loc. cit.,* p. 95.

requires no more than all our hearts, and never blames us for not having larger natural capacities. The gospel aims to recover us to love God only with all our hearts, but makes no provision for our having any new natural capacity; as to our natural capacities, all is well. It is in our temper, in the frame and disposition of our hearts, that the seat of all our sinfulness lies.[8]

That paradox of Bellamy's rhetoric—"the more unable to love God we are, the more we are to blame"—became characteristic of the school. Inability, instead of being accepted as an excuse, was itself ground for greater repentance, because it was voluntary. It will be said, of course, that the theory of the will underlying such statements affords no real ground for them, because giving no real ability. It was enough, however, that Bellamy supposed that there was a real ability, and that he preached it as such. No one can get from his words any other impression. It was this impression that prevailed. The theory of the doctrine does not appear in his pages to disturb the mind; the fact of ability is stated with great popular power. Such preaching had its natural effect, and the way was prepared for the improvement of the theory.

Out of such preaching began another style of exhortation to the impenitent which was soon to break up the old paralysis which had crept over the New England churches. Men had ability to repent, and the duty of the minister was to exhort them to exercise this ability. They were no longer to "read the Scriptures," or to "pray," or to "choose God as their best good and last end," and *remain impenitent through it all,* as in former times they had too often done. But, under the preaching of Bellamy, they were exhorted not "to do any duty in an unholy manner, to hear the word in a disposition to hate and reject it," but to hear "in a disposition to love, believe, and practice it." In short, the preaching became the preaching of *immediate repentance.*

[8] *Ibid.,* p. 100.

2. *Original sin.*—In respect to this doctrine Bellamy followed Edwards quite closely, teaching that by divine appointment Adam stood and acted as our public head. This was as well for us in every respect, and better in some respects, than if our condition had been made to depend entirely upon our own acts. He did not, however, follow Edwards into his speculations as to the method of our connection with Adam. Leaving that, and every other speculative element, he enforced in the following manner the direct and unmodified responsibility of the sinner for himself:

> Let it be by Adam's fall, or how it will, yet if you are an enemy to the infinitely glorious God, your Maker, and that voluntarily, you are infinitely to blame, and without excuse; for nothing can make it right for a creature to be a voluntary enemy to his glorious Creator, or possibly excuse such a crime. It is, in its own nature, infinitely wrong; there is nothing, therefore, to be said; you stand guilty before God. It is in vain to make this or any other pleas, so long as we are what we are, not by compulsion, but voluntarily. And it is in vain to pretend that we are not voluntary in our corruptions, when they are nothing else but the free, spontaneous inclinations of our own hearts. Since this is the case every mouth will be stopped and all the world become guilty before God, sooner or later.[9]

Like Edwards, Bellamy also teaches that our natural corruption, though real, is something privative, so that God does not bring us into the world infected with any positive taint.[10]

3. *Election.*—This is brought out in the clearest terms. The divine sovereignty is exalted in connection with it. God does not elect this or that man for anything that he himself does, or for any goodness that there is in him. The condition of mankind is but one, and that is rebellion and opposition to the will of their Maker. At times, in order to exalt the sovereignty of grace, expressions are used by Bellamy which seem to imply that God acts arbitrarily.

[9] *Loc. cit.,* p. 99.
[10] See *Works,* Vol. I, p. 153; cf. also pp. 138, 139.

But this is not his meaning. If he says, "It is evident that his designs of mercy took their rise merely, absolutely, and entirely from himself," he adds in the next member of the sentence: "from his own infinite benevolence, from his self-moving goodness and sovereign grace." [11]   And again: "God does not appear to be a Being influenced, actuated and governed by a groundless, arbitrary self-will, having no regard to right reason, to the moral fitness and unfitness of things." [12]

Election is thus taken out of the realm of the absolutely unaccountable, and one of the most serious objections against it is removed. This is the retroactive effect of the Edwardean theory of virtue. If right be founded, as has been so often said, in the will of God, then it may be that God proceeds in election according to his arbitrary will. It will then be right, for that is what right is. But if right is right in the nature of things, and God himself is obligated to exercise love and to act for the welfare of being, then not even the interests of sovereignty can justify the use of phrases which put the divine action above reason. More and more was this feature to be emphasized in New England theology.

4. *The atonement.*—Upon this topic Bellamy's services were epoch-making, for he introduced to New England thinking an entirely new theory of the atonement, although it was left for another, his pupil Jonathan Edwards the Younger, to propose it in such a way as to secure its general adoption.

It will be necessary, in order to understand Bellamy's work, to review briefly the course of an obscure rivulet of thought, the existence of which has been generally forgotten. In the year 1617 Hugo Grotius, a learned jurist and

[11] *Ibid.*, p. 249.
[12] *Ibid.*, p. 258.

theologian of Holland, published a *Defence of the Satisfaction of Christ,* in which he presented a new theory of the atonement, which has received the name of the "governmental theory" because it explains the atonement as a governmental necessity, and transfers the central point of the theory by teaching that God is, in this matter, not the "offended party," but the supreme "Ruler." This work was early known in New England. William Pynchon apparently referred to it. John Norton quotes it in 1653. Charles Chauncy had evidently read it in 1659. Baxter, who adopted the theory, and Samuel Clarke, who improved it somewhat, were both read in New England. Grotius' complete works were in the library of Yale College in 1733. It is pretty certain that the younger Edwards and later New England divines read the *Defence.* It is quite probable that Bellamy also did.[13]

Grotius' main suggestion must have been a very welcome one to Bellamy. As long as the divine justice was conceived as a single unrelated attribute, and theologians talked of the necessity of the satisfaction of justice by the sacrifice of Christ, the position that God acted as the offended party was the logical one. But as soon as God is conceived as acting always from love, and his justice becomes modified both in what it demands and in the reason for its infliction by this conception, then God must act in the matter of punishment from general motives, dictated by love, or he must act as a general person, and in this case as the divine Governor. Bellamy immediately adopted this line of thought, and put at the very head of his discussion the term "moral Governor of the world" as descriptive of the position of God in the atonement. To this

---

[13] A fuller account of the historical setting of the Grotian theory, and of its connection with New England thought, has been given by the present writer in his "Historical Introduction" to his translation of the *Defence* (Andover, 1889). In some respects the present account supersedes the former.

he consistently adheres. He thus effected the transfer of the center of gravity in the New England theory to this new point, and thus determined in what path it should move. This may seem strong language, especially when Bellamy's inconsistencies of expression are remembered. Professor Park claimed for him only that he "directly or indirectly suggested the Edwardean theory.[14] But he did far more than that. He took the two positions which rendered the theory a necessity if they should be firmly held and consistently applied. For his use of the word "Governor" was no mere verbal change in phraseology. Turretin had employed the term "Ruler of the Universe" as the appropriate designation of God when inflicting punishment; but he had never really changed the determinative conception that God was the offended party. Bellamy, however, in his explanation of the term is everywhere governed by the great conceptions of the theory of virtue, and these compel a real change of position. Thus he says:

God does not appear to be a being influenced, actuated, and governed by a groundless, arbitrary self-will, having no regard to right reason, to the moral fitness and unfitness of things; nor does he appear to be a being governed and actuated by a groundless fondness to his creatures. . . . . He considers the happiness and good of his creatures, his intelligent creatures, as being what it is. He sees what it is worth, and of how great importance it is, and how much to be desired in itself, and compared with other things: he sees it to be just what it really is, and has an answerable disposition of heart, that is, is desirous of their happiness and averse to their misery, in an exact proportion to the real nature of the things in themselves.[15]

No one familiar with Edwards can fail to see the watermark of the master's theology here. Nor is this an isolated passage. For pages the same style of discussion is continued. "Yea, if it was put to his own case, if we could possibly suppose such a thing, he [God] would make it ap-

    [14] "Introductory Essay" to *The Atonement; Discourses and Treatises,* p. xxxix.
    [15] *Works,* Vol. I, pp. 258 f.

pear that *he does as he would be done by,* when he punishes
sinners to all eternity." [16] "Rewards and punishments
. . . . are visible public testimonies borne by the Governor
of the world to the moral amiableness of virtue on the one
hand and to the moral hatefulness of vice on the other."[17]
He also many times defines the atonement in terms like
the following, which are a full expression of the new theory:

> To the end that a way might be opened for him to put his de-
> signs of mercy in execution, consistently with himself, consistently
> with the honor of his holiness and justice, law and government, and
> sacred authority, something must be done by him in a public manner,
> as it were, in the sight of all worlds, whereby his infinite hatred of
> sin, and unchangeable resolution to punish it, might be as effectually
> manifested as if he had damned the whole world.[18]

Bellamy also taught the doctrine of general atonement.
The older Calvinism had taught that the atonement,
though sufficient for all men, was *designed* only for the
elect. This position Bellamy expressly denies again and
again. For example:

> And indeed, was not the door of mercy opened to all indefinitely,
> how could God sincerely offer mercy to all? Or heartily invite all?
> Or justly blame those who do not accept? Or righteously punish
> them for neglecting so great salvation? [19]

Or, at greater length:

> Besides, if Christ died merely for the elect, that is, to the intent
> that they, only upon believing, might, consistently with the divine
> honor, be received to favor, then God could not, consistently with his
> justice, save any besides, if they should believe; "for without shedding
> of blood, there can be no remission." If Christ did not design, by
> his death, to open a door for all to be saved conditionally, that is
> upon the condition of faith, then there is no such door opened; the
> door is not opened wider than Christ designed it should be; there
> is nothing more purchased by his death than he intended; if this
> benefit was not intended, then it is not procured; if it be not pro-
> cured, then the non-elect can not any of them be saved, consistently

[16] *Loc. cit.,* p. 259.   [17] *Ibid.,* p. 260.
[18] *Ibid.,* p. 267.   [19] *Ibid.,* p. 294.

with divine justice. And, by consequence if this be the case, then, first, the non-elect have no right at all to take any, the least encouragement from the death of Christ, or the invitations of the gospel, to return to God through Christ, in hopes of acceptance; for there are no grounds of encouragement given. Christ did not die for them in any sense. It is impossible their sins should be pardoned consistently with justice; as much impossible as if there had never been a Savior; as if Christ had never died; and so there is no encouragement at all for them; and therefore it would be presumption in them to take any; all which is apparently contrary to the whole tenor of the gospel, which everywhere invites all, and gives equal encouragement to all.[20]

Thus Bellamy laid down the fundamental positions of that theory of the atonement which was later to be called the New England. He did more than this; for we shall see, when we are brought in the progress of our history to the proper point, that he had prepared every element for the hand of that man who gave it its place in the new theology, who was, moreover, the pupil of Bellamy, and had probably derived his entire scheme from his teacher. But of this at the proper place.

5. *Total depravity.*—This common position of Calvinism was firmly held by Bellamy. No one could state it more uncompromisingly than he did in this definition:

The very best religious performances of all unregenerate men are, complexly considered, sinful, and so, odious in the sight of God. They may do many things materially good, but the principle, end, and manner of them are such as that, complexly considered, what they do is sin in the sight of God.[21]

The new element in his view was the reason which he gave for this position. This was derived from the new theory of virtue. Negatively, all acts of unregenerate men were sinful because they lacked the one motive which alone could make them acceptable, since they were not performed from love to God. Positively, they were sinful because they were performed from a motive thoroughly sinful, the mo-

[20] *Ibid.*, p. 294.   [21] *Ibid.*, p. 156.

tive of selfishness. Bellamy thus propounds the doctrine, which was to become of more importance in later writers, that all sin is selfishness; but he does not go into any proof of it. The gain he makes is simply in the suggestion that it is the life-motive which makes all the acts of the sinner sinful.

So much for the treatise upon *True Religion*. We pass now to a new field of theological effort, opened by Edwards, in which Bellamy is the first of the New England writers formally to labor—that occupied by the treatise upon the *Permission of Sin*.

Like all the rest of Bellamy's work, this was suggested by the problems which press themselves upon a preacher of repentance. The difficulties which trouble the minds of inquirers call for an argumentative style of preaching. Edwards had set the example, for the vein of argumentative defense of Christian truth runs everywhere through it, as it does through all strong preaching. From his *Miscellaneous Observations* a tolerably comprehensive system of Christian evidences could be constructed. Bellamy could not fail to meet the objection to the goodness of God which is constantly drawn in practical life from the pain which men suffer. If he answered this by a reference to the fact of sin, it was only to have the objection return with all the more force: How could a good God permit sin to enter the world? To the full answer of this objection he addressed himself in the treatise before us, and thus began that long line of effort culminating in the famous Taylor controversies, and in the so-called New Haven theology. It was issued in the darkest period of the French and Indian War (March, 1758). "These sermons are the rather published at this season," says Bellamy, "when the state of the world and of the church appears so exceedingly gloomy and dark, and still darker times are by many expected, as they are

calculated to give consolation to such as fear the Lord and
are disposed to hearken to his holy word." [22]

The work is divided into four discourses. The first
defines what is meant by the permission of sin and defends
the wisdom of God in permitting it. By God's permitting
sin we are not to understand that he loves sin; nor that he
deprives the sinner of his free will in permitting it. It
consists simply in his not hindering it. He does not permit
it in the character of an unconcerned spectator who does
not care how affairs go, but only because, all things considered, he judges it best not to hinder it. He may at times
interfere to prevent individual sins, and when he does so,
this is justifiable, commendable, and praiseworthy.[23] In
all this Bellamy does not pass beyond the Westminster
Confession.

Thus Bellamy seeks by his earliest definitions to disarm
the objection which was commonly made—that, upon the
Calvinistic system, God foreordains sin. His relation to
sin is merely one of permission. Bellamy thus appropri-
ates the phrase of Edwards in his *Freedom of the Will.*
We may regard his treatise as the natural supplement to
Edwards' somewhat restricted remarks. But it is noticeable that, as he writes the first formal treatise upon this
subject, so he falls short of Edwards in the philosophical
part of the matter. The philosophy of motives is not introduced to explain the method of God's providential government.

Bellamy then proceeds to justify the ways of God in
thus permitting sin. He conducts the argument by means
of a multitude of scriptural examples in which he shows
how God overrules the sin of men to work out in the best
way possible his own plans. The final result, for example,
of the course of wickedness on the part, first of Joseph's

---

[22] *Loc. cit.*, Vol. II, p. 5.   [23] *Ibid.*, p. 9.

brethren, and then of the Egyptians and especially Pharaoh, was to reveal the heart and character of God as it could not otherwise have been revealed, to give his creatures a true specimen of themselves, and thus to advance his own glory and their good. For the greatest thing we can possibly have is an increased knowledge of God and of ourselves.

This ends the first discourse, and here Bellamy has touched only upon the problem of justifying the wisdom of God in permitting sin when it has once entered the world. But how shall his wisdom in permitting it to enter be justified? This is the topic of the second discourse.

He takes as his starting-point the position that God in creating the world has chosen the best of all possible plans, and that this is, accordingly, the best possible world. He says:

In the days of eternity, long before the foundation of the world, this system, now in existence, and this plan, which now takes place, and all other possible systems, and all other possible plans, more in number perhaps than the very sands of the seashore, all equally lay open to the divine view, and one as easy to Almightiness as another. He had his choice. He had none to please but himself; beside him there was no being. He had a perfectly good taste, and nothing to bias his judgment, and was infinite in wisdom: this he chose; and this, of all possible systems, therefore, was the best, infinite wisdom and perfect rectitude being judges. If, therefore, the whole were as absolutely incomprehensible by us as it is by children of four years old, yet we ought firmly to believe the whole to be perfect in wisdom, glory, and beauty.[24]

This will remind every reader of the optimism of Leibnitz.[25] Every Christian, indeed, must be an optimist.

[24] Loc. cit., p. 28.

[25] Probably Bellamy had read Leibnitz. I find a book, published in England after Leibnitz' death, entitled, A Collection of Papers Which Passed between Mr. Leibnitz and Dr. Clarke, quoted by Stephen West in his Essay on Moral Agency (1st ed., p. 139). Evidences of Malebranche's influence appear in the same author and book (p. 47). Edwards, in his Original Sin, advances the doctrine of continued creation. Evidently, .her, a decided influence from these philosophers upon New England is to be assumed.

If God is infinitely wise and good, he must be able to produce the best possible world, and he must have the goodness
and the will to do this. Thus, says Bellamy, "were there
no instance in which we could see the wisdom of God in
the permission of sin," this argument would alone convince
us that it must be wise to permit it. But we have more
than this. God's ways are uniform, and what is true of
particular parts of the universe will be true of all. If wisdom is evident in the particular parts which we can behold
and estimate, then it will be found in the rest of the system,
though we may not be able to examine the whole. Now,
such wisdom is evident in limited portions and ranges of
experience—as, for example, in the history of Joseph and
Israel in Egypt already cited. Therefore, could we but
examine more widely, we should everywhere find traces
of the same wisdom, till its proof was complete.

This positive argument is strengthened by the answer
of objections which is next presented. Bellamy insists
upon the ignorance of man. This is so great that our inability to see the meaning of any particular action or course
of action cannot be employed as an argument against the
wisdom of such action. Under the darkest circumstances
perhaps God may have such plans in view as justify his
course. And with the light shed upon the subject by the
Scriptures we have positive reason for believing this in
spite of seeming difficulties.

So far the second discourse. In the third, Bellamy advances still nearer the heart of the subject. God, he says,
does not act arbitrarily, but upon good and sufficient reason. Relying upon this truth, we may advance with confidence in the attempt to discover the reason of this great
mystery.

God acts reasonably. What, now, in the first place,
was exactly that which he did? He erected a grand and

noble theater, the world, fit to be the scene of so great
events. Upon this he placed man, a noble creature, an
intelligent free agent, capable of moral action, and a proper
subject of moral government. He treated him with distinguished goodness in making him capable of knowing,
loving, and obeying God; and in giving him all things
necessary for his comfort in such abundance. Man was thus
under the highest obligations to love God, his Maker, and
to dedicate himself to his service. These obligations God
specially revealed to him, put him under a law, and told
him the penalty which would be inflicted upon him in case
he disobeyed. God thought that he had now done enough,
and that he might reasonably suspend the destiny of man
upon his own action, without taking further precautions
for his safety. Man rebelled, sinned, and fell.

Now, here were three designs: man's design, to gain
rapid and surprising advance in knowledge and happiness;
Satan's design, to thwart the purpose of God by ruining
man; and God's design, to permit Satan to succeed so far
in his attempt as to furnish God with an occasion to attain
more honor, to make the holy part of his creation more
humble, holy, and happy, and to defeat Satan in his
schemes as effectually as he did Pharaoh when he overwhelmed him in the Red Sea. How was God's design
justifiable?

It belongs essentially to the nature of finite beings to be
mutable and peccable. Consequently holiness can be absolutely maintained only when sin is positively prevented, or
when God himself becomes surety that a given individual,
or number of individuals, shall not sin. He must *confirm*
such beings in holiness.

But innocent, holy beings, though mutable, if they have
never felt the least inclination to sin, do not feel themselves exposed to the danger of sin. Was it possible for

Peter to feel that he was in danger of denying his Lord? He felt the greatest aversion from such a deed, and only repeated experience of his weakness could teach him the possibility of such a fault.

Now, if God had confirmed these holy, mutable beings in holiness, so as to prevent all apostasy on the part of any of them, although the kindness done them would be infinitely great, and so perceived by God himself, they would have been in no position to perceive God's goodness, and so their knowledge, both of God and of themselves, would have been inadequate. They were, therefore, not fit to be confirmed; and to have confirmed them would have been to deprive the universe of a great portion of its knowledge of God and of itself, which would have been a great loss to it. Hence it was better not to confirm them till their need of confirmation was evident. But this involved the permission, and resulted in the actuality, of sin.

The fourth discourse adds nothing essential to the argument. It meets the principal objection to this line of thought, which is thus phrased: "But was there no other way in which God could have made angels and men as holy and happy, without the permission of sin?" The answer is: "Not if there was no other way in which he could so fully reveal himself. For aught I or the objector knows, this, of all possible plans, may be the best contrived to give a full and clear manifestation of deity. And its being chosen by infinite wisdom before all others, demonstrates that this is actually the case." Thus Bellamy closes the argument where he began it—in the assumption that this is the best possible world.

This doctrine is that which has been condensed in the phrase, "sin a necessary means of the greatest good." The greatest good involves the fullest possible knowledge of God. This cannot be attained without the existence of sin.

Therefore sin, because it is necessary to a complete divine self-revelation, which is the greatest good, is permitted. This is the first position taken by New England divinity upon this theme.

The following year (1759) a reply to Bellamy appeared in the form of a tract by S. Moody [26] (anonymously printed), entitled *An Attempt to Point out the Fatal and Pernicious Consequences of the Rev. Mr. Joseph Bellamy's Doctrines respecting Moral Evil.* If Bellamy's treatise had been an epoch-making one, this reply was also epoch-making. It was not merely an evidence that every theological proposal in New England was sure to receive the fullest and freest discussion—itself a most important fact, and one promising that theological innovation should result in theological progress; but it also revealed the fact that the young school of thought which was now slowly coming to the front was but one of the profoundly earnest and progressive movements of the day, and that these several movements, even when opposing each other, had much in common. If most of them came to naught, and if one of them took later a wrong direction and cut itself off from the line of evangelical advance, while New England theology held a straighter course and came to a sounder result, it was not because they did not all feel the same great influences. The superiority of the one school was in its leaders; and their superiority consisted in their mingled conservatism and radicalism. Underneath the whole seething surface of the controversies lay the question of human freedom. Apparently the only safeguard just then against an abuse of the idea of freedom was a restriction of the idea. Edwards had given this restriction; and in his theory of virtue he had at the same time given a great impulsive power toward a better view of man. The co-operation of these two tend-

[26] See Dexter, No. 3380.

encies kept the Edwardean school from many a premature position and many an error.

Mr. Moody objected against the idea that "it is most for the glory of God and the good of the moral system that there should be moral evil." [27] While he conducts the discussion upon the surface of the theme, and seems scarcely to be conscious what his fundamental difference from Bellamy is, they really held irreconcilable ideas of the nature of man and of his freedom. Moody could not see anything but evil in sin, and referred it in its whole entirety to man, as a free agent acting in opposition to God. He thus gave the creature an independence before God which Bellamy was in no condition to admit. And when Bellamy urged his *a priori* line of argument by which God must always do the best, since he was infinite and perfect, Moody put in the reply of the agnostic, that such positions are speculative and beyond our powers. [28]

Moody begins by pointing out fallacies in Bellamy's fundamental principles. He has no right to argue that "because God educes many happy consequences from moral evil . . . . therefore he thought best that moral evil should be introduced into a system where all were perfectly holy;" [29] nor that "the sight of the distress of others greatly enhances our pleasure in this state: therefore a view of the misery of those who fell made a prodigious increase of the happiness of those who continued innocent and holy;" [30] nor that God "must *necessarily* always will and do that which is most for his own glory." [31] His thought in this last is that "in no definite period of time, in no given quantity of space can there be a full discovery of God's glories." [32] He questions whether this present scheme can

---

[27] *Attempt*, p. 4.

[28] *Ibid.*, p. 5.

[29] *Ibid.*, p. 6.

[30] *Ibid.*, p. 9.

[31] *Ibid.*, p. 12.

[32] *Ibid.*, p. 13.

be properly said to be God's. To God belong its "order, good, and happiness;" "all the sin, confusion, and misery to Satan and wicked men." [33]

He next presents a number of the common objections, such as that the theory of Bellamy makes God the author of sin, and sin a good, not to be opposed or lamented, etc. And then he presents the argument which in N. W. Taylor's hands, long afterward, was to be one of the principal arguments to destroy the idea that sin was the necessary means of the greatest good; viz., this, that if all rational beings had continued holy and perfect, there would have resulted an amount of blessedness which would have been more to the glory of God than the present existing evil.[34] Finally he objects to the reasoning of Bellamy: The present scheme is a fact; therefore it is best.[35]

The meaning of the whole pamphlet was, therefore: Bellamy makes sin the necessary means of the greatest good; to sustain this, he makes all the steps necessary, leaves no place for man's responsible personal action, and throws upon God's purpose an *onus* which belongs upon the will of man.

Bellamy issued the following year (1760) a *Vindication* [36] in reply. He does not touch the point really at issue, nor advance anything essential to his view of the subject, and hence the book need not detain us long. He shows, however, one of the first qualifications of a controversialist, when he tries to find common ground with his adversary, and specifies eight points in which they agree.[37] The "grand point of difference" he understands to be the optimism of his position, whether "God's present plan is,

[33] *Loc. cit.*, p. 15.

[34] *Ibid.*, pp. 20 ff.; found also in Butler's *Analogy.*

[35] *Ibid.*, p. 25.

[36] *Works*, Vol. II. Quotations here from the original edition.

[37] *Vindication*, pp. 5, 6.

of all possible plans, the best." [38] The proposition to which the book is directed is that "God, who is a being of infinite wisdom and perfect rectitude, always conducts agreeably to his own most glorious perfections;" [39] and this he carries out in a very skilful dialogue, in which he puts aside the unnecessary agnosticism of his opponent. The real gain of this controversy was therefore the negative result—not then fully understood, because the point of the whole had not been brought out—that to defend the freedom of man the overruling government of God must not be so treated as to reduce it to a nullity.

But the process which was hereafter to distinguish the history of New England theology had begun. Our divines, who were so absorbed in the practical labors of the ministry, which demand certainty and consistency of teaching, as constantly to overlook many of the implications of their own positions, were to be gradually pushed on by their adversaries, whom they confuted at some points, but from whom they had to learn at others, into greater and greater modification of their original system. The problems of the day were perceived by many minds; the progress of conviction was the same at points apparently very diverse; the evolution of New England theology was more the work of the age than of the leaders in whose works it was gradually formulated.

We pause here in our review of Bellamy,[40] to recur to him as to minor points repeatedly in connection with his successors. It was evident to his cotemporaries that a new force had appeared in American theology, and we can now see that it was a new school. Upon central portions of the theological system a number of valuable suggestions are

[38] *Ibid.*, p. 7.   [39] *Ibid.*, p. 9.

[40] Another pungent treatise of Bellamy's was his *Blow at the Root of the Refined Antinomianism of the Present Age,* etc. (Boston, 1763; reprinted at New York, 1812).

made, all deriving their force from a new theory of man, as embraced in the ideas of virtue and of freedom, which had entered into the thinking of the times, partly in consequence and partly in spite of the labors of Edwards; and at the central point of all, in the doctrine of the atonement, the theory is propounded which is to constitute the principal service of New England theology to the world, and is adequately presented in its leading idea and in the reasons for this.   Above all, a new air breathes through Bellamy's writings—the air of freedom; and a new intellectual disposition is everywhere manifest—the disposition to discuss, not merely in order to refute, but also to learn, and to meet new difficulties by new propositions suited to the day. It is the unmistakable influence of Edwards that we see here.   The protagonist has passed through the first great struggles of a new epoch, and come to a knowledge of himself and his work; his successor stands already in the full freedom of the new position gained and in the joyous consciousness of his powers addresses himself to the task prescribed by the situation.   It was with a feeling of great expectation that men looked forward to the future, to its struggles and to their outcome.   And this feeling of buoyant hope long continued to be the dominant feeling of the New England school, as it was of the entire new American nation.

CHAPTER VI

SAMUEL HOPKINS

It was fortunate for the new theology of New England that so rich a nature, with so warm a heart and so intensely practical interests as Bellamy had, stood at its fountainhead to direct its course. The other colaborer with Edwards, Hopkins,[1] was naturally of a more prosaic and exclusively intellectual turn; but he too was a pastor, and was thus made constantly solicitous for the practical usefulness of every theological theory. He was, perhaps, not so large a nature as Bellamy, but he was violently uprooted from his retirement in the depths of the western wilderness and transplanted to one of the principal seaports of the country, and here, amid the opportunities and under the incitements of a busier life, be became involved in larger attempts, and performed a larger service, than fell to Bellamy's lot. His theological service was larger, for he gathered his theology into the first New England "system;" but he was also a reformer, laboring against intemperance, slavery, secret societies, etc., gave the impulse which finally brought into existence the American Board of Commissioners for Foreign Missions, and engaged in large miscellaneous literary labors, becoming, in particular, the editor of Edwards' literary remains. It is as a portion of a widely extended activity that we are to view those labors which fall under our present examination.

Hopkins' system of theology was a growth in his own mind, and was formed by prolonged study, and in constant

[1] Samuel Hopkins, born in Waterbury, Conn., September 17, 1721; died in Newport, R. I., December 20, 1803; entered Yale in 1737, graduating in 1741; studied theology for a short time (eight months) with Edwards; settled in Great Barrington, Mass., 1743; dismissed in 1769; installed in Newport 1770. Beginning his writing in 1759, he published constantly during his Newport pastorate, closirg with his *System of Doctrines* in 1793, and a volume of sermons (1803?).

contact with other minds. It was presented in many partial views in a series of controversial writings beginning with the very unpopular tract, *Sin through the Divine Interposition an Advantage to the Universe* (1759). It was finally gathered up in one full presentation in his *System of Doctrines* (1793). But meantime there had been a long and varied theological history, in which many different minds had been engaged, from some of whom Hopkins took much. The full understanding of his work therefore requires that it shall be divided, and, that after its earlier portions have been considered, and the foundations which he laid have been traced, attention shall be turned to the controversies going on about him and to the work of other laborers. Only thus shall we be able to understand the *System* when it comes.

The title of the first tract,[2] already mentioned, was "so shocking to many that they would read no further." Such is Hopkins' own account. But it was a serious and reverent handling of the great theme which Bellamy had discussed but a little before—the permission of sin. Hopkins' first proposition is that sin is the occasion of great good. The case of Joseph, of Pharaoh, and of the Savior are cited, very much as Bellamy had cited them. Hopkins also declares under this head that God could have made intelligent creatures and kept them from sin without destroying their free agency. The second proposition is that the result of sin in accomplishing good is no excuse for it. The argument is chiefly biblical, consisting of examples which illustrate the vileness of sin, thus bringing to the heart and conscience of the reader the principles to which heart and conscience must ever respond. Sin is not the occasion of good because of any tendency to good in itself.

---

[2] *Works* (Boston edition of 1852, which will be uniformly cited in the following pages), Vol. II, pp. 491 ff.

Bellamy had uncompromisingly declared, on the basis of the Leibnitzian optimism, that sin was the necessary means of the greatest good. Hopkins was also an optimist, and may have shared Bellamy's view. But there are two distinct interpretations of optimism possible—one that there can be no world better than the present, and the other that there can be none so good. Bellamy takes the latter position; but Hopkins may have taken the former. Though he says, "God's greatest and most glorious work is to bring good out of evil . . . . to make sin in general, which is the greatest evil, the means of the *greatest* good," [3] he is elsewhere cautious to a degree that implies some hesitation from fully following Bellamy. He says: "Christ will make sin the occasion of so much good, that the world shall be *at least as good* a world as if sin had never been introduced." [4] His last word upon the theme is the supposition: "*If* God saw that sin's entering into the world would be the best means of answering the greatest and best ends . . . . would be the occasion of the greatest good . . . . a means of the world's becoming *better,* more excellent and glorious *than otherwise it would be,"* etc.[5] But he never introduces the thought that the revelation of God could not be perfected without sin, or any other position that must involve Bellamy's radical affirmation.

Hopkins' next work was his *Inquiry concerning the Promises of the Gospel* (1765),[6] written in reply to two sermons of Dr. Jonathan Mayhew,[7] pastor of the West Church in Boston, which were entitled, *Striving to Enter in at the Strait Gate . . . . and the Connection of Salvation Therewith* (1761). Mayhew was entering a protest against certain applications of that same doctrine of inabil-

---

[3] *Ibid.,* p. 503. [4] *Ibid.,* p. 506.
[5] *Ibid.,* p. 50. [6] *Ibid.,* Vol. III, p. 183.
[7] Born October 8, 1720; died in Boston, July 9, 1766; graduated at Harvard 1744; pastor of West Church, 1747–66; D.D. (Aberdeen), 1749.

ity, inherent in the ancient Calvinism, against which New England theology was about to make equal protest. He seems to have come already upon the ground of Edwards so far as to teach that the character of God was comprised in his love, and to draw the consequences that later gave the New England doctrine of the atonement.[8] He had in mind certain extreme statements of the doctrine of prevenient grace, which led men to "deny there is any sort of connection between the most earnest endeavors of sinners and their obtaining eternal life."[9] He was writing of the "unregenerate," but it is not quite certain that he did not mean by that term the "unsanctified." His terms are a little nebulous. Hopkins understood him to mean those who have not received the new heart by the special operation of the Holy Spirit. Whatever he meant at this point, so much is clear, that he taught that one who is "at least a speculative believer in the gospel," and has "some sense of his sin, guilt, and misery," has "his heart engaged in this matter as a thing of the last importance to him," earnestly prays, strives against sin, and intends to persevere "not for a month, a year, or any definite, given time, but as long as it shall please God to continue him in the world,"[10] may "strive to attain holiness and eternal life," and that, "if they strive in the manner they may and ought to do . . . . God will certainly afford them all the influences of his Spirit and grace which are necessary to that end."[11] The impression which the book makes as a whole is that, in resisting certain evil tendencies of the times, Mayhew had unconsciously gone over into substantial Pelagianism, ascribing the gift of converting grace to the divine response to efforts of the sinner.[12]

[8] *Loc. cit.*, pp. 63 ff.

[9] *Striving to Enter*, etc., p. 82.

[10] *Ibid.*, pp. 11–20.

[11] *Ibid.*, p. 45.

[12] Mayhew is an illustration of a fact elsewhere noted in these pages, viz., the general prevalence of the theological ferment of that day in New England,

Mayhew accordingly favors the use of "means" by the unregenerate, and ascribes to them some degree of acceptableness before God for such use. He does not exhort them to enter in at the strait gate, but to strive to enter, and the exhortation seems to Hopkins to have the force of urging them to strive in such a way as not to enter in actually.[13] Hopkins had had bitter experiences of the effect of such exhortations in suppressing the Christian life in his own personal history. The book before us was written out of an inner necessity of the writer's mind. It was the first, but not the last, effort to strip such opinions of all their disguises and reveal them in themselves and in their baleful effects upon individual piety and the prosperity of the churches.

The new theory of virtue might have given Hopkins a means of complete logical refutation of Mayhew's views. If there is such a thing as a separate virtue, a single act of the will, which, without regard to the great end for which man is living, has a virtue in itself as an individual act, then there may be a prayer pleasing to God which yet falls short of being a full surrender of all the powers of the man to his service. But the Edwardean theory insisted first upon the exercise of "love to being in general," or that all things must be done from the supreme motive of love to God, and thus excluded every form of service of God which did not involve this. Such was Hopkins' position, and he, no doubt, saw clearly the inconsistency

and the common sharing of many ideas which in the New England school served to sustain evangelical religion, but which with others developed into Unitarianism. Thus in *Two Sermons on the Nature, Extent, and Perfection of the Divine Goodness* (1763) Mayhew presents the Edwardean idea of the character of God: "Perfect goodness, love itself, is his very essence, in a peculiar sense; immeasurable, immutable, universal, and everlasting love. And nothing that is in any manner or degree inconsistent with such love has any place in God" (p. 44). And he presents a thoroughly Grotian view of the atonement, and identifies the justice of God with public justice" (pp. 63 ff.).

[13] Of the same general cast were Samuel Williams' two sermons on *Regeneration the Most Important Concern* (Boston, 1766).

of Mayhew's teachings with this fundamental idea. But it is remarkable that he does not conduct the argument upon this basis. To have done so would have been to prejudice his case before a public which knew little as yet about the theory of virtue, which was, indeed, published the same year with Hopkins' tract under his editorial supervision (1765).

The question in dispute between Mayhew and Hopkins turned upon the doctrine of total depravity. Mayhew thought that the unregenerate might have such desires and strivings after holiness as were pleasing to God, though they were still unregenerate. Hopkins declared that if they had such acceptable strivings, they were regenerate; and if they were unregenerate, they did not have them. "All must see, I think, by this time," says Hopkins, "that in order to understand and settle the question before us, it must be first determined what can be justly predicated of the doings of unregenerate sinners, and that a just solution of this will put an end to the dispute." To the resolution of this issue Hopkins now addresses himself.

The expression "desiring salvation," if it means anything which it should mean, must, according to Hopkins, involve the choice of salvation; and this signification, he thinks, is contained in many expressions of Dr. Mayhew's. Now, it will not be difficult to prove that all who come with such a desire will obtain salvation, for all the promises of the gospel are made to them. The question is simply whether the unregenerate have any such desires.[14] This the Scriptures deny in such passages as this: "No

[14] He should have said choices. We note here the old ambiguity between "inclination" as a desire and as a choice, which so vitiated much of Edwards' reasoning, returning to plague this argument. Mayhew could insist upon the emotive side of desire, and rightly maintain that the sinner had such a desire for salvation, from which position he could not be driven out. Hopkins was insisting upon its volitional side, and his argument would have gathered both clearness and power if his phraseology had always made this evident.

man can come to me except the Father which hath sent me, draw him." This drawing is regeneration, before which there is no true "coming." Says Hopkins:

There must, therefore, be a distinction kept up between regeneration, which is the work of God in giving a new heart, and in which men are perfectly passive, and active conversion, in which men, being regenerated, turn from sin to God in the exercise of repentance towards God and faith towards our Lord Jesus Christ, and in consequence of which they are pardoned and received to favor and a title to eternal life, and have the gift of the spirit to dwell with them forever, as an abiding principle of life and holiness. All this, with every benefit which men receive by Christ, is promised to those who believe or heartily embrace the gospel, and not to regeneration; for to this, considered as antecedent to all action, and only as the foundation of right exercise, no promise is made.

Neither are those influences by which men are regenerated in this sense meant by giving or receiving the Spirit, as the Spirit of promise, by which believers, and they only, are sealed to the day of redemption. But men receive the Spirit, in this sense, as a Spirit of adoption, by which all God's children are led by faith, or a hearty receiving Christ with all his benefits. (See John i. 12. Gal. iii. 14, 26. Eph. i. 13.) They who will not make and understand this distinction, must think and talk in some measure unintelligibly on this point. This change, therefore, called *regeneration,* by which a new heart is given, as the foundation of all true discerning of the things of God's moral kingdom, and of all right exercises of heart; this change, I say, wrought by the Spirit of God, immediately and instantaneously, and altogether imperceptibly to the person who is the subject of it,— it being impossible that he should know what God has done for him but by a consciousness of his own views and exercises, which are the fruit and consequence of the divine operation,—these views and exercises of the regenerate, in which they turn from sin to God, or embrace the gospel, are often in Scripture spoken of as included in that change which is called *a being born again;* as all the change which is perceptible, and in which man is active, consists in this. And this is sometimes called, by divines, *active conversion,* to distinguish it from regeneration, or that change in which men are passive.[15]

Hopkins here has in view the subjective motive leading to the action of the will. "Things that exist in the view of the mind," says Edwards, "have their strength,

[15] *Works,* Vol. III, pp. 235 f.

tendency, or advantage to move or excite the will from many things pertaining to the nature and circumstances of the thing viewed, the nature and circumstances of the mind that views, and the degree and manner of its view." To give this subjective condition, in the critical matter of regeneration, is the act of God, and before it the will never acts in accordance with the law of God. Yet this philosophical argument is never introduced by Hopkins, who no more quotes the *Freedom of the Will* than he does the *Nature of Virtue,* but advances other arguments more readily accepted by his audience. For example, he says: "That there are no promises of regenerating grace made to the exercises and doings of the unregenerate may be argued from passages of the Holy Scriptures;"[16] and then proceeds to quote the requirements of the Scripture to repent and believe, and not to do anything short of this. He might have said: "This theory of regeneration puts it in the act of man, whereas it is the sovereign act of God." But he does not use this argument; he proceeds with his quotations. "To be carnally minded is death. . . . . All unregenerate persons are according to this in a state of condemnation and death and are in the way to eternal destruction." And he says, again: "That there are no promises of salvation made to the exercises and doings of the unregenerate will be evident if it be considered that such do, with their whole hearts, oppose the way of salvation by Christ and reject the salvation offered them."

Now, that exercises of enmity against Christ, and opposition to the gospel, and the salvation therein revealed and offered, or those which are consistent with this, are made the condition of a title to, and interest in, this salvation, so as that all the promises of the gospel are made to such exercises and acts, I presume none will believe.

If salvation is offered to all who heartily desire it, really choose

---

[16] *Loc. cit.,* pp. 237 ff.

and accept of it, and so truely ask for it, it is offered on terms low enough, as low as any can reasonably desire; yea, on the lowest conceivable or even possible terms. But no unregenerate person comes up to these terms. Therefore, salvation is not offered or promised to any doings of the unregenerate.

But, now, if the unregenerate are not accepted of God and blessed in their prayers and in the use of the other "means of grace," so called, what is the proper office of the Word in preaching, of the services of the sanctuary, of the reading of the Bible, of prayer, etc.? In reply, Hopkins emphasizes truth as "the grand medium of grace and salvation, and, strictly speaking, the sole medium." [17] The whole object of the use of these means by Christians is to make the truth come home with greater power to men's hearts. And unconverted men are themselves also to use these means; that is, they are to seek every help in gaining a larger knowledge of the things relating to God's moral government and kingdom.

But if regeneration is, after all, God's work, what will be the benefit of this? Hopkins' answer is that the degree of knowledge thereby gained, while not a discernment of the true beauty of divine things, is the necessary condition of such a discernment.

This [true discernment] is a kind of knowledge which is peculiar to the regenerate, the foundation of which is laid in their having a new heart. The former is necessary in order to the latter, as it is supposed and implied in it; for there can be no discerning of the beauty of those objects of which the mind has no speculative idea.[18]

But, still further, what is the true condition of the unregenerate under the use of these means? Are they the better or the worse for them? Hopkins answers, in entire consistence with the positions he has taken previously, that there is no true holiness in such use of means, but that,

[17] *Ibid.,* p. 259.
[18] *Ibid.,* p. 263.

on the contrary, if the sinner continues to reject the gospel,
he does not grow

better, but rather grows worse, by all the instruction and knowledge
he gets in the use of means. And awakened, convicted sinners, with
whom most means are used, and who are most atttentive to the concerns of their souls, and most in earnest in the use of means, are commonly, if not always, really more guilty and odious in God's sight,
than they who are secure and at ease in their sins. Their greater sinfulness does not, indeed, consist in their concern about themselves, in
a sense of the sad, dangerous state they are in, and in their earnestly
desiring deliverance and safety, or in the pains they take in order
hereto; but in their continuing to hate God and his law, and to oppose
and reject the Savior; even under all their concern, exercises, and endeavors, and with all the light and conviction they have.[19]

But if all these efforts and all the use of means only
make the sinner worse and worse, what is he to do? Shall
he continue to use these ineffective means? Yes, says Hopkins, they are necessary to salvation, inasmuch as their
absence is a fatal bar in the way of salvation.

God can, doubtless, as easily change the heart of the most ignorant, deluded Mahometan, or heathen, yea, the most blind, stupid Hot-
tentot in the world, as that of the most awakened, enlightened sinner under the gospel. But if he should do so by the regenerating influences of his Spirit, there could be no right and proper exercises of
Christian virtue and holiness; because such a one is without any right
speculative knowledge of those truths, in the view of which alone
Christian holiness is exercised. And giving a new heart, or a right
taste and temper of mind, would not remove this darkness. This only
prepares the mind to discern and relish the beauty and sweetness of
divine things, when set before it in the use of means, but does not give
any new speculative ideas or knowledge. Therefore, we have no
reason to think God ever does so.[20]

Hopkins' hopes for the heathen were not greater than
Luther's, though the rational ground of his despair was
not precisely the same.

To sum up, then, the substance of this treatise in a few
words: Hopkins taught that the sinner is totally wicked; is

[19] *Loc. cit.*, p. 264.
[20] *Ibid.*, p. 266.

under immediate obligations to repent; and nothing short of this is acceptable before God. He is bound to use the means of enlightenment, but in a holy manner, repenting of his sins as fast as he discovers them, casting himself wholly upon God, and choosing his service. Every promise is made to him under such circumstances, and nothing less can be or will be accepted by God. But if he refuse to give God his heart, all that he does is wicked, and the more he strives to put something else in the place of this simple, easy, and single duty, the more wicked he is. Such is the meaning of Hopkins; and the positions he thus laid down became at once and remained commonplaces in the New England school.

The men who opposed Hopkins so violently in this "new doctrine" claimed to be good Calvinists. It is therefore interesting to ask what were the actual relations of Hopkins' teaching to Calvinism, and especially to the Westminster Confession. The answer is brief. Hopkins was simply reaffirming the Westminster doctrine, in almost the very words of the Confession. We read:

Works done by unregenerate men, although for the matter of them they may be things which God commands, and of good use both to themselves and others, yet because they proceed not from a heart purified by faith, nor are done in a right manner, according to the Word, nor to a right end, the glory of God; they are therefore sinful and cannot please God or make a man meet to receive grace from God. And yet their neglect of them is more sinful and displeasing unto God.[21]

This contest was the first shock of the battle of the new divinity with conservative Calvinism. It is natural at the present time to suppose that Edwards' works were recognized, when they first appeared, as possessing the importance which was later ascribed to them, and that his cotemporaries had the same respect for him which pos-

[21] Westminster Confession, chap. xvi, § vii.

terity has felt. But such was not the case. The controversies into which Hopkins fell illustrate the prevalent condition of theological thinking, and thus throw very important light upon the times; but they were also essential steps in the contest which had to be waged in behalf of the new opinions before these could boast of the general acceptance which they finally received, and thus are indispensable topics in a genetic history of New England theology. Into their details it will therefore be necessary to go.

In 1767 Rev. Jedidiah Mills, of Ripton, Conn., wrote an *Inquiry concerning the State of the Unregenerate under the Gospel,* etc.[22] This essay was particularly called out by the tenth section of Hopkins' tract against Mayhew, in which he dealt with the use of means and the condition of the unregenerate while using them. Mr. Mills did not approve of the position that the unregenerate, under conviction of sin in consequence of the application to them of the means of grace, are more sinful than they would be in a state of indifference and neglect of the means.[23] This seemed to him an extreme against which he wished to protest.

His own starting-point it is somewhat difficult to determine, for he does not seem to have been a clear and incisive thinker. He sometimes describes the "unregenerate" man in a way which applies only to the regenerate.[24] In such passages "unregenerate" would almost seem equivalent to "unsanctified." He implies that it is the duty of the "unregenerate, as a means among others, to pray for regenerating grace."[25] He speaks of them, though unregenerate, as "less wicked, and, in the true sense of Scripture, in a state brought nearer to the kingdom of God"

---

[22] New Haven, 124 pages.   [23] *Op. cit.,* p. 5.

[24] *Ibid.,* p. 7.   [25] *Ibid.,* p. 41.

when awakened and convicted.[26] He does not intend by this to abandon the Calvinistic system in favor of the Pelagian, although he approaches the latter; he is deeply interested in one main thing—in avoiding discouraging impressions as to the outcome of "using the means," in order that the unregenerate may not be led to neglect them.

However vague, rambling, and weak Hopkins felt the book to be, as it was in no small degree, he saw in it an epitome of the objections with which his work was being met, and proceeded to answer it at length.[27] It is often more difficult to answer a vague and weak man than one strong and exact. With the thoroughness of Edwards himself, he set out to demolish the adversary and all he represented. It will obviously be unnecessary to follow the controversy into all its ramifications, for we are concerned here only with getting before us the contributions that came from it to the growing system of New England thought. But the main positions of Hopkins we must note, and they were these:

After remarking that Mr. Mills had "carefully kept the character which I give of the unregenerate sinner under true awakenings and convictions of conscience out of view," and had "done it through his whole performance," Hopkins redefines his position in the following paragraph:

The unregenerate sinner, who is under genuine and thorough awakenings and convictions of conscience respecting his own state and circumstances and the truths of the gospel, particularly respecting this truth, that salvation is freely offered to him through a Mediator, which he is obliged by the strongest ties of duty and interest immediately to accept and embrace, being at the same time wholly without any excuse for his neglect in not embracing it, and for the opposition of his heart to Christ, of which he is conscious, and who yet continues, under all this light, and contrary to the plain dictates and pressing, painful convictions of his own conscience, obstinately to

[26] *Ibid.,* p. 59.
[27] *Works,* Vol. III, pp. 277–497 (large octavo!).

oppose and reject Jesus Christ; such a one is, on the account of this his impenitence and obstinacy under this clear light and conviction of conscience, more guilty, vile, and odious in God's sight than he was before he had this light and conviction and was in a state of security and ignorance, whatever alteration or reformation has taken place in him in other respects.[28]

He then goes into an elaborate discussion of "the true state and character of the unregenerate sinner under awakenings and convictions," [29] in which he maintains that he is "an enemy to God;" [30] and that, "however distressed and anxious he is about his case, ... he is as real and as great an enemy to the divine character as ever." [31] Then he illustrates as follows:

Many a profligate wretch, who has long indulged himself in uncleanness and debauchery, when he has been brought into such circumstances that his wickedness is likely to be discovered so as to bring disgrace and contempt upon him and ruin him in all his worldly interests, has been filled with anxiety and distress, so that he could find no quiet night nor day; he has been convinced of his folly, condemned himself, and reformed his vile practices, being afraid to indulge himself in the least degree as he had done, and resolved that he would carefully avoid such conduct for time to come, and has used unwearied attempts to escape the evil he feared; and in this time of his fear and distress has made many prayers to God, hoping that he would interpose in his behalf, so that he might escape the evil he feared. But when his fears were over and nothing was, in his view, in the way of his going into his former practices without danger of punishment or a discovery, he has returned to them with as much delight and eagerness as ever. In this case every one will be sensible how little in his favor was his reformation, and that under all his fears and terrors and earnest endeavors to avoid evil, his heart was really no better than it was before, and was as much in love with sin. This may in some measure illustrate the case of the awakened sinner with respect to what I have just now been speaking; for there is no more virtue and goodness in fearing evil in the future world, even the punishment of hell, than worldly evil; and the reformation of any particular practices from such fear is from no better principles and no more an evidence of real opposition of heart to sin than in the instance just mentioned.[32]

[28] *Loc. cit.*, pp. 288, 289.   [29] *Ibid.*, p. 292.   [30] Also *ibid.*, p. 292.

[31] *Ibid.*, p. 292.   [32] *Ibid.*, pp. 295, 296.

"This," says Hopkins again, "is carefully kept out of sight" by Mr. Mills; and—

he represents the unregenerate as not wholly to blame for their unregeneracy, their unbelief, and not embracing the gospel, but as being under an impotence which does in some measure, if not wholly, excuse. This representation runs through his whole book, ... and is laid as the foundation of all his opposition to me.[33]

In other words, here was again the old paralyzing doctrine of inability, which was to Hopkins a "refuge of lies." [34]

The dispute between the parties gathered, then, as Hopkins says, "about the true character of the unregenerate sinner." [35]

At a later point Hopkins takes up the question whether "the apathy of the awakened sinner is an encouragement to the abandoned sinner." [36] He answers this by a consideration of the ruling motive of sinners, which he finds in their selfishness. He sketches the efforts of such a sinner, under fear of hell, to secure salvation; and declares that, if the sinner is convinced that "attendance on means" will bring salvation, he will not be deterred by any idea of increased guilt, for *it is not his guilt that disturbs him,* but his *danger.*

If, therefore, he does neglect means, and live in known ways of open sin, under a pretence that he is afraid of that greater sin he shall be guilty of if he attends on means and becomes a convinced sinner, it is certain it is but a pretence, in which there is no truth; for if he is afraid of greater sinfulness, why not of less; why does he go on in known sin? If he hates sin and hence sincerely desires to be delivered from it, why does he not leave off sinning and fly to Christ, the only deliverer? [37]

Thus Part I of the answer. Upon this follows a Part II,[38] which is entitled: "Wherein it is inquired, whether

[33] *Ibid.,* p. 300.
[34] *Ibid.,* p. 299; cf. p. 428.
[35] *Ibid.,* p. 303.
[36] *Ibid.,* pp. 406 ff.
[37] *Ibid.,* p. 409.
[38] *Ibid.,* p. 418.

God has given any commands to unregenerate sinners, which they do truly comply with and may perfectly obey while unregenerate?" Hopkins' line of argument is already familiar to us. He insists on the "heart" [39] or the motive, necessary to fulfil *any* command of God's, and this is that element which only the regenerate have. And, finally, we need only notice, near the end of his treatise, and after much other discussion, his summary of the evil tendency of Mr. Mill's *Inquiry*.[40] This consists in his "representing sinners more to blame for other sins than for the sin of unbelief," in the tendency "to prevent sinners from coming to any proper, true, and thorough conviction of their guilt," to flatter the superficially interested, and to discourage "every sinner who has any good degree of true, genuine conviction," etc., etc.

A second antagonist arose in the person of Rev. William Hart, who wrote a small tract upon President Edwards' theory of virtue.[41]

Mr. Hart had evidently been repelled by the style of Edwards, especially by his excessive abstractness and the unusual significations given to his terms, which mark this brief treatise on virtue more than any other of Edwards' writings. That he had taken little pains to penetrate the hard shell to the kernel and come to an understanding of what Edwards really meant is equally evident; unless, indeed, we are to suppose him too indefinite in his own thinking to be able to follow another as logical as Edwards was.

[39] *Loc. cit.*, p. 419.

[40] *Ibid.*, p. 481.

[41] The full title: "Remarks on President Edwards' Dissertations concerning the Nature of true Virtue: Shewing that he has given a wrong Idea, and Definition of Virtue, and is inconsistent with himself. To which is added an Attempt to shew wherein true Virtue does consist. By William Hart, Pastor of the first Church in Say-Brook. Great men are not always wise. Elihu. Beware lest any Man spoil you through philosophy and vain deceit, after the tradition of men, after the rudiments of the world, and not after Christ. Paul. New Haven, etc., 1771." (53 pages.)

As an illustration of his attitude we may note the following passage:

Is true religious love to God such as Mr. Edwards here represents it? Does the virtuous or holy mind first entertain a benevolent affection for being in general, abstractly considered, simply as intelligent, and in the next step direct this benevolence chiefly to God, considering him as having the greatest share of mental being? and thus viewing him as most benevolent and beneficent to being simply considered, does the benevolent mind rise in greater benevolence to him, and settle in complacence in him, on this account, from a sort of gratitude to him, as thus befriending the grand object of his primary love? Does not this represent being simply considered as the supreme object of virtuous regard, and make it an idol, and virtue itself idolatrous? Does it not in effect represent love to God as the result of our own virtuous love to simple being, virtue's idol, rather than of his virtuous attraction, and quickening love to us while we were sinners? Do we receive any such ideas from inspired teachers in holy scripture?—These views are too shocking.[42]

The historical process by which a man comes to love God is here confounded with the logical relations of ideas. Being simply considered is taken as if it were a different being from God, in opposition to the most express cautions and explanations of Edwards. The last sentence is also characteristic, for the work is pervaded by a kind of holy indignation, which provoked Hopkins to some sarcasms that, however deserved, might have been better omitted.

The argumentative value of the work was not great, for, though he tries to catch Edwards in inconsistencies with himself, he never grapples with the true question at issue between them, which was in fact the question between Calvinism and Pelagianism.[43] And when, in the last chap-

---

[42] *Remarks*, p. 9.

[43] Hart seems, from an extract from a "Letter to Dr. Whitaker" given by Hopkins (*Works*, Vol. III, p. 87), to have been, at least half-and-half, a Pelagian. He said: "The Holy Spirit accompanies this ministration of the word of life with some degree of his influence, as a common grace. If sinners improve this, and the outward helps they have by the gospel, *as far as they are improvable by them*, I believe he will crown his common influence with special and effectual, leading them on to saving faith, and so regenerate them." This is *Dei gratiam secundum merita nostra dari*.

ter but one, he attempts to state the "real nature and essence of true virtue or real holiness," he approaches very
near to Edwards, for he defines it thus: "It consists in
right and equitable dispositions and actions towards God
and our fellow servants."

Still another antagonist had to be met in the person of
Rev. Moses Hemmenway,[44] of Wells, Mass., who in 1767
published *Seven Sermons on the Obligation and Encouragement of the Unregenerate to Labour for the Meat
Which Endureth to Everlasting Life.* They seem to have
had a purely practical purpose—to increase the attendance upon the means of grace by the uncoverted—and
are by no means marked by extremes of any sort. Under
the head of "mistaken ends of religious duties"[45] he
guards against a number of the same misunderstandings
which Hopkins was laboring against. "No one is required
to do anything to atone or satisfy for his past offences;"
"nor are these duties to be required as meritorious of the
favour and kindness of God, or as rendering us worthy
objects of his mercy;" they are not "a condition of acceptance with God;" they have not "a promise of faith, or the
grace of regeneration annexed to them;" and "the duties
or endeavors which God has prescribed to the unregenerate
are not prescribed because there is any spiritual goodness
in the performances of such persons." The positive doctrine which he is inculcating is summed up in the following sentences:

They ought to repent and believe the gospel and obey all the
precepts therein contained, from a true faith in God and in his Son,
Jesus Christ the redeemer, from a holy reverence, love, and gratitude, for the majesty and grace displayed in the work of redemption.
But they are morally incapable of acting from such views and ends
as these, till they have a spiritual knowledge of the glory of God in

[44] Born at Framingham, Mass., 1735; graduated at Harvard, 1755; ordained
pastor at Wells, Mass., August 8, 1759; died there August 5, 1811.

[45] *Op. cit.,* pp. 39 ff.

the face of Jesus Christ; yet they are capable of performing the matter of the duties required from lower views, from natural principles, and a different kind of light and influence from the Holy Spirit. And it is their duty and they have encouragement to do what God has required of them, in such a manner and for such ends as these, however defective, rather than not at all. Till their hearts are divinely renewed and their minds savingly enlightened, they are to attend upon the instituted means of grace from a conviction of conscience that God has commanded them to do so, and it is their duty to obey. They are to do it from a desire of further light and instruction, which God has directed them to seek for in this way. They are to do it from a serious concern, if it may be, to find rest to their weary souls, to flee from the wrath to come, and obtain reconciliation with God.[46]

When, now, Hopkins put forth his *True State and Character of the Unregenerate* in reply to Mr. Mills, Hemmenway found himself as much attacked as Mr. Mills. He therefore issued (1772) a *Vindication,* which will answer the question which will have arisen in the mind of every reader: how it was that, when he was so near to Hopkins, he could not come nearer. That answer will be given by the fact that he had by no means accepted the new Edwardean philosophy, whether of the will or of the nature of virtue.

He could not, in the first place, accept the distinction which Edwards had made between natural and moral ability and inability.[47] He could not understand what was meant by natural inability (defined by Edwards as inability because of "some impeding defect or obstacle that is extrinsic to the Will"), because he could not get at the precise meaning of "will" in such a connection. He is not ready to accept the division of the soul into faculties; for "some, who have been no mean philosophers, have thought that no real and natural distinction could be made between the faculties, habits, acts, and objects of the understanding and the will." He mentions the threefold, and Ed-

[46] *Ibid.,* pp. 58 f.

[47] *Vindication,* pp. 11 ff.

wards' twofold, division of the faculties, but decides for neither, and is indeed averse to such discussions, for "it is not surely fit that a distinction of so much importance as this, between that inability which excuses and that which does not, should turn upon so nice and abstruse a point as whether the defect or obstacle lies in the understanding or the will." [48]   He notes the ambiguity which attended Edwards' use of the word "inclination," [49] but does not press this as he should.

When he comes to state what he himself understands under the inability of the unregenerate, he distinguishes between the powers or faculties of the soul, in respect to which it is "indifferently capable of sin or holiness," [50] and its "habits," which he otherwise terms "secondary powers of moral action," [51] and which are "any principle, disposition, or propensity which is the foundation of men's loving or hating particular objects, or acting in a particular manner." It is the lack of such a habit (comparable to skill in speaking a particular language),[52] "disposing them to holy affections and actions," [53] which constitutes the inability of the unregenerate.

It is for the purpose of still further clearing up this topic that Hemmenway now passes to the nature of true holiness; and here his second great difference from Edwards appears. "Holiness," he says, "consists in conformity to the preceptive will of God." [54]   He does not mean thereby that right and wrong are founded in the will of God. God has commanded us to be holy "because it is right."

Now, one would expect, if there was to be a difference from Hopkins established here, that Hemmenway should

[48] Loc. cit., p. 15.

[49] Ibid., pp. 16 ff.

[50] Ibid., p. 22.

[51] Ibid., p. 23.

[52] Ibid., p. 25

[53] Ibid., p. 26.

[54] Ibid., p. 31.

next declare that an outward act, such as attendance upon the public worship of God, performed by an unregenerate person, might be holy, at least in some respect, because it is "in conformity to the preceptive will of God." Indeed, he does use expressions which hint at this. He speaks of an action as "not absolutely holy, though in some particulars it may be good." [55] But when he comes to define the "principles of holy obedience," they are (1) "a supernatural habit communicated in regeneration," (2) "a true faith in God, in Christ," (3) "the special influence of the Holy Spirit dwelling within us," (4) "love, the greatest of Christian graces, without which we with all our endowments and works are nothing." [56] This falls very little short of being Edwardean. But it is not intended to be that, for a little later, with explicit reference to Edwards, Hemmenway says of true holiness that "it seems not to be an exact and just definition to say, 'its essence consists in general benevolence.' " [57] He continues:

For, though it be true that general benevolence is a holy affection, yet holiness does not consist wholly in right affections. Not only love but good works are required in the divine command. Effective acts of the soul are as really of the nature of holiness as immanent exercises, when they are in themselves, and in their circumstances and qualifications, conformable to the will of God. . . . . And, besides, there is a rectitude of nature comformable to the law, distinct from all exercises of the soul whatever. This definition then appears to be defective, narrow, and inadequate.

With the true meaning of Edwards he does not, therefore, grapple. He is both more pointed and more successful in refuting Hopkins' statement that "the unregenerate act wholly from self-love." [58]

The final outcome of all his discussions is perhaps sufficiently embraced in the following paragraph in the sec-

[55] *Ibid.*, p. 36.   [56] *Ibid.*, p. 41.
[57] *Ibid.*, p. 46.   [58] *Ibid.*, pp. 60 ff.

tion entitled, "the unregenerate able and obliged to do actions materially good:"

It has been proved that the unregenerate who enjoy gospel privileges are able, by the common assistance of divine providence and grace, to reform their lives; to break off from courses and acts of open sin in opposition to the dictates of their own conscience; to do actions materially good, and that seriously and conscientiously according to their present light. They have both faculties and principles of action sufficient for these things. If these things are enjoined upon them by and contained in those commands which God in his word has laid upon them, then it is their duty thus to reform their lives, and attend the means of grace, that is, something is their duty which they have a power to do before regeneration.[59]

A serious problem was now presented to Hopkins. With Hart's *Remarks on President Edwards' Dissertation* and Hemmenway's *Vindication* before him, he saw that the true difficulty as to "unregenerate doings" was the failure to understand, or at least to accept, the doctrines of the will and of virtue which the master had set forth. He determined, therefore, in order that he might introduce these doctrines to the thinking of the day, to reply to these last tracts by a new presentation, in his own language, of the theory of holiness which Edwards had originated. This he did in 1773, issuing his *Inquiry into the Nature of True Holiness,*[60] to which were added appendices in which he paid detailed attention to his opponents. He confessed his entire agreement with Edwards, and our treatment of the book may, therefore, be the briefer.[61]

[59] *Loc. cit.,* p. 104.

[60] Hopkins' *Works,* Vol. III, pp. 1–141.

[61] Hopkins had issued Edwards' treatise upon virtue in 1765. The same year Thomas Clap, president of Yale College, issued an *Essay on the Nature and Foundation of Moral Virtue and Obligation,* etc., for his pupils in college. It serves to show the atmosphere into which Edwards' treatise was introduced. Clap made the nature of virtue to be "conformity to the moral perfections of God" (p. 3); or "it is an imitation of God in the moral perfections of his nature." He paid particular attention to Cumberland and Hutcheson (pp. 17, 22), and rejected their theory because it did not provide for the divine justice and truth. His theory was essentially atomistic.

The preface, however, contains a remark which may attract our attention:

I humbly conceive there has been too little attention to the nature of holiness among divines in general, and that a proper and intelligible definition of it is not easily to be found in bodies of divinity or elsewhere. And most of those who think it a very easy matter to tell what holiness is, and that we are all agreed in this, have been contented with a set of words which express no distinct ideas, but leave the thing wholly in the dark. They will perhaps say, God's holiness is his purity. If it is asked, In what does this purity consist? the common answer is, In that which is opposite to all sin, the greatest impurity.[62] We have now got what, I think, is the most common definition of holiness. But who is the wiser? This does not help us to any idea of this purity, unless we know what sin is. But this can not be known so long as we know not what holiness is; for we do not learn what holiness is by first obtaining the idea of sin, but we must first know what holiness, or, which is the same, what the divine law is, in order to the knowledge of sin.[63]

The method of Hopkins in traversing the ground which Edwards had so fully covered was evidently governed by the reasons which led him to write the treatise. He does not begin at a point so remote from the thinking of ordinary men as Edwards did, nor seek to ground his theory so entirely in one fundamental principle. Yet it will be noted that his method is substantially the same. Thus he begins, not with ideal harmony in the universe, nor with virtue as beauty, but with a series of plain statements as to holiness—that it is reasonable, as the greatest good in the universe, the highest possible excellence, the most perfect and beautiful union of intelligent beings, the same thing in all beings, simple, etc. He then advances to his proposition,

[62] It would almost seem as if Hopkins had just been reading Vincent's *Explanation of the Shorter Catechism,* written at least before 1666, and reprinted in this country as late as 1805. We read in that luminous work, in answer to the question, "What is the holiness of God?" this reply: "The holiness of God is his essential property whereby he is infinitely pure, loveth and delighteth in his own purity and in all resemblances of it which any of his creatures have; and is perfectly free from all impurity and hateth it wherever he seeth it." In other words, holiness is—holiness.

[63] *Works,* Vol. III, p. 6.

"Holiness consists in Love," which he proves from the Scriptures exclusively. Then follows the question, "What is that love in which all true holiness consists?" and he defines it as "universal benevolence, or friendly affection to all intelligent beings." This is more intelligible than Edwards' "love to being in general." Then, after discussing self-love, Hopkins goes over all those particulars which he laid down in the opening section, and shows that universal, "disinterested" (his favorite and characteristic term) benevolence satisfies all those statements. After some further Scripture proofs, and the brief discussion of objections, his treatise is brought to an end.

But Hopkins did not suppose himself to be merely restating what Edwards had already stated. He viewed himself as having made certain substantial and important "improvements."

The chief of these consisted in his statement of the "opposition of holiness to self-love." The improvement does not consist in any new view of self-love in itself, for the definition given by the two divines is substantially the same. Edwards says: "Self-love . . . . signifies a man's regard to his confined, private self, or love to himself with respect to his private interest."[64] Hopkins says: "It is a man's love of his own self as self, and of nothing else." According to both, such self-love is sinful, for a man must love himself for the same reason as he loves other men, or else, not having the right motive in it, such love is not virtuous. He must love himself and consider his own interests as a part of being in general. Thus alone will he be able to subordinate his own good to the good of others, and thus only to love his neighbor as himself, and God supremely.

But Hopkins deemed that he added to the doctrine of

[64] *Works,* Vol. III, p. 119.

Edwards a valuable element when he taught that "all sin consists in self-love and what is implied in this."[65] We have already considered Edwards' definition of sin. Sin, according to him, is *any other* elective preference than that of the good of being in general. The whole treatise is in accordance with this idea, and gives no indication of Hopkins' new position. Edwards' chapter in the *Nature of Virtue* upon self-love is engaged in showing how many supposed virtues may flow from nothing but self-love, and so have no really virtuous character, however amiable they may appear. Hopkins does not stop with this plain proposition that all selfishness is sin, but converts it and maintains that all sin is selfishness.

There is something attractive about the proposition to reduce sin to one principle, as virtue may be reduced to one; for there is a certain symmetry thereby introduced into ethics. But it is doubtful if sin is a very symmetrical thing. Hopkins has probably presented this matter as strongly as any of his successors, many of whom adopted his view. But he does not prove his case. His arguments may be briefly summarized thus:

1. "Self-love is in its whole nature and in every degree of it, enmity against God." True; but this is only to say: "All selfishness is sin."

2. "Self-love, exercised and indulged, blinds the heart to every true moral excellence and beauty: this does not suit the taste of the selfish heart but gives it disgust." In other words, selfishness is injurious; but it does not show that every injury of the kind arises from selfishness.

3. Self-love is the source of all the profaneness and impiety in the world." This is not proved. Is there not some impiety which develops from another root than selfishness?

[65] Hopkins' *Works*, Vol. III, p. 29. The same doctrine was maintained by Dr. Samuel Spring. See *Disquisitions*, pp. 16 f.

4. A final argument is rather implied than stated by Hopkins. It may be put in modern phrase thus: The opposition between holiness and selfishness is that between a wholly disinterested affection and a wholly interested affection. As the disinterested affection comprises the whole of holiness, so the interested affection comprises the whole of sin. This is as strong a statement of the argument as can be made; but it derives its whole force from the idea of symmetry above alluded to, and that force falls short of proof. The rest of the argument is conspicuously fallacious. It is the simple conversion of the universal affirmative proposition without limitation. It is as absurd as to maintain that all white men are Englishmen, because all Englishmen are white.

Another particular in which Hopkins attempted to improve upon Edwards was in the answer to objections. The most important of these at the present day, and the most plausible in itself, was that which appealed to the biblical use of rewards to induce men to repent. They suppose that men have self-love, and that it is proper to be influenced by this. But if so, it cannot be sinful. Hopkins makes short work with this. They are, after all, not addressed to self-love, because they are rewards of a character which will never appeal to a selfish man; and the evils which the Bible uses as threats are such as a selfish man will dread, but also such as will lead him to forsake his selfishness with his sin.

The honor which the proud man seeks is not the same which Christ promises to him who humbleth himself, but entirely of a different nature and contrary to it. A person who humbles himself renounces that self-exaltation and honor in comparison with other beings which pride and selfishness seek, and places his honor and happiness in abasing himself and becoming the servant of all, by exalting God and promoting his glory, and serving his fellow creatures, ministering to their greatest good in the exercise of universal benevolence; and so obtains true exaltation and honor which is most contrary to selfishness and pride.[66]

Hopkins thus brought out more clearly than Edwards had done the absolute inconsistency of selfishness with religion. He recognized how largely the religion of some men consists in selfishness and lacks the elements of true religion. Much preaching consisted of little else but appeals to selfishness, thus attempting to build up the people in holiness by fostering the very principle in which Hopkins saw the essence of all sin. Accordingly, in his "inferences," he attacked the same point again, and here advanced the doctrine which, probably more than any other feature of his teaching, excited the opposition of his critics and reflected discredit in their eyes upon its author, viz., the doctrine that a man, in order to be saved, must be willing to be damned.[67]

This doctrine comes in under the second inference, as to the nature of true self-denial. The question is suggested whether persons are to give up their eternal interest in self-denial so as not to have a selfish regard to this in their religious exercises. The answer is sufficiently strenuous:

Whatever temporal good any one gives up for the sake of his own eternal interest, and wholly from selflove, he is, by the supposition, as selfish in this as he can be in anything whatsoever; and therefore there is no selfdenial in it, if selfdenial is acting contrary to self or denying ourselves. So that he who does not know how to deny himself with respect to his eternal interest, is really a stranger to selfdenial. . . . . But let it be kept in mind that in the practice of the greatest selfdenial a person does not divest himself of a love of happiness; . . . . but he places his happiness, not in his own private interest, but in a good more worthy to be sought, viz., the glory of God, and the prosperity of his church and kingdom. For the sake of this he gives up the former and forgets himself.[68]

Or, as he says a little below, we are to love God "with-

[66] *Works*, Vol. III, p. 54.   [67] *Ibid.*, p. 59.
[68] *Ibid.*, p. 59.

out making any conditions in regard to ourselves." [69]   The
further question is then asked: "How can our eternal interest be inconsistent with the greatest display of God's
glory, and the highest interests of his kingdom?"   And
the answer is:

> If we know that we are true Christians, we may be sure that it is
> for the glory of God and good of the whole that we should be
> eternally happy in his kingdom. But even in this case we are capable
> of making the supposition that it would not be so; and, on this sup-
> position, we shall be disposed to give up all our personal interest, so
> far as we are in the exercise of disinterested affection and willing to
> deny ourselves. But if we do not know that we have embraced the
> gospel, we cannot be sure that it is, on the whole, most for the
> honor of God and the glory and happiness of his kingdom that our
> eternal happiness should be secured; so we have opportunity to try
> how we shall feel and be disposed on such a supposition. [70]

This doctrine excited so much opposition that Hopkins
thought it best to defend it in a special tract, which he entitled *A Dialogue between a Calvinist and a Semi-Calvin-
ist* [71]—which, by the way, shows his idea of his own thor-
ough-going Calvinism. He reiterates the doctrine that *if*
being cast off by God is necessary in order to secure a
greater good than his own salvation, the Christian ought
to be willing thus to be cast off. It is a very large *if;* as
Hopkins repeatedly says, "a supposition," an "impossible
supposition;" [72] but it is a supposition which it is well to
make in order "to show that there may be a greater evil
than the damnation of one individual."

The objections to his view which Hopkins answers in
this tract show his estimate of the importance of the idea.
One of them is "that it would be wicked: for we are com-

[69] This was not a new position for the young New England school. Bellamy
had already copiously defended it in a tract, *Remarks on the Rev. Mr. Cros-
well's Letter to the Rev. Mr. Cumming* (Boston, 1763), pp. 36. See Dexter, nos.
3437, 3445, 3452.

[70] *Loc. cit.,* p. 61.

[71] *Ibid.,* pp. 143 ff. A posthumous work.

[72] *Ibid.,* p. 144.

manded to do that which is directly contrary to this, viz., to desire and to seek to escape damnation and to be saved." The reply is that by being willing to be damned is not meant being pleased with it, or desiring and choosing it for its own sake, but only being willing if it be necessary to secure some greater good. Another objection is: "It is impossible that a man should be willing to give up all good and to be miserable forever for the sake of the good of others, be it ever so great." The answer is that it is not impossible, for it is reasonable, and men, like St. Paul who was willing to be accursed from Christ for his brethren's sake, have actually been thus willing. A third objection is: "We ought to make the glory of God our supreme end; but this will be so far from making us willing to be damned that it will lead us to desire and pursue our salvation, that he may be glorified in that and that we may glorify him forever." The reply rests upon the doctrine advanced in the sermons upon the permission of sin, that the damnation of unrepentant sinners is for the glory of God. It runs:

But it is not for the glory of God that all should be saved, but most for his glory that a number should be damned; otherwise all would be saved. We will, therefore, now make a supposition, which is not an impossible one, viz., that it is most for God's glory and for the universal good that you should be damned; ought you not to be willing to be damned on this supposition, that God could not be glorified by you in any other way? [73]

The objector now takes another position: "But suppose he knows he loves God, and therefore knows that it is for the glory of God that he should be saved?" To which Hopkins:

No man can know that he loves God until he really does love him; that is until he does seek his glory above all things, and is disposed to say, "Let God be glorified whatever may be necessary in order to it," without making any exception. And this is to be willing to be damned, if this be necessary for the glory of God. [74]

[73] *Ibid.*, p. 147.   [74] *Ibid.*, p. 148.

And finally the objector says that this is a puzzling doctrine, tending to perplex and discourage Christians, and should therefore be avoided. Hopkins replies that it may puzzle half-hearted Christians, or true Christians who have never considered these matters, but it will powerfully tend to expose the weakness and wickedness of the former when understood, and will confirm the latter and establish them. And hence it is a doctrine exceedingly important to strip false professors of all disguises and bring them really to Christ.

The intensely earnest and radical spirit of Hopkinsianism appears here more clearly, perhaps, than anywhere else. What will such a spirit effect in the development of a new theology? We are to see what it did effect.

But to return from this digression to the treatise upon holiness. The first appendix is taken up with a more detailed answer to Hart's *Remarks,* which have already been summarized. The book would seem to have required little reply in any case, and to have received all it needed in the exhaustive discussions which Hopkins had just finished in the body of his new presentation of the theory of virtue. But it was a critical moment in the fortunes of the new theology; and Hopkins felt called upon, as Edwards had before him, to pulverize all opposition. He therefore seized upon every weak point and exposed every inconsistency in his adversary. Three special points needed a more substantial consideration: Hart's objections to Edwards' "being simply considered," his confusion as to the meaning of Edwards' "secondary beauty," and his own attempts to state the nature of true virtue. His reply to the first of these we may summarize in the phrase that by such expressions as "being simply considered," being "in general," etc., Edwards meant being as such, or for its own sake. We are commanded to love God for his own sake, for what he is in himself. The answer to the second was as follows:

Mr. Edwards observes there are two kinds of beauty. One is moral beauty, or the beauty of true virtue or holiness, which is the highest kind of beauty, and consists in cordial agreement and harmony, or general benevolence, and is discerned and approved of by such only who love true holiness, which love is itself the exercise of holiness. The other is natural beauty, which consists in natural harmony or agreement, and takes place in the natural and material world in numberless instances. And this same kind of beauty is found in things immaterial and mental, as well as in other things, and there is a natural beauty in virtuous exercises of the mind, and the fruit of those exercises, which is entirely distinct from the moral, holy beauty, and of a different nature; even the same kind of beauty which is found in the material world. . . . . This natural beauty is found . . . . especially in relative duties between man and man, according to their different stations and relations, which may be relished and delighted in by those who have no virtue, as a taste for this natural beauty is natural to all men, and does not emply disinterested benevolence, but is consistent with the highest degree of selfishness and sin.[75]

As to the last point, Hopkins declared that Hart really agreed with Edwards:

Thus we see Mr. H. represents his equitable affection as a *friendly* love, which is really *universal* benevolence, which is love to being in general. And he says, "This spirit of equitable, *friendly regard* will dispose the virtuous mind to behave to every one in a manner suitable to their various characters, offices, and relations." This "friendly regard" is benevolence and nothing else; and it must be universal benevolence if it will dispose to behave to *every one* in a suitable manner. And this must be true virtue in its essential nature, and comprehend the whole of holiness, as this will lead to all right exercises and conduct towards every one.[76]

The third appendix [77] took up in like manner Mr. Hemmenway's *Vindication*. It does not attempt to go to the bottom of Hemmenway's differences, for this has already been done in the body of the work. If he could be brought to accept the Edwardean doctrine, he would relinquish

[75] *Loc. cit.*, p. 74.
[76] *Ibid.*, p. 95.
[77] *Ibid.*, pp. 109 f.

his minor errors of himself. But Hopkins did not excuse
himself for this reason from a more detailed consideration
of these minor errors. He attempted to show how they all
rested upon confusion of thought. Hemmenway's "act of
the will *ab extra*," considered without reference to its motive and in this aspect possessing something of an acceptable quality before God, Hopkins declared to be inconceivable, because, if you abstract from the motive, the act
is not moral at all, and so does not enter into the consideration. But he does not pause here; he pushes Hemmenway to the wall, after the manner of this school of terrible
dialecticians, by showing that Hemmenway has really
acknowledged as much by what he said of Judas, when he
said it was not "matter of duty" but "vile treachery, in
Judas, to kiss his Lord in order to betray him." Hopkins
disposes of the supposition in one sentence: "If matter of
duty was the effective act of the will abstracted from all
circumstances, then Judas did the matter of duty as much
as any one can." [78] He also brings out Hemmenway's inconsistency in still another position, in supposing that acts
of duty may be done from self-love, an innocent principle,
and so be externally right. In discussing inability [79] a
more fundamental question was touched upon, and Hopkins pushed Hemmenway hard when he urged the question how a "natural inability" could be maintained which
did not excuse the sinner. The advantage here was divided between the contestants, for Hemmenway was right
in affirming that Edwards' moral inability was really a
natural inability, and Hopkins was right in emphasizing,
upon the basis of the new theory which was beginning to
emerge in his own mind, that the sinner was subjected to
no real natural inability. In one sentence Hopkins planted
himself entirely upon the "exercise" platform, when he said

[78] *Loc. cit.*, p. 111.   [79] *Ibid.*, p. 132.

that Hemmenway ought to "have offered some proof" that there is "a holy principle, distinct from all *exercise of the heart,* necessary in order to all holy acts of the will." [80]

These were the principal controversies in which Hopkins engaged. Other controversial writings of a minor character will be noticed in their appropriate connections. Those we have just reviewed led him to a more precise formulation of his thought, and developed him as a constructive theologian, as well as gave him fame and influence throughout New England. He has thus proved his power and given sample of his work. Will he do still more, and will he inscribe his name among the great systematic divines of the world? The next chapter must show.

[80] *Ibid.,* p. 134.

CHAPTER VII

HOPKINS' SYSTEM OF THEOLOGY

The progress of our history has brought us to the last decade of the eighteenth century. From the moment that Edwards began to exert his mighty personal influence, we have found New England seething with thought. Even the distractions of war have not been able to put a stop to theological reconstruction. The new school has been marked by great independence and originality, by great force and logical power. It has engaged in controversy in various directions, and has passed over a wide field of investigation and discussion; but its results have been somewhat miscellaneous and unsystematic. The time has now come for summing up what has been gained, and for presenting the system of theology, which Willard had last drawn out (1707) in entire conformity with Westminster, with the modifications which the study of three-quarters of a century had produced. This work fell to the lot of Samuel Hopkins, who published his *System of Doctrines* in 1793.[1]

While the situation of our divines in the small and retired hamlets of a new country prevented them from being great readers of books, evidence has continually presented itself that they diligently improved such opportunities as they had, and that they were adequately equipped with a knowledge of the best that had been written upon the themes which they treated. Professor Park has spoken of Hopkins' learning in the following words:

He was a diligent reader of commentaries, particularly of Poole's *Synopsis*. He read through the whole of Poole's five folios in Latin. He commented three several times on every chapter of the Bible in his

[1] Found in the first volume of the *Works*.

expository discourses; and this extensive exposition required of him, what he pursued, a diligent perusal of the critics. . . . . Among the authors which are most familiarly mentioned by him are Calvin and Van Mastricht (both of whom he studied in their original Latin), Saurin, Owen, Manton, Goodwin, Bates, Baxter, Charnock, Prideaux, Sharp, Matthew Henry, John Locke, Whitby, Dr. S. Clarke, Dr. John Taylor, Mosheim, Doddridge, etc., etc.[2]

We shall therefore not be surprised to find in Hopkins' system a due appreciation of the past. It was, in fact, the old system reproduced, for it rests throughout upon the ancient theological foundation, and is in essential agreement with Westminster and Dort. And yet it is a new system. It is permeated with new ideas, which do not fully reveal themselves or are not fully applied to the great subjects under consideration, but which are already beginning to work powerfully in remodeling and improving the system, and still more powerfully in preparing the way for subsequent improvement.

The affinity of the system with its predecessors among Calvinists is evident from the slightest examination. Its general course of topics follows closely the Westminster Confession. We have: Revelation; God; Decrees; Providence; the Fall; Redemption; the Redeemer; Regeneration; Faith; Justification; Sanctification; Eschatology; the Church; the Christian Life. Repeated allusions to the Confession are made, as when decrees are defined in its language. The idea of a true system was warmly embraced by Hopkins. He explains:

Is not a system of divinity as proper and important as a system of jurisprudence, physic, or natural philosophy? If the Bible be a revelation from heaven, it contains a system of consistent important doctrines, which are so connected and implied in each other that one cannot be so well understood if detached from all the rest, and considered by itself; and some must be first known before others can be seen in a proper and true light.[3]

2 "Memoir," in Hopkins' *Works*, Vol. I, p. 53.
3 Preface to the *System*.

Thus the presupposition which underlies Edwards' theory of virtue appears again in this form in Hopkins, that there is ultimate harmony in the universe. If this be so, truth is a harmony and is capable of being stated in a systematic and consistent form. To deny this, or to slight it, is to do violence to one's thinking. In the last analysis there must be a system of truth, or there is no such thing as truth, nor even such a thing as thinking.

As to the Scriptures Hopkins did not differ from the generality of his predecessors. The proofs given are the usual ones. The definition of scriptural infallibility and authority as the standard of faith and practice is the same with that of the Westminster divines. The effect of the controversy with the Deists is at once evident by the pains taken to show that unaided human reason is not enough to give man a knowledge of "every necessary and important truth." For the same reason, proofs are subjoined that these writings are not forgeries. The evidence of miracles is also discussed, though the question of their possibility is not argued at length, and the reliability of the Scripture record is assumed upon such proof as has already been suggested. The argument from prophecy is also considered. But the great reliance is placed upon the general view of the contents of the Scriptures, upon their harmony, and upon the truths revealed. In this Hopkins is in full accord with the Confession. "The greatest and crowning evidence" are the "contents of the Bible." The perfections and works of God, the rule of duty, etc., commend themselves to every reasonable mind. But

the honest virtuous mind only, which does discern and relish the beauty and excellence of truth and virtue [i. e., the converted mind], will see and feel the full force of this argument for the divinity of the Holy Scriptures. . . . . To such the true light shines from the Holy Scriptures with irresistible evidence, and their hearts are established in the truth. They believe from evidence they have within themselves, from what they see and find in the Bible.[4]

Thus the Scriptures are proved from themselves, and Hopkins has the immense advantage of employing the Bible in the construction of the whole system, including the doctrine of God. At one point only does he fall short of the Confession—in not ascribing the illumination of the Christian, by which he perceives the truth, directly to the Holy Spirit. But this lack is made up in other parts of the work. No distinction is made between revelation and inspiration, and no special proof of inspiration is attempted.

Hopkins immediately takes advantage of the ground thus occupied in the development of the existence and character of God. All knowledge of God "depends greatly if not wholly on divine revelation." But, "when once suggested to us, it becomes an object of intuition in a sense, so that, though there be reasoning in the case, it is so short and easy that it strikes the mind at once, and it is hardly conscious of any reasoning upon it." [5] Hence Hopkins gives briefly some rational arguments for the existence of God, but soon comes to the Scriptures whose mere existence is a proof of God's existence, but whose testimony is itself the great proof. The Scriptures are immediately employed as the chief source of knowledge as to God's attributes, and almost entirely so as to his moral character. Here we have introduced the distinguishing principle of New England divinity, the theory of virtue, and the moral character of God is defined as consisting in his holiness, which is comprehended in love. The proof of the love of God is scriptural, and the great example of it cited, and great proof of it, is the sacrifice of Calvary. And thus the benevolence of God is proved before difficulties are raised about the existence of evil, and the proof is made from Christ as the cen-

---

[4] *Works*, Vol. I, p. 24.　　　[5] *Ibid.* p. 33.

ter and substance of the divine revelation. Here Hopkins
passes far beyond the Westminster Confession in the spiritual character of his theology, and develops the best thought
of his master, Edwards.

In the doctrine of the Trinity there is nothing new or
different from the general course of presentation in the
early church. There are references to some new opinions
or to the revival of old ones, now becoming evident. The
preacher of the sermon on the divinity of Christ in the Old
South, Boston, in 1768, enters somewhat fully into the
refutation of Socinian errors in the system of 1793. At one
point there is an interesting connection between Hopkins
and the subtle speculations of the Greek Fathers of the
Nicene age. They held that the doctrine of the Trinity occupied the true mean between the polytheism of heathenism
and the abstract monotheism of Judaism. It displayed God
as the source of the universe, as fitted in his divine nature
to sustain it and communicate himself to it as well as to redeem it. Hence no philosophy which did not contain in it
the essential elements of the Christian Trinity would be able
to explain satisfactorily the origin and history of the universe. So thought the Greek Fathers. And now we hear
Hopkins saying: "Had there not been this distinction of
persons in God, there would have been no foundation or
sufficiency in him for the exercise of mercy in the recovery
of apostate man." [6] He maintains also the usage of the
early Fathers in respect to the terms "Son of God" and
"eternal generation," employing the former of the second
person of the Trinity, and the latter as describing the relation of the Father and Son within the Trinity itself.

The modifying ideas of Hopkins' system, as already
stated, are the Edwardean, or: moral agency consists in
choice; human ability; love, the essence of virtue. As to

[6] *Loc. cit.*, p. 66.

these ideas it may be well to repeat that in the theory of virtue Hopkins had nothing to change in the teachings of Edwards, except to introduce the incorrect idea that all sin is selfishness. In respect to the doctrine of the will there is a considerable difference. Hopkins does not seem to be entirely consistent, but upon the whole it is tolerably clear that the tone of his thought, if not his formulated conclusions, had undergone modifications which carried him somewhat away from the Edwardean positions toward what was finally to be a doctrine of a more genuine freedom. He seems to have been dependent upon Stephen West as well as upon Edwards, as we shall have occasion later to trace.[7]

The new elements to be found in Hopkins' system, derived from these leading ideas, and constituting the gain made by New England up to this point of her history, are the following:

1. Hopkins meant to maintain a *true freedom of the will* —that freedom of which we are all conscious and which we regard as essential to accountability. There are many passages in which he exalts the agency of God, but he maintains with equal steadiness and firmness the liberty of man. He defines this somewhat differently from Edwards, so as to make a real advance upon him. While Edwards had put liberty in the external ability to execute our volitions, Hopkins places it in the volition itself. He says:

The internal freedom of which [a man] is conscious consisteth in his voluntary exercises, or in choosing and willing; that he is conscious that in all his voluntary exertions he is perfectly free and must be accountable, and has no consciousness or idea of any other kind of moral liberty, or that the liberty he exerciseth hath anything, more or less, belonging to it, or that it could be increased or made more perfect freedom by the addition of anything that is not implied in willing and choosing. He may, indeed, *not be able to accomplish the thing* or event which is the object of his choice, and in this respect be under

[7] Cf. his own citations, *Works*, Vol. I, p. 87.

restraint; *but this is not inconsistent with his exercising perfect freedom in his choice* and in all voluntary exertions or in all he does with respect to such object or event.[8]

This is undoubtedly sound. The only further question would be whether Hopkins did not hold a theory of the action of the will and of the influence of motives which, like Edwards', introduced elements which destroyed the possibility of such freedom. He proceeds to examine and reject the so-called "self-determining power of the will" upon the same grounds as Edwards, by reducing it to the absurdity of the infinite series. Then comes the following remarkable passage:

Agreeable to this notion of a self-determining power, and in support of it, it is said that a man cannot be free in his voluntary actions unless he has a freedom to either side; that is, has a freedom to choose or refuse, to prefer one thing or the contrary, or has power and freedom to choose that which is directly contrary to that which is actually the object of his choice. If by this be meant that whenever any one freely chooses any particular object or act or is inclined any particular way, he is at liberty to prefer a contrary object or act and to incline the contrary way if he please, or wills and chooses so to do; this is no more than to say that, in the exercise of liberty, a man must choose agreeable to his choice, or has his choice; that is, must be voluntary, and therefore is not a contradiction to that which has been above asserted, namely, that liberty consists in the exercises of will and choice, or voluntary action.[9]

At first sight Hopkins seems in this passage to deny the power of alternate choice, or, as was later said, "power to the contrary." But the next paragraph makes it clear, although it is a clearness somewhat muddied by the confusing psychology brought down from Edwards, that he is opposing the idea of the perfect indifference of the will as essential to freedom. He says:

If by a freedom to choose either side be meant that, in order to the exercise of a free act of choice, he must at the same time be as much disposed or inclined to choose the contrary, or be no more inclined

[8] *Loc. cit.,* p. 83.

[9] *Ibid.,* p. 86.

one way than the other; there is no need of saying anything to expose the absurdity and inconsistence of this to those who allow themselves to think.

The rejected definition of freedom he understood as supposing an *inclination* to one alternative as great as that to the other. Had he distinguished inclination from choice, the sensibility from the will, he would have rejected as sharply as he did an indifference of inclination, which is certainly contrary to the facts of consciousness. He could then have recognized back of the desire, however strong it might be, a will as yet unmoved. But the inclination was confounded with choice, and then the impossible idea of an indifference of choice and a positive determination of choice in the same act was introduced which must, of course, be immediately rejected. In all this Hopkins does not differ from Edwards.

The first part of the passage quoted suggests, in connection with its surroundings, an advance upon Edwards. If we should ask Hopkins this question, "Before a given act of choice, may not the will choose either alternative?" he would answer first, with the instinctive tendency of the theologian to guard the great doctrines: "It is perfectly *certain* which alternative will be chosen?" "Yes," we might reply, "but, so far as the power of the will is concerned, may it not be exerted in either direction?" I think he would reply, "Yes." And this would be a near approach to the modern doctrine of the will as a first cause.

In confirmation of this interpretation, note (1) that Hopkins insists that the will cannot be compelled to a given choice. "No compulsion can be offered to the will or the freedom of it be any way affected by any operation *or influence* on the mind which takes place antecedent to the exercise of the will and in order to the choice that is made." [10]   (2) In the same line, he enters at one point a

[10] *Ibid.*, p. 374.

disclaimer of any knowledge of the connection which sub-
sists between God's activity and man's. God, "by his own
operation and agency" causes moral evil to take place as he
does as also the holiness which takes place in men; "but as
to the manner of the operation, as the cause of either, we
are wholly in the dark—as much as we are with respect to
the manner of the divine operation in the creation of the
world and the different and various existences." [11]   We
know that Hopkins believed in the immediate operation of
the Holy Spirit upon man in regeneration.   He probably
held Edwards' theory of motives in general; but the fact
that he never introduces that theory in his explanations of
the various questions which gather about the will, the fact
that he declares the manner of God's action inscrutable,
and this doctrine of the immediate operation of the Spirit
in regeneration, unite to show that he did not regard that
metaphysical explanation as enough to exhaust the case.
In other words, he purposed to hold fast to the freedom of
the will, and in doing this found insuperable difficulties in
the Edwardean scheme.

2. The next feature of Hopkins' system was his strong
emphasis upon the *doctrine of decrees.*

It is always a question whether a theologian, in modifying the Calvinistic doctrine of the will in favor of a larger
recognition of human freedom, will go in the direction of
Arminianism.   The New England school was kept from
this by the influence of Edwards, who, having in mind the
Arminianism of his own surroundings, which was associated with many departures from evangelical theology, had
put forth his mightiest efforts directly and openly against
it.   Hopkins entertained the sentiments of Edwards as to
the essential character of Arminianism, and therefore laid
the more emphasis upon the distinguishing features of Cal-

[11] *Loc. cit.,* pp. 139, 140.   Such expressions suggested Emmons' doctrine.

vinism. In fact, he was a high Calvinist—higher than his Calvinistic contemporaries.

Decrees are the plan of God in the government of the universe. This plan is the best conceivable, for God had all possible plans before him when he created the world, and he chose the best. This is the Leibnitzian optimism of Bellamy repeated. God chose the best plan, and he executes it in the best way, because he is himself infinitely good. And hence the divine decrees are founded in the love of God. This is a necessary consequence of the Edwardean theory of virtue. The following passage will exhibit this, and will also show, what needs to be borne in mind with reference to subsequent questions as to Hopkins' system, that the love of God is not first exercised when creatures have been brought into being, but respects primarily himself.

The moral excellence and perfection of God consists in *love,* or goodness, which has been proved in a former chapter. This infinite love of an infinite Being, is infinite felicity. This consists in his infinite regard to himself as the fountain and sum of all being; and his pleasure and delight in himself, in his own infinite excellence and perfection; and in the highest possible exercise, exhibition and display of his infinite fulness, perfection and glory. And his pleasure in the latter, so as to make it the supreme and ultimate end of all his works, necessarily involves and supposes his pleasure and delight in the happiness of his creatures. If he be pleased with the greatest possible exercise, communication, and exhibition of his goodness, he must be pleased with the happiness of creatures, and the greatest possible happiness of the creation, because the former so involves the latter that they cannot be separated; and may be considered as one and the same thing; and doubtless are but one in the view of the all comprehending mind; though we, whose conceptions are so imperfect and partial, are apt to conceive of the glory of God, and the good of the creature, as two distinct things, and different ends to be answered, in God's designs and works.

Thus whatsoever comes to pass from the beginning of time to eternity is foreordained, and fixed from eternity by the infinitely wise counsel and unchangeable purpose of God.[12]

[12] *Loc. cit.,* p. 73.

This is the point upon which Hopkins—and I may also say the whole line of New England divines—laid the chief emphasis. Few men would be so bold as to deny that God has a plan in the government of the world, and few so foolish as to deny that this plan is governed by infinite love. The tendency of Hopkins' whole scheme is thus to maintain the loving government of God. If there be any other element in this problem, it must be interpreted so as to preserve, not only the *fact* of his loving government, but the *emphasis* which belongs to this fact.

The fact of the divine decrees is proved from the Scriptures and from the divine foreknowledge.

But Hopkins has an eye also for the difficulties of the theme, and he states them with great force. The crucial objection is that decrees seem to destroy freedom, to make vice necessary, and thus to impugn the character of God. The reply is from the Scriptures. Cases are cited to show that God did decree certain acts, which were nevertheless free acts of men. Decrees, he says, include the freedom of man, because God makes use of that freedom to carry out his decrees. Particularly does freedom consist in volitions; and when God decrees that men shall be saved, it is that they shall be saved through their volitions—that is, that their freedom shall be preserved. This is not a philosophical defense of the doctrine. As we have seen, Hopkins had no theory of the action of the will which he was willing to introduce for such a purpose. He many times intimates that in a limited sphere we readily see how God through motives can govern man without infringing upon his freedom, and this proves that there is nothing *in the nature of volition* to prevent control of a free agent. But into any hopeless attempt to uncover the point in our subconscious nature where the divine and human action join, Hopkins does not go.

The second principal objection to decrees is derived from the existence of evil which the doctrine seems to charge home upon God. Hopkins' answer is the same as in his earlier treatise, except that he now states, without the slightest qualification, that sin is the necessary means of the greatest good.[13] Next, the objection was raised that the doctrine made God the author of sin. Here no new points are brought out. But the great plainness of his language gives occasion to an important query. He says:

That God did will the existence of moral evil, in determining, at least, to permit it, when he could have prevented it, had he been pleased to do it, must be granted by all who would avoid ascribing to Him that imperfection, impotence, and subjection to that power, be it what it may, which introduced sin, contrary to his will; which is indeed shockingly impious, and real blasphemy, to every considerate, and rationally pious mind. We may infer from this, with the greatest certainty, that it is, all things considered, or in the view of the omniscient God, *wisest* and *best* that moral evil should exist. For to suppose that it was his will that it should take place; or that he has permitted it, when he could have prevented it; and yet that it was not wisest and best in his sight, that it should exist, is beyond expression impious, and at once strips the Deity of all moral good or holiness; and gives him the most odious and horrid character![14]

Finally, he sums up the whole subject of the divine and human operation in the volition of man in the following terms:

Here are two distinct agents, infinitely different; God, absolutely independent, and almighty; and a creature absolutely dependent for every thought and volition, having no power and sufficiency, that is not derived immediately[15] from his Maker: and the agency or operation is as distinct and different as the agents. The creature's agency is as much his own as in the nature of things can be, and as it could be if it were not the effect of the divine agency, if this were possible. And the creature acts as freely, as if there were no agents concerned but himself, and his exercises are as virtuous and holy; and it is really and as much his own virtue and holiness, and he is as excellent and

[13] *Loc. cit.,* pp. 89, 90, 91, 98.

[14] *Ibid.,* p. 108.

[15] It is the emphasis of such expressions as this that gives Emmons his justification for claiming entire agreement with Hopkins.

praiseworthy, as if he did not depend on divine influences for these exercises, and they were not the effect of the operation of God.[16]

The question which is thus pressed upon us is whether Hopkins had escaped from the supralapsarian predestination of Willard and his predecessors in general. His treatment of this theme, as of all the remaining topics of theology, is marked by a certain largeness. He does not engage himself with mere scholastic details, but goes at once to the heart of his subject. Thus he never raises the question of the "order" of the decrees. But supralapsarianism is at bottom not a question of order, but of the universal prevalence of the divine decree to the exclusion of human agency. He might have escaped from such a theory by emphasizing the theory of virtue; for it leaves that place for humanity which Hopkins' evident tendencies toward a better doctrine of human freedom, elsewhere noted, should have led him to welcome. He does partially escape by this very path, for he makes decrees the realization of the *love* of God,[17] and not of his "justice and grace" with which supralapsarians are so much engaged. In fact, justice merges with him into love. But decrees still continue to cover all the action of men as well as that of God.[18] No place is left for an undecreed freedom of the fall, as Augustine seemed to leave it. The freedom of man is the mystery, not the decree of God. It is a mystery imbedded in the decree and providence of God. Its ultimate explanation must admit of the view that all things are finally done by God. He is the first, and in the last analysis, the only cause. Thus there is nothing placed in the will of man in distinction from the will of God, or done by man and not done by God.[19] The day of struggle

16 *Loc. cit.*, p. 139.
17 *Ibid.*, p. 73.
18 *Ibid.*, pp. 90, 103, 104; and very strongly, p. 124.
19 *Ibid.*, p. 141.

with supralapsarianism had come, indeed, but not the day of deliverance from it.

3. *Original sin.*—Hopkins' doctrine is summarized in his own words as follows:

> On the whole, it is hoped that the doctrine of original sin has been stated and explained agreeable to the holy scripture; and that it does not imply anything unreasonable and absurd, or injurious to mankind; but is the result of a constitution which is perfectly agreeable to the nature of things, reasonable, wise and good; that the children of Adam are not guilty of his sin, are not punished, and do not suffer for that, any farther than they implicitly or expressly approve of his transgression, by sinning as he did;—that their total moral corruption and sinfulness is as much their own sin and as criminal in them, as it could be if it were not in consequence of the sin of the first father of the human race, or if Adam had not sinned;—that they are under no inability to obey the law of God, which does not consist in their sinfulness and opposition of heart to the will of God;—and are therefore wholly inexcusable, and may justly suffer the wages of sin, which is the *second death.*[20]

The intimate connection of Hopkins with Edwards in all this is evident both from his phraseology and his ideas. He speaks of the "constitution" in the same language as Edwards. Even his figures are drawn from Edwards. There is no imputation "considering men as sinners when they are not," but sin is imputed because they are sinners. But how can they be sinners antecedent to any sin of their own? Is not all sin voluntary sin? "Yes," says Hopkins:

> This sin, which takes place in the posterity of Adam, is not properly distinguished into original, and actual sin, because it is all really actual, and *there is, strictly speaking, no other sin but actual sin.* . . . . If the sinfulness of all the posterity of Adam was certainly connected with his sinning, this does not make them sinners, before they actually are sinners; and when they actually become sinners, they themselves are the sinners, it is their own sin, and they are as blamable and guilty as if Adam had never sinned, and each one were the first sinner that ever existed. The children of Adam are not answerable for his sin, and it is not their sin any farther than they approve of it, by sinning as he did: In this way only they be-

[20] *Loc. cit.,* p. 235.

come guilty of his sin, viz., by approving of what he did, and joining with him in rebellion. And it being previously certain by divine constitution, that all mankind would thus sin, and join with their common head in rebellion, renders it no less their own sin and crime, than if this certainty had taken place on any other ground, or in any other way; or than if there had been no certainty that they would thus all sin, were this possible.[21]

It will require but a brief review of Edwards' positions upon this topic to show how entirely Hopkins is following his master in all this. There is the same "union" established between Adam and his descendants, the same "consent" to his sin, the following imputation, the consequent guilt for the sin consented to. With both Hopkins and Edwards the consequence of Adam's sin is to establish the certainty of this evil consent, and thereby to make all men sinners.

The first and most important result of this method of viewing the subject for Hopkins was that he accepted thoroughly the doctrine that all sin was voluntary, or that there is no sin but actual sin. His expressions of this principle are clearer than Edwards', though the substance of his doctrine is merely a repetition of what Edwards had laid down. We may see the preparation for a transfer from the theory of a constitution to that of the voluntary character of all sin under which the connection with Adam becomes a natural one (e. g., through heredity), in such a passage as this: "The posterity of Adam become guilty and fall under condemnation by consenting to his sin and by a union of heart to him as a transgressor; that is, by sinning themselves."[22] More explicitly he says in the longer passage just quoted: "This sin which takes place in the posterity of Adam is not properly distinguished into original and actual sin, because it is all really actual, and there is, strictly speaking, no other sin but actual sin."

[21] *Loc. cit.*, pp. 224, 230.   [22] *Ibid.*, p. 464.

4. *Ability and inability.*—The fall being included in the
decrees of God, there is no reason why the condition of
man before the fall should be a "probation" in any sense
in which it is not later. Hence Hopkins taught that man
after the fall is in a state of probation—that is, under a
moral government—with the alternatives of life and death
set before him, and with the full ability to choose the one
or the other. Upon the subject of ability Hopkins is specially emphatic. Though he teaches total depravity, and
emphasizes it against the Deists, it is a moral depravity.

Man has not lost any of his natural powers of understanding
and will, etc., by becoming sinful. He has lost his inclination, or is
wholly without any inclination to serve and obey his maker, and entirely opposed to it. In this his sinfulness consists . . . . and in
nothing else; and the stronger and more fixed the opposition to the law
of God is, and the farther he is from any inclination to obey, the
more blamable and inexcusable he is.[23]

If there could have been any question, after the revival
preaching of both Edwards and Bellamy, and after Bellamy had emphasized so strongly the ability of man to repent, whether that paralyzing doctrine of inability which
had wrought unspeakable disaster to early New England
was to be repudiated and replaced by a doctrine of ability which should pave the way for aggressive preaching
and for the winning of souls, it was now settled favorably
to progress by the clear adhesion of Hopkins to ability.
From this point we shall have occasion only to mark the
different forms given to the rationale of the doctrine. The
conviction and the usage of the whole New England school
is henceforth uniform.

5. *The atonement.*—We should also expect that Hopkins would fall in with the course of progress upon this
doctrine already marked out by Bellamy (1750) and Dr.
Edwards (1785). How far this expectation is realized
we are now to see.

[23] *Ibid.*, p. 233.

He begins by exalting the law of God.   This is the eternal, unchangeable rule of righteousness.   It cannot be abrogated.   An essential portion of it is its penalty threatened against the disobedient.   This is as unchangeable as the law itself.   Man by transgression has fallen under this penalty.   By the nature of law, it must be executed in the true meaning and spirit of it, or else God himself joins with the sinner in dishonoring the law, and favors, justifies, and encourages rebellion.

This otherwise insuperable difficulty, this mighty bar and obstacle in the way of shewing any favour to man, and escaping eternal destruction, is the ground of the necessity of a Mediator and Redeemer by whom it may be wholly removed, and man be delivered from the curse of the law; and saved consistent with the divine character, with truth, infinite rectitude, wisdom and goodness; and so as not to set aside and dishonour, but support and maintain the divine law and government.[24]

The fundamental idea of Hopkins' theory, then, is the necessity on God's part of a mediator before he could forgive sin; or, he teaches distinctly the objective theory of the atonement.

The work of the atonement consists of two parts: first, that accomplished by the suffering of Christ, and, second, that accomplished by his obedience.   At first sight it would appear that Hopkins accepted exactly the old theory whereby the sufferings of Christ were the literal penalty of the law suffered in the place of sinners.   Christ was to make atonement for the sins of men "by suffering in his own person the penalty or curse of the law under which by transgression they had fallen." [25]   The sacrifices of the Old Testament are quoted to prove the doctrine of vicarious sacrifice.   Christ "by his sufferings took on him the *penalty of sin*, and bore the punishment of it so as effectually to put

[24] *Loc. cit.*, p. 322.
[25] *Ibid.*, p. 324.

it away from all who believe in him that it may never be laid to their charge to condemn them." [26]

But modifying expressions begin soon to appear. In commenting upon the favorite text of subsequent divines (Rom. 3: 25, 26), Hopkins says:

Here the design of the Redeemer is expressed, and the great thing he is to accomplish *is to maintain and declare the righteousness,* the rectitude, and unchangeable truth and perfection *of God in opening a way by* his blood, *his sufferings unto death, for the free pardon of sinful man, consistent with his rectoral justice* and truth, and *doing that which is right and just both with respect to himself, his law and government, and all the subjects of his kingdom.*[27]

Note the phrases "rectoral justice," "right and just both with respect to himself, his law and government, and all the subjects of his kingdom." This points to a new understanding of the suffering of the penalty. A new kind of justice is introduced. Hopkins was perfectly familiar with, and accepted Edwards' doctrine that mere "natural justice," though having in itself a kind of beauty, had no moral beauty or virtue, and therefore was not fit to be the governing motive of the divine action, and could, accordingly, never be executed by God. The demands of love might make the execution of justice the only course left to the divine being. But a mere and exact satisfaction of natural justice as such could have no place in his government.

The word "equivalent" is often used to express the relation of the sufferings of Christ to those required by the law.[28] They were equivalent because of the greatness and worth of his person. Says Hopkins further:

Thus we see how Christ suffered for sin, was made a curse, that is, suffered the curse of the law, the curse of God: and in his sufferings, he, in a sense, suffered and felt the displeasure and wrath of God; and the anger of God against sin and the sinner was in a high

[26] *Ibid.,* p. 326. [27] *Ibid.,* p. 323.
[28] *Ibid.,* p. 328.

and eminent degree manifested and expressed in the sufferings and death of Christ, consistent with his not being displeased, but well pleased with Christ himself, and loving him because he laid down his life for his people.[29]

We see here how completely Hopkins, in spite of infelicities of diction, has adopted the new theory of the atonement, how he has changed the view of God's position from that of the "offended party" to that of "Governor," has made the sufferings of Christ an example rather than the literal suffering of punishment, and brought the whole transaction under the rectoral, or public, justice of God.

At the heart of the matter Hopkins is, therefore, altogether Grotian (or Edwardean) in his theory of the atonement. But in the second portion of his doctrine, that referring to the obedience of Christ, he seems to remain with the older Calvinism. The Westminster Confession taught that the obedience of Christ was the price with which positive blessings were purchased for believers, and that his righteousness was imputed to them. Hopkins followed the Confession, and yet in his own fashion. The suffering of Christ atoned for the sins of men, and procured for them forgiveness. But it

only delivers from the curse of the law, and procures the remission of their sins who believe in him, but does not procure for them any positive good: It leaves them under the power of sin, and without any title to eternal life, or any positive favour, or actual fitness or capacity to enjoy positive happiness. This would be but a very partial redemption, had the Redeemer done no more than merely to make atonement for sin, by suffering the penalty of the law for sinners, and in their stead. It was therefore necessary that he should obey the precepts of the law for man, and in his stead, that by this perfect and meritorious obedience, he might *honour the law*[30] *in the* preceptive part of it, and obtain all the positive favour and benefits which man needed, be they ever so many and great.[31]

The foundation of this idea is the doctrine of the federal

[29] *Loc. cit.,* p. 339.
[30] This is a Grotian turn to the thought.
[31] *Loc. cit.,* p. 345.

headship. Adam was a federal head. His obedience,
though he owed it for himself, would have gained certain
benefits for his posterity, and they would have been positively blessed with good and granted eternal life. But he
fell, and so the federal headship resulted in their being
sinners and lying under the wrath of God. Just as his
obedience might have procured them blessings, so the
obedience of Christ procures them blessings. But as
Christ is of far greater dignity than Adam, he procures
blessings far greater than would have been bestowed in
consequence of Adam's obedience.

By the obedience of Christ all the positive good, all those
favours and blessings are merited and obtained, which sinners need,
in order to enjoy complete and eternal redemption, or everlasting
life in the kingdom of God. By this he has purchased and obtained
the Holy Spirit, by whom sinners are so far recovered from total
depravity, and renewed, as to be prepared and disposed to believe on
Christ and receive him, being offered to them; and he carries on a
work of sanctification in their hearts, until they are perfectly holy.[32]

We perceive immediately that the conception of imputation here involved, like that already considered under the
head of "original sin," is different from that ordinarily
held by the Calvinistic divines of Hopkins' time. It will
be best for us to defer our special consideration of its
nature, however, until a later point.

In conclusion, under this head, Hopkins teaches general
atonement:

The Redeemer has made an atonement sufficient to expiate for the
sins of the whole world; and, in this sense, has tasted death for
every man, has taken away the sin of the world, has given himself
a ransom for all, and is the propitiation for the sins of the whole world,
so that *whosoever* believeth in him may be saved, and God can now
be just, and the justifier of him that believeth in Jesus. Therefore,
the gospel is ordered to be preached to the whole world, to all nations,
to every human creature. And the offer of salvation by Christ is to
be made to every one, with this declaration, that whosoever believeth,

[32] *Ibid.*, p. 348.

is willing to accept of it, shall be delivered from the curse of the law, and have eternal life.[33]

6. *Regeneration.*—The distinction between regeneration and conversion, which Hopkins early established, enables him now to distinguish sharply between the divine and human part in conversion. God regenerates; man converts. The former is the rendering of the man willing; the latter is the performance of holy exercises by the man himself.

There are no express statements, so far as appears, which exhibit clearly Hopkins' views as to the nature of the depravity which men derive from Adam. It is, however, probable from not obscure intimations,[34] that he accepted Edwards' theory that it consisted in no positive impairment of our faculties, but only in the results of one positive cause —that is, the withdrawal of the Holy Spirit. If this be so, it is easy to understand why he puts our corruption wholly in the will, not the understanding (the second of the two faculties of the mind), and makes regeneration consist in an immediate operation upon this. There is no need of more light or of the use of any other means, in Hopkins' view, because the trouble is not with the intellect, but with the will. Man has light enough, only as his intellect is darkened by his perverse will. It is to the will, then, that the remedy must be applied. Here God works immediately and miraculously.[35] When the will is inclined to the right by the Holy Spirit, the man's exercises become right, and he is himself right.

Regeneration is thus but one, though the chiefest, illustration of the "Divine illumination." The regenerated man now sees the being and perfections of God in their true nature, sees and approves of the law of God, discerns the character of Christ and the way of salvation; and, in view

[33] *Loc. cit.*, p. 365.   [34] *Ibid.*, pp. 219 ff.
[35] *Ibid.*, p. 371. This again, prepares for Emmons.

of these great motives now rendered accessible to him, he turns to God, accepting that law, obeying, believing, choosing, loving, all of which are essentially the same, or putting forth the holy volition, which is disinterested benevolence. This is conversion. I pause to quote a paragraph in which is not only described this "divine illumination" but also given the foundation of that "testimony of the spirit" upon the basis of which Hopkins constructed the proof of the Scriptures.

The real Christian is, in becoming such, turned from this darkness to marvelous light, which is effected by the omnipotent influences of the Spirit of God in the renovation of the heart, which was before totally corrupt, forming it to disinterested, universal benevolence, and so making it an honest and good heart; and forming the single eye, by which the truths revealed in the Scriptures relating to the being and perfections of God, his law, and moral government, the state and character of man, the character and works of the mediator, the way of salvation by him, the nature of duty and true holiness, etc., are seen in their true light, as realities, beautiful, divine, important, excellent, harmonious, glorious, and above all things else interesting and affecting, and the mind is filled with this spiritual, marvelous, glorious light. By this all the powers of the mind are enlarged and strengthened. Reason and judgment, being no longer biased by an evil heart, are rectified, and the reasoning, speculative faculty is exerted in an honest, attentive pursuit in the investigation of truth.[36]

Here, again, we have seen the application of the theory of virtue.

Conversion, wrought by man in connection with the action of God in regeneration, an act of the will, is instantaneous. Hopkins says:

This change, of which the Spirit of God is the cause, and in which he is the only agent, is instantaneous; wrought not gradually, but at once. The human heart is either a heart of stone, a rebellious heart, or a new heart. The man is either under the dominion of sin, as obstinate and vile as ever, dead in trespasses and sins; or his heart is humble and penitent; he is a new creature and spiritually alive. There can be no instant of time, in which the heart is neither a hard heart, nor a new heart, and the man is neither dead in trespasses and sins,

[36] *Ibid.*, p. 416.

nor spiritually alive. The Spirit of God finds the heart of man wholly corrupt, and desperately wicked, wholly and strongly, even with all the power he has, opposed to God and his law, and to that renovation which he produces. The enmity of the heart against God continues as strong as ever it was, till it is slain by the instantaneous energy of the divine Spirit, and from carnal it becomes spiritual, betwixt which there is no medium, according to scripture and reason.[37]

This is an advance in clearness of view upon his predecessors and prepares the way for the revival preaching of subsequent times. When conversion was viewed as instantaneous and human efficiency was exalted to its proper place, then it became natural to preach to men that conversion was their own work, that they could *then and there,* before leaving their seats—yes, while listening to the preacher—repent, believe, and be saved. Thus the last strand in the old doctrine of inability was broken. Immediate repentance became the distinguishing point urged by New England revival preaching, and was the source of its great effectiveness.

As to the nature of saving faith, Hopkins says concisely: "It is considered and represented as consisting in the exercise of the heart and choice of the will: this being essential to it and including the whole." [38] This is the foundation of its instantaneous character, and also of its being an object of command. The belief of the truth of the gospel is also implied in it; holy love is essential to it; true repentance is included in it; obedience is connected with it; its ultimate nature is love. The formal definition of it is not as good as the enumeration of particulars just given. It is this: "Saving faith is an understanding, cordial receiving the divine testimony concerning Jesus Christ and the way of salvation by him; in which the heart accords and conforms to the gospel." [39]

[37] *Loc. cit.,* p. 367.   [38] *Ibid.,* p. 423.
[39] *Ibid.,* p. 448.

We are now prepared to consider more closely Hopkins' idea of imputation, which was deferred from an earlier point. The definition of justification contains no real imputation.

The justification of a sinner, now under consideration, consists in forgiving his sins, or acquitting him from the curse and condemnation of the law; and receiving him to favour, and a title to all the blessings contained in eternal life; which is treating him as well, at least, as if he never had sinned, and had been always perfectly obedient.[40]

The sinner is received to favor, not for what he has done, because there is nothing in it to recommend him to God's favor; but for Christ's sake, because the believer is united with Christ. The righteousness of Christ is not transferred to the sinner that he may be regarded righteous. He is treated as though he were righteous, although he is not, for Christ's sake. There is a natural fitness that he "whose heart is united to Christ, as it is by believing, should be recommended to favour and justified by his worthiness and righteousness to whom he is thus united and in whom he trusts." [41] So Christ gains by the merit of *congruity,* through his obedience, the title to eternal life for the believer.

We have thus passed in review the first complete, indigenous system of theology issued in New England. Distinguished by marked independence, it is nevertheless built upon the foundations laid by Hopkins' predecessors in dogmatic work from the beginning of Christian history, and is thus conservative and historical. Particularly does it maintain the historic connection of our theology with English Puritanism, and with its embodiment in the Westminster Confession. The great spiritual elements of this Confession it maintains without abridgment. It even am-

[40] *Ibid.,* p. 458.
[41] *Ibid.,* p. 472.

plifies them. The authority of the Scriptures is derived from the divine witness in the soul, and they are then employed in the development of all the system, by which circumstance the exaggerated emphasis given to the rational element in later New England theologians is avoided, and the distinction between natural and revealed theology, current since the days of Butler, is obliterated. The great ideas of Edwards are incorporated in the system, and already determine its character, though not yet perfectly wrought out. The work is great for its adherence to facts, and for its faithfulness to the Scriptures as the source of religious knowledge. It is pervaded by a marked religious purpose, for every major section is followed by an "improvement," as the application of a discourse was technically called in New England. On the whole, for comprehensiveness, thoroughness, high tone, power of reasoning, independence, ethical and spiritual value, and solid contributions to the advancing system of thought, it deserves to be called a great work—great in comparison with the great systems of the Christian world, and unsurpassed within its own special school. It illustrates the Ritschlian canon that the true spirit of a movement will be found in its earliest documents. He who will thoroughly know the New England school must read deeply in the system of Samuel Hopkins.

THE DEVELOPING SCHOOL

CHAPTER VIII

ESCHATOLOGY AND ATONEMENT

From the two leaders whom we have just studied, Bellamy and Hopkins, proceeded two streams of theological influence which differed somewhat from each other. Not that there was any strong or divisive difference; for they themselves labored in entire harmony, and both contributed to the forming of many of their colaborers and successors. Still it may be said that there was a "school" of Bellamy, and there was a school of the followers of Hopkins sufficiently marked to give rise to the common name "Hopkinsians." The line proceeding from Bellamy has for its principal names Edwards the Younger, Smalley, Dwight, Taylor, Beecher, and Tyler; and that from Hopkins, Emmons, Woods, and finally Park.

Among the first generation of the pupils of Bellamy the most conspicuous name is the younger Edwards.[1] When he came to Bellamy, it was with a letter of introduction from Hopkins, with whom he had been at Great Barrington for about nine months.[2] He was no "Edwardean" when he arrived at Hopkins', but the instruction of this friend of his father's soon brought him into cordial accord with the teachings of the first Edwards. With Bellamy he remained but three months, when he was licensed to preach (1766). He thus drew from both of these teachers, and might be thought to be a Hopkinsian rather than a follower of Bellamy. But because of his temper and relations to the gen-

[1] Jonathan Edwards the Younger, called often Dr. Edwards to distinguish him from his father, was born at Northampton in 1745; died 1801; graduated at Princeton, 1765, and was successively pastor at White Haven (1769–95) and at Coleridge (1796–99), both in Connecticut, when in 1799 he was elected president of Union College in Schenectady, New York.

[2] See Hopkins' *Works*, Vol. I, "Memoir," p. 59.

eral movements in Connecticut, he belongs with the latter rather than with the former.

In spite of all the disturbance involved in the Revolu· tionary War, theological thought in New England continued to move steadily on. The close of the war was to be signalized by the more open appearance of a movement which threatened the very existence of the new divinity, and delivered the mightiest blow against New England Congregationalism which it ever received—Unitarianism. But still earlier there was another movement, of a kindred nature, and itself assuming ultimately a Unitarian form, which called out some of the most important treatises which fall under our view in the whole history of New England —Universalism. And from this attack there resulted, not only a thorough discussion of eschatological questions, but also the general introduction among the New England divines of Bellamy's Grotian theory of the atonement.

The introduction of Universalism [3] into America was performed by Rev. John Murray, who came to this country in 1770. He was a follower of James Relly, of London, who, in a book entitled *Union; or A Treatise of the Consanguinity and Affinity between Christ and his Church,* propounded the doctrine of salvation *en masse* in its extremest form. He says:

> Christ's righteousness is upon all his seed; by his single act, before they had any capacity of obeying after the similitude of his obedience, or of assenting to what he did or suffered. This manifests such a union to him, such an inclusion of the whole seed in him, as renders his condition theirs in every state which he passes through. Insomuch that his righteousness, with all the blessings and fruits thereof, is theirs, before they have known it, believed it, or ever were conscious of existence. Thus by the obedience of one are many made righteous.[4]

[3] For a considerably fuller account of this controversy and of all the New England publications upon these themes, the reader may compare a series of articles by the present writer in the *Bibliotheca Sacra*, extending from January, 1886, to January, 1889.

[4] *Union* (Am. ed.), pp. 26, 27.

Murray always preached upon the basis of this theory.[5] Hosea Ballou 2d, than whom there could be no better authority, summarizes his teaching as follows:

A few are elected to obtain a knowledge of the truth in this life, and these go into Paradise immediately at death. But the rest, who die in unbelief, depart into darkness, where they will remain under terrible apprehensions of God's wrath until they are enlightened. Their sufferings are neither penal nor disciplinary, but simply the effect of unbelief. Some will believe and be delivered from their darkness in the intermediate state. At the general judgment, such as have not been previously brought into the truth will "come forth to the resurrection of damnation;" and, through ignorance of God's purpose, they will "call on the rocks and mountains to fall on them," etc. . . . . Then the Judge will make the final separation, dividing the "sheep" or universal human nature, from the "goats" which are the fallen angels, and send the latter away "into everlasting fire." [6]

The effects of Murray's preaching began to be immediately felt in New England. A small community of Universalists was gathered and organized into separate churches. What the influence of the Rellyan mode of thought was upon theologians it is difficult to say. That it achieved some influence is evident from the fact that in 1796 there appeared a posthumous work by Rev. Joseph Huntington, D.D., long the pastor of Coventry, Conn., under the title *Calvinism Improved,* which is complete Rellyanism, though the disciple is in this case greater than the master. These ideas must have long been in his mind, and it cannot be said in how many others'. Huntington founds salvation upon the divine election, and declares that "the

---

[5] See, for example, his *Universalism Vindicated* (Charlestown, undated; in Harvard College Library), a discourse from the text Gen. 28:14—"In thy seed shall all the families of the earth be blessed"—in which the federal headship of Christ is urged to the point of the inclusion of all men—that is, all individuals of the human race—in all the acts of Chris'. Thus "when our Savior was suspended on the cross between heaven and earth, he contained *in himself* as the *second Adam,* the fulness of the human nature." Hence, as all men have in Christ died to sin, they are all in that fact already eternally saved. See particularly pp. 16 ff.

[6] *Universalist Quarterly,* January, 1848.

elect body is all human nature."[7]   But the foundation of
election is in the atonement.   Christ is strictly a substitute
for us.   "The true doctrine of the atonement is in very deed
this.   A direct, true, and proper setting all our guilt to the
account of Christ, as our federal head and sponsor, and a
like placing his obedience unto death to our account."[8]
Hence, as the atonement was made for all men, their guilt
is removed by it, and "by a true and proper imputation"[9]
its benefits are immediately communicated to the race.
Huntington goes so far as to answer expressly the arguments which New England men were beginning to use,
founded upon the idea that personal guilt and righteousness
cannot, in the nature of things, be transferred.   This is possible because property can be transferred, and all "men are
God's property, absolutely and wholly so; and of consequence [!] all their doings are equally his property."[10]
Through their "union with Christ" the character of men becomes the character of Christ when he is to be punished for
them, and then his obedience becomes their obedience, thus
giving them salvation.[11]   This is the Rellyan idea, and it is
often expressed in phrases strikingly like Relly's.[12]

Against such a movement, which was beginning to draw
away their people from evangelical truth, and which was
having an influence, more or less certain, among thinkers,
the New England school must protest.   They did this with
one consent; and they would not have been the children of
the Puritans if they had not.

The Edwardeans had always shown a decided interest
in questions of eschatology.   Edwards himself preached
some powerful and famous sermons upon this theme, led

[7] *Op. cit.,* p. 81.   [8] *Ibid.,* p. 98.

[9] *Ibid.,* p. 108.   [10] *Ibid.,* p. 111.

[11] *Ibid.,* pp. 67, 83, 127, 171. In 1791 he had himself published at New-
buryport, *Thoughts on the Atonement of Christ,* in criticism of the Edwardeans.

[12] E. g., see *ibid.,* pp. 55, 130, 133, 165, 183.

thereto by the prevailing indifference and spiritual sluggishness of the times, and the disposition to deny the doctrine already manifest in many quarters. He discussed
it with great power and vividness. His great positive arguments were brought to the support of the position that
eternal punishment is just. This is so because an infinite
evil demands an infinite punishment, because of the greatness of man's depravity, because of God's honor, and because of the good results which follow upon punishment.
He also went into the refutation of errors, discussing two
principal ones—annihilation and final restoration. Annihilation is a relief, whereas future punishment, as represented
in the Bible, seems to have no such element. And restoration implies a future probation, as to which there is no
Scripture evidence for it, and nothing in the way of a manifest superiority to the present probation to warrant it.

Bellamy also turned to this theme, and contributed an
epoch-making discussion of the probation of the heathen,
teaching that

all mankind have not only sufficient natural powers but also sufficient
outward advantages to know God and perfectly conform to his law,
even the heathen themselves; and that the very reason they do not is
their want of such a temper as they ought to have, and their voluntary, rooted enmity to God, and love to sin.[13]

The new note of freedom and true ability to repent inherent
in all men was here struck, which was later to sound still
more loudly.

Among these earlier writers upon eschatology the first
place belongs to Samuel Hopkins, who published in 1783
*An Inquiry concerning the Future State of Those Who Die
in Their Sins.*[14] It was a tract springing out of the
discussions of the times, but it did not mention Murray by
name, and was throughout of a strictly impersonal char-

[13] *Works,* Vol. I, p. 111.
[14] *Works,* Vol. II, p. 365.

acter. Only Jeremiah White, a writer of the previous century, whose *Salvation for All Men* had been recently published, receives direct answer. Hopkins intended to take up every important phase of the subject, thoroughly ground the doctrine in Scripture and reason, and answer every important argument against the eternal punishment of the finally impenitent. He even incorporated a sufficient answer to Murray.[15] But he did not judge the movement inaugurated by this extremist of as great importance as it later seemed to be, and hence passed over it without detailed notice.

The central idea controlling Hopkins' eschatology is his lofty conception of the government of God. It comprises peculiar views of the being governed, man, of the Being governing, and of the character of that government. As to man, Hopkins exalted him to a very high position. Not only did he give great scope to man's natural ability, and emphasize his responsibility, but he viewed him as clothed with the most exalted intellectual powers. He was totally depraved; that is, he was totally turned away from God and engaged in his own pursuits. But, though thus morally fallen, his intellectual powers were unimpaired,[16] and he was capable of piercing by their exertion to the counsels of eternity, and certainly of knowing fully, and with the most absolute clearness and distinctness, his duty toward God and man. As to God, Hopkins' new ideas may be compendiously stated in the single phrase that he viewed him more constantly than others had done as a Governor. Under this conception it was his intention to make his readers feel the infinitely lofty and amiable character of the divine government as the reflection of the divine character, which was summarized in the word "love." Holiness is the lofti-

---

[15] *Loc. cit.*, p. 467.
[16] Cf. Vol. I, pp. 229, 369, 370.

est thing in the universe. A God of love, who chooses the well-being of the universe, must choose its holiness first of all. Love of holiness is the same as hatred of sin. God hates it for what it is toward himself, who is the chief Being in the universe; he hates it, as a Governor, for its harmful tendency to his government; he hates it *in that* he loves holiness, for this hate and love are as inseparable as the two sides of a piece of paper. Thus he punishes it; and his punishment of sin is as amiable as his rewarding of righteousness, for the one motive extending through all his actions is love.

The general course of his argument is simple. In the first section he proves that the Scriptures "teach that the wicked will be punished in the future state." The text is almost continuous quotation. Then he advances to the proof that this punishment will be "endless." His discussion includes a careful treatment of the words employed to express the idea of endlessness, which, if it has not prevented later attempts to limit them in various ways, ought to have done so. But the argument is not petty. It pays suitable attention to the general impression of the Bible. It then passes to the passages which have been supposed to teach another doctrine. Incidentally, among these, I Pet. 3:19 is discussed, with the result that the preaching was done by Noah to the men about him at the time of their sin.

The fourth section treats the rational argument. Hopkins was disposed to teach that "reason, without the help of divine revelation, can determine nothing with certainty about future and endless punishment." But this position did not shut out all argument upon it as improper; and he believed that thorough reasoning would do much to establish the doctrine by showing that it was in perfect accord with right reason. His first argument was the one already elaborated by Edwards, that sin was an infinite evil, and so deserving of an infinite—that is, unending—punishment. The magnitude of a sin is measured, he says, by the being against whom it is committed. Now, all sin is ultimately against God, who is the infinite Being. Hence it is an infinite evil. Hopkins adds the thought that the infinite evil of sin is also seen in the evil which it naturally tends to produce, and will produce unless it is prevented.

It tends to dishonor and dethrone the Almighty; to destroy all his happiness, and to ruin his whole interest and kingdom; to introduce the most dreadful confusion and infinite misery, and render the whole universe infinitely worse than nothing, to all eternity. . . . . Nothing short of an endless punishment can be its proper reward.

And he illustrates the argument thus:

If one who has defamed the character of a worthy personage, being prosecuted, convicted, and condemned, should be punished only by paying a small fine, viz., one penny or shilling, the language of this would be that the character of the person defamed was worth no more, and, therefore, would be so far from answering to the injury, and wiping off the reproach, that it would really fasten the disgrace upon him, and his character would suffer more than if the criminal had not been condemned and punished. [So] a temporary punishment only . . . . would be infinitely worse than none.[17]

This argument, with its utter neglect of the second party in the matter, man, is now given up. It is, indeed, in flagrant antagonism to the principle which New England theology was to bring forward, that obligation and ability are commensurate. But, held by Hopkins in all its rigidity, it is easy to see why he would not hear to the various excuses that were offered, as if man were too insignificant or too ignorant to commit an infinite evil. "If a finite being can affront and abuse his Creator," if he can desire to dethrone his Maker and destroy his kingdom, he can commit an infinite evil.

Another striking argument in the same line is derived from the atonement. "One end of the atonement which

[17] *Works*, Vol. II, p. 445.

Christ made for sin was to show what evil there is in sin and its ill desert. But this is every way sufficient to atone for sin which has an infinite ill desert; therefore this declares sin to be an infinite evil, or to deserve infinite or endless punishment." In modern phrase, God will not put forth more energy in the atonement than the occasion demands. He continues: "To deny that there is infinite evil in sin is, in effect, to deny the divinity of our Saviour." To understand the historical significance of this last sentence, we must remember that Hopkins lived in the shadow of the two great coming controversies, the Unitarian and the Universalist, which he thus recognizes as closely allied.

Hopkins gave fuller expression than his predecessors to the argument that good will arise from the eternal punishment of the wicked. It maintains the divine government, which is a good. It promotes the perfect display of God's character, his displeasure and anger with sin, and thus his righteousness and goodness. Hence it will promote the highest good of the blessed. He expresses himself in the characteristic passage, more candid and powerful than adroit or circumspect:

The smoke of their torment shall ascend up in the sight of the blessed forever and ever, and serve, as a most clear glass, always before their eyes, to give them a constant, bright, and most affecting view of all these. And all this display of the divine character and glory will be in favor of the redeemed, and most entertaining, and give the highest pleasure to all who love God, and raise their happiness to ineffable heights, whose felicity consists summarily in the knowledge and enjoyment of God. This eternal punishment must therefore be unspeakably to their advantage, and will add such immense degrees of glory and happiness to the kingdom of God, as inconceivably to overbalance all they will suffer who shall fall under this righteous judgment, and render it all, in this view and connection, an infinite good.[18]

It was upon this passage that the caricature was issued which represented Hopkins as "entertained" at the suffer-

[18] *Ibid.*, p. 459.

ings of the lost. Yet the passage reads: "This *display of the divine character* . . . . will be most entertaining;" and: Punishment is *"in this view and connection,* an infinite good." The passage cannot be said to breathe a spirit of sympathy or tenderness; and yet Hopkins was not without sensibility to the dreadful character of the sufferings of the lost, considered in themselves. His constant thought is that, if sin were not, a happy universe, ultimately without trace of suffering, would be the only one consistent with the perfections of God. But sin having entered by the free choice of man, punishment increases the glory of God.

One final thought was contributed by Hopkins: that the number of the saved will be much greater than that of the lost, "it may be, many thousands to one." Even granting that the most part living in the first six thousand years of the world's history perish, yet there is to come a seventh thousand, the blessed period of the millennium, when so great multitudes will live upon this earth, all of whom will be saved, that the great disparity will be completely wiped out. Upon this thought of the millennium Hopkins expatiates at great length and with delight in the appendix to his *System.* His eschatology, stern and rugged at it is, ends nevertheless in a prophecy of unutterable glory. Says Channing: "Whilst to the multitude he seemed a hard, dry theologian, feeding upon the thorns of controversy, he was living in a region of imagination, feeding upon visions of a holiness and a happiness which are to make earth all but heaven." [19]

From this digression we must now return to the course of our history. We had noted the arrival of John Murray in America, and the character of the Universalism which he had derived from James Relly, and which he preached.

---

[19] *Works* (Boston, 1875), p. 428. This sermon ("Christian Worship") gives an excellent view, from an Unitarian standpoint, of Hopkins' system of theology.

But our digression has not been in vain, for we have seen the materials which were in the hands of those who finally came to the reply to Murray and Relly, which had been gathered together by their predecessors in this field. A few years had necessarily to elapse before this reply was called for. No teacher comes to his full power at once; and the labors of Mr. Murray could not at once produce results sufficient to call for general public notice. In 1779 he organized the first Universalist church in Gloucester, Mass. By the year 1785 Universalists were numerous enough in Massachusetts to justify the calling of a convention. In 1784 Rev. Charles Chauncy, D.D., minister of the First Church, Boston, issued his *Salvation of All Men,* the first marked evidence that Universalism was beginning to find a place among the Congregational clergy. Hence it was in the year 1785 that the New England divines first published upon the new theories, when there appeared three works: Smalley's Wallingford sermon, "delivered by particular agreement, with special reference to the Murryan controversy;" Dr. Edwards' *Three Sermons* upon the atonement; and Stephen West's *Scripture Doctrine of Atonement.* In 1789 Edwards replied to Chauncy, and in 1796 Nathan Strong to Huntington. The object of all these treatises was to refute the Rellyan Universalism which had appeared, and all sought to do it by the same method, by correcting the false premises upon which Relly had based his argument. The result of them was to introduce into New England theology, as already remarked, a new theory of the atonement.

Smalley's [20] reply to Rellyanism was introduced by the following statement of its argument. "God is obliged in

[20] John Smalley, born at Columbia, Conn. (then Lebanon), June 4, 1734; studied theology under Bellamy, 1736–37; ordained at New Britain, 1758; died at New Britain, June 1, 1820. The sermons quoted are reprinted in Park's *Collection of Discourses and Treatises upon the Atonement* (Boston, 1863).

justice to save men as far as the merit of Christ extends: but the merit of Christ is sufficient for the salvation of all men; therefore God is obliged in justice to save all." Smalley had been a pupil of Bellamy, who taught that Christ died for all men. Hence he naturally said:

The minor proposition I dare not deny. I question not the sufficiency of the merit of Christ for the salvation of all mankind. . . . . The only thing therefore which I have to dispute in this argument is the obligatoriness of the Redeemer's merit on the Supreme Being: or, that it is of such a nature as to afford any ground to demand salvation from God as a just debt.

That is to say, he questioned the major premise, which was to question the whole idea that the death of Christ was a satisfaction to justice, as Calvinism had hitherto held. He thereby followed Bellamy farther, and with him made God a governor, and not the offended party, in the matter of sin and forgiveness, as is evident from his whole discussion. He had apparently read Grotius, for he cites an illustration which Grotius gives, the act of self-mutilation by Zaleucus, by which he spared one eye to his son who had broken the law the penalty of which was to lose both eyes. Smalley's contention is, therefore, that justification is an act of free grace, to which God is in no sense obligated in justice, and which he freely performs unto believers alone. His two sermons are in full accord with what other writers were bringing out about the same time upon the atonement, but he was too much restricted by the practical aim of his efforts, the refutation of Murray, to present the new theory in the most comprehensive way or to give to it the best analytical statement.

This special service has, by general consent, been ascribed to Dr. Jonathan Edwards, who delivered at New Haven, also in the year 1785, *Three Sermons* [21] on the necessity of the atonement and its consistency with free

[21] In Park's collection of essays, *The Atonement*, pp. 1 ff.

grace. A somewhat fuller account of Edwards' discourses will therefore be required to put the theory in its historical setting.

The first sermon is from the text: "In whom we have redemption through his blood, the forgiveness of sins, according to the riches of his grace" (Eph. 1:11). Forgiveness is here said to be in the exercise of grace, and at the same time in consequence of a redemption by the blood of Christ. How are these two parts of the proposition consistent? This, Edwards says, "has been to me one of the gordian knots" of theology. He seeks to loosen it by proposing three successive questions.

I. "Are we forgiven through the redemption or atonement of Jesus Christ only?" This question he answers in the affirmative. The Scriptures clearly teach it. Then "the necessity of the death and atonement of Christ sufficiently appears by the bare event of his death. . . . . We cannot suppose . . . . that the infinitely wise and good Father would have consented to the death of his only begotten and dearly beloved Son . . . . if there had not been the most urgent necessity." With this *a posteriori* argument, which is Calvin's, he supports an argument otherwise entirely scriptural.

II. Our next inquiry is, what is the reason or ground of this mode of forgiveness? or why is an atonement necessary in order to the pardon of the sinner? I answer, it is necessary on the same ground, and for the same reason, as punishment would have been necessary, if there had been no atonement made. The ground of both is the same. The question then comes to this: Why would it have been necessary, if no atonement had been made, that punishment should be inflicted upon the transgressors of the divine law? This, I suppose, would have been necessary to maintain the authority of the divine law. If that be not maintained, but the law fall into contempt, the contempt will fall equally on the legislator himself; his authority will be despised and his government weakened. . . . .

"When moral creatures are brought into existence, there must be a moral government. . . . . This is the dictate of reason from the nature of things. Besides the nature of things, we have in the present instance fact, to assist our reasoning. . . . . But in order to moral law, there must be a penalty; otherwise it would be mere advice, but no law. In order to support the authority and vigor of this law, the penalty must be inflicted upon the transgressors. . . . . It is no impeachment of the divine power and wisdom to say that it is impossible for God himself to uphold his moral government over intelligent creatures when once his law hath fallen into contempt. He may, indeed, govern them by irresistible force, as he governs the material world; but he cannot govern them by law, by rewards and punishments. . . . . For these reasons it appears that it would have been necessary, provided that no atonement had been made, that the penalty of the law should have been inflicted, even in every instance of disobedience: and for the same reasons doubtless was it necessary, that if any sinners were to be pardoned, they should be pardoned only in consequence of an adequate atonement. The atonement is the substitute for the punishment threatened in the law; and was designed to answer the same ends of supporting the authority of the law, the dignity of the divine moral government, and the consistency of the divine conduct in legislation and execution. By the atonement it appears that God is determined that his law shall be supported; that it shall not be despised or transgressed with impunity; and that it is an evil and a bitter thing to sin against God."

This is the substantial part of the first sermon. Its concluding portion is taken up with the consideration of a number of objections, such as this, that, if God had seen fit to order it so, we might have made atonement for our own sins, etc., all derogating from the strict necessity of Christ's death.

The second sermon proceeds:

III. "Are we, notwithstanding the redemption of Christ, forgiven freely by grace?" After considering several ways of bringing in the word "grace," when the theories upon which forgiveness was explained, like those of Relly and of the older Calvinists, really rendered its application improper, he continues the exposition of his own theory. He begins by defining the terms "justice" and "grace." The word "justice" is used in three distinct senses. "Sometimes it means *commutative* justice," which "respects property and matters of commerce only and secures to every man his own property." Sometimes it means *distributive* justice, which "consists in properly rewarding virtue or good conduct, and punishing crimes or vicious conduct. To treat a man justly in this sense is to treat him according to his personal character or conduct." Sometimes it means *general* or *public* justice, which "comprehends all moral goodness; and though the word is often used in this sense, it is really an improper use of it. In this sense, whatever is right is said to be just, or an act of justice; and whatever is wrong or improper to be done, is said to be unjust, or an act of injustice. To practise justice in this sense, is to practise agreeably to the dictates of general benevolence, or to seek the glory of God and the good of the universe.

"The term grace comes now to be explained. Grace is ever so opposed to justice that they mutually limit each other. Wherever grace begins, justice ends; and wherever justice begins, grace ends. Grace, as opposed to commutative justice, is gratuitously to relinquish your property, or to forgive a man his debt. And commutative injustice is to demand more of a man than your own property. Grace as opposed to justice in the distributive sense, is to treat a man more favorably or mildly than is correspondent to his personal character, or conduct. To treat him unjustly is to use him with greater severity than is correspondent to his personal character. . . . . With regard to the third kind of justice, ... as it comprehends all moral goodness, it is not at all opposed to grace; but comprehends that, as well as every other virtue, as truth, faithfulness, meekness, etc. . . . . And even grace itself, which is favor to the ill-deserving, so far as it is wise and proper to be exercised, makes but a part of this kind of justice.

"We proceed now to apply these explanations to the solution of the difficulty under consideration. The question is this, Is the pardon of the sinner, through the atonement of Christ, an act of justice or of grace? To which I answer, That with respect to commutative justice, it is neither an act of justice nor of grace, because commutative justice is not concerned in the affair. We neither owed money to the deity, nor did Christ pay any in our behalf. His atonement is not a payment of our debt. If it had been, our discharge would have been an act of mere justice, and not of grace. . . . . With respect to *distributive* justice, the discharge of the sinner is wholly an act of grace. This kind of justice has respect solely to the personal character and conduct of its object. . . . . With regard to the case now before us, what if Christ has made an atonement for sin? This atonement constitutes no part of the personal character of the sinner; but his personal character is essentially the same as it would have been if Christ had made no atonement. And as the sinner in pardon is treated not only more favorably, but infinitely more favorably, than is correspondent to his personal character, his pardon is wholly an act of infinite grace. . . . . In the third sense of justice before explained, according to which anything is just which is right and best to be done, the pardon of the sinner is entirely an act of justice."

There are a number of other discussions in this sermon, some of which are marked by great dialectical keenness. We hasten on to the third sermon, which is occupied with "inferences and reflections." Of these it will be necessary to note here only four, and these very briefly.

"The atonement of Christ does not consist in his active or positive obedience," for this "would never support the authority of the law and the dignity of the divine government." Again, in requiring an atonement, "God acts, not from any contracted, selfish motives, but from the most noble benevolence and regard to the public good. It hath often and long since been made a matter of objection to . . . . the

atonement of Christ that it represents the deity as having regard merely
to his own honor and dignity, and not to the good of his creatures,
and therefore represents him as deficient in goodness." But this is
far from the case. [This is, of course, not an adequate treatment of
the point whether God acts as the offended party or as Ruler, but it
will be noted that it covers that point.] Still again, the atonement of
Christ is not a satisfaction to distributive justice, but only to general
justice, or the well-being of the universe. And, finally, God was under
no obligation in distributive justice to accept the atonement of Christ,
though "the glory of God and the greatest good of the moral system"
did require him to accept it, and in this sense obligate him.

This treatment of the subject is hampered by the circumstances which called it forth, so as not to afford a complete
view of the atonement, or to present it from its proper
starting-point. It is only inferentially that the great difference between it and the old Calvinistic theory is introduced, the change of the view of God from that of "offended party" to "ruler." Nor is the theory of virtue applied as it should be, although God is said to act with a view
to the highest good of all. But from this time on, the rectoral theory of the atonement took the place of the satisfaction theory, and as time went on received better statements from successive theologians. The progress of our
history will lead us to pass later presentations in review.
But we must tarry still a little upon the other original statements of it, noticing next West's.[22]

West presented his views, as was possible in an essay of
more than two hundred pages,[23] in a much fuller and more
satisfactory form than Edwards had done, but in complete
accord with him as to the positions taken. He carries back

[22] Stephen West, born at Tolland, Conn., November 13, 1735; died at
Stockbridge, Mass. (where he was minister from 1758 to 1818), May 15, 1819.
Educated at Yale, graduating in 1755, he studied theology with Rev. Timothy
Woodbridge at Hatfield, Mass., probably in 1757. He published *Essays upon
Moral Agency* (1772) and *Evidence of the Divinity of Our Lord Jesus Christ*
(1816), besides the essay now under consideration.

[23] Entitled *The Scripture Doctrine of the Atonement, Proposed to Careful
Examination* (1785).

not merely the atonement, but the creation, to the character of God as its foundation.

A display, or manifestation, of his own true and infinitely holy character was the chief and ultimate end which God had in view in creation.—As God is most eminently good, it is evident that the real disposition of his infinite mind doth not appear excepting in works of goodness and where some good is actually done. His true character, therefore, cannot otherwise be manifested then in doing good.— The same glorious design which is expressed in creation, will be invariably expressed in preservation, for in strictness of speech, preservation is no more than creation continued. What gave birth to the existence of creatures will direct in the government over them. And should we entertain a thought that God's moral government will not be eternally administered in such a manner as to express to the best advantage his true character, we must at once admit either that he has changed his original scheme, or that the government of so vast and complicated a system is become too unwieldy for its great and original creator, either of which suppositions is atheistical and absurd. The community must have confidence in God; and the confidence of a community in the character of a governor arises in a great measure from the apprehensions they have of his sincere, benevolent regards for the general good. And they can no further confide in his regards to the public good than they believe him to be averse from everything that injures the public. As it is impossible that the love of virtue in any being whatever should exceed his hatred of vice, it is impossible for any one to give evidence of the former when, the object being presented, he neglects expressing the latter in ways becoming his character.—As far as God's love of righteousness and hatred of iniquity can be separately viewed and distinguished from each other, the great end of the death of Christ was to exhibit the latter and not the former. The disposition of the divine mind is perfectly uniform and harmonious. There is nothing in God or in the disposition of his mind but benevolence and love. Yet general good operates in a different manner toward different objects, and obtains different epithets according to these severally different operations. Should we, for instance, conceive no different ideas of divine justice from those which we entertain of divine mercy, it is evident we should have no proper and adequate conceptions of either. Or, should we form no different ideas of God's love of virtue and of his hatred of vice, it is manifest that we should view him as being indifferent to virtue and vice. Yet the very different ways in which God's love of virtue and his hatred of vice express themselves in fruits, and the extremely different effects they produce in the subjects on whom they are severally displayed, naturally lead us to view them as in some respects exceedingly different from each other, and that, however obviously they discover in their several operations beautiful harmony and uniformity in the disposition of the divine mind.

Here we see the government founded upon the character of God, and this presented as goodness, love, which consists in regard for the general good. And what is more important, the maintenance of the government of God is no maintenance of this as a *mere* government, but it is a maintenance of the character *through* the government, and this for the "public good." In other words, the love of God to his creatures, though not this alone, leads him *for their sake* not to forgive without the atonement.

The theory of atonement thus introduced received constant study and exposition in subsequent years, to which the progress of our history will bring us again. Leaving it now in the form in which it was first stated, we return for a brief review of its closing stages, to the early Universalist controversy.

The year 1784 saw, as noted above, the publication of Chauncy's *Salvation of All Men*. This was not Chauncy's first appearance against evangelical theology, for in 1743 he had written against the revivals of that year, and particularly against Edwards' *Distinguishing Marks of a Work of the Spirit of God*. The doctrine he now advocated was "that the scheme of revelation has the happiness of all mankind lying at bottom, as its great and ultimate end." [24] He teaches future punishment, which he designates as "awful misery;" but, however long it may be, or "however many states some of the individuals of the human species may pass through," it will issue in such a change of mind as shall fit men for salvation, and "the Son of God . . . . will not deliver up his trust into the hands of the Father . . . . till he has fully discharged his obligations in virtue of it,

[24] *Op. cit.*, pp. 12, 13.

having finally fixed all men in heaven, when God will be all in all."

The work rests upon what was, doubtless, a well-nigh self-evident proposition to Chauncy—that universal happiness was the designed goal of the universe. Still the argument is carefully exegetical, however defective. On Rom. 5:12 ff. he argues that, as mankind universally is the object of condemnation, "the same mankind must universally be the object of the opposite justification." [25] The discussion of the meaning of the words for "everlasting" in the Greek Testament, αἰών and αἰώνιος, is an extended one. He curiously inverts the argument from Matt. 25:46, robbing it of all power to bear independent witness in the matter. He says:

> The precise duration intended by the words . . . . must be determined by the nature of the thing spoken of, or other passages of Scripture that explain it. When it is affirmed of the wicked that they shall go away εἰς κόλασιν αἰώνιον, into everlasting punishment, the certain meaning of this word αἰώνιος, everlasting, is clearly and fully settled by the above proof of the final salvation of all men.[26]

The reply of Edwards was predominantly rational. He thus recognized the essential rationalism underlying the whole of Chauncy's argument. Not that he neglected the exegetical reply; for this was both elaborate and annihilating. In discussing the words αἰών and αἰώνιος, he counts their occurrences in the New Testament, classifies them, subjoins a concordance. He proves their entire correspondence to our English words "eternity" and "eternal," and shows that the presumption with which we come to the subject of future punishment is in favor of their strict use here. He follows Chauncy into all his windings and confutes him everywhere, manifesting all the keenness and delight in dialectics which his father had shown.

[25] *Ibid.*, p. 60.
[26] *Ibid.*, p. 270.

But the book was more than merely a successful piece of debate. It furthered essentially the understanding of its theme among the New England divines. The same discriminations as to various kinds of justice which appeared in the sermons on the atonement are applied to this theme. It is to be noted that the principle of all virtue is beginning to modify even the definition of distributive justice; for, while distributive justice respects the "personal character" of the sinner, the nature and amount of a just punishment are determined by the proportion which ought to exist between it and the crime. A punishment is just "when by the pain or natural evil of the punishment it exhibits a just idea of the moral evil or ruinous tendency of the crime, and a proper motive to restrain all intelligent beings from the commission of the crime."[27] This is to determine distributive justice by the consideration of the general good, or to convert it into public justice. Thus the relation to the goodness of God of his punishment of men is brought in at this early point; but there is also a special discussion of this relation. In order to answer Chauncy's fundamental assumption, Edwards asks the question "whether the damned deserve any other punishment than that which is conducive to their personal good."[28] If they do not, and do not receive any other, then it is perfectly easy to reconcile their punishment with the divine goodness, for it is nothing but an exercise of the divine goodness toward them. Edwards answers the question affirmatively, because of the words which the Scripture employs to designate this punishment —"curse," "vengeance," "great evil," etc.—which are irreconcilable with Chauncy's idea. But, now, how is future punishment consistent, upon this basis, with the divine goodness? Edwards replies: Pain inflicted in this life, and

[27] Edwards' *Works*, Vol. I, p. 74.
[28] *Ibid.*, p. 24.

some punishment in the world to come (which, it will be remembered, Dr. Chauncy did not deny), are evidently for the good of the universe *upon the whole*. "Why may not *endless* misery be so too, *provided* it be just?" [29] Thus Edwards answers the objections by an irrefutable hypothesis. He compels his opponent to prove a universal negative, if he will maintain the irreconcilability of eternal punishment with the divine goodness; viz.: Endless punishment answers no good end. But he does not stop here; he goes on with an argument positively supporting the consistency of punishment with goodness. To *make* a law which is inconsistent with goodness is just as bad as to execute it. But here is a law threatening eternal punishment. To execute it is no worse than to make it. Both must be consistent with goodness, if either is. But, since sin is in the world, God must punish it. If he

were never to punish it, it would seem that he is no enemy to it. Or, if he punish it in a far less degree than it deserves, still it would seem that his displeasure at it is far less than it is and ought to be. . . . . But will any man say that it is conducive to the good order and happiness of the intellectual system, that God should appear to be no enemy, but rather a friend, to sin? [30]

One more work must be briefly reviewed, and then we may turn away, for a time, from the Universalist controversy. This is Dr. Nathan Strong's reply to Huntington's *Calvinism Improved*.[31] This is one of the best books of the series. It is, however, in so perfect harmony with the works already examined, in the carefulness of its exegetical discussions, in its emphasis of the new theory of the atone-

[29] *Ibid.*, p. 124.

[30] *Ibid.*, p. 140.

[31] Nathan Strong, born at Coventry, Conn., October 16, 1748; died December 25, 1816. He graduated from Yale College in 1769, was tutor there in 1772 and 1773, and was ordained minister of the First Church in Hartford in the fall of 1773. He held this position till his death. He published a number of sermons, was the founder of the *Connecticut Evangelical Magazine,* and one of the founders of the Connecticut Missionary Society. He received the degree of D.D. from Princeton in 1801.

ment as the proper answer to Rellyanism, and in the thoroughness with which it pursues the antagonist through all the intricacies of his argument, that we should be only repeating what has already been presented if we indulged in special citations. He repudiates with great force Relly's doctrine of "union." And the divergence of Huntington from evangelical theology is shown by the difference of his doctrine of saving faith.

At this point we may break off the discussion of Universalism for a time. The work of the New England divines did not stop the spread of the movement, for it founded a small number of churches, which had for many years a lingering existence, and have perpetuated themselves to the present day. But these powerful collections of argument did arrest the tendency toward Universalistic views of the future among the New England churches, and determined that the course of New England theology should embrace no such divergence from the evangelical theology of the past.

We return, therefore, to the history of the doctrine of the atonement which we broke off with the essay of Stephen West. We had found him presenting more fully than his predecessors the origin of the atonement in the love of God, though leaving something to be desired in respect to the orderly development of this great central thought. His successors remedied this defect with increasing plainness of statement.

Dr. Nathaniel Emmons (1745–1840) expresses the connection between the love of God and the atonement by a more orderly deduction. He says: [32]

All the moral perfections of the Deity are comprised in the pure love of benevolence. God is love. Before the foundation of the world there was no ground for considering love as divided into various and distinct attributes. But after the creation new relations

[32] Park's *Discourses and Treatises*, pp. 116, 117.

arose; and in consequence of new relations, more obligations were formed, both on the side of the Creator, and on that of his creatures. Before created beings existed, God's love was exercised wholly towards himself. But after moral beings were brought into existence, it was right in the nature of things that he should exercise right affections towards them according to their moral characters. Hence the goodness, the justice, and the mercy of God are founded in the nature of things. That is, so long as God remains the Creator, and men remain his creatures, he is morally obliged to exercise these different and distinct feelings towards them. . . . . Now, there never was any difficulty in the way of God's doing good to the innocent, nor in the way of his punishing the guilty; but there was a difficulty in sparing and forgiving the wicked. . . . . This was a difficulty in the divine character, and a still greater difficulty in the divine government; for God had revealed his justice in his moral government. . . . . How then could grace be displayed consistently with justice? This question God alone was able to solve. . . . . By inflicting such sufferings upon Christ, when he took the place of a substitute in the room of sinners, God as clearly displayed his hatred of sin, and his inflexible disposition to punish it, as if he had made all mankind personally miserable forever.[33]

Thus again, the government of God is founded upon his character, and ruled in accordance with it. There is still something of the juridical and external in the form of presentation, however, and it needs, perhaps, to be corrected by emphasizing the fact that the government which is here to be maintained is not a government of brute force, but a moral one, a government of moral agents by means of influence. Emmons says:[34]

It belongs to God not only to exercise a natural government over the natural world, but to exercise a moral government over the moral world. The proper mode of governing moral subjects is by laws, rewards, and punishments.[35]

[33] The discussion from Emmons to the end of this chapter appeared originally in the *Bibliotheca Sacra* for October, 1890 (pp. 575 ff.).

[34] *Works* (ed. 1842), Vol. VI, p. 182.

[35] An objection sometimes made to the statement that the interests of God's government required the atonement is, that God is able to take care of his government, and nothing that a sinner can do on account of the free forgiveness of men can ever weaken it. It will be seen upon reflection that this objection views the government of God as a government of force, and not a moral government. It is important, therefore, with reference to the

We may pass on, however, for a more satisfactory treatment of this joint, to Dr. Edward D. Griffin (1770–1837), whose treatise upon the extent of the atonement emphasized topic, and so had occasion to dwell more at length upon the nature of a moral government. Whatever difference there is, is more of form, however, than of substance. Griffin says:

Considered in relation to its dominion over the mind, a moral government may be called a government of motives; for these are the instruments by which it works. It is a course of acting, not upon the disposition by insensible influence, but upon the reason and conscience of a ̇ rational being by manifest motives. . . . . In a limited sense a moral government is the mere administration of law; but in a more general and perfect sense it includes the whole treatment which God renders to moral agents. . . . . A moral government wields all the motives in the universe. It comprehends the entire system of instruction ̇ intended for creatures. The Bible lies wholly within its bounds. It comprehends the public dispensation both of law and gospel, with the whole compages of precepts, invitations, promises, and threatenings. It comprehends the atonement, and all the covenants made with men, and all the institutions of religion, with the whole train of means and privileges. . . . . It comprehends a throne of grace, with all the answers to prayer. It comprehends a day of probation, with all the experiments made upon human character. . . . . It comprehends the day of judgment. . . . . It comprehends all the sensible communion between the Infinite and finite minds; all the perceptible intercourse between God and his rational offspring; all the treatment of intelligent creatures viewed otherwise than as passive receivers of sovereign impressions.[36]

Caleb Burge (1782–1838), whose *Essay on the Scripture Doctrine of Atonement* is one of the very best of the New England treatises upon the subject, reproduces these ideas in various forms. He employs certain forms of expression, not common elsewhere, which present with special felicity the substitute which New England theology has to

objection, to note, as we proceed, the true conception of the government of God which underlies the governmental view. It will be evident at last that it is the force-theory which is "external," and not the view resting upon the thought of a moral government.

[36] Park's *Discourses and Treatises*, pp. 293–98.

offer for the doctrine that the atonement satisfied the distributive justice of God. Its emphasis upon the individuality of man forced it to the position that, as justice demanded the punishment of the sinner himself, no other arrangement could satisfy exactly this demand. Yet there was something in God himself which must be satisfied by an atonement, which Burge styles his "justice to himself." He says:

> Every good being, in order to do justice to his own character, must manifest his goodness. A wise being, in order to do justice to his character, must manifest his wisdom; or, at least, he must not manifest anything which is opposite to wisdom. All must allow that if one being should knowingly give a wrong representation of the character of another, who is wise and good, he would be very unjust. But if a good and wise being should give a wrong representation of his own character (if this were possible) there would be the same injustice done which there would, if the same representation were made by another.[37]

Hence, in order properly to represent his own character, and be *just to himself,* God must forgive only upon a provided atonement. This is the truth underlying the incorrect statements of the strict satisfaction theory.

We pass on rapidly to Dr. N. W. Taylor (1786–1858). He placed the moral government of God in the forefront of his theology, and two-thirds of his printed lectures are more decidedly the freedom of man in connection with this topic. But they are only the development of what had been taught from the first in New England. This appears in the very form of the definition of a perfect moral government given at the beginning of the treatise. Taylor defines thus: "The influence of the . . . . rightful authority of a moral governor on moral beings, designed so to control their action as to secure the great end of action upon their part, through the medium of law." [38] Moral beings are defined

[37] *Ibid.,* p. 450.
[38] *Lectures on the Moral Government of God* (1859), Vol. I, p. 7.

as "beings capable of moral action." The points which
Griffin had emphasized, form the main staple of Taylor's
argument, except that they receive new force from the new
theory of the constitution of the mind, which, beginning
with Asa Burton, had now in Taylor's hands given American theology a better division of the faculties of the mind,
and, by separating the sensibility and the will, had made a
reasonable theory of moral action for the first time possible.
The "control" spoken of is a control through influence,
and this is the influence of authority. The law promulgated requires "benevolence . . . . as the best kind of
action and as the sum of obedience." Taylor views "benevolence on the part of the moral governor and its manifestation as one essential ground of his authority."

In this fact is involved another. The moral governor who is truly
and perfectly benevolent, must feel the highest approbation of right
moral action and the highest disapprobation of wrong moral action on
the part of his subjects. These particular emotions in view of the
true nature and tendency of right and wrong moral action are inseparable from the nature of benevolence in every mind. Again, benevolence, in the specific form of it now stated as the character of the
moral governor, must, from the very nature and design of his relation be supremely concerned and absolutely committed to secure so
far as he is able, right moral action in every instance, and to prevent
wrong moral action in every instance by the influence of his authority.[39]

Even the legal sanctions ratify God's authority by manifesting his benevolence. And so, when men have sinned,
their salvation can be given only upon an atonement, since
otherwise God would not appear to hate sin, or would disregard the obligations imposed by benevolence to maintain
the authority of the law. In the development of this line
of thought he is particularly strong. The immutability of
God's character is the foundation of the immutability of
his law, which is the expression of that character. The im-

[39] *Loc. cit.*, p. 86.

mutability of the law is the same as the immutability of its sanctions. Hence, as God is what he is, he must maintain the authority of his law, and hence the principle: *the perfect equity or justice of a moral governor can be reconciled with mercy to transgressors only through an atonement.* He shuts up the objector to an atonement successively to denying the benevolence of God, or else to maintaining the future exact retribution of this wicked world, or else to admitting an atonement. He does this with so great cogency and force as almost to amount to a new proof of the necessity of the atonement. The necessity lies in the demands of real and comprehensive benevolence.[40]

It is unnecessary to quote from the writings of Charles G. Finney (1792–1875). The same views would be found to be repeated in connection with his more radical and correct opinions upon the freedom of the will. The meaning of a moral government; the character of God as love, which constitutes the divine response to the immediate affirmations of his own intellect as to obligation; love as having respect to the moral system as a whole and demanding a satisfaction to "public justice;" and the perfect adaptation of the divine government and of the atonement to securing the best good of all concerned, are brought out by him in terms largely identical with those employed by his predecessors, but with the added clearness which correcter views as to the nature of the mind and moral agency rendered possible.

Our whole review up to this point has shown us that, while the New England writers emphasized the divine government as the sphere within which the atonement was wrought, they all with increasing clearness founded that government upon an ethical idea, a conception of the character of God as love, which redeems the theory from the

<hr />

[40] Cf. *ibid.,* Vol. I, pp. 270 ff.; Vol. II, pp. 149 ff.

charge of artificiality and superficiality, though they did not seek to make the ethical idea prominent, or generally to deduce the whole theory from the ideal basis of it. But even the points already discussed cannot be made as full and clear as they should be, till we have read further. We therefore pass on without delay to the relation of election to the atonement.

The question of the extent of the atonement was prominently brought before the New England writers from the first of their investigations upon the subject. The Universalists had made the proposition that Christ died for all a principal step in their argument. The old theories had avoided their conclusion only by denying that he died for all; but this truth was too plain to admit of denial, in the opinion of the New England thinkers. So, from the first, they taught the doctrine of a general atonement.

Dr. Edwards says nothing in particular upon this point in his three sermons. West, however, proceeds to draw the conclusion which could but follow so soon as the premises of the new theory were adopted.[41] The atonement was sufficient for the whole world, not in the sense that it "superseded all use of punishment in the divine government," but in the sense that it made "such a manifestation of divine displeasure against the wickedness of men as is enough to convince every candid spectator that the disposition of the divine mind is perfectly conformable to the true spirit of God's written law." "The direct end of atonement is answered," he says, "and such a manifestation made of divine righteousness as prepared the way for a consistent exercise of mercy. Now, God would not appear to give up his law even though he pardoned the sinner." West then dwells largely upon the dignity of the

41 *Loc. cit.*, pp. 135 ff.

person of Christ as exalting the atonement made by him, and contributing to its perfection, and so to its universality.

Emmons is axiomatic and incisive, as usual. The proposition of his sermon upon the necessity of the atonement is: "That the atonement of Christ was necessary entirely on God's account," i. e., not at all upon man's. Hence he argues:

> Then it was universal, and sufficient for the pardon and salvation of the non-elect. . . . . If it has rendered it consistent with the justice of God to exercise pardoning mercy to one sinner, it has rendered it equally consistent with his mercy to exercise pardoning mercy to all sinners. . . . . It opens as wide a door of mercy to the one as to the other.[42]

If the only obstacles were upon God's part, once removed they were removed.

The great treatise upon this part of the subject was, however, Griffin's. We shall not fully understand his argument unless we have somewhat clearly in mind the course of New England thought upon the whole subject of the will, for Griffin seeks to find a solution of the difficulties between the maintainers of limited and of general atonement by sharper distinctions upon moral agency. We are therefore conpelled partly to anticipate the discussion to which the next chapter is to be devoted. The freedom of the will, as needs scarcely to be recalled, was the great first question which engaged New England theology when Edwards began his contest with the Arminians. His solution, while providing for the divine sovereignty, and an external freedom of the man to do what he willed, did not provide for the freedom of the will itself. This was felt by his contemporary and successor, Samuel Hopkins, who brought forward the idea that freedom was an inalienable attribute of the will as such, and made it to reside, not in Edwards' external freedom, but in the very exercise of

[42] Park's *Discourses and Treatises*, p. 119.

volition. Emmons, who was fond of paradoxical forms of statement, emphasized human agency as much as he did divine sovereignty, and often employed much the same terms to describe each. God governs man through motives, and yet when motives have been presented, he acts upon the will, which without his action never could respond to their stimulus. Thus God "produces" our volitions. In fact, all action in the universe is God's. But, on the other hand, by a mysterious connection between man and God, man acts exactly as if God did not act. He is perfectly free, and this in the same sense as God himself is. Under his universal agency, man has a real agency, which must no more be neglected than that of God. With varying success as to the theory of the will, the deepening tendency of the New England school was to view the divine and human operations in the matter of volition as if they were two concentric spheres. The ultimate question as to the possibility of the communication of independence to man they did not attempt to solve. The fact of natural powers was enough.

Now Griffin approaches the problem very much after the manner of Emmons. His purpose is to reconcile the two schools of thought upon the extent of the atonement, and he says:

One party contemplate men as passive receivers of sanctifying impressions; and their question is, How many did God intend by regenerating influence to make partakers of the benefit of the atonement? The answer is, The elect. And so say we. The other party contemplate men as moral agents; and their question is, How many did God intend to furnish with a means of pardon which they should be under obligations to improve to their everlasting good? The answer is, All who hear the gospel. And so say our brethren. . . . . The mistake of our brethren, as we view it, has arisen from not keeping these two characters of man distinct [viz., passive subjects and agents]. . . . . The two characters are about as distinct as body and soul; and on their marked separation the solution of almost every difficulty in metaphysical theology depends.[43]

This idea is more fully brought out as follows:

None but moral agents bear any relation to law, obligation, guilt, pardon, rewards, or punishments. . . . . This is what we mean when we say that the atonement was a measure of moral government. . . . . Now one of the things which essentially belong to a moral agent is, that he must act, and on his action his happiness depends. . . . . You cannot therefore contemplate a man as needing an atonement, without contemplating him as one, who, if he has opportunity, is to act towards the atonement, and is to enjoy or lose the benefit according as he receives it or rejects it. . . . . Anything, therefore, which is done for a moral agent is done for his use after the manner in which things are for the use of free moral agents, or creatures governed by motives and choice and bound to act. That is, it is done that he may use it if he pleases, and that he may be under obligation to use it.[44]

The statement of Griffin's fundamental thought here is as follows:

The foundation of the whole divine administration towards the human race lies in this, that men sustain two relations to God. As creatures they are necessarily dependent upon him for holiness, as they are for existence, and as such they passively receive his sanctifying impressions; and they are moral agents. Now the great truth to be proved is, that these two characters of men (passive receivers and moral agents) are altogether distinct and independent of each other. And the proof is found in the single fact, that their moral agency is in no degree impaired or affected by their dependence and passiveness, nor their passiveness and dependence by their moral agency. That is to say, they are none the less dependent (as Arminians would make us believe) for being moral agents; and on the other hand (and this is the main point to be proved), they are none the less moral agents (as Antinomians seem to suppose), that is, are none the less susceptible of personal and complete obligations, for being dependent. For instance, they are none the less bound to believe because faith is "the gift of God," nor to love because love is "the fruit of the Spirit." Their obligations rest upon their capacity to exercise, not on their power to originate; on their being rational, not on their being independent. On the one hand, the action of the Spirit does not abate their freedom. The soul of man is that wonderful substance which is none the less active for being acted upon, none the less free for

[43] *Loc. cit.*, pp. 252 f.   [44] *Ibid.*, pp. 262, 263.

being controlled. It is a wheel within a wheel, which has complete motion in itself while moved by machinery from without. While made *willing,* it is itself voluntary, and of course free. On the other hand, the absence of the Spirit does not impair the capacity on which obligation is founded. The completeness of moral agency has no dependence on supernatural impressions, and on nothing but a rational existence combined with knowledge. The bad, equally with the good, are complete moral agents, the one being as much deserving of blame as the other are of praise; otherwise (which forever settles the question), the unsanctified are not to blame and cannot be punished.[45]

The argument is continued:

I have shown you two independent characters on earth. If God acts towards these according to truth, there will be a counterpart of them in the heavens; he himself will sustain two characters . . . . altogether independent of each other. As he stands related to the moral agent, he is the Moral Governor; as he stands related to the mere passive receiver, he is the Sovereign Efficient Cause. . . . . Now the atonement was certainly provided by the Moral Governor, because it was a provision for moral agents. It follows, then, that in making this provision he had no regard to the distinction of elect and non-elect [in distinguishing between which he acts as the Sovereign Efficient Cause]. An atonement made for agents could know nothing of passive regeneration or any decree concerning it.[46]

These ideas represent the highest point attained by the New England writers upon the subject. They all re-echo more or less distinctly the teaching of Griffin. Burge says:

The atonement of Christ is, in a strict and proper sense, for all mankind. Christ tasted death for every man; for the non-elect as much as for the elect. Indeed, election has nothing to do with atonement, any more than it has with creation, resurrection from the dead, or the general judgment.[47]

He adds immediately:

From the necessity and nature of the atonement it is evident that its extent is necessarily universal. . . . . The death of Christ completely removes them [the obstacles which stood in the way of God's pardoning sinners].

But we hasten to consider the artificial elements of the

[45] *Loc. cit.,* pp. 264, 265.   [46] *Ibid.,* pp. 269, 273.

[47] *Ibid.,* p. 525.

doctrine which these writers rejected. Among these the principal is the doctrine of imputation, with its associated idea of the strict equivalency of Christ's sufferings to our punishment. Doubtless the prime motive force in this modification of the old theology was the sense of reality and spirit of honesty which were characteristic of the New England thinkers. It is interesting to note the workings of President Edwards' mind upon these topics. His treatise upon original sin we have seen to be the most important of his works as illustrating the operations of his mind and the character of his theology in their relations to conservatism and progress. On the one hand he will have nothing to do with "treating men as" they are not; but, on the other, he cannot avoid a connection with Adam and a guilt for Adam's sin; and so he struggles with theories of identity and with ideas of divine constitution, till he makes us one with Adam in some sense, and yet declares that we are not guilty of Adam's sin by imputation till we are participators in it by "consent." But such efforts in behalf of imputation were in vain. Edwards' successors regarded the idea with more and more distrust, and the Universalist controversy put an end to every effort to retain it. At this time it became an evangelical interest which contended against the theory. Universalism and some forms of orthodoxy maintained that there was no grace in saving men, since the atonement had merited salvation for them, and the merits of Christ were directly imputed to believers. Hence eternal life was bestowed as a thing which had been duly bought by this infinite price. The New England thinkers found this too abhorrent to the gospel. We are saved by grace, they said, and they devoted a large part of those various discourses and treatises, which we have been reviewing in this chapter, to proving that an atonement is consistent with the exercise of grace. Smalley protests against forms of expression which the revered Thomas Hooker, of Hartford, had once employed, as if the sinner could *claim* forgiveness from God. "Where do we find," he asks, "our infallible Teacher instructing his disciples to make such challenges from the Father, even on his account, of deliverance from all evil and the bestowment of all good, as their just due?" [48]   Emmons answers the question from the standpoint of the New England theory of the atonement, as when he says:

> Though Christ suffered, the just for the unjust, though he made his soul an offering for sin, and though he suffered most excruciating pains in the garden and on the cross, yet he did not lay God under the least obligation, in point of justice, to pardon and save a single sinner. . . . . By obeying and suffering in the room of sinners, he only rendered it consistent for God to renew or not renew, to pardon or not to pardon, to reward or not to reward, sinners; but did not lay him under the least obligation, in point of justice, to do either of these things for them. [49]

But he also appeals to our sense of the majesty of God, who "is above being bound by any being in the universe." And, in general, he rests upon the fundamental absurdity of teaching that the character of one man can be transferred to another, since a character consists in acts which, done by one man, cannot be also acts done by another. Burge is perhaps as pointed as any of these writers. He says:

> The righteousness of Christ, like that of every other holy being, consists entirely in his actions, feelings, and attributes. Essentially it consists in his love to God and other beings, and is as unalienably his as is any other attribute of his nature. Is it even possible that the actions which Christ performed while here on earth, in which his righteousness in part consists, should be so transferred from him to believers as to become actions which they have performed?

He says trenchantly, in reference to the idea that believers receive the righteousness of Christ by faith:

[48] *Loc. cit.*, p. 52.   [49] *Ibid.*, p. 121.

It is confidently believed that neither Scripture nor reason affords any more warrant for the opinion that it is even possible for the believer's faith to receive Christ's faith, or love, than for the opinion that a believer's walking in the highway receives Christ's walking upon the water.

When it is said that "God views and represents them [sinners] as righteous, by virtue of the righteousness of Christ; then the inquiry which arises is, Whether God do not view and represent things precisely as they are?" [50] In all this, which is the style of remark pursued by later New England divines as well, it should be remembered that what the antagonist had in mind was the ignorant Universalist preacher with his Rellyan doctrine of "union." But though the form of answer was thus determined, the New England divines held that the substance of their argument was valid also against the exaggerations of the Old School.

We have thus outlined the course of the doctrine in the New England writers; have shown the determining influence of the doctrine of Edwards as to the nature of virtue, which furnishes the ideal side of the theory; the influence also of increasing light as to the freedom of the will; and the strong effect of the idea of individuality introduced into the school by its founder. The theory underwent no essential change from this point during the progress of the New England school. In the theology of Professor Park it received some enrichment by his steady effort to incorporate whatever of good he found in other writers wherever laboring. Our study of this subject will therefore come to its legitimate conclusion while we are considering the theology of Park, to which time further discussion is deferred.

[50] *Ibid.*, pp. 504–6.

CHAPTER IX

THE DEVELOPMENT OF THE THEORY OF THE WILL

At the time at which we have now arrived in the progress of this history (1795), the air was full of the portents of the great controversy, commonly styled the Unitarian controversy, which was soon to engage the energies of the churches and to rend them into two hostile divisions. One brief campaign with an allied movement, the Universalists, had already been fought. It might have seemed as if such struggles were enough to exhaust the attention of our divines. But it was not so. Out of many a quiet pastor's study came a book, the product of profound reflections upon themes suggested by no immediate issue, which after a little called forth a reply from some other study where the same great themes had been meditated in all retirement and seclusion. So the debate went on; and many a movement of thought, destined in the end to find a close application to the practical necessities of troubled days, was carried on in entire unconsciousness of any such probable application.

One of these movements, in many respects the most important, certainly the most tragic, we must now turn aside to describe. It is that which resulted in great practical modifications of the theory of the will, as derived from Edwards, from which flowed other and great modifications in both theory and practice. Modifications of Edwards' views began with the very first writers who carried on his work, as we have already had occasion to remark. These became considerable in the process of time and brought the school to the very verge of a doctrine of genuine freedom. Many of the results of such a doctrine were actually incorporated in the received systems of theology. But the tragic element was not wanting, for upon the whole, even in the person of its final and greatest representative, Professor Edwards A. Park, the New England theology did not break loose from the substantial supralapsarianism in which Edwards had left it. Every great reasoner upon this theme believed himself to be in entire accord with Edwards. So profound was their admiration for their great leader that his successors scarcely conceived it possible that they should disagree with him, except in some small details of phraseology, or possibly, now and then, of thought. Whether they did differ or not we are soon to see; but the outcome of this intense loyalty to one man and one book was that they remained restricted by both phraseology and thought to the narrow limits there found. Their mighty struggles to escape, all incomprehensibly futile, remind one of nothing so much as of a lion caught in a net.

When we look at the so-called "New England" writers exclusively, we are in danger of thinking that they represent the whole of New England, and that Edwards' work upon the will was received with the universal conviction of its unanswerable greatness with which they were impressed. But this was not so, and the progress made in the theory of the will was the result of the action and reaction of many minds, of which some were decidedly hostile to the whole Edwardean theology. For twelve years the silence of the opposing party was unbroken, and then appeared an *Examination* [1] by Rev. James Dana, of Wallingford, Conn., which very sharply and effectively called Edwards to account. Its view of Edwards' theory was precisely that taken in this history. It rested upon the contrary theory of a self-determination of the will, by which was intended a real and originative causality, conceived as

[1] Issued anonymously (Boston, 1770).

the special and distinctive peculiarity of man. The examination begins with an inquiry into the connection of motives with the action of the will, and an indication is soon given that, in the examiner's opinion, President Edwards must view every volition as an immediate and necessary effect of the supreme cause, God.[2] This intimation soon becomes a vigorous argument, and the chief merit of the book is its strongly maintained thesis that upon the Edwardean foundation the divine efficiency becomes the only efficiency in the universe. Finally he asks:

> To what extrinsic cause, then, or to whom, are the volitions of men to be ascribed, since they are not the cause of them themselves? By whom or what is the state of men's will determined? According to Mr. Edwards, it is the strongest motive from without. But motives to choice are exhibited to the mind by some agent. By whom are they exhibited? In regard to sinful volitions, we know that one man enticeth another, and Satan enticeth all mankind. But this will not be given as an answer to our question, since the sinful act of one sinner in enticing another, and of Satan in tempting all men, must be determined by a previous cause—an antecedent highest motive exhibited by some other agent. (Though, by the way, it may be difficult to show how one man can be the cause of sin in another, when he cannot be the cause of it in himself.) What we are inquiring after is the cause of "the first and leading sinful volition, which determines the whole affair." Nor is there any stop, till we arrive at the first cause, whose immediate conduct Mr. Edwards saith is first in the series of events, connected with nothing preceding.[3]

ˆ Edwards was himself so merciless in the pursuance of any infelicity of diction into which an adversary might fall, like the selection of the word "self-determination" to express originative and causal action on the will's part, that it may be interesting to remark that Dana held him squarely to the implications of that remarkable passage in which he identified the choice and the motive. Dana writes:

> As no authority can be of equal weight to overthrow this main position as the author's own, we beg the reader would consider the

[2] *Op. cit.*, p. 6.

[3] *Ibid.*, pp. 48 f.

following passage; which is so full to our purpose that we are saved the trouble of a labored confutation of the principle alluded to. "I have rather chose to express myself thus, that the will always is *as* the greatest apparent good, or *as* what appears most agreeable, than to say that the will is *determined by* the greatest apparent good or by what seems most agreeable, because an appearing most agreeable or pleasing to the mind, and the mind's preferring and choosing, seem hardly to be properly and perfectly distinct. If strict propriety of speech be insisted on, it may more properly be said that the voluntary *action,* which is the immediate fruit and consequence of the mind's volition or choice, is determined by that which appears most agreeable, than the preference or choice itself." Here it is fully declared that, "properly speaking," volition and the highest motive are not distinct things—that the former is only *as* the latter, and not determined by it. Motive cannot be the ground and determiner of volition and at the same time the act of volition itself. It is not the cause of volition, but the *thing,* "if strict propriety of speech be insisted on." Instead of the strongest motive's being the cause of volition, the real truth is that volition is the cause of *external action.*[4]

And on this basis he later affirms that the whole question, What determines the will? is "unanswered, and yet returns." [5]

It is unnecessary to quote at greater length from Dana, since the work which it called out, the *Essay on Moral Agency,* by Stephen West, of Stockbridge (1772), was an independent treatise rather than a detailed reply.

West's essay is divided into two parts, of which the second is occupied with the problem of the existence of evil. It takes the general Hopkinsian position that sin is the necessary means of the greatest good.[6] The first part is occupied with the theory of the will, and hence particularly calls for our present attention.

West professes his general agreement with Edwards. He agrees with him in the first and determinative peculiarity of his treatise, in the view of the constitution of the mind. Evidence of this appears upon the earliest pages of

[4] *Ibid.,* pp. 17 f.   [5] *Ibid.,* p. 29.

[6] West's *Essay,* p. 178.

the book.[7]   He rejects the idea that "the action and preference of the mind" may be "so different from each other
as that they might properly be treated of as cause and
effect." [8]   He speaks of the "moral beauty and deformity
of affections." [9]   Again, motives "obtain the appellation of
motives only in the mind's feeling their influence, or being
in actual motion in view of them." [10]   "When the mind
feels or perceives the influence of a motive, it is then too
late for the motive to produce effects in the mind—exciting
it to motion, choice, or action; the mind being already
moved, the will exerted, towards some common object; and
choice having gained existence." "In the mind's perceiving anything . . . . is really all the choice which is ever
made of it." [11]

In his definitions of moral agency, while in the main
agreeing with Edwards, West reminds us frequently of
Hopkins, who was the friend under whose influence he had
made the transfer of himself from Arminianism to Calvinism. "When we talk of moral agency . . . . it is agreeable to the common sense . . . . of men to consider him
[man] as in exercise." [12]   Freedom is made to reside not
in "liberty to do as we please," as Edwards makes it, but
in "spontaneous, voluntary exertion." [13]   "To be free and
to be voluntary in any action whatsoever, whether internal
or external, I suppose are one and the same thing." [14]   But,
whereas in Hopkins this position looked toward greater
freedom of the will, in West it looks toward less.

Advancing still farther upon the path which Edwards
had marked out, but still in essential accord with him,
West emphasizes the fact that we can have no *conscious-*

[7] *Loc. cit.,* p. ii.   [8] *Ibid.,* p. 37.

[9] *Ibid.,* p. 48.   [10] *Ibid.,* p. 59.

[11] *Ibid.,* p. 59.   [12] *Ibid.,* p. 18.

[13] *Ibid.,* p. 19.   [14] *Ibid.,* p. 21.

ness of a power to choose "distinguishable from actual choosing." [15] He says:

Minds are conversant only with their own ideas: they perceive and are immediately conscious of nothing beside their own exercises and ideas. However they may reason and infer concerning other things and form premises and make conclusions with a great degree of justice or precision, still those things of which they attain knowledge in such a way as this are not the objects of direct, immediate perception. If liberty is what we perceive actually to exist in the mind, it can certainly be perceived no otherwise than in its exercise: just as a power of choice can be perceived only in actual choosing.[16]

He thus attempts to cut the nerve of the argument for freedom from consciousness.

West's discussions of the subject of power form the most original and important part of his book. He was brought to some difference with Edwards upon certain points, but with regard to the relations of power to moral agency he remains exactly where Edwards was. "Power . . . . is not essential to moral agency, virtue, or vice." It is an external matter. "When an event taketh place upon our choosing it and in consequence of our choice, according to the use and import of the word in common language, we have the power of that event, or power to produce it." [17] "Power implieth a connection between the volitions of the agent and the event which is the object of the volition." [18] It was natural that the question should arise upon this view of the matter: Who established this "connection"? West has removed from the idea of power the idea of efficient causation, so far as man is concerned, when he has said that we have power over an event if it "taketh place upon our choosing it," for we have no more real causation under such a definition than under John Stuart Mill's "invariable consequence" upon unchanged antecedents. But the question as to the efficient cause of an

15 *Ibid.*, p. 22.   16 *Ibid.*, p. 22.
17 *Ibid.*, p. 45.   18 *Ibid.*, p. 47.

event cannot be suppressed. Accordingly West says: "Power, therefore, strictly speaking, is no more than a law of constant divine operation." [19] That is, when I will, God operates in a predetermined manner, producing the corresponding event. He thus introduces the idea of occasionalism, derived from Edwards or directly from Berkeley, to explain our efficiency.

And now we have arrived at the critical point of the whole question. West has left us no true efficiency in the external world; will he maintain the same position as to the internal world? This is the next step, and it is boldly taken in the following discussion of motives. After a number of useful distinctions in respect to motives, he says:

> It appeareth that there is an utter impropriety in saying that the mind is governed and determined by motive, if the expression is designed to represent motive as the cause, and choice or volition its effect. . . . . To view the matter in such a light as this would lead to evident inconsistency and confusion.[20] Motives are not the causes of volitions. When we are inquiring into the sources of things and the cause of their existence; as in the natural, so in the moral world, we are compelled to resolve all into the divine disposal and a certain law or method of constant divine agency and operation. What are usually termed secondary causes have no productive agency or efficiency in them. . . . . When motives are represented as the causes of volition . . . . the word cause . . . . implieth nothing more than an *occasion* of the event.[21]

Here, then, lie West's difference from Edwards, and his contribution to the thinking of the school, the idea that moral agency consists in *exercises,* and that *these are the action of the deity* as the sole efficient cause.

So far as the work is intended as a reply to Dana, it accepts at this important point the doctrine to which Dana intended to drive the Edwardeans, that God was the true efficient cause of volitions.

[19] *Loc. cit.,* p. 48.
[20] *Ibid.,* p. 61.
[21] *Ibid.,* pp. 66, 67.

The relation of this position to Hopkins' doctrine of the will is even more interesting. Hopkins contributed all the elements of this conclusion which West has only been consistent in drawing; but he did not himself draw it. He taught that God is the cause of our volitions, but he did not say exactly how, whether through motives or immediate agency, and evidently intended to leave place for the agency of man. He had place in his philosophy for second causes, and a difference between God's immediate and mediate agency. Yet he says: "All power is in God, and all creatures which act or move, exist and move or are moved in and by him." [22] And again: "The divine hand of power and energy is as really and as much concerned and exerted . . . . as if no instrument, agent, or second cause were used or had any concern in the matter." While he was thus moving toward a doctrine of freedom, as already said, his movement was quite capable of being reversed, and West reversed it. He reversed it effectively for more than one theological generation; and although at last some of the later members of the school refused to follow in the direction thus prescribed to them, the influence of Edwards prevented them from giving a consistent form to the new truths they dimly saw.

The controversy between Dana and West did not stop here, for Dana replied with an *Examination . . . . Continued,*[23] which considered some topics of the controversy more fully, particularly defining self-determination better, and discussing the questions connected with moral evil and the divine foreknowledge. He did not, however, make any large contributions to the theme, nor did West when, in an appendix to a new edition of his *Essay,*[24] he took special

[22] *Works,* Vol. I, pp. 140 ff.   [23] Published, New Haven, 1773.
[24] Of the year 1794.

notice of Dana's second book. He merely reiterated Edwards' arguments, especially that of the infinite series involved in the idea of self-determination. The matter was left where it was before, every suggestion of a better view of the subject being rejected with emphasis.

Of course, so downright contradiction of the protest which Dana had attempted to put in against the strangling of all human freedom by Edwards' treatise could not be allowed to pass without another effort to give it effective utterance. This was made by Samuel West,[25] of New Bedford, in his *Essays on Liberty and Necessity,* in the year 1793. It was the fruit of long reflection and no mere hasty reply to an obnoxious tract. It is said that he disputed with his teacher, who superintended his preparation for college, against the common necessitarian ideas of his day. He probably had embraced the old Arminian system which Stephen West had also earlier embraced, from which arises his reputation as a "Unitarian." The book was brief, exercised but little influence, and has now become exceedingly rare;[26] but Dr. Edwards, who answered it, called it the ablest thing which had appeared upon that side. It was in fact revolutionary, and ought to have called forth that decisive change in New England psychology which it was reserved for Burton to produce. But it suffered the misfortune of being ahead of its times.

West begins his treatise by proposing a threefold division of the faculties of the mind. Stephen West, he says, confounds the perception of an object, in which we are entirely passive, with a volition, in which we are active.

---

[25] Samuel West, born 1730, graduated at Harvard 1754, D.D. 1793, pastor at New Bedford, Mass., 1761–1803; died 1807.

[26] The full title of the book was: "Essays on Liberty and Necessity in which the true Nature of Liberty is stated and defended, and the principal Arguments used by Mr. Edwards and others, for Necessity are considered. By Samuel West, DD., Pastor of the First Church of Christ in New Bedford . . . . 1793." Reissued in 1795 with a second part. Citations from the reissue.

Hence he observes that there are three main faculties of the mind—"the perception, the propension, and the will."[27]

The last only is properly the active faculty of the mind. . . . . The active faculty is exerted to acquire many of our perceptions, but still perceptions are not acts of the will. . . . . In demonstrating the truth of a proposition, a man is active in orderly arranging the several steps of the demonstration; but when he has done that, the perception of the truths demonstrated depends not upon an act of his will. By propension I mean to include inclination, affection, passion. These are all entirely distinct from the will. That bodily appetites, such as hunger, thirst, drowsiness, etc., are involuntary, I suppose will be allowed; and we may say the same of mental propensions, such as fear, love, anger, etc. . . . . A man may love a person whom he knows to be utterly unworthy of his affections, and may really choose to eradicate this propension from his breast; and yet he may find this passion rising in his breast in direct opposition to his will and choice.[28]

This is a perfectly clear and comprehensive description of the essential elements of the case. And, if it was, as it may have been, derived from Locke, it is clearer than his. West also seems to see the confusing effect of Edwards' philosophy upon his theory of the will, for he says: "He everywhere confounds the propensity of the mind with volition. Hence he tells us, 'The affections are only certain modes of the exercise of the will;' whereas I think the propensities of the mind, whether you call them inclinations, affections, or passions, are as different from the exercises of the will as light is from darkness." [29] But he fails to bring out the exact nature of the fallacy under which Edwards labored, for he goes on to say: "It is very evident . . . . that the will and the propensities are so distinct that they may be in direct opposition to each other; and that though these propensities may be so strong as to hinder us from doing what we choose, yet they cannot take away the freedom of the will; that is, the freedom of the will, or a self-determining power, is consistent with the

[27] *Essays*, p. 12.   [28] *Ibid.*, pp. 12, 13.
[29] *Ibid.*, Part II, p. 29.

strongest habits of virtue or vice." [30]   He adds below: "I believe, now, that it will appear, my notion of self-determination is very different from that which Mr. Edwards opposes, being a kind of medium between that and the doctrine of necessity." [31]   There is nothing further upon this point. A positive, Edwards-like annihilation of his adversary was called for if West could hope to make an impression upon the obstinacy with which the New England writers were still prepared to follow their great leader; but it was not forthcoming.

Upon the basis of this division of the mind, yet without consistent application of it, West now proceeds to make several forcible objections to Edwards' theories. His fundamental objection to necessity goes to the bottom of the subject. He says: "We certainly feel ourselves agents —feel ourselves free and accountable for our conduct— we feel ourselves capable of praise and blame. How all these things can be reconciled to a doctrine of necessity I cannot conceive." [32]

In opposition to Edwards' theory he therefore teaches that the will is self-determined. He expresses his meaning in a variety of ways. He says: "By liberty or freedom we mean a power of acting, willing, or choosing: and by a power of acting we mean that, when all circumstances necessary for action have taken place, then the mind can act or not act." [33]   Again: "The sense in which we use self-determination is simply this, that we ourselves will or choose; that we ourselves act; that is, that we are agents and not mere passive beings; or, in other words, that we are the determiners in the active voice, and not the determined in the passive voice." [34]   Again: "There is no in-

[30] *Loc. cit.*, p. 30.   [31] *Ibid.*, p. 31.
[32] *Ibid.*, p. 18.   [33] *Ibid.*, p. 15.
[34] *Ibid.*, p. 16.

fallible connection between motive and action." [35]   He defines self-determination by reference to the Deity, who, he
says, "has a self-determining power . . . . being the first
cause."   He often says "Volition is no effect."   And,
finally, he holds that by divine communication we have the
same self-determining power, or power of first causation,
which the Deity has.[36]   Certainly these distinctions are
clear enough to have called attention, if anything could
have done so, to Edwards' misinterpretation of his antagonists, and to the merely verbal character of his argument
when he pressed the term "self-determination" in a way
acute and strong, but in no relation to their real meaning.
If there is any idea expressed by the phrase "first cause"
whatever, then it is no absurdity to apply it to man, whether
the application is correct or not.

In defense of this doctrine West denies the Edwardean
doctrine that motives are the causes of volitions.   He maintains that, if motives are causes, they must be efficient
causes, and hence minds, which is absurd.[37]   He appeals
to experience to show that "when motives have done all
that they can do," the mind may act or not act.[38]   If volition is an effect, then man is passive in willing; and if so,
then he is active in nothing else; that is, he is no agent.[39]
If volition were an effect, we could not be causes of effects,
and so could never have the idea of cause.[40]   He even reduces Edwards to the absurdity of the infinite series, which
may be said to be carrying the war into Africa.   If volition is the activity of the mind, as Edwards maintains,
and at the same time caused from abroad, then our only
activity is caused.   But it is caused by some mind, which
in its activity needs another mind to cause it, which in its

[35] *Ibid.*   [36] *Ibid.*, p. 26.

[37] *Ibid.*, p. 10.   [38] *Ibid.*, pp. 16, 17.

[39] *Ibid.*, p. 22.   [40] *Ibid.*, p. 23.

turn needs another mind to cause it, and so *ad infinitum*.[41] He also says that motives cannot be compared so as to obtain the strongest motive which Edwards seeks as the cause of action.

In order to compare motives together to enable us to determine which is the strongest, the motives compared must all belong to the same faculty of the soul; and if they belong to different faculties of the mind no comparison can be made between them. Thus we find ourselves possessed of two different faculties, reason and propensity. Objects that are agreeable to our propensities are easily compared: thus of different kinds of food . . . . we can easily tell which we have the greatest relish for. . . . . We can also compare things that are agreeable to reason and judgment. . . . . But how can we compare things together that belong to different faculties of the mind? For example, one has an inordinate thirst after strong drink though his reason tells him it will ruin his health, his estate, and his reputation, etc.[42]

Turning now to the work of Stephen West, Samuel West notices the idea that the efficient cause in human volitions is the Deity. He himself prefers the doctrine that the Deity produces all the requisites for action in the mind, and that then it is capable of acting or not acting. But, he says, if volition is the immediate action of the Deity, then there is no action in the mind but the divine action, and, since action is essential to the life of every mind, it will follow that the Deity is the only living principle in the mind, and so in the universe, and that there is no such thing as a creation. Hence there is no Creator who has made and who governs all things by his power and providence.[43]

But Edwards would have objected to West's arguments against necessity that he himself was defending only certainty. This leads West to consider the natural and moral necessity and ability taught by Edwards, which, in agreement with Dana, he finds to be one and the same thing.[44]

---

[41] *Loc. cit.*, pp. 25, 26; cf. pp. 11, 12, 21 for other applications.

[42] *Ibid.*, Part II, pp. 5, 6.   [43] *Ibid.*, p. 8.

[44] *Ibid.*, p. 7.

He also maintains that the certainty of future events does not involve their necessity. "The deity," he says, "being himself uncaused, must be possessed of an underived, self-existing knowledge, which is independent of any cause or medium whatever." [45]

Thus an attack, strong in its main positions, however defective in amplitude of statement or dialectic form, had been made upon the New England theory and upon its latest exponent. Would it produce any effect?

Upon one man at least it produced an effect; but he was only led to reject it as a part of the old "Arminianism" against which he had long set himself. This was the younger Edwards, who came to the defense of his father and of Stephen West in a considerable treatise entitled *A Dissertation concerning Liberty and Necessity,* etc.[46] It was strictly a reply to West and other Arminians, and therefore does not present any distinct and systematic theory of the will. It was, however, said by Professor Park to be the best exposition of President Edwards' theory. We may dismiss it for this reason with the briefer consideration, occupying ourselves with the points in which it lends its aid to the current already so strongly setting in in the work of Stephen West. As a reply it is a masterpiece. It has the Edwardean thoroughness. Its favorite method is to show that West really meant, and often said, precisely what President Edwards had said, and that nothing but consistency is necessary to make him a full-fledged Edwardean. Its keenness makes it constantly interesting, and even absorbing, to everyone who loves thought. And yet, fundamentally, it concerns itself with words rather than realities, and Edwards fails to understand the important and new truth which his adversary was so richly offering him.

[45] *Ibid.,* p. 30.   [46] *Works* (Boston, 1850), Vol. I, pp. 295 ff.

The great contribution which West had made to the discussion of the will was the proposal of the division of the faculties of the mind into three—perception, propension, and will. This made no impression upon Edwards. He noticed it, but did not seem to understand it. And yet, by that strange mental obliviousness by which men repeatedly miss great opportunities in every department of human thought, he once came near both understanding and accepting it, only, however, to do neither! When engaged in refuting West's theory as to our choice between objects of equal eligibility, he says that President Edwards ascribed "a great part of our volitions to disposition, inclination, passion, and habit, *meaning certain biases of the mind distinct from volition and prior to it.*" [47] If he could have seen that they were radically distinct from volition, he would have been ready to understand West. But he let the issue drop without adequate thought. He left to others to reap the benefits and the glory of accomplishing this forward step.

West's irrefutable argument from self-consciousness is evaded in the same way as Stephen West would have evaded it. Samuel West had expressed himself as if freedom were the object of immediate consciousness, for he said, "We feel ourselves free." But he had also expressed his idea in better form by saying that we "feel ourselves accountable for our conduct, and capable of praise and blame." Hence he would reason to freedom. This is the decisive argument, and was made by Lotze, for example, the turning-point of the argument for freedom. But Edwards contents himself with bringing out the fact that we cannot be conscious of freedom, but only of volitions.[48] He does not enter into the significant and vital question which West had started: What is the freedom we must

[47] *Loc. cit.,* p. 331.   [48] *Ibid.,* pp. 388, 421.

conceive human agents to have to render them responsible? This is the crucial failure of his reply.

West's arguments against the causative power of motives seem to have made more impression upon him. In reply he has recourse to Stephen West's doctrine of occasionalism. He says that President Edwards has "explained himself to mean by cause no other than occasion, reason, or previous circumstance necessary for volition." [49] It is true that President Edwards did include every antecedent of a volition in its cause, and that he can be interpreted, as his son here interprets him, by straining his language. Hence arose that school of Edwardeans of which mention is to be made at length later. Dr. Edwards constantly reverts to this explanation, and it constitutes his standard interpretation of his father. That it was false we have already seen. Indeed, Dr. Edwards only presents it in this instance to cancel it effectually almost in the article of proposing it; for he continues:

> I do not pretend that motives are the *efficient* causes of volition. If any expression importing this have dropped from any defender of the connection between motive and volition, either it must have happened through inadvertence, or he must have meant that motive is an efficient cause in no other sense than rain and the rays of the sun are the efficient cause of the growth of vegetables, or than medicine is the efficient cause of health.

Now, in accordance with the Berkeleian idealism which pervaded, whether consciously or unconsciously, the whole New England school at this point of its history, physical causes had no efficient power. Hence Edwards could deny that motives—which, it should be strictly marked, he puts in the same category with these physical causes—had efficient causation. But if one was not an idealist, and attached to the physical causes of events real power and a consequent efficiency, then *to him* the causation of motives

[49] *Ibid.*, p. 344.

became an efficient causation, and West's interpretation of Edwards must become his interpretation. Dr. Edwards proceeds now to carry out his line of defence to its consequences. If motives have no efficient causation, where is the causative force efficiently producing volitions? He says:

It is denied that man himself is the efficient cause of it [volition]. He who established the laws of nature so-called is the primary cause of all things. What is meant by the efficient cause in any case in which an effect is produced according to established laws? For instance, what is the efficient cause of the sensation of heat from fire? If it be answered: Fire is the efficient cause; I also answer that the motive is the efficient cause of the volition and doing aforesaid. If it be said that the Great First Cause is the efficient of the sensation of heat, the same Great Agent is the efficient cause of volition, in the same way, by a general law establishing a connection between motives and volitions, as there is a connection between fire in certain situations and the sensation of heat.[50]

Here the son is true to the father, who said that the difference between causation in the moral and physical realms lay, not in the nature of the connection, but in the nature of the things connected. Thus the milder interpretation proposed by Edwards really vanishes, and the critics of the original treatise of the elder Edwards are abundantly justified.

But Dr. Edwards goes still farther. He has banished efficient causation from the physical universe, and he now proceeds to banish it from the universe at large. The Deity, says Edwards, "is no more the efficient cause of his own volitions than he is of his own existence." [51] How mightily the lion is struggling in the entanglements of the invisible net! This is utter confusion of thought, and should have brought Edwards back to the error lurking in his premises. But he remains entangled in the result of his own consistency. God is, however, he grants, the efficient cause of *our* volitions. Certainly, these sentences constitute a *reductio ad absurdum,* perpetrated by Edwards himself, greater than all the infinite series of his father together!

Emmons [52] closes this drift of thought. He puts the theory of the divine agency in its extremest form. Men act freely in view of motives. They act freely because they act voluntarily, since these two are one and the same thing. When they act in view of motives, God "exhibits the motives and then excites them to act voluntarily in view of the motives exhibited," "for the bare perception of motive is incapable of producing volition." [53] Thus God "produces" our volitions. For producing, Emmons often uses the word "creating," and the operations of God in creating the material world and governing it are made exactly parallel with his operations in renewing the hearts of men. He expressly rejects the idea "that God only upholds moral agents in existence and preserves their active powers without exerting any influence upon their wills which moves them to act in every instance according to his pleasure." "Adam could not be the efficient cause of his own volition."

But this is only a part of Emmons. Extreme as his statements are, they must be understood in the light of equally extreme statements upon the other side. He also says: "How God operates on our minds in our free voluntary exercises, we are unable to comprehend." He proposes therefore to hold the fact that God so operates, and also to hold every other fact, let them be consistent or inconsistent. Therefore he teaches that God has made men free moral agents. They are this in the same sense that he is. Under his universal agency, human beings have a true agency. In the divine mind this consists in volition, and in the human mind it consists in the same. Moral agency and

---

[52] Nathaniel Emmons, born 1745; pastor at Franklin, Mass., 1773-1827; died 1840.

[53] *Works* (Ide's edition), Vol. IV, pp. 352 ff., for all these citations.

moral character consist in "exercises." God works in men
to lead them to perform the ordinary actions of life, such
as sowing, planting, etc., in the same way as he does to
produce the religious actions, such as repentance. Man is
as free in the one class as the other. He has all the freedom of which he can conceive.[54]

Up to this point the tendency of New England theology
has been to destroy more and more completely the freedom
of the will. The two tendencies characteristic of Calvinism
and Berkeleianism—to exalt the agency of God, and to
deny to second causes efficiency and even existence—have
been reducing man more and more to the position of a
mere puppet upon the stage of human history. But now
there was introduced by a remarkable book, written by an
obscure country minister, the idea which was finally to reverse the current and set this theology in motion toward
a doctrine of freedom. It did not break with the prevailing

[54] Professor Park, who is the profoundest student of the history of New
England theology that has yet appeared, maintains that Emmons did believe in
the reality of second causes, and continues:

"His allusions to second causes are so much more infrequent than his allusions to the great First Cause that even Professor Stuart misunderstood him to
teach that there is in fact only one real cause in existence. The objector asks:
Does not Emmons affirm that man is not the efficient cause of his own choices?
He does, sometimes; but *then* he means by efficient cause, that agent who produces a volition by previously choosing to produce it; and a man does not produce
his choice, his first choice, for example, by previously choosing to produce it.
Man does not begin his moral action by choosing to choose. He does not put
forth his first preference as an effect of his antecedently preferring to put it
forth. On this point, Emmons is the truest representative who has appeared
of the Edwardean philosophy. But, rejoins the critic, Does not Emmons affirm or
imply that God is the only efficient cause in the universe? He does. But here he
uses the word efficient as denoting independent. He teaches that all other choices
are put forth by the intervention of powers which absolutely depend on the
first eternal choice of the First Cause. That first eternal choice is the only
independent, and, with this meaning, the only efficient cause in the universe.
. . . . Although his language is more nervous than perspicuous, more compressed than precise, on this theme, yet it may be understood by considering
the general scope of his theology, and by remembering his favorite principle,
that *agency in God is like agency in man,* that *causation in God is like causation
in man.* If man, therefore, be not a real cause, God himself is not a real cause."

See the "Memoir," Boston edition of Emmons' *Works,* pp. 385 f., with the
cross-references.

necessitarianism, and so was not denied a hearing at the very start, as its predecessors upon the same path had been. This was Asa Burton's *Essays on Some of the First Principles of Metaphysicks, Ethicks, and Theology* (1824) [55] which is one of the classics of New England theology, and one of the great influential philosophical books of the world.

All the previous writers had maintained the twofold division of the mind into understanding and will. As we have seen, Samuel West's clear statement of the threefold division had been without effect. The common-sense which had directed what opposition was made to the prevailing necessitarianism had had no sufficient theoretical basis in a sounder psychology. Burton supplied this basis. After showing that there are faculties in the mind, and developing briefly the fact that there are three main faculties— the understanding, the heart, and the will—he takes up each of these faculties in order. In his treatment of the understanding we find him determining the terminology of a long line of successors. The special treatment of the "taste," as he calls the sensibility, begins upon page 53. He classifies the emotions, desires, etc., as properly belonging to one class of mental affections, and declares that they must have a cause, which cause is the "taste." This he defines as "that preparedness, adaptedness, or disposition of the mind by which the mind is affected agreeably or disagreeably when objects are presented to it." [56] At a later point he distinguishes sharply between the "heart" and the will.[57] It is evident, he says, "that neither a pleasant nor a painful sensation is a volition."

[55] Asa Burton, born at Stonington, Conn., August 25, 1752; graduated at Dartmouth College, 1777; ordained in Thetford, Vt., 1779; instructed about sixty students for the ministry; D.D., 1804; died in Thetford, May 1, 1836.

[56] *Op. cit.*, p. 54.

[57] Pp. 87 ff.

Volitions and desires are not operations of the same faculty. . . . .
Though desire has an object, yet its object is not an action nor an
effect. . . . . I may desire meat or drink . . . . and yet not one effect
follow necessary to obtain them. But when I will these effects, they
follow, they are produced. . . . . Whether objects shall please or disgust us does not depend upon anything in us except our nature; but
whether they shall be chosen or not depends upon our pleasure. . . . .
Pleasure and pain are not produced by choice, neither can choice
prevent them. Whether we will or not, some objects will please us
and others will disgust us. But whether they are chosen or not depends upon our pleasure.

Burton thus brings out distinctly, though not with absolute correctness, the fact that there is a distinction between
the sensibility and the will. We shall see that through
the ambiguity of the word "pleasure" he seems to state
here more than he actually does.

Varying the order of Burton's discussion somewhat, we
now advance to his definition of liberty. Here he makes a
very decided improvement upon any of his predecessors.
Liberty, he says, is not to be predicated of the intellect or
of the desires.[58] The operations of these faculties is necessary. Neither does liberty consist in volition. A person
may be bound and so have no power of motion, though he
wills it. He is not then at liberty, and hence volitions do
not constitute liberty. Neither is it a power which the
mind possesses, as to act or not to act. Burton distinguishes between liberty of action and liberty of will. We
have liberty of will when we can choose objects according to our wish—that is, our strongest wish or desire.
This, evidently, can never be taken from us, and we therefore always have it. Liberty of action is the privilege of
acting externally according to our volitions; and of this
we may be deprived.

We are thus introduced to Burton's theory of the will.
The action of the taste is necessary. Objects excite our

[58] Pp. 111 ff.

desires, and our desires move our wills. Hence the taste
is the "spring of action in all moral agents," and operates
as the cause of volitions. "The will is only an executive
faculty; . . . . its office is to obey the commands of the
heart." The clearest and completest statement of the
theory may be thus condensed:

This internal cause [the taste] by its operation produces every
volition. . . . . Between this cause and volition, God has established
an infallible connection. . . . . Hence the reason why the liberty of the
will [in the sense of a liberty of willing according to our pleasure]
can never be abridged. . . . . This connection is moral necessity, and
this necessity renders liberty of will absolutely sure and certain.[59]

We are thus left by Burton still in the toils of Edwards'
necessity. He has corrected, one by one, the minor errors
of his predecessors, having rejected the position of Hopkins, that freedom consists in voluntariness; of Emmons,
that our mind is a chain of exercises (the extremest result
of the hereditary Berkeleianism), and that our volitions are
"created" by God. He has distinguished between the necessity of the operation of the intellect and that of the will.
But still the will remains necessitated through its dependence upon the taste. Hence, so far as the theory of the
will is concerned, he has given but little relief. It seems
the fate of all sound theological progress to move with ex-
ceeding slowness, by almost infinitesimal increments. It
is as in animal development, where the "variation" is generally minute. But, as we shall soon see, by the distinction
established between the taste and the will he has prepared
the way for an altogether new conception, which he did
not himself attain, and which introduces ultimately the idea
of freedom in its true form. There was need of still
another laborer before the wide-reaching consequences of
Burton's new truth could be brought out.

This successor to Burton's labors and completer of his

[59] P. 126.

work was Nathaniel W. Taylor,[60] the most original, powerful, and widely influential mind which New England
theology ever possessed. He derived his impulse to productive work upon the will from Burton, and alone proved
able to effect anything in the further development of the
doctrine. But he was not solely dependent upon Burton
for he stood in the succession of Yale teachers, and had
been brought by his predecessors in this great school to a
new philosophical position—to the final abandonment of the
Berkeleianism which had been so influential, and so bale-
fully so, up to this time. Dwight [61] had been familiar with
English and Scotch philosophy, and the great master Reid,
and had laid the foundation of the philosophy of common-
sense, which Taylor adopted, and which became the great
offensive weapon of New England apology as well as its
great instrument of constructive reasoning. Day,[62] Fitch,
and Goodrich had taken part in the discussion of the will,
and had cleared the ground somewhat for Taylor. With
all the advantage derived from a new philosophy and a
new method, Taylor, having once seen the wide-reaching
consequences of Burton's discoveries, was able to draw

[60] Born in New Milford, Conn., 1786; died in New Haven, March 10, 1858;
graduated at Yale, 1807; studied theology with President Dwight; pastor of the
First Church, New Haven, 1812; transferred to the chair of theology when the
department of theology was organized in Yale College, 1822.

[61] President Noah Porter says (American edition of Ueberweg's *History of
Philosophy*, Vol. II, p. 449): "Dr. Dwight was, in the main, a disciple of
Edwards. . . . . He was familiar with the works of the leading English and
Scotch philosophers, and discussed their opinions in a popular style. . . . . He
was also more or less familiar with the rational and ethical English divines of
the eighteenth century, and was influenced to some degree at least by the modes
of reasoning and statements with which he became familiar in Berkeley, Butler,
and George Campbell."

[62] Dr. Jeremiah Day, president of Yale College, who contributed two brief
discussions to the controversy, both of them substantially Edwardean, though
manifesting something of the traditional apologetic interpretation, but full of
acute and useful discriminations: *Inquiry respecting the Self-determining Power
of the Will*, etc. (New Haven, 1838) and *An Examination of President Edwards' Inquiry on the Freedom of the Will* (New Haven, 1841).

them without embarrassment and apply them courageously both in theory and in practice.[63]

Taylor followed Burton in adopting the threefold division of the mind. There must be something in the mind of the sinner to which the gospel could appeal, some neutral point not thoroughly corrupted with the corruption of his moral nature, though that corruption, in respect to the will, was entire. Such a neutral point Taylor found in the sensibility, whence the will might be reached. This was a position which commended itself to him because he was profoundly interested in the work of converting men, in which as a pastor and evangelist of great power and eloquence he had long been variously engaged.

Prepared thus to perceive and escape the fundamental fallacy of Edwards, Taylor was ready for various improvements upon his predecessors. He corrected the tendency which had done so much to make theology impossible, by pronouncing for human efficiency. "Moral agents," he says, "are the proximate efficient causes of their own acts." [64] He does not hold them to be the *sole* efficient agents, or the *ultimate,* but the *proximate,* having a true agency. The same efficiency he also ascribes to material objects. "My mind inclines to the belief of the efficiency of second causes." [65] An argument in favor of this is "our consciousness of the existence of created agents of one sort," viz., ourselves.

In possessing this agency, the soul possesses "power to the contrary," or, in any definite choice which it makes, acts under no necessity but with power to make the contrary choice equally with the choice actually made, the cir-

---

[63] For a valuable article upon Taylor see G. P. Fisher's *Discussions in History and Theology* (pp. 285–354), to which I am happy to acknowledge my indebtedness for much of what follows, and for my general view of Taylor's theology.

[64] *Moral Government,* Vol. I, p. 309.   [65] *Ibid.,* Vol. II, p. 311.

cumstances of the choice remaining unaltered.[66]   Taylor
said, in order to avoid the evasions of Edwards: "A man
not only can if he will, but he can if he won't."   He says:

> Moral agency implies free agency—the power of choice—the power
> to choose morally wrong as well as morally right under every possible
> influence to prevent such choice or action. . . . . I now speak of pre-
> venting sin in moral beings, free moral agents, who *can* sin under every
> possible influence from God to prevent their sinning.[67]

At the same time, Dr. Taylor does not deny the influence of motives.   The system under which we live is a
system of moral influence, of law possessing authority and
uttering commands designed to influence men.   In some
way also, however impossible to understand or explain, the
moral system, including free moral agency, with its "power
to the contrary," secures *certainty* as to future moral events.
Moral government "is an influence which is designed and
fitted to give, not the necessity, but merely the certainty of
its effect." [68]   How this is secured Dr. Taylor does not say.
He objects to the theory that it is produced through motives, and prefers to say, "through the constitution of man
and the circumstances in which he acts." [69]   To these
sources we ourselves refer all our actions.   How the constitution and circumstances of man are managed to secure a
definite volition in every case is the point left unexplained.
The theory, as a theory, is therefore still defective, the idea
of freedom, so clearly and decidedly advanced, being left
altogether unadjusted to the sovereignty and foreknowledge of God.   The crux of the New England theology
begins therefore to appear in this hitherto unequaled
thinker.   Will he be able to resolve the difficulty, or will
the lion, now grown greater and more powerful, still prove
himself unable to escape the net in which he is enmeshed?
Meantime Taylor holds to the old distinction between

[66] Fisher, *op. cit.*, p. 312.   [67] *Moral Government*, Vol. I, p. 307.
[68] *Ibid.*, Vol. I, p. 8.   [69] *Ibid.*, Vol. II, p. 312.

natural and moral ability. The natural ability is the true power; the moral ability, the condition of the will. A man is morally unable to will one thing, such as to love God, while he is at the same time willing the opposite thing, such as to love himself supremely. The real difficulty in spiritual struggles consists in the obstinacy of the will, or the actual preference of other things to the service and glory of God.

Taylor has thus seized upon the great advance made by Burton, in adopting the threefold division of the mind, and has at the same time freed himself from the necessitarianism in which Burton had remained, by breaking the bond which in Burton's scheme still connected the action of the will with the condition of the sensibility. While still a most intense admirer of Edwards, he has broken with his distinctive idea also—with the infallible connection between the greatest apparent good and the volition. He stands for a true freedom, upon the basis of consciousness, and will allow nothing to interfere with its reality. But he stands at the same time, upon quite other grounds, for the previous certainty of all human actions.

Another writer, more a psychologist than a theologian, who accepted Burton's new division of the faculties of the mind,[70] and contributed to liberate our philosophy and theology from thraldom to Edwards, was Thomas C. Upham,[71] professor for many years in Bowdoin College. In his *Philosophical and Practical Treatise on the Will* (1834) he issued one of the first original and comprehensive contributions of American scholarship to modern psychology. It embraced descriptions of the phenomena of the mind

[70] Quoting him on p. 29 of *The Will*.

[71] Born in Deerfield, N. H., January 30, 1799; died in New York, April 1, 1872; graduated at Dartmouth, 1818; Andover, 1821; pastor in Rochester, N. H., 1823–24; professor of mental and moral philosophy in Bowdoin College, 1824–67; published also *Elements of Mental Philosophy* (1827), which was widely used.

drawn from a wide range of reading, and was not written with a view of sustaining some preconceived theory. Though not without a purpose, it was not so occupied with its purpose as to select its material with reference to that alone, and confine itself to a single and narrow line of inquiry. It was more largely influenced than many later productions by the conception of psychology which is now controlling, viz., that it is a chapter in the natural history of the soul.

Upham begins with the "General Nature of the Will," in which he sets forth the existence and general relations of the three faculties of the mind, intellect, sensibility, and will. All parts and powers of the mind are connected. The intellectual part is the foundation of the others. The intellect reaches the will through the sensibilities. When an object is perceived, the emotions are excited, upon which follow the desires, and then the will acts. It is an example of the breadth of Upham's view that he pauses here, in the onward movement of his theme, to note that, while the intellect acts on the sensibility, this reacts upon the intellect. The will itself is the controlling power of the mind which maintains the harmony of the mind. It "is not meant to express anything separate from the mind," and may be defined as "the mental power or susceptibility by which we put forth volitions." The term "volition," designating a "simple state of the mind," admits of no definition.

After a concluding chapter on the distinction between the desires and the volitions, necessary in those times, Upham advanced to his second part, in which, by a long discussion of the universality of law, and of various specific laws, he arrives at the conclusion that there are laws of the will. This view is contrasted in his mind with the view that the actions of the will are "without respect to antecedent, and regulated by no conditions." [72] The laws considered are those of causality, those found in moral government, those implied in the prescience of the Deity and the foresight of men, in the sciences relating to human conduct, and those intimated by consciousness, and the influence of motives. In all this wide range of discussion the central idea is that brought out in the following extract:

Every moral government implies, in the first place, a ruler, a governor, some species of supreme authority. The term government itself, separate from any qualifying epithet, obviously expresses the fact that there are some beings governed, which is inconceivable without the correlative of a higher and governing power. And what is true of all other government is certainly not less so of that species of government which is denominated moral. In all moral government, therefore, there must undoubtedly be some supreme authority to which those who are governed are amenable.

Now if men are under government, they are under law. To be governed is obviously to be regulated, guided, or controlled, in a greater or less degree. To say that men are governed and are at the same time exempt from law, is but little short of a verbal contradiction, and is certainly a real one. But when we speak of men as being under laws, we do not mean to assert a mere abstraction. We mean to express something actually existing; in other words, we intend to assert the *fact,* that the actions of men, whatever may be true of their freedom, are in some way or other reached by an effective supervision. But when we consider the undenied and undoubted dependence of the outward act on the inward volition, we very naturally and properly conclude that the supervision of the outward act is the result of the antecedent supervision of the inward principle of will; in other words, the *will has its laws.*[73]

With this principle copiously proved and definitely laid down, but *without attempt to enumerate or describe* the laws themselves, Upham passes to the topic of the freedom of the will. Freedom, he says, is the name of a simple idea (here recurring to Locke's phraseology), and therefore is indefinable. But it is not impossible to gain a tolerably correct view of what Upham meant by freedom. Although

[72] *The Will,* p. 133.
[73] *Ibid.,* p. 150.

he wanders off into a discussion of "mental harmony," by which he means what the Germans designate by their term *reale Freiheit,* in which the powers all co-operate under the guidance of conscience in perfect union with one another, and declares this the only condition in which true freedom can be realized, it is evident on the whole that he means by freedom a true power of causality. He proves it by man's moral nature, gaining evidence of it from the feelings of approval and disapproval, those of remorse, the mere existence of the abstract ideas of right and wrong, the feeling of moral obligation, and men's views of crimes and punishments. He adduces to the same end evidence from language, from occasional suspension of the will's acts, from our control over our own motives, from our attempts to influence other men, and from the language of the Scriptures. And at a later point he also employs the word "self-determining" power [74] to express his doctrine, though he objects to that use of the word against which Edwards had argued. And, while he defers the whole matter of the consistency of the will's subjection to law with the fact of freedom, he affirms that they are consistent, using Emmons' appeal to reason for the idea of law, and to consciousness for the knowledge of freedom. An interesting Part IV on the "Power of the Will" closes the work.

The ideas of Taylor were taken up at Oberlin by President Finney.[75] He adopted the division of the mind into intellect, sensibility, and will. He criticized Edwards' distinction between natural and moral ability, and reduced

[74] *Loc. cit.,* p. 341.

[75] Charles G. Finney, born in Warren, Conn., August 29, 1792; died in Oberlin, O., August 16, 1875. A revivalist, pastor of Broadway Tabernacle, New York, he was called to Oberlin as professor of theology in 1835. In 1837 he became pastor of the First Church. In 1848 he went to England and spent three years there, reissuing his *Systematic Theology* in that country. From 1852 to 1866 he was president of Oberlin College.

them, upon the basis of Edwards' philosophy, to one and the same thing. His definition of freedom was as follows:

Free will implies the power of originating and deciding our own choices, and of exercising our own sovereignty in every instance of choice upon moral questions. . . . . The sequences of choice or volition are always under the law of necessity, and unless the will is free, man has no freedom; and if he has no freedom, he is not a moral agent.[76]

The argument from consciousness for freedom had not escaped the attention even of the Berkeleian period; and we have had occasion to note in Stephen West close distinctions relative to consciousness of power. Now that our theology had passed over to the new basis of the Scotch school, fresh discussions of consciousness might be expected. Finney occupied himself with them somewhat, but gives a rather uncertain answer to the question whether we are actually conscious of freedom. He says: "Consciousness gives us the reasons of the affirmation that liberty is an attribute of the actions of the will." This is probably the phrase by which we gain the true interpretation of another phrase of Finney's: "Man is conscious of possessing the powers of a moral agent." [77] The freedom of the will is an affirmation of the reason upon consciousness of the phenomena which pass on within us.

Finney also maintained the perfect certainty of all future volitions, which are embraced in the purposes of God, so that God's foreknowledge of what will be done depends upon his purposes as to what he will himself do. In respect to all these subjects, however, there is no philosophical discussion; but Finney contents himself with the affirmation of what he regards simple and indisputable truth.

Finney's successor, President Fairchild, presented the same doctrine, but with new and juster emphasis upon the

[76] *System*, Fairchild's edition, p. 15.
[77] *Ibid.*, p. 19.

testimony of consciousness. The intellect and the sensibility are marked in their action by the law of necessity. But
in the case of the will, in view of at least two courses,

we consciously determine for ourselves, by a free choice between the
two, upon which of these courses we shall enter. . . . . In this decision
we are conscious of the fact of freedom, or liberty. We know that
we can will to take either of the attitudes, or pursue either of the
courses open to us; this is the beginning and the end of our freedom. . . . . The proof of our freedom is found only in our consciousness, and can be found nowhere else. We know that we are
free, and that is the end of the argument; it is a fact of consciousness. . . . . The argument for freedom derived from our moral consciousness, the fact that we hold ourselves bound by duty or obligation to a certain course of action, is a good argument for the freedom
of the will. But the perception or conviction of the obligation *presupposes the consciousness of freedom.* The view is sometimes presented that we infer our freedom from our consciousness of obligation.
But it is not merely a logical inference. The consciousness of freedom is doubtless involved in our perception or conviction of obligation. The fact of freedom is the logical antecedent of that of obligation, and the thought of freedom must come before, or with, the thought
of obligation.[78]

Fairchild attempted to make the possibility of freedom a
little clearer by dividing, as Samuel West had done, between the two classes of motives—those which appeal to
the intelligence, and those which appeal to the desires. All
motives reduce to these two classes. Between the two the
will chooses in perfect freedom. In fact, freedom is made
possible by the fact that the two are incomparable as to
their strength, since they appeal to the personality in two
completely different ways.

How do we measure strength of motive? There are two ways—by
the judgment or reason, and by the sensibility or feeling. The two
standards are entirely different, but the will is not always as the
strongest motive, tested by either standard. It is not always as the
best judgment; for the sinner always acts against the true reason as
presented by his judgment. Nor is it always as the strongest feeling; the good man often obeys his judgment, against his feeling.

[78] *Elements of Theology, Natural and Revealed* (Oberlin, 1892), pp. 37 ff.

This is more illuminating than anything that had yet been said. Yet Fairchild did not quite rise to the true height of freedom, for he said:

If motive acts only in the shape of desire, then there is but one kind of motive acting upon us, and *no alternative in action;* only one course open to us, and hence no choice, no freedom. The strongest desire, or the resultant of the desires, must control the will. There is nothing possible in action but to obey the feeling.

This is entirely to surrender freedom; for the fact is that the strength of desires does not touch freedom. Action must, to be sure, "obey the feeling;" but which, of several feelings? It erects the authority which it obeys into an authority in the act of obeying it. Fairchild further held the certainty of all future events, because he maintained God's perfect foreknowledge. But foreknowledge was mysterious. God must be supposed to have "some direct beholding of the future, a power which we cannot explain or understand."

The Oberlin school thus attained the best statement of the meaning of freedom which had yet been given in the New England theology. But its atomistic theory of the will's action[79] prevented it from accepting Taylor's idea of a "primary predominant choice," with all which that involves for the idea of character. For the highest point reached in this development we must turn to Samuel Harris, who in his *Philosophical Basis of Theism* gave a new statement to freedom and rendered many of the old disputations forever unnecessary.

Harris begins his treatment of the will with definitions. To summarize:

The will is the power of a person, in the light of reason and with susceptibility to the influence of rational motives, to determine the end or objects to which he will direct his energy, and the exertion of his energy with reference to the determined end or object. The will is a person's power of self-determination. It is his power of determining

[79] See Chapter XVI, on the Oberlin theology.

the exercise of his own causal efficiency or energy. *He has the power of self-direction, self-exertion, and self-restraint.* . . . . The determinations of the will are of two kinds—Choice and Volition. In choice a person determines the object or end to which he will direct his energies. In volition a person exerts his energies or calls them into action; or he refuses to do so. . . . . Choice is self-direction. Volition is self-exertion or self-restraint. Both are self-determinations.[80]

The distinction here made between choice and volition is vital to Harris' understanding of the subject. It

is essential to the reality of free-will and moral responsibility. If will is merely the volitional power of calling the energies into action, then we no longer determine by free-will the ends or objects of action; and these are determined by the constitutional impulses or motives which are at the time the strongest. And thus all freedom both of choice and volition disappears, since the man has no power of self-direction and can exert his energies only in the direction already determined for him by the unreasoning impulses of nature.[80]

Choice "presupposes a comparison of objects in the light of reason. . . . . After the comparison follows the choice, which is the simple, indefinable determination of the will."

A choice is an abiding determination of the will. It may abide for an hour or a day; it may be a life-long choice or preference. . . . . Choices may be distinguished by their objects as supreme and subordinate. A subordinate choice is the choice of an object as subordinate to an ulterior end; as when one chooses wealth as an object of pursuit, but chooses it simply as a means of political preferment. The supreme choice is the choice of the supreme end of action, to which all other ends are subordinate and which itself is subordinate to no ulterior end. Because man is rational he must choose some supreme end; for he recognizes reason as supreme.[81]

With these definitions the affirmation of freedom is closely connected.[82] "The definition of will is in itself the definition of free-will." "The freedom of the will consists in the fact that the will is a will." "Freedom is inherent in rationality." Edwards was wrong in considering the will "from the point of view of efficient causation," and

[80] *Op. cit.,* p. 349.   [81] *Ibid.,* p. 354.
[82] *Ibid.,* p. 361.

forgetting that it might be exercised (in choice) prior to all causation. The threefold division of the mind, separating sharply between the determinations of the sensibilities and those of the will, is of essential help in maintaining the correct view. "Man's knowledge of his free-will is of the highest certainty." [83] The proof is derived from the immediate affirmations of consciousness, from the consciousness of moral responsibility which involves freedom, from the fact that it "sustains the tests of primitive knowledge," and from human history. The "implication of man in nature," [84] which proves that he is above nature, is considered at length; and then the old historic struggle is taken up in a section upon "the influence of motives." [85] The motive is not the efficient cause of the will's determinations; nor does it determine it to choose this rather than that. The various formulas which have been suggested— The will always is as the strongest motive; as the greatest apparent good; as the last dictate of the understanding— are all aside from the true point. This portion of the subject is summed up in the following paragraph, which also anticipates the substance of a valuable section upon "Sociology and Free-Will:"

The uniformity of human action cannot be explained by any law of the uniform influence of motives on the will. Another factor is concerned in this uniformity; it is the character in the will. By its choice the will forms in itself a character; and by action in accordance with the choice, it confirms and develops the character. This must be recognized in explaining the uniformity of human action. The attempt to explain it by some law of the uniform influence of motives assumes that the will is always characterless. Writers on the will who attempt to explain the uniformity of human action in this way, have much to say about the necessity of finding the laws of the will. But in fact they are seeking for a law of the will which shall be only a necessary uniform sequence of nature; should they succeed they would only prove that the determinations of the will are a part of the

[83] *Ibid.,* p. 365.   [84] *Ibid.,* p. 376.
[85] *Ibid.,* p. 389.

course of nature and subject to the *dictum necessitatis.* This would prove that personal beings do not exist and that nature is all. The real law to the determinations of the will is the moral law which declares the ends to which rational beings ought to direct their energies and the principles which ought to guide them in their actions. If personal beings exist they must at some point rise above the fixed course and uniform sequences of nature and find themselves under obligation to conform their free action to the truths, laws, ideals, and ends of reason.[86]

But this is a disgression. We are here engaged with a theologian who represents a later stage in the history of theology, when the homogeneous and self-centered New England school was giving way to the introduction of a still "newer" theology. We revert, therefore, to Taylor as the propounder of a real freedom, and ask what the effect of this proposal is to be within the strict New England school, of which Taylor certainly was a member, both by training and by his hearty acceptance of its leading positions. What would be done with it in our oldest and then principal school of theology, in Andover, and by the greatest representative of the unmodified New England strain, Professor Park?

The real question for New England theology, after Taylor had led the way in so large a revision of Edwards' positions as substantially to reverse them, was whether the departure from Edwards should be frankly acknowledged, and the development of theological thought be allowed to go unhampered on its way, or whether the overshadowing influence of Edwards should be maintained to the great damage of the constructive processes so actively proceeding. Should the dogmatic or the historic spirit prevail? It was Park's peculiar fate to guide in the latter direction, and to maintain the historic attitude at the expense of perfect clearness and dogmatic success. He so admired and reverenced Edwards that he believed himself at every point

[86] *Loc. cit.,* p. 396.

a follower of the master. Why he thought so is one of the
mysteries of the subject. He was himself a greater mind
than Edwards. He must have known Edwards' entire dependence upon Locke for both doctrine and arguments.
But Park's admiration of the acuteness, elaboration, comprehensiveness, and mercilessness in the pursuit of error,
which mark Edwards' work, and of the great service rendered by the perfect timeliness of his writings to evangelical theology, was so great that it blinded him to every other
aspect of the matter. This was the easier on account of
that subtle ambiguity in Edwards' phraseology which we
have already marked, and which gave rise to the interpretation of his father made by the younger Edwards. Park
seized this interpretation and declared it the true interpretation, and thus concealed from himself his greatest divergence from Edwards. His further divergences could then
the more easily remain hid from his own eyes.

These divergences pertained to three points:

1. Edwards followed the old division of the mind into
the understanding and affections, and subsumed the will
under the latter head. He hence confounded the affections
and the will, and made a hundred times the fallacy of glid-
ing from "inclination" considered as a desire to inclination
as a volition, without being conscious of it; which, of
course, was the fallacy of "ambiguous term." Park, on
the contrary, followed the threefold division into intellect,
sensibility, and will, and was always consistent in the distinction.

2. Park denied the *causal* connection between motives
and choices. Hence he interpreted the maxim, which he
himself preserved, "The will always *is* as the greatest apparent good," as embodying the *usage,* not the necessitated
action, of the will. It *might* at any moment choose the

least apparent good; but it never *does,* and it never *will.* This was the younger Edwards' interpretation of his father.

3. Park gave a new meaning, and above all a new force, to the idea of natural ability to choose, which he would have made a real freedom but for the shackles laid upon him by that maxim, which he thought he had evacuated of its mischief, but which, like a tamed cobra, possessed both the power and the will to poison the theory, if not the practical application, of any theology cherishing it.[87]

These divergences were of the utmost importance for subsequent thinkers, but it was chiefly because of their extension and enlargement on account of practical considerations. We now concern ourselves with the question of the theoretical adjustment of the idea of freedom, and of the success of Park in maintaining a true freedom.

Park maintains that the will always *is* as the greatest apparent good. Take any human being, from Adam down, and he comes into a world of goods, already fixed independently of his volitional action. His own balance of desires and tendencies (subjective natural motives, in Park's terminology), previous to his first choice, is also fixed independently of himself. Now he chooses—puts forth his *first* choice. It *is* as the greatest apparent good. What that good presented to him is, is independent of himself. What there is about it, or about him, that renders it apparently good is independent of him. The "greatest apparent good" is absolutely *objective* to him considered as a free, choosing being; and his will *is* as that good. The same is true of every subsequent choice, for if the will, the previous choice, is at any moment operative in determining what he

---

[87] Shedd (*Dogmatic Theology,* Vol. II, p. 219) reveals this inner contradiction in Edwards thus: "These positions [bondage of the will not "natural inability;" "moral inability" not "inability proper"] bring Edwards into contradiction with himself and open the way for a different anthropology from that contained in his writings generally, and particularly in his treatise on *Original Sin.*"

desires and thus modifies the "appearance," it was itself not *his*, but was *as* the (previously) apparent good. Hence two things follow:

1. Such a connection between motives and will is *causative;* and hence Park has not avoided the abyss of Edwards' necessity—nor that of Spencer or even Spinoza.

What is a causative connection between phenomena? I see a spark applied to powder and then I see an explosion. This is the uniform fact. The explosion always *is* as the application of the spark. I apply heat to ice and it melts. Whenever I see invariable connection of antecedents and certain consequents, I say the former are the *cause* of the latter. Professor Park elsewhere reasons in this way. He is thoroughly opposed to John Stuart Mill's theory of causation. He says that *whenever* we see the invariability which Mill affirms, we go farther than Mill, and declare that there is *power* there; and we thus arrive for the first time at the true idea of causation. Apply the same reasoning to his own maxim; and whenever we perceive that the "will *always is* as the greatest apparent good," we say: "The good is the *cause* of the action of the will;" *and we cannot say anything else while we have the powers of human reasoning left.*

Park, of course, perceived that this objection would be made to him, and his answer was ready. This uniformity is uniformity of *usage*. The will can choose the greatest apparent good freely—as freely as it could a lesser apparent good. And it always *does* freely choose the greatest apparent good. That it always does it freely, however so many times, is evident from consciousness; for consciousness declares of every choice that it is free.

We may rejoin that we are not conscious that every choice is free, for many are not; as, for example, my choice this morning to brush my hair with my brush. But of free choices—for man does make such, and of these only, is our discussion here—consciousness not only declares that the choice is free, but it often declares also that the choice is *not* one of "the greatest apparent good." It is an abuse of language as well as of morals to declare that the drunkard choosing the cup believes or feels it in any sense "good!" So that consciousness, if it is for freedom, as it is, is against the uniformity of the Edwardean maxim!

It is the more strange that Park did not see this because, if the will always is as the greatest apparent good, then, on his theory of virtue, *there can never be any sin.* Sin is the choice of the lower instead of the higher or greater good. If a man chooses the greatest apparent good—that is, the thing which on the whole seems best to him—that act is a virtuous act. And as every act is such a choice, according to Edwards, every act is virtuous. This argument can be met only by saying that the "greatest apparent good" is that which appeals most to the man, affords the greatest total present gratification, is the easiest to choose, has the most desire for itself. But if it is these, it is *truly* the greatest good, *unless* the man knows all the time that to choose it he must forsake duty for it, and that the desire it will gratify is an *evil* desire which he ought *never* to harbor. But then it is neither good nor apparently good! It is bad, and nothing but bad.

In fact, the term "greatest apparent good" is another example of the "ambiguous middle" in Edwards' reasoning of which "inclination" is the first and principal. Now it means the preponderating object of the sensibility, and now that of the conscience or of the whole harmonious man. No one can tell when it oscillates from one to the other; and hence *any* argument *may* be vitiated by it, and *most are.*

2. This theory is essentially supralapsarianism. The de-

crees of God are eternal. They surround the first, equally
with every, act of the will. There is never a moment of
freedom, of action not predetermined. Augustine made
man free in his fall; Edwards and Park made him no more
free there than anywhere else. In view of this, all questions of the *order* of the decrees are trivial. Was the decree to make man sin prior or subsequent to the decree to
damn him? Who cares? The main fact is that *all* of
every man's action and of all men's is decreed—his fall, his
sin, as well as his punishment for sin. God's decree embraces everything. It was not that God *foresaw* man's sin,
and then decreed to punish him. He did not *foresee,* he
decreed man's sin. There is not one atom of freedom, one
moment cf personal responsibility, deliberation, individual
and uncaused action on the part of man, anywhere. All is
necessitated.

Professor Park, of course, elaborately denies these positions, and, as we are about to show, escapes them—but not
consistently. We are now holding him strictly to his theories as they must be interpreted, if he consistently maintains the Edwardean theory of the will, as he says he does.
He says: God does not *positively* decree the sin of Adam or
of any other man. But he "circumstances and places" man
so that he "will certainly sin," and Adam as much as any
son of his. Now that is, in plain words, *surrounding him
with motives* leading to sin—and motives are *causes* producing sinful action. The distinctions utterly evaporate as
soon as the maxim, "always *is* as the greatest apparent
good," is remembered. That is *causation.* Thus Park was
a supralapsarian, forced to that position against his choice
by his theory of the will. True, he treats supralapsarianism
in a special section, and rejects it by saying of it that it is
"unreasonable and arbitrary;" but he does not give any
reason for this condemnation. This is the stranger because

he had in his theory of virtue the means of pulverizing it as no theologian before him had been able to do. He might have said: "Supralapsarianism is the theory that, irrespective of the fall, and without prevision of the same, God, from all eternity, for the glory of his mercy and the praise of his justice, separated men into two classes, and foreordained the one unto eternal life and the other unto eternal death. This theory is *impossible;* for (1) it regards men, antecedent to all sin, either as mere mathematical units, or as merely sentient beings, their moral nature and questions of desert being disregarded. (2) As mere mathematical units they can be the object of no moral judgment, and so neither condemned nor acquitted. (3) As merely sentient, they must become the objects of the divine *benevolence,* by which God *must choose to do them good, and good only,* and hence none of them can be reprobated. (4) Hence in neither case can there be the separation described." But Park does not say this. Why? The answer, I believe, is to be found in his determinism, which made substantial supralapsarianism necessary to him, however unwelcome. *This discord between the nature of virtue and the theory of the will is the great defect of Park's system, and would have been fatal to it had there not been a corresponding inconsistency in the theory of the will itself.* We are, accordingly, approaching rapidly to the deepest secret of Park's theology. It is his *crux.*

The charm of such a view of the will's action, by which this grim and inhuman theory of absolute predestination retained its hold upon the minds of Edwards and Park, is to be found in its relation to the concept of God. God was viewed by them both as unchangeable in all his perfections, in his wisdom, knowledge, blessedness, etc. His government was perfect also. Now, if there had been any true grief in God, his eternal blessedness would have been impaired; if any ignorance, even the slightest, of the future free acts of man, his infinite knowledge would have disappeared; if any failure to control any, even the least act of man, even so little an act as putting the finger *at random* on any square of a checker board (which example Edwards elaborately discussed), then there would be no divine government left whatever! The perfection of the logician, of the systematician—a geometrical perfection—was thus demanded in respect to life, even the life of God; and these great men continued to demand it in entire obliviousness of the fact that they were now discussing, not the Living God, but an intellectual abstraction, as cold as an iceberg, and as unreal as the Olympian Zeus. A colossal blunder certainly, but one of which "only colossal minds could be guilty."

The third peculiarity by which Park departed from Edwards undid, however, most of the harm of these supralapsarian positions. Following Bellamy, Hopkins, and Taylor, he gave a new meaning to "natural ability." This he defined as real ability, the ability to choose freely either right or wrong. "Moral ability" is not properly ability at all, since it is mere willingness. But natural ability is true, spontaneous, primal, causality. A man has natural ability to repent, always, everywhere, without the influence of the Holy Spirit, without church or Bible; but he *never* will so repent. He hasn't "moral ability;" that is, he *won't*. But he *can*.

Now, Park himself may have been perfectly consistent here with his Edwardean positions. He may have maintained that "natural ability," while complete, was *never* exercised, even in so small a matter as lifting the finger to brush away a fly, without "moral ability" conjoined—that is, without a balance of motives for such an action. His emphasis on certain positions, however, and the elaborateness with which he defined and removed objections when discussing the subject of decrees, would imply not. The toil would have been so futile unless the pupil, and the master, got for the time out from under the burden of Edwards' "certainty!" His pupils made an adjustment, even if Park did not, and the impression and total outcome of the system for them at this point were something as follows:

1. The will of man is free. He can, at any moment, choose right or wrong. This is the emphasis which Park constantly threw upon "natural ability." His statements were as extreme as the most ardent devotee of free will could desire. "Man can perfectly obey the law of God, because he can love God supremely and his neighbor as himself, and can maintain such a love, and exemplify it in every individual choice." "He can do right just as easily as he can do wrong." "He can break every decree of God relating to his own conduct." "He can repent at any moment without any aid from the Holy Spirit." Such were forms of expression Park constantly used. And out of them his pupils drew the doctrine that the will has a true, unchanged, primal causality, by which man truly originates action, and is himself the one, and the only, cause of his own action.

2. Motives, however, have a real influence on man; that is, a real tendency to move the will in this direction or that.

3. God's moral government is exercised through motives, influencing human wills. The action of a man can be determined, within reasonable limits, by his fellow-creatures, as they plan to bring such or such other motives to bear upon him. God can in a far greater sense control men's action by the same method, because he has far greater knowledge of all the conditions, internal and external, which affect the operation of those motives.

4. The scope of this government thus includes the volitions of men, and extends far beyond the reach of finite

comprehension. Has it any limits? Only such, whatever they may be, as God himself has given.

5. God set in motion a universe resulting in some degree of sin. Of course, he *purposed* to permit that sin. The explanation of that permission Park had already given. Sin entered by the free act of man; and that man was as able not to commit the sin he did commit, as he was to commit it. But God foresaw that man *would* sin; and he prepared for it.

6. The condition of things now is such that, left to themselves, men will sin. This is not a necessity, but it is a fact.

7. God interferes with the course of sin as largely as he can consistently, and calls some men unto salvation. This is *election*. It is not absolute in the sense that it renders faith necessary, for any elected man *can* persist in sin and be lost; and he can be saved only by exerting this same power of freedom in the way of repentance, faith, and reformation. Are any elect thus lost? Park would say, "No!" His pupils would say: "Possibly some are."

8. Those whom God must, to be consistent with the best interests of all, leave without such influence as will *actually* bring them to repentance, he so leaves. This is "praeterition," passing over, not "reprobation." But there is no absolute or complete praeterition. Men have grace enough to be saved, everyone. And they have "natural power," true freedom, to repent and be saved without *any* grace.

9. God never lets the world get out of his control. No "permissive decree," no "praeterition," ever implies that he stands by as a silent and helpless spectator, and sees the world going evil ways which he cannot hinder. He so guides and controls, even in the darkest times, as to bring

all out eventually to his own glory. This is his perfection, but it is a living and not a mere geometrical perfection.

Park thus never accepted for himself fully an idea which is essential to his defense of the benevolence of God in the permission of sin—the idea of the divine self-limitation. He admitted it in respect to the permission of sin, for he taught that God, having made man as he did and given him the faculty of free will, *could* not then consistently do so and so. He never explicitly recognized the fact that God limits himself even when he creates matter; for he cannot thereafter proceed in the universe, matter having its fixed qualities, forces, and laws, exactly as he otherwise could. He expressly rejected the suggestion of Julius Müller and other Kenotics, that the divine Logos limited itself in the incarnation. He really wanted a self-limitation which should be at the same time no limitation; which should explain the permission of sin, and yet not infringe the absoluteness of God's control, foreknowledge, and eternal decree, which with differences was to cover everything alike. He erred here in maintaining a doctrine of the Absolute—the truly Unconditioned—which is impossible when once sin, incarnation, atonement, and forgiveness are introduced. He should have listened here to Kahnis, with whom he once studied, and to the great Thomasius.

This, then, may be said to be the outcome of the New England theology in respect to the doctrine of the will. The great idea of a true freedom, born of the revival efforts of the great leaders of the school, struggled in the minds of the successive thinkers as they labored at making the system of theology more true and more consistent, but was not able to attain clearness of statement even from the greatest of them—from him who was in most respects the representative and consummation of the whole move-

ment. Here, then, the theology resulted in handing down
to its successors the imperative problem of a better settlement of this pivotal doctrine—a settlement which should
take the doctrine for itself, and discuss it upon its own evidences, and, having developed it in accordance with the
facts of a sound psychology, should then give it its place,
and its due influence in determining the other doctrines of
the Christian system. New England theology, to the end,
sacrificed the doctrine of freedom to that of the divine
perfections. It hence failed at getting a true doctrine;
and this was its crux.[88]

[88] In default of any published system from the hands of Professor Park,
I am compelled to present his system as I find it in my own stenographic notes
of the year 1875–76. I have often compared these with those of Rev. Henry
M. Tenney, of the year 1865–66. While the lack of an authoritative final
statement from Professor Park's own hand is greatly to be deplored, I have
not thought that posterity ought to be deprived of the illumination which is
thrown upon this history by his work, when hundreds of authentic reports of
his lectures are still in existence. In fact, this history, but for the light which
Professor Park's work throws upon it, could not have been written. It is
his completing work which shows the meaning of the course of the whole
school.

THE GREAT CONTROVERSIES

CHAPTER X

THE UNITARIAN CONTROVERSY

From the digression which we have made in the last chapters, we must now return to the regular progress of our history. We had been brought to the year 1795, or thereabout, by which time the new doctrine of the atonement had been set forth, and the first system of theology, Hopkins', had appeared. It was a time of great theological ferment. The Unitarian controversy was impending, and already monitions of its outbreak had been frequent. In this year Timothy Dwight came to Yale as its president, to find the college honeycombed with French infidelity, the legacy of French co-operation in the War of the Revolution. We are therefore called next to the study of this great crisis in the history both of the theology and of the organization of the New England churches. Was the new theology, which had sought to prepare the way for more effective evangelistic work, to go down before the attacks of English rationalism within its own fold and of French materialistic infidelity from without? So it seemed for a time. But the stress into which it was brought served only to show the stuff of which it was made.

The Unitarian movement in Massachusetts can be understood only by a careful review of a long history. Its roots stretch back to the very beginning of English Protestantism. In the milder tendencies of the English Reformation is to be found in part the explanation of the Arminianism which, under the influence of the powerful reaction from the high Calvinism of the Commonwealth, culminated in various forms of heterodoxy after the Restoration. Arminianism developed into Latitudinarianism, and Latitudinarianism into Arianism and Unitarianism. Samuel Clarke, a powerful writer upon apologetics, was an Arminian with a strong leaning to high Arianism, to say the least. Daniel Whitby was first an evangelical Arminian, and then a Unitarian. And then came a number of lesser writers, such as John Taylor, of Norwich, whose treatise on *Original Sin,* it is interesting to observe, was answered by both Jonathan Edwards, the Calvinistic revivalist of America, and John Wesley, the Arminian revivalist of England; and such as Emlyn, the author of the *Humble Inquiry into the Scripture Account of Jesus Christ,* etc., etc. Meantime also Deism, beginning with Herbert of Cherbury away back in the time of James and Charles I, was running its course. By the time of Wesley there was desperate need of an evangelical revival, if English theology or the English church was to be saved from complete destruction.

Long before this final stage of degeneration was reached in England, a parallel history of decline had begun in New England. The history of this, so far as it was the result of purely indigenous causes, has been already traced. Incidentally we have also repeatedly seen the influence which English writers constantly exercised in New England, and how Clarke, Whitby, Taylor, and others were read. Theological degeneration followed upon religious and moral decline. The steps of it, it is difficult, if not impossible, to follow. The principal writers remained still orthodox. The dissenters said little and wrote less. Still, dissent existed. We have seen that Arminianism became "prevailing," in the opinion of Edwards. But there was deeper divergence than mere Arminianism. Unitarianism was not professed, or publicly advocated, in New England circles during the eighteenth century; but, if we may judge from the writings of orthodox divines, there must have been a good deal of favor shown it in private, for, beginning with Samuel Mather's tract on the *Necessity of Believing the Doctrine of the Trinity,* in 1718, there was a considerable series of defenses of the doctrine by divines little known, such as Kent, Burr, Barnard, and Alexander,[1] the last of whom wrote in 1791. The leaders of New England opinion were no less concerned, for Edwards once wrote to Wigglesworth, professor of divinity in Harvard College, warning him against the rise of an alien system of thought, but to no purpose. In 1758 Bellamy printed a *Treatise on the Divinity of Christ,*[2] exclusively exegetical.[3] In 1768 Hopkins preached in Boston a sermon upon the divinity of Christ, "under a conviction," as he says, "that the doctrine was much neglected, if not disbelieved, by a number of ministers in Boston." [4] There were some open signs of this fact, for in 1756 "a layman" had caused to be printed in Boston extracts from the *Humble Inquiry* of Emlyn, above mentioned, which gained an astonishing influence. The book is so essentially weak that it provokes examination to discover, if possible, why it seemed so convincing to many.

The argument of the first chapter is "that the term God is used in the Scriptures in different senses, supreme and subordinate;" and "that our Lord Jesus Christ speaks of another as God, distinct from him, and owns this God to be above or over him." The reasoning has no points of novelty to one acquainted with discussions upon the Trinity. Emlyn lays special stress upon the passage which speaks of the subjection of the Son, "that God may be all

---

[1] A pretty good bibliography of this minor controversy may be had in Dexter's *Congregationalism,* Bibliography, Nos. 2908, 2958, 2962, 2964, 3123, 3232, 3350, 3421, 3525, 3642, 3786, 3815, 3867, 3954, 3973.

[2] *Works,* Vol. I, pp. 417–41.

[3] Rev. John Barnard, of Marblehead, preached a "public lecture" in Boston, July 16, 1761, on "The True Divinity of Jesus Christ."

[4] Reviewed in *Spirit of the Pilgrims,* Vol. III, pp. 582–91.

in all" (I Cor. 15:24–28). The texts he quotes to show
that there are different senses of the word "God" in the
Scriptures are: Ps. 8:5; Ex. 4:16; Eph. 1:3, 17; that
Jesus speaks of another God: Matt. 27:46; John 7:17;
that the Father is superior to Jesus: John 14:28; 10:29;
5:20; 6:38.

All this contained nothing novel or in any way convincing to a theologian. The influence of the work must have
largely depended upon the representations of the second
chapter. Emlyn here argues that "our Lord Jesus Christ
disclaims those infinite perfections which belong only to
the supreme God, underived power, absolute goodness, unlimited knowledge." For this assertion he refers to the
texts: John 5:30; Matt. 19:17; Mark 13:32. He then
asks: What evidence is there of these "two natures" which
are brought in to explain the difficulties presented by the
passages cited:

> Our Lord Jesus Christ, if himself was the supreme God in any
> nature, could not have said such things as that he "did not know the
> day nor the hour" etc. . . . . He puts not the distinction of two
> natures between the Son of Man and the Eternal Word, but between
> the Son and the Father, "not the Son knows, but only the Father." [5]

Emlyn then dwells upon the necessity of taking Scripture
in its obvious meaning, etc., etc. He thus sharply brought
forward the question whether the orthodox party could
maintain its ground in the forum of ratiocination. Was
the theory of the two natures correct? Was it so managed
as to meet the difficulties raised by the evident limitations
laid upon the attributes of Christ? He thus smote the
weak point of the historic Calvinism, which had been open,
from the time of Calvin down, to the charge of substantial
Nestorianism—not a Nestorianism of profession or inten-

[5] Emlyn himself gathered together in 1719 twelve of his own tracts, reach-
ing from the *Humble Inquiry* of 1702 to 1710. He discussed, among other
things, the text I John 5:7, and showed good critical ability. Dependent upon
Mill.

tion, but of inability to bring the two natures of Christ into anything more than a formal union. Calvinism held to "the unity of the person" which Chalcedon had declared, but it treated the divinity and humanity so as to render any true unity impossible. The demand was now sharply thrust upon the Calvinism of New England either to justify her exegesis by a satisfactory theology, or to surrender her doctrine of the trinity. This was the significance of Emlyn's book, and, I think, the secret of its influence.

The confusion caused by the Revolutionary War put a stop to the open discussion of the subject, and the general unpopularity of Unitarian views led, by a natural tendency, to pass them over with little mention. But soon after the close of the war, King's Chapel in Boston, the original Episcopal church of Massachusetts, became Unitarian under the lead of its pastor, James Freeman (1785). The liturgy was modified to omit all passages objectionable to Unitarians. In 1786 Mr. Freeman sought ordination from Bishop Seabury in Connecticut. At an examination which he sustained before the convocation, he declared his belief in the unity of God and the entire distinction of Christ from God, and explained the divine attributes of Christ— omnipotence, omniscience, etc.—as derived from the Father.[6] He was accordingly refused ordination, and subsequently ordained by his own church, congregationally. He remained in the pastorate of King's Chapel till his death, exercising a wide influence. His preaching was attractive, polished, plain, and practical. That he never rose to the height of the sublimest themes of the gospel may easily be seen from the volume of sermons published in 1821. Upon Good Friday he preached upon "The Tenderness of Jesus," at Christmas upon "Jesus Christ the

---

[6] I depend here upon Sprague's *Annals*, Unitarian. Freeman does not seem to have been specially influenced by the peculiar trend of Emlyn's book.

Prince of Peace," in which sermon, after mentioning the work of Christ as consisting in two particulars—that God in him reconciles us to himself, and that the Savior is the author of inward peace, or tranquility of heart—he goes on to discuss the latter under the heads that Christ (1) teaches us the value of true humility, (2) creates true piety, and (3) teaches us to practice true benevolence. Under (2) he incidentally gives us his view of the character of God, which is a kind of abridgment of his whole theology. He says:

> He came . . . . to reveal to the whole of the human race the most important of all truths, which was before known to one favored nation only,—that there is one God, who has always existed and always will exist; whose power is unlimited, and who is everywhere present; who is not blind and insensible like fate, but who possesses moral attributes, and can be adored and feared and loved; who is wise, just, and good; who created the heavens, the earth, everything which we behold, and which we can even conceive; who gives us every blessing which we enjoy; who never sports with the miseries of his creatures, but who delights in making us happy, and whenever he afflicts us, has a wise and gracious design; who is not only our maker and governor, but our friend; who has compassion on our infirmities, is ready to pardon our sins as soon as we repent, and pities us as a father pities his own children; and who in particular so loved the world as to send his son to reveal these consolatory truths. We need hear no more. If there is such a being, our hearts are at rest. The prince of peace has expelled every doubt and terrour.

Thus Unitarianism in its essential features—in its denial of the divinity of Christ, of total depravity, of the expiatory nature of the atonement [7]—and in the characteristic style of its preaching, was established in Boston before the close of the eighteenth century, though not yet in any of the original Congregational churches, at least professedly.

In Connecticut two clergymen were removed from their parishes by council about the beginning of the century,

[7] See Ellis, *Fifty Years*, p. 46.

one of whom, Rev. John Sherman, published at Worcester, in 1805, a work defending Unitarianism, entitled *One God in One Person Only and Jesus Christ a Being Distinct from God,* etc., in which he went over the entire argument for the Trinity and attempted to overthrow it at every point, principally by exegetical arguments. He was somewhat dependent upon Emlyn.

In 1795 Timothy Dwight had been called to the presidency of Yale College, to find that institution thoroughly permeated with the spirit of French infidelity.[8] He grappled with the situation at once, and by the strength of his character as well as his mind soon produced a great revulsion of sentiment and a general return to evangelical religion. About the year 1800, largely in consequence of influences emanating from New Haven, a revival of religion spread over southern New England, resulting in a new period in the religion and theology of America. Massachusetts and Harvard had suffered in like manner with Yale, although the theological tendency was quite another, as our history has detailed. The revival seems to have had little or no influence here, and no such man as Dwight appeared who could reverse the current; and soon a decisive step was taken which confirmed the influence of Unitarianism for long years.

The chief position of theological influence in Massachusetts was the professorship of divinity in Harvard College, founded in the early part of the eighteenth century by Thomas Hollis, an English Baptist. This professorship fell vacant in 1803, and was filled in 1805, after a sharp contest, by the appointment of Henry Ware. It was generally understood, and soon became certain, that he was a Unitarian. Some discussion of the propriety of this step

[8] For some of the reasons of this see I. W. Riley, "The Rise of Deism in Yale College," *American Journal of Theology,* Vol. IX (1905), pp. 474 ff.

followed, and a good many fugitive tracts were published upon the main question, but no general controversy arose. It was, however, felt that Harvard would no longer be a suitable place for the education of orthodox ministers, and a theological seminary was founded in Phillips Academy at Andover (1808).[9]

In 1810 appeared Noah Worcester's *Bible News,* one of the most original and respectable of these earlier discussions, the unsophisticated boldness of which was perhaps the chief reason why it seemed to have little influence on the Unitarian side. His doctrine is "that the self-existent God is only one person . . . . that Jesus Christ is God's own Son . . . . that by the Holy Ghost is intended the fullness of God, or the efficient, productive emanations of the divine fullness."[10] "Person" he defines as "intelligent being," and therefore denies three persons in one God as being a contradiction.

The most important portion of the book is that occupied with the person of Christ.

Two ideas are naturally suggested by the title, the Son of God, viz., divine origin and divine dignity. By divine origin I do not mean that the Son of God is a *created* intelligent being; but a being who properly derived his existence and his nature from God. . . . . Adam was a created being; Seth derived his existence from the created nature of Adam. . . . . So it is believed that the only begotten Son of the Father derived his existence from the self-existent nature of God.[11]

His argument for this position is the plain meaning of the term "Son." The divine dignity of the Son came from his

[9] See Professor Leonard Woods, *History of the Andover Theological Seminary* (Boston, 1885), p. 58. There was, however, another distinct line of influences, arising from the necessity of further instruction for the ministry, such as had been furnished by Bellamy, Emmons, Backus, and a number of others, before any doubt had been thrown upon the character of the Hollis professorship, and from the wish of the Hopkinsians to maintain what they regarded as genuine Calvinism, which would have led to the formation of a seminary without regard to the events at Harvard. This is brought out in Wood's *History* with great fulness.

[10] *Op. cit.,* p. 26.

[11] *Ibid.,* p. 57.

divine origin and from the communication to him of the divine fulness, whereby he did divine works, creation, etc. This pre-existent Son of God "became the Son of man by becoming himself the soul of a human body." [12] Incidentally Worcester brings out many suggestions as to the unity of the person of Christ to which the orthodox should have paid more attention, as when he speaks of the "identity of the Son of God and the Son of man." [13] The possibility of the suffering of Christ in his divine nature he grounds in his difference from the underived and self-existent God, who is impassible. To this Son are due divine honors because of "the will of God." [14]

With such discussions as these [15] Unitarianism progressed slowly. But without exciting much attention, till in 1815 there was republished in Boston a part of a life of Lindsley by Belsham, both English Unitarians, in which the progress of Unitarianism in America was described to Lindsley by letters from Unitarians in this country. The work was reviewed by the *Panoplist,* and a sharp controversy arose upon the necessity of a separation between the orthodox and the Unitarians. Channing wrote upon this topic; [16] but the beginning of the theological controversy was made by him in a sermon preached at the ordination of Jared Sparks, subsequently president of Harvard College, in the year 1819.

Upon the eve of this controversy, by far the most important event in the history of Congregational theology,

[12] *Ibid.,* p. 102. [13] *Ibid.,* p. 108.

[14] *Ibid.,* p. 35. In 1814 Worcester published an *Appeal to the Candid,* chiefly controversial.

[15] Rev. J. S. J. Gardiner, rector of Trinity church, Boston, joined in the discussion with a sermon on *A Preservative Against Unitarianism* (Boston, 1811). So did Thomas Baldwin, D.D., pastor of the Second Baptist Church, *Supreme Deity of Christ,* Illustrated (Boston, 1812). Also G. B. English, *Grounds of Christianity Examined* (Boston, 1813), which took the ground that Jesus was not the Messiah, and attacked the character of Paul.

[16] *The System of Exclusion and Denunciation in Religion Considered.*

it is necessary that we pause to review briefly the leading positions which New England theology had gained. We have now followed it to a point of high development, from its very beginning. We have seen that the occasion of modification in every case was the presence of some real danger to the faith: with Edwards, of Arminianism; with the younger Edwards and his associates upon the doctrine of the atonement, of Universalism: or else it was the inherent power of a new principle; with Hopkins, that of disinterested benevolence; with Emmons, that of agency as exercise. In their own conception the New England fathers were always defending the truth, not by giving it up, but rather by stating it better. Thus they remained in conscious sympathy with their Calvinistic fathers, and thus called themselves Calvinists, and quoted and taught the Westminster Catechism, though in fact they had substantially abandoned the philosophy and many of the minor doctrines of the Westminster scheme. For the arbitrary will of God they had substituted his character, love; for a sinful nature, a nature occasioning sin; for imputation, a strict personal responsibility; for a limited, a general atonement; for a bound, a free will; for a satisfaction to justice in the atonement, a governmental example; for irresistible grace, unresisted. Not all points were clear; not all antitheses as sharp as later; not all necessary details worked out. Hence their reply, when they were first attacked, was bungling, confused, and largely ineffective. On the other hand, the assailant, Channing, was a product of advanced orthodox thinking. At first himself substantially orthodox, he had followed out certain of the principles of the new divinity far beyond their logical conclusions into an extreme which, while false, was so clear and comprehensible, as extreme positions when superficially considered often are, that it was rendered easy for him to avail himself of his great power of luminous and trenchant discourse to give plausibility, attractiveness, and large influence to his views. We shall see that the natural result followed, that the favorable moment of acknowledging what was good, of pointing out what was extreme in the positions of the Unitarians, and thus of winning them back to the evangelical theology, was lost, while only slowly did the orthodox learn what the controversy had to teach them, and that at the expense of costly contentions among themselves.

Channing's sermon, preached upon the occasion of the ordination of a professed Unitarian, in a city, Baltimore, where such views were novel and regarded with the greatest suspicion, left the usual path of ordination discourses for an elaborate exposition and defense of Unitarianism.[17] It treated its subject under two heads: principles adopted in interpreting the Scriptures, and the doctrines drawn by this interpretation from the Scriptures. Under the first head the principles of interpretation generally recognized by sound exegesis were detailed, such as the necessity of attention to the context, the subject discussed, the purpose, etc., of the writer, and the genius of the language employed. In all this there was little to be criticized, except some indications of the manner in which the principles enumerated would be applied. A defense of human reason is also introduced, denying its depravation so as to be unworthy of our confidence, emphasizing our responsibility for a right use of it, and rejecting the possibility of believing manifest contradictions under the guise of truths above reason.

We ought, indeed, to expect occasional obscurity in such a book as the Bible, which was written for past and future ages as well as the

[17] It may be found in the popular edition of Channing's works, published by the American Unitarian Association in 1875, and widely distributed (pp. 367–84).

present. But God's wisdom is a pledge that whatever is necessary for *us,* and necessary for salvation, is revealed too plainly to be mistaken, and too consistently to be questioned, by a sound and upright mind. It is not the mark of wisdom to use an unintelligible phraseology, to communicate what is above our capacities, to confuse and unsettle the intellect by appearances of contradiction. We honor our Heavenly Teacher too much to ascribe to him such a revelation. A revelation is a gift of light. It cannot thicken our darkness and multiply our perplexities.[18]

Under the second head the first doctrine considered was the unity of God, "or that there is one God, and one only."

We understand by it that there is one being, one mind, one person, one intelligent agent, and one only, to whom underived and infinite perfection and dominion belong. . . . . We find no intimation that this language was to be taken in an unusual sense, or that God's unity was a quite different thing from the oneness of other intelligent beings.

He continues:

We object to the doctrine of the Trinity that, whilst acknowledging in words, it subverts in effect, the unity of God. According to this doctrine, there are three infinite and equal persons, possessing supreme divinity, called the Father, Son, and Holy Ghost. Each of these three persons, as described by theologians, has his own particular consciousness, will and perceptions. They love each other, converse with each other, and delight in each other's society. They perform different parts in man's redemption, each having his appropriate office, and neither doing the work of the other. The Son is mediator, and not the Father. The Father sends the Son, and is not himself sent; nor is he conscious, like the Son, of taking flesh. Here, then, we have three intelligent agents, possessed of different consciousnesses, different wills, and different perceptions, performing differents acts, and sustaining different relations; and if these things do not imply and constitute three minds or beings, we are utterly at a loss to know how three minds or beings are to be formed. It is difference of properties, and acts, and consciousness, which leads to the belief of different intelligent beings, and, if this mark fails us, our whole knowledge falls; we have no proof that all the agents and persons in the universe are not one and the same mind. When we attempt to conceive of three Gods, we can do nothing more than represent to ourselves three agents, distinguished from each other by similar marks and peculiarities to those which separate the persons of the Trinity; and when

18 *Edit. cit.,* p. 370.

common Christians hear these persons spoken of as conversing with each other, loving each other, and performing different acts, how can they help regarding them as different beings, different minds? [19]

This is the principal argument, though the usage of the New Testament is variously urged. "We challenge our opponents to adduce one passage in the New Testament where the word God means three persons, where it is not limited to one person, and where, unless turned from its usual sense by the connection, it does not mean the Father." [20] The impossibility of stating the doctrine in scriptural language is urged. The injury of the doctrine to devotion, "not only by joining to the Father other objects of worship, but by taking from the Father the supreme affection which is his due and transferring it to the Son," [21] is commented upon. "The worship of a bleeding, suffering God . . . . awakens human transport rather than that deep veneration of the moral perfections of God which is the essence of piety." [22]

The second doctrine considered is the unity of Christ. Channing delivers his objection to the orthodox doctrine in the following terms:

According to this doctrine, Jesus Christ, instead of being one mind, one conscious, intelligent principle, whom we can understand, consists of two souls, two minds; the one divine, the other human; the one weak, the other almighty; the one ignorant, the other omniscient. Now we maintain that this is to make Christ two beings. To denominate him one person, one being, and yet to suppose him made up of two minds, infinitely different from each other, is to abuse and confound language, and to throw darkness over all our conceptions of intelligent natures. According to the common doctrine, each of these two minds in Christ has its own consciousness, its own will, its own perceptions. They have, in fact, no common properties. The divine mind feels none of the wants and sorrows of the human, and the human is infinitely removed from the perfection and happiness of the divine. Can you conceive of two beings in the universe more distinct?

[19] *Ibid.*, p. 371.   [20] *Ibid.*, p. 371.
[21] *Ibid.*, p. 372.   [22] *Ibid.*, p. 373.

We have always thought that one person was constituted and distinguished by one consciousness. The doctrine that one and the same person should have two consciousnesses, two wills, two souls, infinitely different from each other, this we think an enormous tax on human credulity.[23]

He objects to the orthodox doctrine, therefore, principally in the name of simplicity and clearness of thought, but he also urges against it the teaching of the New Testament.

Other Christians, indeed, tell us that this doctrine is necessary to the harmony of the Scriptures, that some texts ascribe to Jesus human, and others divine properties, and that to reconcile these we must suppose two minds, to which these properties may be referred. In other words, for the purpose of reconciling certain difficult passages, which a just criticism can in a great degree, if not wholly, explain, we must invent an hypothesis vastly more difficult, and involving gross absurdity. We are to find our way out of a labyrinth by a clue which conducts us into mazes infinitely more inextricable.[24]

In opposition to this he propounded the doctrine that Christ was "one mind, one being, and a being distinct from the one God." The Scripture argument may be compressed in the single paragraph:

He is continually spoken of as the Son of God, sent of God, receiving all his powers from God, working miracles because God was with him; judging justly because God taught him, having claims on our belief because he was anointed and sealed by God, and as able of himself to do nothing. The New Testament is filled with this language. Now we ask what impression this language was fitted and intended to make? Could any who heard it have imagined that Jesus was the very God to whom he was so industriously declared to be inferior?[25]

The argument from the relations of the doctrine to the atonement is also considered, and the infinity of the atonement denied because only the human nature could have suffered. Indeed, this fact reduces, according to Channing, the whole humiliation to a fiction, since the God, who was

[23] *Loc. cit.*, p. 373.   [24] *Ibid.*, pp. 373 f.
[25] *Ibid.*, p. 374.

the real Christ, "was infinitely happy at the very moment of the suffering of his humanity."

What exactly Christ was, whether mere man or angelic being, Channing does not at all attempt to say.

Up to this point Channing had said little to betray his own connection with the New England school. His vindication of the reason was, indeed, the position which anyone who had at all imbibed the spirit of the bold speculation of these theologians from Edwards down must take. He is presenting a new issue, and forcing it upon the attention of his contemporaries. It is the same great objection which Emlyn had made—the call for a justification or a surrender of an unintelligible doctrine of God and Christ. What had been done in public consideration of that objection as yet was entirely inadequate. Channing not only demanded, he secured a new consideration. This was his position and service in the controversy.

He advances next in the Baltimore sermon to the "moral perfection of God."

We believe that God is infinitely good, kind, benevolent, in the proper sense of these words,—good in disposition as well as in act; good not to a few but to all; good to every individual, as well as to the general system.[26]

He maintains also God's justice, but it is a justice consistent with the benevolence of God, which he defines as "God's infinite regard to virtue or moral worth expressed in a moral government; that is in giving excellent and equitable laws and conferring such rewards and inflicting such punishments as are best fitted to secure their observance." [27] All this is in entire agreement with Hopkins, from whom Channing cordially acknowledged that he had received many ideas. But the application of the principle was entirely different from that of Channing's New Eng-

[26] *Ibid.*, p. 376.　　　　　[27] *Ibid.*

land predecessors. The two doctrines of total depravity, both in its original Calvinistic form, and in the form which it had taken under the modification of Edwards, and of election, are declared inconsistent with God's moral perfection, and to be rejected.

> According to the plainest principles of morality, we maintain that a natural constitution of the mind, unfailingly disposing it to evil, and to evil alone, would absolve it from guilt; that to give existence under this condition would argue unspeakable cruelty; and that to punish the sin of this unhappily constituted child with endless ruin would be a wrong unparalleled by the most merciless despotism.[28]

The next doctrine considered is the atonement. Jesus came to effect "a moral or spiritual deliverance of mankind." He accomplishes this by a variety of methods, by his instructions and example, and by his death. As to the force of his death, Channing says that Unitarians are not agreed. Some think "that we ought to consider this event as having a special influence in removing punishment, though the Scriptures may not reveal the way in which it contributes to this end."[29] He strongly objects to all views, as dishonorable to God, which maintain that his disposition toward men is changed by the death of Christ; and, particularly, the doctrine of satisfaction to justice, even in the form that the death of Christ is in any sense an equivalent for the punishment of men, is unbiblical and impossible. "According to this doctrine, God, instead of being plenteous in forgiveness, never forgives."[30]

The sermon closes with a head upon the nature of Christian virtue, in which the positive doctrine is Edwardean, but the negative part consists in objections to irresistible grace and infused character, with remarks upon the duty of charity and love, against which nothing is to be said, except that possibly a subtle plea for latitudinarianism was hidden under the phraseology employed.

[28] *Loc. cit.*, p. 377.   [29] *Ibid.*, p. 378.   [30] *Ibid.*, p. 379.

Channing engaged again in the controversy, but, except in form, or in greater fulness at certain points, he added little to the contribution which he made in this historic sermon. In the sermon upon "Unitarian Christianity Most Favorable to Piety" (1826) he objects very strongly to the doctrine of the incarnation as infringing upon the spirituality of God, and renewed his objections to the doctrine of an infinite satisfaction for sin, comparing the cross to "a gallows in the center of the universe," and terming the idea of a satisfaction "wholly delusion." Nowhere is his power of felicitous statement more conspicuous than in this sermon, and nowhere is his fundamental objection to all Calvinism more evident. He rejects it because it is, as he thinks, a contradiction of the reasonableness of the divine love.

Thus we see that Channing was intimately acquainted with the teachings of our New England leaders, especially with those of Hopkins,[31] and that in some respects his positions had grown out of theirs and represented the extreme to which those positions could be pushed. It was therefore incumbent upon New England orthodoxy, not only because of the force with which he had presented it with a new issue, vital to itself in common with all evangelical theology, but because its own essential character and the validity of its own positions and their evangelical soundness were all put to the question, to answer Channing thoroughly.

The challenge of Channing was taken up by Moses Stuart,[32] professor of sacred literature in Andover Seminary, in *Letters* published at Andover (1819). He ac-

[31] He has a very interesting passage on Hopkins in his sermon on "Christian Worship."

[32] Moses Stuart, born at Wilton, Conn., March 26, 1780; died at Andover, January 4, 1852; graduated at Yale, 1799; admitted to the bar, 1802; ordained and settled in New Haven, 1806; called to Andover, 1810; served as professor till 1848. "The father of biblical learning in this country."

cepted with some slight criticisms Channing's general discussion of the principles of interpretation, and then passed
to the treatment of the main doctrines discussed.

On the Trinity he began the discussion with the
words:

> Admitting that you have given a fair account of our belief, I
> cannot see, indeed, why we are not virtually guilty of tritheism, or
> at least of something which approximates so near to it that I ac-
> knowledge myself unable to distinguish it from tritheism. But I
> cannot help feeling that you have made neither an impartial nor a cor-
> rect statement of what we believe and what we are accustomed to
> teach and defend.[33]

But it is evident that some justification for his understanding of current orthodoxy might have been urged by
Channing, as even Stuart was ready to admit. Emmons,
for example, who had been, ten years before, the most
prominent figure among the New England leaders, uses
the following language in his sermons upon the Trinity:

> The Scripture represents the Father, Son, and Holy Ghost as dis-
> tinctly possessed of personal properties. The Father is represented as
> being able to understand, to will, and to act of himself. The Son is
> represented as being able to understand, to will, and to act of himself.
> And the Holy Ghost is represented as being able to understand, to will,
> and to act of himself. According to these representations, the Father,
> Son, and Holy Ghost are three distinct persons or agents.[34]

He speaks also of "society" [35] in the Godhead, of the
different persons making a "covenant of redemption," and
teaches that there are three persons, not in one *person,* but
in one *being.*[36] This is a denial of the uni-personality of
God. In a word, almost all the phrases to which Channing
objects are to be found in Emmons, as well as in many a
lesser light of orthodoxy.

[33] I employ, at the present writing, the reprint by Stuart himself, of 1846.
See p. 15.

[34] Emmons' *Works,* Vol. II, p. 134.

[35] *Ibid.,* p. 142.

[36] *Ibid.,* pp. 132 f.

Stuart's positive reply to Channing consisted in emphasizing, first, the *numerical* unity of the Godhead.

I am now prepared to say that I believe that God is *one, numerically one, in essence and attributes.* In other words, the infinitely perfect Spirit, the Creator and Preserver of all things, the Father, Son, and Holy Ghost, has *numerically* the *same essence,* and the *same perfections,* so far as they are known to us. To particularize; the Son possesses not simply a *similar* or *equal* essence and perfections, but *numerically the same* as the Father, without division, and without multiplication.[37]

He next affirms that "the Son (and also the Holy Spirit) does, in some respect *truly* and *really,* not merely nominally or logically, differ from the Father." The objection of Channing had been, however, that this difference was so conceived as to destroy the unity which Stuart had just now reasserted. He consequently felt himself compelled to adjust the two ideas, which he attempted to do by a discussion of the word "person."

The common language of the Trinitarian symbols is, that *"there are three persons in the Godhead."* In your comments upon this, you have all along explained the word *person,* just as though it were an established point, that Trinitarians use this word in such a connection, in its *ordinary* acceptation as applied to *men.* But can you satisfy yourself that this is doing us justice? What fact is plainer from church history, than that the word *person* was introduced into the creeds of ancient times, merely as a term which would somewhat strongly express the disagreement of Christians in general with the reputed errors of the Sabellians, and others of similar sentiments, who denied the existence of any *real* distinction in the Godhead, and asserted that the Father, Son, and Holy Ghost, were merely *attributes* of God, or the names of different ways in which he revealed himself to mankind, or of different relations which he bore to them, and in which he acted? The Nicene fathers meant to deny the correctness of such views, when they used the word *person.* They designed to imply by it, that there was some *real,* not merely *nominal,* distinction in the Godhead; and that something more than a mere diversity of relation or action of the Godhead in respect to us, was intended. They used the word *person,* because they supposed it approximated nearer to expressing the existence of a

[37] *Letters,* p. 18.

real distinction, than any other which they could choose. Most certainly, neither they, nor any intelligent Trinitarian, could use this term in such a latitude as you represent us as employing it, and as you attach to it. We profess to use it merely because of the poverty of language; merely to designate our belief of a *real* distinction in the Godhead; but not to describe independent, conscious beings, possessing separate and equal essences and perfections. Why should we be obliged so often to explain ourselves on this point? Is there any more difficulty here, or anything more obnoxious, than when you say: "God is angry with the wicked every day"? You defend yourself in the use of such an expression, by saying, that it is only the language of rhetoric and figure; that it is merely intended to describe that in the mind of the Deity, or in his actions, which corresponds in some measure, or in some respect, to anger and its consequences in men; not that God is really affected with the passion of anger. Why will you not permit me, then, to say that we speak of *persons* in the Godhead, in order to express that which in some respect or other corresponds to *persons* as applied to men, i. e., *some distinction: not* that we attach to it the meaning of three beings, with a *separate* consciousness, will, omnipotence, omniscience, etc.? Where, then, considering the poverty of language in respect to expressing what belongs to the Deity, is our inconsistency in this, or how is there any absurdity in our language, providing there is a real foundation in the Scriptures on which we may rest the *fact* of a distinction, which we believe to exist? [38]

He says further:

I receive the fact that it exists, simply because I believe that the Scriptures reveal the fact. And if the Scriptures do reveal the fact that there are three *persons* in the Godhead (in the sense explained); that there is a distinction, which affords grounds for the respective appellations of Father, Son, and Holy Ghost; which lays the foundation for the application of the personal pronouns, *I, Thou, He;* which renders it proper to speak of *sending* and *being sent;* to speak of Christ as *being with God, being in his bosom,* and of other things of the like nature in the like way, and yet to hold that the divine nature belongs equally to each; then it is, like every other fact revealed, to be received simply on the credit of divine revelation.[39]

This was, in a sense, the reduction of the Trinity to **its** lowest terms—to a form of statement in which there could be nothing to quarrel about because it was so low

[38] *Loc. cit.,* p. 20.
[39] *Ibid.,* p. 23.

and indistinct. Yet some elements of definiteness were left. He continues:

In regard to this distinction, we say: *It is not a mere distinction of attributes, of relation to us, of modes of action, or of relation between attributes and substance or essence,* so far as they are known to us. We believe the Scriptures justify us in these *negations.* But *here* we leave the subject. We undertake (at least the Trinitarians of our country with whom I am acquainted undertake) *not* at all to describe *affirmatively* the distinction in the Godhead. When you will give me an affirmative description of underived existence, I may safely engage to furnish you with one of *person* in the trinity. You do not reject the belief of the divine self-existence, merely because you cannot affirmatively define it;' neither do we of a distinction in the Godhead, because we cannot affirmatively define it.

And he warns Channing against confounding *"terms* which are *unintelligible,* and *things* which are *undefinable."* [40]

Stuart then brings forward a number of examples from church history to show that early writers, particularly Tertullian, had not succeeded very well in presenting clear affirmative definitions of the distinction between the different "persons" of the Trinity. He does not find the Nicene Fathers themselves to have been more successful. The doctrine of "eternal generation" which they presented Stuart did not find to possess any "definite meaning" to his mind. Any intimation of the derivation of the divine nature of the Son he regards as trenching upon his supreme divinity, which, if it is divinity at all, must be underived. "The Nicene creed then is not, I must confess, sufficiently orthodox for me," he says.[41] He thus briefly indicated as a part of his reply to Channing the elimination from the theology of the Trinity of the doctrine of eternal generation. He later expanded these ideas in letters to Dr. Miller on his *Eternal Generation.* His position, as more clearly expressed there, was as follows:

[40] *Ibid.,* pp. 24, 25.   [41] *Ibid.,* p. 31.

The subject necessitated "two inquiries, viz., Is the generation of the Son eternal? and, Is that generation voluntary or necessary? . . . . In other words, Did the early Fathers believe that the Logos was not only eternal, but that he was Son eternally?" [42]   Stuart believed that the Logos was "truly eternal," but he questioned whether he was "eternally the Son of God." He was thus led into an elaborate examination of the Fathers and of the various definitions of eternal generation which have been given, with the general result that they are full of contradictions both of expression and of thought. The "generic idea of eternal generation" he finds to lie in the "general idea of derivation and dependence, in some respect or other, of the Logos upon the Father." [43]   This idea he conceives to be inconsistent with self-existence, and so to be impossible of application to the Logos, who is God, and therefore self-existent.[44]

The following passage expresses his fundamental objection to the doctrine:

Any theory, then, respecting the person of the Son of God which makes the Logos a derived being, destroys the radical principle—an elementary ingredient, of his true and proper divinity. I believe that the Logos is really and verily divine—self-existent, uncaused, independent, immutable in himself. Derivation in any shape or in any measure; as to all or part of his essential predicates as God—whether you apply to it the name generation, emanation, creation, procession, or any other term which has been used—derivation, I say, appears essentially incompatible with proper divinity. And so plain does this appear to my mind that, if I once admit the proper derivation of the Logos (be the derivation eternal or in time), the idea of the supreme divinity vanishes in a moment; and the Logos ranks with those who are called God only from some resemblance, either of station or of office, or of moral or intellectual qualities, to the self-existent deity.[45]

His own doctrine of the sonship is as follows: (1) "Christ is called the Son of God because, in respect to his

42 *Letters* (Andover, 1822), pp. 17 ff.   43 *Ibid.*, pp. 88, 90.
44 *Ibid.*, pp. 91, 92.   45 *Ibid.*, pp. 92 f.

human nature, he is derived from God." He refers at this point to Luke 1 :35. "John says not a word concerning the Son until he has mentioned the incarnation of the Logos." [46] (2) As Messiah.[47]

This thoroughgoing rejection of the "eternal sonship," which is an essential part of the New England answer to Unitarianism, as formulated by Stuart, though not technically belonging to the reply to Channing, relieved somewhat the difficulties raised by him. But Stuart had more fundamental answers to make. He declared that Unitarians were as incompetent to define the unity of God as the orthodox were his trinity. He thus anticipated in everything but sharpness of form N. W. Taylor's exposure of the fundamental fallacy of Unitarianism, which consisted, as he said, in the assumption, totally unwarranted, that the unity of God is like our unity, and, because this is a perfect simplicity, that of God's must also be.

Familiar as the assertion is, in your conversation and in your sermons, that God is one, can you give me any other definition of this oneness, except a negative one? You deny plurality of it; you say God is but one, and not two, nor more. All this is mere negation. In what, I ask, does the divine unity actually and positively consist? God surely has different and various faculties and powers. Is he not almighty, omniscient, omnipresent, holy, just, good? Does he not act differently, i. e. variously, both in the natural and in the moral world? Unity, therefore, is not an universal sameness of attribute or of action. Does it consist, then, appropriately in his essence? . . . . Is it possible to show what it is, which constitutes the internal nature of the divine nature or attributes? To show how these are related to each other, or what internal distinctions exist? . . . . The assertion that God is one means, when fairly and intelligently understood, nothing more positively than that he is numerically one, i. e. it simply denies polytheism. . . . . That God is one, does not mean that there is but one simple element in his nature (for this we do not and cannot know), but that there

[46] *Ibid.*, p. 111.

[47] *Ibid.*, p. 115. Stuart expressed some surprise that his treatment of the sonship of Christ had met with so sharp criticism, and declared that his views were those common in New England. In this statement he is confirmed by Noah Worcester, *Bible News*, pp. 169, 170.

is in him only one intelligent agent. . . . . In respect to principle, then, what more difficulty lies in the way of believing in the threefold distinction of the Godhead, than in believing in the divine unity? [48]

He closes this portion of the discussion by an ingenious answer to the brief and common argument of Unitarians: "How can three be one, and one three?"

In no way, I readily answer, provided the one and the three both relate to the same specific thing, and in the same respect. "How then is the doctrine of the Trinity in Unity to be vindicated?" In a way, I would reply, which is not at all embarrassed by these, or by any of the like, questions. . . . . Supposed I should affirm that two subjects A and B are numerically identical in regard to what may be called X, but diverse or distinct in regard to something else called Y; is there any absurdity or contradiction in this affirmation? . . . . We do not maintain that the Godhead is three in the same respects that it is one, but the reverse. In regard to X, we maintain a numerical unity; in regard to Y we maintain a threefold distinction. [49]

Stuart now advanced to Channing's second and more vital point—his objection to the orthodox doctrine as destructive of the unity of Christ. The reply is all summed up in the one sentence that the doctrine of the two natures in Christ is "a fact with which natural religion has no concern; at least, of which it has no knowledge." [50] The determination of the dispute must therefore lie exclusively in the sphere of exegesis. But rational elements could not, of course, be wholly excluded, and Stuart recognizes the difficulty which Channing had formulated afresh, which was the old difficulty handed down from Chalcedon unsolved: how to conceive of Christ, while both divine and human, as truly one person, possessed of a single consciousness. Chalcedon itself had so balanced the two natures over against one another as almost to render a true unity impossible. Calvinistic theology since had emphasized the twofoldness at the expense of the unity. Stuart did the same. He intended to maintain the unity, for he

[48] *Loc. cit.*, p. 41.   [49] *Ibid.*, p. 43.

[50] *Ibid.*, p. 49.

says that we "recognize and distinguish, in this complex being, but *one person,* and therefore speak of but one." [51] He even went so far as to make some suggestions as to how this union was effected.

> God cannot divest himself of his essential perfections. . . . . In whatever way, then, the union of the two natures was effected, it was so brought about that it neither destroyed nor essentially changed, either the divine or human nature. . . . . One person in the sense in which each of us is one, Christ could not be.

The last sentence might seem to deny the unity of the person of Christ; but the context shows that Stuart meant one person, *made up in the same manner as we,* Christ could not be.   He continues:

> One person in the sense in which each of us is one, Christ could not be. If we, with some of the fathers, make God the soul and Jesus of Nazareth the body of Christ, then we take away his human nature, and deny the imperfection of his knowledge. But may not God have been, in a manner altogether peculiar and mysterious, united to Jesus, without displaying at once his whole power in him, or necessarily rendering him, as a man, supremely perfect? In the act of creation, God does not put forth *all* his power; nor in the preservation of created things; nor in sanctification; nor does he bring all his knowledge into action, when he inspires prophets and apostles. Was it necessary that he should exert all his attributes to the full, when he was in conjunction with the human nature of Christ? In governing the world from day to day, God does not surely exhaust his omnipotence, or his wisdom. He employs only so much as is necessary to accomplish the design which he has in view. In his union with Jesus of Nazareth, the divine Logos could not, of course, be necessitated at once to put forth all his energy, or exhibit all his knowledge and wisdom. Just so much of it, and no more, was manifested, as was requisite to constitute the character of an all-sufficient and incarnate Mediator and Redeemer. When necessary, power and authority infinitely above human were displayed; when otherwise, the human nature sympathized and suffered like that of other men.

This passage contains suggestions which Stuart never expands and which received scanty attention from his contemporaries. It is a little uncertain what he meant.   He

[51] *Ibid.,* p. 50.

may have foreshadowed the same ideas which were later embraced in the theory of the "kenosis;" or, more probably, he was echoing the Lutheran theory that Christ "surrendered, during the period of his humiliation, the *use* of the divine attributes." But though he intended to maintain the unity of Christ's person, he repeatedly surrendered it in this brief passage. "God . . . . united to Jesus:" consistent maintenance of Christ's unity would put it, "God united with humanity," for there was no Jesus till that union was complete, and Jesus was that one person who was both God and man. "Rendering him *as a man* supremely perfect:" here you have the division of the one personality so that some things are to be true of his consciousness as man which are not true of that same and undivided consciousness as God; which is rending the unity. And then that word "conjunction," what does that mean? The divine and human were not in conjunction, but in union. Neither was the divine Logos in "union with Jesus of Nazareth." And his later and more formal definition is equally defective: "When we say that the two natures of Christ are united in one person, we mean to say that divinity and humanity are brought into such a connection in this case, that we cannot separate them, so as to make two entirely distinct and separate agents." [52] How far short that falls of maintaining two natures in the unity of a single consciousness.

Inasmuch as this is all of the rationale of the matter which Stuart presents, confining himself hereafter to proving from the Bible the reality of each of the two natures in Christ, he must be judged to have failed in answering the sharp demand of Unitarianism since the days of Emlyn for an intellectual justification of the doctrine of the person of Christ. To this extent the orthodox reply upon the

[52] *Loc. cit.*, p. 52.

whole was a failure, for others did no better than Stuart did. No one in this period, except the Unitarians, made a reality of the unity of the Redeemer's person. Hence there was no advance in the doctrine of Christology. The Unitarians surrendered the divinity to maintain the unity, and their opponents surrendered the unity, in all but words, for the sake of maintaining the two natures. The controversy at this point only serves to illustrate the nature and urgency of the problem. It is at least doubtful whether the orthodox even saw what the problem was.

The real strength of Stuart's reply, and the element which enabled the evangelical churches to maintain themselves and cast off the Unitarian attack, lay therefore elsewhere. In the battles of thought, as of those of arms, the precise gage thrown down is seldom taken up. Stuart had the larger justification of his method in the fact that he was an exegete and not a dogmatician. In him, for the first time in the history of New England theology, a thoroughly scholarly critic of the New Testament appears upon the stage. The meaning and importance of a genuine theological seminary were beginning to be seen. Emmons had taken for his text, when about to preach his initial sermon upon the Trinity, the spurious text of the three heavenly witnesses (I John 5:7). Stuart fell into no like mistake, but with scholarly accuracy, and with an amplitude of learning which had had no precursor and had no rival, he set forth the biblical argument for the divinity of Christ in the forms which it has since maintained in New England. Christ is called God; there are ascribed to him divine attributes and works—omniscience, omnipotence, eternity; and divine honors are paid to him. The true humanity is also treated at considerable length. Channing, as Stuart remarks with surprise, had never maintained clearly that Christ was truly and properly a man. But Stuart left no doubt upon this subject. In all this we may the more confidently judge that Stuart was, in general, right, that the standard exegesis seems now to have accepted the biblical argument as conclusive, if the investigator accepts biblical authority at all. The position of modern opposers of the Trinity is curiously different from that of the early Massachusetts Unitarians. Instead of denying that John, for example, taught the divinity of Christ, in order to obtain support for their own rejection of it, they at once and most cordially admit that he did and then proceed to get rid of this fact by taking it as a proof that "John" was not written by John, but is the product of a much later period. As that eminent Unitarian scholar, Dr. George E. Ellis, once said, upon the basis of the view of the inspiration and authority of the Scriptures which was common to orthodox and Unitarian at this time, the orthodox certainly had the best of the argument.

The total effect, however, of Stuart's method of reply was in one respect damaging to evangelical theology. Orthodoxy came out of the battle victorious, but maimed. The doctrine of the divinity of Christ was rescued so as to become a practical portion of the faith of our churches, and the real basis of its worship and spiritual life. But the doctrine of the Trinity, viewed as a mere fact, totally inexplicable, and reduced to the simple matter of "distinctions" within the Godhead, lost its place as the great fundamental doctrine of the system. Men did not know what to do with it. It has almost been regarded as a burden upon the system of Christianity. Its apologetic value, especially in the defense of the eternity of God and the doctrine of the creation of matter; its relation to Christian consciousness, as a consciousness of sin and redemption; and its constructive part in the erection of Christian theology, incarnation, atonement, and the rest—have all been largely forgotten. The fear of tritheism has led many a thinker to occupy at times a position scarcely distinguishable from unitarianism. Rationalism can be defeated only by rationalism; and when the false rationalism of the Unitarians was met only by a biblical argument, and not by a true rationalism, the poison of that false rationalism entered to a considerable degree into the theological man and made him too often, in the later days of the school, himself a rationalist.

Stuart's vigorous book brought out soon a sharp answer from a writer who was afterward to be famous as a professor of theology at Cambridge—Andrews Norton, in his *Statement of Reasons for Not Believing the Doctrines of Trinitarians respecting the Nature of God and the Person of Christ* (1819). It seems to have been regarded as conclusive by the Unitarians, for they left it to stand as their only serious attempt at an answer. It was, however, comparatively weak upon the exegetical side, where Stuart was strong, and only strong upon the dogmatical side, where he had been weak.

Norton's fundamental objection to the Trinity is that it is incredible. Thus he says: "Three persons . . . . are three Gods. A person is a being. . . . . The doctrine of the trinity, then, affirms that there are three Gods." [53] And this is a contradiction to the doctrine of one God also affirmed by Trinitarians. After some just criticism upon the phrase "fountain of divinity" used in the ancient church of the Father, who, if the Trinity is eternal and necessary, can be no more underived than the Son or the Spirit, Norton declares that Stuart's doctrine of three "distinctions" is "a mere evasion introduced . . . . for the purpose of rescuing it from the charge of absurdity," [54] and then charges him, with less justice, with immediately relapsing

[53] *Op. cit.,* p. 4.   [54] *Ibid.,* p. 7.

into the common belief.   If he were consistent, Stuart
would teach a merely nominal Trinity.[55]   He affirms, says
Norton,

that there is a threefold distinction in the divine nature, that is in the
nature of this one person.   But of the nature of any being we can know
nothing but by the attributes or properties of that being.   We conceive that this is at the present day a fundamental and undisputed principle in metaphysics.   Abstract all the attributes or properties of any
being, and nothing remains of which you can form even an imagination.   These are all which is cognizable by the human mind.   When
you say therefore that there is a threefold distinction in the nature of
any being, the only meaning which the words will admit (in relation
to the present subject) is that the attributes or properties of this
being may be divided into three distinct classes, which may be considered separately from each other. . . . . But this is nothing more than
a modal or nominal trinity.

Norton then passes to Christology, where he adds nothing
to Channing but certain forcible statements of the
argument.   He shows, however, distinctly that Christ was
a true man; and then puts his argument briefly: Because
he was a man, he was not God.   One new argument as to
the Trinity which lay outside of the province of a sermon
like Channing's, he introduced, viz., a review of the history
of the doctrine, in which he traced it to Greek philosophy,
and presented "its gradual introduction, its slow growth to
its present form, the strong opposition which it encoun-
tered, and its tardy reception among the great body of common Christians" [56] as conclusive proofs of its falsity.   He
had, naturally, no conception of a development of doctrine,
and demanded of the primitive church a nineteenth-century
philosophic statement of every doctrine which she might
legitimately hold, as he did of the Scriptures a perfect dogmatic statement of every position which they should be
permitted to teach.   His exegesis was by no means competent to meet such a scholar as Stuart.   Unitarianism was

[55] *Loc. cit.*, p. 9.
[56] *Ibid.*, p. 35.

too clearly the truth, in his mind, to admit of the plodding
and exact studies of words and constructions which was
characteristic of the new learning as Stuart managed it.
His easy treatment of Phil. 2:5 is an illustration of his exegetical defects.[57] "It is now conceded that the passage is
incorrectly rendered. But Professor Stuart, though he
allows this, still thinks the text of too much value to be
given up; and by retaining a part of the old mistranslation
(supposing ισα to denote *equality* instead of *likeness*) and
substituting a new one instead of that which is lost (understanding μορφη to mean *being* or *nature*) he has contrived
to press it again into service." Norton himself says:
"Ισος is used sometimes to denote equality, and sometimes likeness. The reasons which determine us to adopt
the latter signification in the present passage are *sufficiently
obvious.*" They are!

We conclude our review of Norton with his brief statement of the Unitarian position at this time:[58]

Christianity, we believe, has taught the Unity of God, and revealed
him as the Father of his creatures. It has made known his infinite
perfections, his providence, and his moral government. It has directed
us to look up to him as the Being on whom we and all things are entirely dependent, and to look up to him with perfect confidence and
love. It has made known to us that we are to live forever; it has
brought life and immortality to light. Man was a creature of this
earth, and it has raised him to a far nobler rank, and taught him to regard himself as an immortal being, and the child of God. It has opened
to the sinner the path of penitence and hope. It has afforded to virtue the highest possible sanctions. It gives to sorrow its best and
often its only consolation. It has presented us, in the life of our great
Master with an example of that moral perfection which is to be the
constant object of our exertions. It has established the truths which
it teaches upon evidence the most satisfactory. It is a most glorious
display of the benevolence of God and of his care for his creatures of
this earth.

Stuart had replied only to those portions of Channing's

[57] *Ibid.*, p. 49.   [58] *Ibid.*, pp. 61 f.

sermon which dealt with the Trinity and Christology. Unable to continue the work, he requested his colleague, Leonard Woods,[59] to review the remaining topics of the sermon. This he did in his *Letters to Unitarians* (1820).[60] We shall be the briefer in our review of this tract because it does not further the development of New England theology particularly, since it is a defense rather than a piece of constructive work. To a considerable extent it is engaged with showing that many of the positions which Channing had implied belonged to the Unitarians, were equally maintained by the orthodox.

After some preliminary remarks, Woods therefore begins his reply with the topic of the moral perfection of God. He accepts, as Channing had done, the Hopkinsian theory that love expresses the whole moral character of God, but passes immediately to the moral government of God as growing out of his love. God promotes the happiness of his kingdom by laws, accompanied with promises and threats. These are good, and so is their execution. The fatherhood of God is next touched upon, and necessary qualifications in the analogy between divine and human paternity drawn. And then Woods passes over to the consideration of total depravity, against which Channing had objected, and which was to become the principal subject of discussion, as it, indeed, lay at the foundation of the whole controversy. The reply consisted in defining the doctrine in the following terms: "That men are by nature destitute of holiness; or that they are subjects of an innate moral depravity; or, in other words, that they are from the first inclined to evil, and that, while unrenewed, their moral

[59] Born June 19, 1774; died August 24, 1854; graduated at Harvard, 1796; pastor at Newbury, Mass., 1798–1808; professor of Christian theology at Andover, 1808–46. A man of the largest practical services, in the founding of the seminary and of numerous benevolent organizations, he was characterized as a theologian by moderation and sense, as well as by competent learning.

[60] I employ at the present writing the reprint in the *Works*, Vol. IV, pp. 1 ff.

affections and actions are wholly wrong." [61] This proposition he established by a long Scripture argument, in which his endeavor is simply to show that the depravity mentioned is a fact. Incidentally he takes occasion to express his rejection of the doctrine of imputation.

It should be remarked that Woods's ideas upon the inductive nature of theology are strongly and excellently expressed.[62] He did not prevent the discussion, however, from passing into the sphere of the rational.

Woods then takes up the subject of election. He admits in the beginning[63] that there is some justification from Channing's objections in the form of expression often employed by the orthodox. In reply to his opponent, he first considers the Scripture argument for election, and then criticizes certain incorrect views and representations of the doctrine, such as that election is "arbitrary," [64] "unconditional," when it is meant that there is no condition of atonement and repentance. The charge of injustice in election is then strongly refuted by pointing out that "salvation is in all instances of grace." [65] He suggests that the reasons for election are "reasons of state." He also endeavors to justify the consistency of election with free agency in the following manner, in which no theoretical explanation is attempted:

As I am a creature of God, I exist as I am, namely, a moral agent, according to his purpose. And if God's purpose, determining my existence as a moral agent, is consistent with my actually existing as such; why may not his purpose, determining the exercises of my moral agency, be consistent with the existence of such moral exercises. The following positions, which I think conformable to sound reason and philosophy, express my views in brief. God first determines that man shall be a moral agent, and that in all the circumstances of his existence he shall possess and exercise all his moral powers. And then God determines that, in the perfect exercise of all his moral powers,

[61] Edit. cit., p. 23. [62] Ibid., p. 20.
[63] Ibid., pp. 39, 47. [64] Ibid., pp. 48 ff.
[65] Ibid., p. 54.

he shall act in a certain manner, and form a certain character. The determination of God, thus understood, instead of being inconsistent with moral agency, does in fact secure moral agency. In regard to this subject, it aims at nothing and tends to produce nothing but the uninterrupted exercise of all our moral powers.[66]

The reply to the following points was less important. Woods insisted upon the origin of the atonement in the love of God, and hints, while explaining away certain objectionable expressions, at his own theory of the atonement, the governmental. Still, the immediate connection of the love of God with every feature of the atonement is not brought out. The failure to state the theory upon its ideal side was the relative justification of Channing's objections; but Woods could not supply this defect in his predecessors. Divine influence is then taken up. The leading objection of Channing, that it was irresistible, was answered by saying "that the Holy Spirit operates in such a manner as to offer no violence to any of the principles of an intelligent and moral nature; that it always produces its effects in the understanding according to the essential properties and laws which belong to the understanding, and in the will and affections without interfering with any of the properties and laws which belong to them."[67] The influence is efficacious, but not overpowering.

After some other topics had been discussed, the tract was brought to an end with an estimate of the practical influence of the two systems—an argument essentially invidious and therefore improper in such a discussion.

Professor Henry Ware,[68] who since his appointment as Hollis professor had not engaged in public controversy, now addressed Letters to Trinitarians and Calvinists (Cam-

[66] Loc. cit., p. 58.

[67] Ibid., p. 82.

[68] Born at Sherburne, Mass., April 1, 1764; died at Cambridge, July 12, 1845; graduated at Harvard, 1785; pastor at Hingham, 1787–1805; professor at Cambridge, 1805–45.

bridge, 1820). Upon the unity of God, he said that, although the orthodox professed a belief in the Divine Unity, Unitarians held that orthodox theories rendered it an impossibility.[69] Stuart's mode of stating the doctrine reduced "the trinity to a mere unmeaning name, and were it not an abuse of language of mischievous tendency, would leave nothing on the subject that need be thought worth contending about."[70] Woods, he says, makes no attempt to show the consistency of the doctrine of depravity with the moral perfection of God, but simply tries to show that it is a fact, whereas its consistency with God's character is a part of the evidence, whether it is a fact or not. He therefore charges Woods with failure. He then passes to the natural character of man, which, he declares, is the main question at issue between the orthodox and the Unitarians. His own view he thus expresses:

Man is by nature, by which is to be understood as he is born into the world, as he comes from the hands of the Creator, innocent and pure; free from all moral corruption, as well as destitute of all positive holiness; and until he has, by the exercise of his faculties, actually formed a character either good or bad, an object of the divine complacency and favor. The complacency and favor of the Creator are expressed in all the kind provisions that are made by the constitution of things for his improvement and happiness. He is by nature no more inclined or disposed to vice than to virtue, and is equally capable in the ordinary use of his faculties and with the common assistance afforded him, of either. He derives from his ancestors a frail and mortal nature; is made with appetites which fit him for the condition of being in which God has placed him; but in order for them to answer all the purposes intended, they are so strong as to be very liable to abuse by excess. He has passions implanted in him which are of great importance in the conduct of life, but which are equally capable of impelling him into a wrong or a right course. He has natural affections, all of them originally good, but liable by a wrong direction to be the occasion of error and sin. He has reason and conscience to direct the conduct of life, and enable him to choose aright, which reason may yet be neglected or perverted, and conscience mis-

[69] Op. cit., p. 10.
[70] Ibid., p. 11.

guided. The whole of these together make up what constitutes his trial and probation. They make him an accountable being, a proper subject to be treated according as he shall make a right or wrong choice, being equally capable of either, and as free to the one as to the other.[71]

It subsequently appears that he believes in the universality of sin, in the sense that all men sin, and he even says that the "all have sinned" of Rom. 5:12 means "all who are capable of sinning, all as soon as they are capable of it, all as soon as they are moral agents"[72]—which is just what Woods had said. But he rejects total depravity, maintaining that "there is much of good as well as of evil in the human character and in the conduct of man;" that "as much as there is of wickedness and vice, there is far more of virtue and goodness . . . . and that even in the worst of men good feelings and principles are predominant, and they probably perform in the course of their lives many more good than bad actions."[73] The proof of these statements is chiefly from the results of "observation." With a short proof of the inconsistency of depravity with the character of God, Ware closes this part of his letters.[74]

[71] *Loc. cit.*, pp. 20 f.   [72] *Ibid.*, p. 43.   [73] *Ibid.*, p. 24.

[74] Edward Beecher, in his *Conflict of Ages*, a book devoted to the problem of original sin, particularly to the origination of that native bias to evil with which men are born, lets fall many valuable historical and critical remarks. He traces the repudiation of old-school theories in New England to the necessity of asserting in reference to the action of God "the divine principles of equity and honor." He rightly places the true starting-point of Unitarianism in this necessity. "The strength of the feelings of Unitarians against the doctrine of the Trinity seems to be chiefly owing to its connection with the orthodox doctrine of depravity" (p. 121). Of the argument of Channing, quoted above, he says: "This statement is fully justified by all the orthodox authorities to whom I have referred." Unitarianism was thus simply attempting in a new way what all the rest of New England was attempting by the "New England" theology. The Unitarian explanation was, however, a complete failure, according to Beecher, even in the eyes of the Unitarians themselves. Their scheme was followed by a "reaction" which arose from "facts, from Scripture, and from Christian consciousness" (p. 131). Descriptions of the prevalence and depth of sin in the world, found in Dewey, Norton, and Channing, do not fall short in intensity of similar passages in the orthodox writers. As time went on the bright hopes which the Unitarian leaders had of great improvement from the spread of Uni-

Ware, though thus presenting the barest Pelagianism himself, had somewhat the better of Woods because he had indentified Wood's doctrine with that of the Westminster Confession. This he had a perfect right to do, for Woods had signed the Confession upon entering upon his professorship; and more, his view of the facts of human nature was precisely that of Westminster, though he had already begun to modify the underlying philosophy in connection with the other New England divines. Individual expressions, such as "penal evils" applied to the consequences among his descendants of Adam's sin, were a sufficient warrant for Ware's method of conducting the discussion. Woods was indeed in an unfortunate position, and the root of his difficulty was that he still retained the old twofold division of the mind—the causative nature of motives, and the Edwardean idea of freedom. He was not, therefore, in fact entirely free from the supralapsarianism which tinges the Confession, and had survived even in Hopkins. Hence Ware opened the subject of election by

tarianism gave rise to gloomy forebodings (p. 136). "Sincere, earnest, and indefatigable, as were the efforts of Dr. Channing, the force of the radical and originating causes of such wide-spread actual human depravity was deeper and greater than his system would allow him to understand and consistently to believe." Neither was the new school explanation able to escape a reaction. Its two views, of "an innocent nature so affected by the fall of Adam as always to lead to sin," and the other, of a divine efficiency directly producing our volitions, sinful as well as holy, were neither of them satisfactory to the advocates of depravity or the Unitarian defenders of the divine honor. Neither did it satisfy the new school itself, for they resorted in their defense of it to the same arguments from the inscrutability of the ways of God, or else fell off into a degradation of the idea of free agency, taking "the ground that the moral constitutions of men are as good as the nature of free agency will allow" (p. 181).

Beecher's own solution, as is well known, was that men are not at birth new-created spirits, but have pre-existed, and in this pre-existent state have fallen into sin, and acquired by their own acts the "habit of sin" which is the striking characteristic of the disposition of man to evil. They are sent into this world as a "hospital"—that is, as a sphere of redemption—and hence as a great example of the goodness of God. Thus their tendency to evil is not against the honor and equity of God, but has been brought upon them by their own act, and the fact that they are in this world at all is a new proof and exemplification of his equity, or rather of his more than equity, his long-suffering love.

indentifying the doctrine of Woods with that of Westminster. He states it:

> That, without any foreseen difference of character and desert in men, before he had brought them into being, he should regard some with complacency and love, and the rest with disapprobation, and hatred, and wrath; and, without any reference to the future use or abuse of their nature, should appoint some to everlasting happiness, and the rest to everlasting misery; and that this appointment, entirely arbitrary, for which no reason is to be assigned, but his sovereign will, should be the cause and not the consequence of the holiness of the one and of the defect of holiness of the other.[75]

He then brings in objections which were as keenly felt by the orthodox as by himself, and so has an easy victory over his supposed antagonist. But in all this he had not sharply stated and thoroughly argued the true question. Woods had clearly declared that he believed in reasons for the electing purpose of God. Other New England divines had also made them to reside in the wisdom and goodness of God. There was no objection in any New Englander's mind to making them to consist partly in the foreknowledge of what the man would be; only it must be the foreknowledge of his natural aptitudes, his probable usefulness, the certainty that he would yield to such influences as God could consistently bring to bear upon him, etc. Did God elect upon foreknowledge of *faith?* Or is the holy influence of God the occasioning *cause* of faith? That was the real question; but Ware gives it little attention. In fact, he confounded throughout the love of complacency and that of benevolence as he does in the passage just quoted. No Calvinist ever held that God "without any foreseen difference in character" regarded some "with *complacency.*" Benevolence comes first; upon it election is founded; out of election comes the foreknowledge of holy character; and then first, in view of this holy character, comes complacency.

[75] *Loc. cit.,* p. 59.

It will not be necessary to delay over the remaining portion of Ware's *Letters*. His method is the same in treating of the atonement and of divine influence. Upon the atonement he sharply demanded a new rationale of the doctrine.

According to orthodoxy "it was the same God, the same being, who sent and was sent, who made the atonement and whose anger was appeased by the atonement, who made satisfaction to offended justice and whose justice was satisfied. It is not enough to assert that 'the Father and Son are two as really as Moses and Aaron, though not in the same sense, nor in any sense inconsistent with their being one.' It belongs to him who asserts this to state intelligibly what is the nature and import of the distinction here intended; to explain in what sense two, and in what sense one. No man knows better than Dr. Woods that *until he has done this, he has done nothing to the purpose.* He uses words without meaning, and merely casts a mist where he is bound to shed light."[76]

His own view may be condensed in that statement that the efficacy of the sufferings and death of Christ consist "not in their appeasing the anger of God and disposing him to be merciful, but in their moral influence on men, in bringing them to repentance, holiness, and an obedient life, and thus rendering them fit subjects of forgiveness and the divine favor."[77] "The salvation of the best men is of Grace, not of debt, what they cannot demand as a right, yet may claim on the ground of the divine promise."[78] In this connection he once more makes the yet unanswered Unitarian demand for a rationale.

It is admitted that if the premises are true, the conclusion does follow [that the sufferings of Christ derived their worth from the dignity of his divine nature]; if Jesus Christ is both perfect God and perfect man in one individual person, the defence is complete. But, in the first place, I remark that the possibility of two distinct intelligent natures making but one person, has never been shown to the smallest degree of satisfaction; especially of two natures so distinct and distant as the divine and human, a finite and an infinite mind.

[76] *Ibid.*, p. 83.   [77] *Ibid.*, p. 97.
[78] *Ibid.*, p. 106.

. . . . But this is not all. The identity of person is not only shown to be impossible upon the trinitarian hypothesis. The only ground upon which some of the strongest objections to the trinitarian doctrine, that part of it which consists in the supreme deity of Jesus Christ, can be evaded is by the assumption of two distinct persons in Jesus Christ. . . . . "Of *this* indeed he was ignorant as a man, but he knew it as God, and this he might truly say he was unable to do as man, though as God he could do all things." . . . . With these brief hints I am willing to leave the reader to make up his judgment "how far the views of the orthodox in this case are capable of being defended in a satisfactory manner." [79]

Ware rejected not only the doctrine of irresistible grace, which he must do and did upon the same principles as he urged against election,[80] but also all special grace tending to conversion.

The influence and agency of the Spirit of God is to be acknowledged in the whole of that discipline which is intended to improve, exalt, and perfect our nature, or to correct any wrong tendencies it may have acquired, and restore it to a right direction and its previous purity. . . . . Not a direct and immediate agency, but such as we see exercised in everything else through the universe; God bringing about his ends by a variety of means and employing in them the subordinate agency and instrumentality of his creatures.[81]

The *Letters* close with a defense of the practical influence of Unitarianism.

Woods replied to Ware in the following year in a pamphlet entitled *A Reply,* and incidentally did something to help on the discussion. He brought out the fact that Ware judged the character of men by a wrong standard,[82] viewing them too much in the aspect of their individual deeds, as if these were to be considered each by itself, whereas men are subjects of the moral government of God, and the question as to their character is the question of their fundamental relation to God's law and will. He distinguishes clearly between the natural affections and true moral purpose, between kindliness and holiness. But nothing sub-

[79] *Loc. cit.,* pp. 99 ff.   [80] *Ibid.,* p. 120.
[81] *Ibid.,* pp. 122, 123.   [82] Woods' *Works,* Vol. IV, p. 130.

stantial was added to the argument, nor by the *Answer, Remarks,* and *Postscript,* which were still to come.

With these works the controversy, as a formal interchange of arguments, came to an end. There was a long series of more or less popular discussions, in which many preachers, not inconsiderable theologians, engaged.[83] The full answer of New England theology was not rendered, however, till one more writer, N. W. Taylor, of New Haven, had presented his reply.

Taylor did not deem Stuart's answer to Channing very effective, thinking it quite as possible for a theologian to say too little as to say too much. He vindicated the right of Trinitarians to declare that they meant no contradiction by affirming a Trinity. He then defined the Trinity thus: "God is one Being in such a sense as to involve three Persons in such a sense that by his tripersonality he is qualified for three distinct, personal, divine forms of phenomenal action." He thus gave a personality to each of Stuart's "distinctions," yet not an independent personality. That there may be a being having such a tripersonality Taylor endeavors to show by considering the possibility of Spinoza's conception of the universe as one being, with the result that this conception cannot be declared *a priori* an impossibility. The fundamental error of the Unitarians

[83]This is a convenient point for referring to several books which ought not to be overlooked. Dean Abbadie's *Traité de la divinité de notre Seigneur* (1689) was republished at Burlington in 1802. D. Dana published in 1810 a sermon on *The Deity of Christ,* almost wholly biblical in argument. E. D. Griffin preached a series of *Park Street Lectures* on total depravity, regeneration, election, and perseverance in 1815. Thomas Robbins published in 1820 a series of sermons preached in East Windsor on *The Divinity of Christ,* chiefly exegetical. The veteran Stephen West came out in 1816 with his *Evidence of the Divinity of the Lord Jesus Christ, Collected from the Holy Scriptures.* Wardlaw's *Discourses* were reprinted at Andover in 1815, and Yates's *Vindication* at Boston in 1816, to be followed by Wardlaw's *Reply,* also reprinted at Andover (1817). These books were much read, and in this way entered into the current of New England theology. The atonement was often discussed, one of the best books upon the Unitarian side being Noah Worcester's *Atoning Sacrifice* (1829). For an excellent, though by no means complete, list of the polemical essays of this period, see the bibliography of Dexter's *Congregationalism.*

consists, he declares, in their pretending to be able to decide positively that such conceptions are impossible *a priori*. They take the common phenomenal conception of being, derived from our own consciousness, as the only and universal conception; and then affirm that it excludes tripersonality. When they reflect upon the unity of God, they declare that the utter want of all evidence from the *unity* of God for his tripersonality is decisive proof that he is not tripersonal. He then discusses the presumption in favor of the Trinity from the work of Christ, and thus incidentally touches upon Christology, without, however, contributing anything to meet the repeated demand of the Unitarians for a rationale. He finally discusses the interpretation of the Scriptures upon these doctrines, and maintains, on the one hand, that the Unitarians acknowledge that there is something peculiar in the language of the Bible requiring special interpretation, and, on the other hand, that the older Trinitarians, in their doctrines of generation and procession, have not shown that the modified use of language which they demand for the expression of their position is *de usu loquendi*.

The position in which New England theology was left by this controversy may be summarily expressed by the following heads:

1. The doctrine of the Trinity itself was more firmly than ever believed to be grounded in the teachings of the Scriptures, though it had taken a depotentiated form from which it did not recover during the career of the school.

2. The divinity of Christ was established afresh as a biblical doctrine, and its practical effects upon life and worship were well secured; but the doctrine of his person was thrown into even greater confusion than it had previously been in, the unity of his person, still nominally maintained,

being almost lost in consequence of the style of argument adopted to maintain his divinity.

3. In the anthropological portion of the debate the New Englanders had found themselves greatly hampered by the unsatisfactory condition of their theory of the will. But they took practically the position that man is truly free and an uncaused agent in his own volitions. Thus maintaining the corruption of human nature and the universality of sin, they affirmed, though without successful adjustment, both the freedom of man and his voluntariness in all sin, and the certainty of his future sinful actions. The priority of grace, and the foundation of gifts of grace in the divine purpose, they maintained with as great constancy.

4. The benevolence of God in respect to both of these elements—both the entrance of sin into the world with its resulting corruption of our nature, and the election of men with its consequent "praeterition" of some—was defended with a success only modified by the weak spot in the theory of freedom, and became tenfold stronger as an inalienable component of the system.

5. Something was done, though not much as yet, to exhibit the connection of the atonement with the love of God, as its consummate and necessary expression.

CHAPTER XI

THE UNIVERSALIST CONTROVERSY CONCLUDED

The real interest of the Universalist controversy to the New England theologians ceased when the Unitarian movement began to absorb their attention. The one was a movement among the obscure, and was comparatively unimportant, since it attracted to itself but few; the other had its source in the high places of the land, seemed about to sweep away everything in its irresistible course, and dealt with the most vital portions of the faith. And, further, Universalism soon became Unitarian in its theology, and resistance to the one movement was resistance to the other. Hence, for a long time, little mention is made of the lesser innovation, and few books are devoted to it.

The progress of Universalism from the high Calvinism of Relly to Unitarianism is, however, not without interest to the critical student of theological movements.

Elhanan Winchester, originally a Baptist, is the next great Universalist leader after Murray. He founded his proof of Universalism upon orthodox premises. He defended the Trinity.[1] His statements as to the ruined condition of man without a Redeemer are as satisfactory as those of his opponents. The absolute need of repentance to forgiveness was a foundation stone of his system. None could be forgiven who did not repent. But his fundamental idea was that all will finally repent—some before death, in which case they will be received immediately to glory; others during the intermediate state before the judgment; but finally, under the long and serious discipline of the "aionian" punishment, all who may have remained in-

[1] *The Divinity of Christ Proved from the Scriptures* (undated).

corrigible by the means that have been used for their recovery before.

He justifies the belief that the punishment of the ages after the judgment will issue in the repentance of all souls, upon the following grounds:

Punishment to a certain degree inflames and enrages in a most amazing manner; but continued longer and heavier, produces a contrary effect—softens, humbles, and subdues. . . . . Some sins are so daring and presumptuous as to provoke God to threaten that they shall not be purged away in this life; and perhaps their malignancy may be so great that nothing that can be used here is able to subdue them. . . . . Thus punishments are designed for the humbling of the proud: but if they fail of answering that purpose as administered in the present state, they will be continued and increased in future periods to such a degree as shall bring all down in due time.[2]

Winchester received, however, comparatively little attention from the New England divines. He was too soon superseded by Hosea Ballou, who, first publishing in 1804, had speedily gained the highest influence among his denomination and effected its transfer from the Trinitarian to the Unitarian basis. On account of his determinative influence, he deserves a fuller consideration.[3]

The book in which the revolutionary change wrought by Ballou was effected was his treatise on the atonement. We shall restrict ourselves at this time to a sketch of this work.[4]

Ballou's decisive, and among the Universalists epoch-making, work sought to go to the foundation of the subject. Its title intimates as much as this; for, though it was intended as a means of propagating the Universalist faith, and had its sufficient *raison d'être* therein, it dealt pro-

---

[2] *Dialogues*, p. 180.

[3] The remaining portions of this chapter first appeared in the *Bibliotheca Sacra* for October, 1888, and January, 1889.

[4] The edition before us is that of Dr. Miner. The title runs: *A Treatise on Atonement*, by Hosea Ballou; with an Introduction by A. A. Miner. (Fourth edition, Boston, 1882.)

fessedly with the atonement. It purposed to root out all
the old theories and doctrines which were the foundation
of the orthodox scheme, and thus lead to the positions
where Universalism was the only consistent conclusion. It
is a system of doctrine culminating in Universalism. It is
divided into three parts, which deal respectively with sin,
atonement, and the consequences of atonement. In general, the argument is straightforward, does not intentionally beg the question or misrepresent opponents, and
seeks to remove objections before they shall occur, rather
than answer them when they are forced upon the writer.
Still, the limitations of Mr. Ballou's mind in the department of metaphysical and exact thinking are often very
manifest.

The definition of sin with which he begins is this: "Sin
is the violation of a law which exists in the mind, which law
is the imperfect knowledge men have of moral good." [5]
The "legislature" which prescribed the law to all moral
beings is "the capacity to understand." Since this is finite,
"sin in its nature ought to be considered finite and limited,
rather than infinite and unlimited, as has by many been
supposed." [6] To the proof of the proposition that sin is a
finite evil Ballou devotes considerable space. He thus designed to meet squarely one of the strong positions of his
opponents. He directly opposes Edwards' arguments in
fact, though he does not mention him by name [7] when he
sets up against the idea of obligation measured by the
being to whom it is due—viz., God—this idea of a finite
"legislature," the mind of man. How important he deemed
this point may be seen by the frequency with which he returns to the topic. And yet he did not thereby rise to the

[5] *Loc. cit.,* p. 41.

[6] *Ibid.,* p. 39.

[7] *Ibid.,* p. 40. Cf. *Bibliotheca Sacra,* Vol. XLIII, pp. 8, 9.

height which the New England divines had themselves already attained.

But certain of Ballou's fundamental assumptions appear also in these opening pages. He says:

Now to reason justly, we must conclude that, if God possess infinite wisdom, he could never intend anything to take place or be, that will not take place or be; nor that which is or will be, not to be at the time when it is. And it must be considered erroneous to suppose that the Allwise ever desired anything to take place which by his wisdom he knew would not; as such a supposition must in effect suppose a degree of misery in the eternal mind equal to the strength of his fruitless desire! [8]

The root of this conception, as we shall see, is a denial of all true freedom on the part of man, which makes God's will all in all, and leads to the express denial of those distinctions between the secret and revealed will of God which are introduced into Calvinistic systems to save human responsibility. [9]

By a strange coincidence, ideas also appear here as to the nature of evil which agree in form of expression strikingly with Samuel Hopkins. Ballou says: "If by the real evil be meant something that ought not to be in respect to all the consequences which attend it, I cannot admit of its existence." [10] He also maintains that "the consequences of an act do not determine whether the act be good or evil." [11]

Passing now from the nature of sin to its origin, Mr. Ballou refers the entire theory of the fall to the "chimerical story of the bard Milton." Viewing the whole as an attempted explanation of the introduction of sin into the universe, Ballou propounds the crucial difficulty in saying that it does not account for the case of Satan himself.

Was not the angel holy in every faculty? Was not the command for him to worship the Son holy and just? All answer, Yes. Then from such causes, how was sin produced? The reader will easily see, the question cannot be answered. [12]

[8] *Ibid.*, p. 41.   [9] E.g., *ibid.*, p. 250.   [10] *Ibid.*, p. 48.
[11] *Ibid.*, pp. 44–48.   [12] P. 53.

Our author's own solution of the problem is as follows:
God had a design in making us, the whole of which "must
be carried into effect and nothing more, admitting him to be
an infinite person." [13]   Sin is therefore in the plan of God.
To arrive at a satisfactory account of the entrance of evil
into the world, we must begin with natural evil.   This is a
natural result of our physical organization.   In the combi-
nation of the various elements entering into the composi-
tion of our bodies, there is provision for the rise of all manner of disorders.   The same feature is found in our senses,
which are at the same time the "origin of our thoughts and
volitions."   Hence physical evil is the source of moral evil.
"Want unsatisfied is an evil; and unsatisfied want is the first
movement to action or volition."   Let now the element of
confusion enter into our desires, and the introduction of
sin is explained.   "From our natural constitution, com-
posed of our bodily elements, we are led to act in obedience
to carnal appetites, which justifies the conclusion that sin is
the work of the flesh."   This language, derived from an
earlier edition, conveys the thoughts of the later one before
us in simpler form.   Ballou subsequently clothed his theory
in an expository form, but without much gain in clearness.[14]

But, says the objector, this is to make God the author of
sin.   No, says Mr. Ballou, it is to make God the author of
that which is in a limited sense sin.[15]

In this connection comes in the discussion of the freedom of the will.   As Mr. Ballou's great doctrinal argument
for universal salvation is that the plans of God will certainly be carried out, he is compelled from his standpoint
to remove the objection that the will of man may interpose to persist in sin.   He does it by denying that the will

13 P. 57.   14 Pp. 57-63.
15 Ibid., pp. 64 ff.

has freedom. "In order for a choice to take place, the mind must have the perception of two or more objects; and that object which has the most influence on the judgment and passions will be the chosen object; and choice in this instance has not even the shadow of liberty." Other expressions which he employs show that Mr. Ballou believes in strict determinism.[16]

In treating of the consequences of sin, our writer rejects the doctrine that they are spiritual, temporal, and eternal death. Temporal death is incidental to our constitution, since we are by nature mortal. As for eternal death, the whole discussion pertains to this; but Mr. Ballou puts in a disclaimer here, that the effects of sin are limited to the state in which they are committed.[17]

In treating the subject of the atonement, to which he now comes, Mr. Ballou transgresses the proprieties of a sober discussion by the bitterness of his expressions against orthodox theories. Or, waiving this, he shows too little sympathy for, or understanding of, what his opponents meant to say, to inspire us with much confidence that he will contribute to the theme.[18] We shall not delay upon his criticisms of other theories, but shall content ourselves with reproducing Ballou's own. It is substantially as follows: Jesus Christ was not God. To suppose this is to involve one's self in inextricable difficulties. "To say of two persons, exactly of the same age, that one of them is a real son of the other, is to confound good sense." "If the Godhead consists of three distinct persons, and each of these persons be infinite, the whole Godhead amounts to the amazing sum of infinity multiplied by three."[19] It will be noted that it is necessary thus to diminish the dignity of Christ

[16] *Ibid.*, pp. 65, 66, 71, especially 95 ff. See also *Select Sermons* (Boston, 1832), pp. 306 ff.

[17] *Ibid.*, p. 95.   [18] *Ibid.*, pp. 103 ff.

[19] *Ibid.*, p. 134.

to establish the view of atonement which is to follow. The dissatisfied party needing reconciliation is man, not God.[20] The sin of Eden produced two errors in Adam's mind, which have remained in the mind of man ever since: (a) He believed God to be his enemy. (b) He believed that he could reconcile his Maker by works which he could himself do. But, on the contrary, God loved Adam after his sin as much as before. He did not regard himself as the injured party, for the only party injured by the sin of man was man himself. His love for his Creator was interrupted, and his views of him were corrupted. The atonement was necessary to renew man's love to God. God himself sought to effect this, and so the atonement did not *produce* love in God toward man, but was the result of that uninterrupted love. And so the atonement consists in manifesting God's love to us, and so in causing us to love him. The temporal death and the literal blood of Christ did not make the atonement. Apparently Mr. Ballou did not have any clear place for the death of Christ in his system.[21]

Incidentally the writer has introduced a discussion at this point of endless punishment as the penalty of the law.[22] It is not necessary (a) to maintain the law and secure the government of God, since he is almighty; nor (b) to reclaim the delinquent, for of course it is especially calculated not to reclaim him, since it is endless; nor (c) is it necessary to deter others from crime, for through the sin of Adam the entire race would be involved in endless punishment, and there would be no one to deter. And (d) endless punishment involves endless sin; but to inflict endless sin is against the law which requires endless holiness.

We now enter upon the closing portion of the work, the most important from the author's point of view—the con-

[20] *Loc. cit.*, pp. 140 ff.   [21] Cf. *ibid.*, pp. 167, 233.
[22] *Ibid.*, p. 126.

sequences of the atonement to mankind. These are, in general, the universal holiness and happiness of the race.

This statement has no sooner been made than the influences of Mr. Ballou's surroundings become evident in his pausing to discuss the supposition that eternal punishment is necessary to the greatest final amount of happiness. The speculations of the Hopkinsians were before his mind here, though the statements which Mr. Ballou makes of their positions are very objectionable. His great answer is derived from the conception that what is meant by these reasoners is that pain is an object of enjoyment in and of itself. We may therefore pass, without stopping on this topic, to the positive arguments which Mr. Ballou now begins to propose for universal salvation.

Certain objections are first noticed.[23] That derived from Rev. 14:10, 11, he answers by referring to the present time as the period of punishment. But it is objected that millions go out of this world unreconciled, and therefore shall remain so to all eternity. But, says Ballou, this implies that there will be no change after death, and, if this is so, saints will not increase in holiness, which is too absurd to need refutation. The answer to the objection from moral agency consists in repeating the denial of the freedom of the will.[24] Or, on the ground of the objector, which Ballou always tries to take, it gives men an opportunity of repentance and salvation, and thus is no obstacle to universal salvation. Again, the word "everlasting" does not mean endless. If the "day of judgment" of the Scriptures be an objection to universal salvation, the proper understanding, according to Mr. Ballou, substantiated by a long exegetical discussion, is that the "coming of the Lord," and the "day of judgment" were accomplished by the de-

[23] *Ibid.*, pp. 187 ff.; formally from p. 193.
[24] *Ibid.*, p. 190.

struction of Jerusalem.[25] The account of Dives and Lazarus
is not literal. In Matt 12:31, 32 (neither in this world
nor in that which is to come), "world" means dispensation;
"this" world, the legal priestly dispensation; and "that
which is to come," the gospel.[26] And, finally, Mr. Ballou
thinks that endless misery demands a principle to support
such misery, in the divine nature.[27]

The treatise closes with the reasons for believing in universal salvation, and with them our review shall close.
They open with the argument from the goodness of God,
with which we are already familiar. Further arguments
are:[28] (a) There is an immortal desire in every soul for
future existence and happiness. "Why should the Almighty implant this desire in us if he never intended to
satisfy it?" (b) All wise, good, and exemplary men wish
for the truth of the doctrine. "If it be God's spirit in us
which causes us to pray for the destruction of sin, is it
reasonable to say that this same spirit has determined that
sin shall always exist?" (c) If any of the human race are
endlessly miserable, the whole must be, provided they know
it, on the principle of sympathy. (d) The world is a place
of education. Sin is a mistake, and is it conceivable that
men should never find this out, unless the school is to be a
failure? (e) Mankind in their moral existence originated
in God. They must finally be assimilated with the fountain
from which they sprang. (f) Finally, the Scripture proof.
This is to be of the plainest sort. "I am determined to
admit no Scripture as evidence in this case that needs any
interpretation to cause it to mean what I wish to prove:
therefore I shall produce but a small part of the Scriptures
which I conceive have a direct meaning in favor of Universalism." We are relieved by this fact from the necessity of

[25] Loc. cit., p. 224.   [26] Ibid., p. 225.
[27] Ibid., p. 227.   [28] Ibid., pp. 229 ff. ,

entering into the discussion of the separate passages. The most obvious meaning which will tell in favor of the doctrine of Universalism is the one which Mr. Ballou has in mind. We therefore append a list of the passages and leave the reader to make the examination for himself.[29]

It may be said that in a large degree the Universalism of Ballou was a reply to itself. Not many books were written especially against Ballou, and the reason is not far to seek. So long as the Universalist movement was favored by leading men like Chauncy, who in general maintained their reputation for orthodoxy and their position in the churches, or appeared unexpectedly among obscurer men like Huntington, whose defection was not known till revealed by a posthumous publication, it alarmed the orthodox and earnest men who formulated the New England theology, for the safety of their churches and the truth. But when it became identified with Unitarianism, and that at the moment when the large prevalence of the Unitarian movement was being revealed, in 1815, by the publication of the Belsham letters, it was no longer an object of special apprehension. What answered the one movement answered the other.[30] The churches were coming gradually into the right position as to the Unitarian movement, and they might be safely left to reject a Unitarian Universalism. It is evident from contemporaneous accounts that the vulgarity of many Universalist ministers and of much of the

---

[29] These occur upon pp. 240 ff. They are: Acts 3:20, 21; Col. 1:20; Eph. 1:10; Gen. 12:3; 49:10; Ps. 72:11; 37:10; 22:27; 2:7, 8; Col. 1:19; Isa. 25:6, 7, 8; I Cor. 15:54; Rev. 21:4; Jer. 33:20; Ezek. 17:22-24; I Tim. 2:4; Eph. 1:11. Especially I Cor., chap. 15; Rev. 5:11, 12, 13, 14; John 5:22, 23; Isa. 45:22-25; Rom. 8:22, 23; II Cor. 5:14.

[30] Ballou, in a sermon entitled "Commendation and Reproof of Unitarians" (*Select Sermons* [Boston, 1860], p. 321), declared that the Unitarians were Universalists and yet would not confess it. In the *Spirit of the Pilgrims* for 1830 (p. 205) is a review of this sermon, the object of which is to show that Mr. Ballou's declaration is correct. It was not long after this, perhaps in consequence of it, that the Unitarians came boldly out upon the side of restorationism.

Universalist preaching excited disgust, and assisted in nulli-
fying their influence.[31]   Ballou himself receded more and
more from reason and common-sense, and hence removed
more and more all necessity for special efforts against him.
In 1817 he "became entirely satisfied that the Scriptures
begin and end the history of sin in flesh and blood; and that
beyond this mortal existence, the Bible teaches no other
sentient state but that which is called by the blessed name of
life and immortality."[32]   The doctrine of no future punishment whatever was so manifestly contrary to the Bible,
as well as to the teachings of former leaders among the
Universalists themselves, that it needed no reply[33] until it
was presented under a professedly exegetical form.   This
was soon given to it, but not by Ballou.   The honor, if it be
such, of supplying this place in the Universalists' argument,
and of presenting their theory with learned apparatus and
in a series of volumes, belongs to Walter Balfour.

[31] See, for example, the testimony of Matthew Hale Smith in his instructive book, *Universalism Examined, Renounced, and Exposed* (Boston, 1844).

[32] See Eddy, *op. cit.*, Vol. II, p. 265, where a sketch of the progress of
Ballou's opinions may be found.

[33] Ballou preached much in different parts of the country, and received
transient attention from the local ministry.   Of such a character was the
amusing episode at West Rutland, when Lemuel Haynes, the minister of
the church, replied to Ballou at the close of the latter's sermon.   Dr. Eddy
has not quite apprehended the circumstances of the case in his account
(Vol. II, p. 110).   The church was Mr. Haynes's own.   He had been intend-
ing to be absent on a pastoral expedition to another part of the parish, but
remained to please the people.   After the sermon, as he had been urged to
speak by Mr. Ballou, who was fond of controversy, like all Universalist ministers of that day, Haynes arose and delivered a discourse upon the first
Universalist preacher, from Gen. 3:4.   It was satirical, and offended Mr.
Ballou deeply; but Mr. Haynes intended doubtless to say to his people, as
forcibly as possible, that he deemed the doctrine of Mr. Ballou hazardous
to their souls.   As their pastor such was his duty.   He knew best how to reach
them and counteract the effect of what they had just heard; and the fact that
he carried them with him is the best proof that his judgment was correct.
Though Dr. Eddy calls it "low-witted," the *Panoplist* said that its satire "was
managed with Christian sobriety."   The whole affair and the subsequent controversy of Haynes with Ballou may be examined in the pages of Dr. Cooley's
Sketches of the Life and Character of the Rev. Lemuel Haynes, A. M. (New
York, 1839).

Balfour's first work was his *Inquiry,* published in 1824.[34] As we learn from the preface of the third edition,[35] the author's attention was directed in this work exclusively to the endless duration of future punishment, since he was not then prepared to deny limited future punishment. His object was to investigate the supposition "that a place called Hell in a future state is prepared for the punishment of the wicked." [36] He says that

all the principal writers on both sides of this question proceed on this ground that there is a place of future punishment and that the name of it is Hell. Winchester, Murray, Chauncy, Huntington, and others all admit that Hell is a place of future punishment. Edwards, Strong, and others who oppose them, had no occasion to prove this, but only to show that it was to be endless in its duration.

The place Balfour occupies in the discussion is thus defined by himself. He comes to the conclusion that there is no place of eternal punishment.

Balfour first takes up the word "Sheol." Following the lead of a certain Dr. Campbell, he brings out by various quotations and discussions the fact that Sheol properly signifies the state of the dead, or the place of the departed. Hence, the argument is, it never signifies the place of punishment. Even Ps. 9:17 ("The wicked shall be turned into hell and all the nations that forget God") is thus explained. "The Psalm in which the words stand is treating of God's temporal judgments upon the heathen nations." [37] He continues: "Surely, no one who has attended to all the above texts in which Sheol occurs, can continue to believe that Sheol here has such a meaning. . . . . It is the same hell in which the Savior's soul was not left," etc. In conclusion

---

[34] *An Inquiry into the Scriptural Import of the Words Sheol, Hades, Tartarus, and Gehenna, all translated Hell in the common English Version* (Charleston, 1824; large 8vo, 448 pages). It was issued in several subsequent editions.

[35] Boston, 1832, p. v.

[36] First edition (from which all subsequent quotations are made), p. v.

[37] *Ibid.*, p. 24.

he affirms that the Old Testament writers and Christians of this day are "hardly agreed in a single idea about hell." He then takes up the word "Hades." The reasoning and conclusion are the same. The account of Dives in Luke is a parable. Whatever Hades is, it shall finally be destroyed. Tartarus, a portion of Hades, shall share its fate, and hence none of these terms denote the place of endless punishment. In fact, Balfour suggests very strongly that the idea of Tartarus was imported into Christianity by heathen converts from the Greek religions.[38]

To this point the difficulties in Balfour's way have been comparatively slight. He puts forth greater exertions in overcoming the force of the word "Gehenna," but arrives successfully at the same goal. He objects strongly to the transfer of the meaning of the word from "the valley of Hinnom" to "hell." The Old Testament, he thinks, makes it an emblem of the "future temporal punishment to the Jews as a nation."[39] This interpretation he derives from Jer., chap. 19, and 7:29 to end. With this clue he comes to the New Testament and interprets all such passages as Matt. 23:33 ("Ye generation of vipers, how shall ye escape the damnation of hell?") of the temporal calamities connected with the fall of Jerusalem.[40] A long and labored distinction between the Greek terms $\psi v \chi \acute{\eta}$ and $\pi \nu \epsilon \hat{v} \mu a$ led to the conclusion that even if Gehenna should be a place of future punishment, the spirit never enters it, and this discovery prepared the way for his later essays upon the immortality of the soul.

Balfour's general conclusion to his first inquiry is therefore that there is no word used in the Bible to designate the place of endless future punishment, and hence that there is no such punishment. The work made the greatest possible

---

[38] *Loc. cit.*, p. 88.   [39] *Ibid.*, p. 110.
[40] *Ibid.*, p. 134.

impression upon the Universalists. They had had hitherto only comparatively uneducated men who had been able to appeal only to the English Bible in substantiation of their position; but here was a scholar who freely handled the original tongues of the Scriptures. The popularity of his writings was so great that Balfour issued in 1826 a second *Inquiry*,[41] in which he arrived at the similar result, that there is no really existent devil, and that the opinion that he exists is derived from heathenism. The last 154 pages of the book are devoted to the discussion of the terms *olim* [for *olam*], *aion*, and *aionios*. Into the details of this argument we cannot follow him. Enough to say that the argumentation is in principle that, because these words do not always mean strictly "everlasting," it can never be successfully maintained that they do in respect to future punishment. Notions derived from the investigation as to Gehenna reappear, and numerous cases of "everlasting punishment" are referred to the destruction of Jerusalem.[42] A substantial summary of his position is made in the following passage:

I conceive that all the everlastings of which the Scriptures speak stand in some shape or other connected with God's dispensation of love and mercy to man through Jesus Christ. The ages or everlastings began with him, and shall terminate when Christ hath subdued all things, and the last enemy death is destroyed. Hence the state after this does not appear to me to be described in Scriptures by the expression "everlasting life," but by other words and phrases. For example—the dead are said to put on incorruption or immortality. Mor-

[41] We have before us only the second edition: *An Inquiry into the Scriptural Doctrine concerning the Devil and Satan, and into the Extent of Duration expressed by the terms olim, aion, aionios, rendered everlasting, forever, etc., in the common version, and especially when applied to punishment,* etc. (Charlestown, 1827; 8vo, 359 pages.)

[42] The witty Parsons Cooke, in his *Modern Universalism Exposed,* took the pains to count up the discourses of our Lord which are recorded in the Gospel of Matthew and refer to the destruction of Jerusalem according to Balfour, and found that they exceeded by one chapter his entire preaching upon all other subjects. Cooke suggested that the name of the New Testament should be changed to "The Destruction of Jerusalem Foretold" as more appropriate to its contents.

tality is then said to be swallowed up of life. They cannot die any more, but are equal unto the angels, being sons of the resurrection, their inheritance is incorruptible, and fadeth not away, and they are to be forever (*pantote*) with the Lord.[43]

The last sentence of this extract suggests the final contribution of Balfour to his system, which was made in 1828 in his *Three Essays*.[44] Here he promulgated the doctrine that the souls of men are not immortal; that the spirit returns unto God who gave it, in the sense that it is laid up with Christ in God, unconscious, to be restored to man in the resurrection at the last day, at which time all men shall be immediately admitted without judgment into felicity, from which they shall never depart.[45]

All these gradual discoveries and communications to the public only made the Balfourean system more popular with the Universalists. It spread rapidly, was eagerly read, and learned by heart by multitudes of the people, and filled the air with the clamor of controversy. Doubtless the New England teachers were not idle, and there were many faithful parish sermons like one of Emmons upon "The Plea of Sinners against Endless Punishment."[46] There are five principles, he says, upon which the Universalists argue in favor of their doctrine. These are: "The universal goodness of God; the universal atonement of Christ; the universal offers of salvation; the universal goodness of mankind; their universal punishment in this life." The arguments of the first four heads are those with which we have already become familiar. Under the last he intends evi-

---

[43] *Inquiry*, p. 354.

[44] *Three Essays on the intermediate State of the dead, the Resurrection from the dead, and on the Greek terms rendered judge, judgment, condemned, condemnation, damned, damnation, etc., in the New Testament*, etc. (Charlestown, 1828; 8vo, 359 pages.)

[45] See p. 205. It is noteworthy that this theory drove Balfour back to the orthodox interpretation of I Peter 3:18 ff., that "the time of the preaching of Christ by the spirit and their disobedience was one and the same time" (p. 45).

[46] *Works*, Vol. V, pp. 592 ff.

dently to meet the form of Universalism before us. He says:

> They affirm that there is not a threatening in the Bible respecting any future and eternal punishment of sinners. But all men of plain common sense who have read the Bible and whose understanding has not been darkened by the blindness of the heart and by the sophistry of deceivers, know that God has plainly threatened future and eternal punishment to the finally impenitent and unbelievers.[47]

And thus, with the most summary quotation of certain passages, he dismisses their position. In a sermon there is little room for prolonged discussion, and yet Emmons desired to strike at the root of the exegesis by which Balfour had now attempted to support Universalism. So he declares that the method of the Universalists is wrong. They come to each passage of Scripture which they quote, determined to make it support their own false principles. Single texts should be interpreted in the light of the whole Bible.

> No doctrine can be proved or refuted by merely marshalling one class of texts against another without explaining them according to some sound and accepted principle. Texts ought never to be adduced to explain and establish any first principles; but first principles are to be adduced to explain and establish the sense of every text of Scripture.[48]

This sounds like a plea for the most pronounced sort of dogmatic exegesis. But such is not Emmons' intent. He is complaining of the dogmatic exegesis of the Universalists. What he means is determined by the significance he attaches to the phrase "first principles," and this he has explained by pointing to those great and fundamental doctrines which constitute the substance of the Christian religion, and which are derived from the Bible itself. He mentions "the true meaning of God's universal goodness as consisting in universal benevolence and limited com-

[47] *Ibid.*, p. 598.
[48] *Ibid.*, p. 599.

placence" and the "true sense of the universal atonement of Christ." Reason was to have its place, though not the supreme place, in interpretation. He complains of the Universalists that

they never lay down principles and explain them, nor construe Scripture according to the dictates of reason. But those who hold to a limited salvation lay down principles and explain them. . . . . They do not set one text of Scripture against another, but explain every text agreeably to the great principles which they have established and explained.[49]

But opposition to Ballou's and Balfour's views arose among those Universalists who were still inclined to favor the doctrine of Restoration. Among these, Charles Hudson, pastor of a Universalist church in Westminster, Mass., published *A Series of Letters* addressed to Mr. Ballou[50] in which, from an intimate knowledge of the Universalist literature, he brought materials to set forth fully the doctrines he wished to refute. As is well known, this disagreement with Ballou ripened into a movement which separated from the Universalist denomination in 1831, and maintained, under the name of the "Restorationist Association," a separate existence till 1841.[51] Hudson was a sharp and witty antagonist, and when he turned his weapons against Balfour, the latter could not endure his sarcasm. He summed up the first *Inquiry* very well in the following words:

In order to ascertain whether Mr. B. has succeeded in refuting future or eternal punishment, it is proper to leave all that he has said upon Sheol, Hades, and Tartarus out of the question; for surely, if they do not mean misery at all, as Mr. Ballou contends, they do not have the least bearing in deciding the question whether misery

[49] *Loc. cit.,* p. 601.

[50] *A Series of Letters addressed to Rev. Hosea Ballou of Boston, being a Vindication of the Doctrine of a Future Retribution against the Principal Arguments used by him, Mr. Balfour and others,* etc. (Woodstock, 1827; 8vo, Vol. II, 308 pages.) For a complete review of Mr. Hudson's literary activity see Eddy, *op. cit.,* Vol. II, p. 321.

[51] Eddy, *op. cit.,* Vol. II, chap. iv.

be endless. . . . . The only word he allows to signify misery is Gehenna; and wherever it occurs in the New Testament, it is, he says,
applied to the Jews, and expresses those judgments, and those only,
which fell upon that nation at the destruction of Jerusalem. . . . .
So the whole of Mr. Balfour's labors comes precisely to this :—
If the destruction of Jerusalem does not mean endless misery, that
doctrine is not taught in the Scriptures! He has written more than
four hundred pages to show that there can be no punishment in a
future state because Jerusalem was captured in this![52]

Hudson complains also repeatedly of Balfour's apparent desire to "pull down and not build up"—a fundamental and
just criticism.

Hudson's remarks irritated Balfour extremely, as was
usually the case, for he did not seem to be able to bear criticism with equanimity, and in some remarks upon Hudson's
Letters, which he attached to his *Three Essays,* he indulged
in petty personalities. One good argument refuting Hudson's own theories is, however, found here. Punishment
arising from

"the internal state of mind" alone, and not from any external application, he says, leaves the abandoned sinner with nothing to fear in
the future world. "The more hardened he dies, so much the better
for him in the world to which he goes. . . . . If he can only contrive
to keep himself hardened in hell, what in God's universe can distress him, upon Mr. Hudson's system of future punishment?[53]

Hudson replied in a small book,[54] in which, among other
things, he pricked the fallacy of Balfour's methods of exegesis, but he succeeded in setting up no sufficient method
for himself.[55]

Less noted orthodox ministers did not neglect the subject in their parish sermons. Edward R. Tyler, of Middletown, Conn., delivered a series of *Lectures on Future Punishment* to his church which he afterward published.[56]

---

[52] *Series of Letters,* p. 167.   [53] *Three Essays,* p. 321.

[54] *A Reply to Mr. Balfour's Essays,* etc. (Woodstock, 1829; 12mo, 209 pages).

[55] *Ibid.,* pp. 37 ff.

[56] Middletown, 1829; 8vo, 180 pages. It was reviewed in the *Christian Examiner,* New Series, Vol. III (1830), pp. 392 ff., by a writer who only men-

Direct reference is made to Balfour's ideas [57] in the discussion of Gehenna. The book was a faithful and useful discussion of the whole theme. It shows how the ministry of that day overcame the danger from Universalism—by openly combating it in the pulpit.

But now a more formidable antagonist of Universalism appeared upon the scene in the person of Moses Stuart. The success with which Balfour had met among his coreligionists had induced him to call loudly for a refutation. Stuart had been frequently mentioned as the man who should undertake it, and probably it was in response to direct solicitations that he finally published, first in the *Panoplist,* and then in a separate form, his book entitled *Exegetical Essays on Several Words Relating to Future Punishment.*[58] It was not formally a reply to Balfour, and for the sake of avoiding "a polemic attitude" mentioned but one writer of opposing teaching, and him only in a short appendix. Yet it was Balfour's works which drew out the treatise, and his first *Inquiry,* and that portion of the second which referred to the words *aion,* etc., were substantially met.

The work opens with remarks upon the importance of the subject and the impossibility of answering inquiries as to the future state by the light of reason. Ancient philosophy failed even to establish the immortality of the soul. Our appeal must then be to the Bible, which must be exam-

tioned the book and then devoted himself to a statement of his own views. According to the Unitarian policy of his day, he is not very explicit. He teaches that we have "the power of forming character for heaven" (p. 293). The implication of the whole is that the character formed here determines the reward there. There is no proper punishment, for all unhappiness which follows upon wickedness works itself out. There seems to be no opportunity in the next world to form character (p. 398). He does not state explicitly that there is no opportunity for a change of character in the next world, but seems to hint that the result will be the annihilation of the wicked (p. 399).

[57] See, for example, pp. 17, 22.

[58] Andover, 1830; 8vo, 156 pages.

ined without prepossessions, candidly, and impartially. Such an examination Stuart sets himself to make.

The words αἰών and αἰώνιος are first examined. Their classical use is presented, and then in various classes the cases quoted in which they appear in the New Testament, and the meaning exhibited in each case. The presentation is fair, the summing-up convincing and the conclusion is expressed with force in these words: "Whenever αἰών is employed for the purpose merely of designating future time, as a period of duration, it designates an indefinite, unlimited time in all cases; those of future punishment being for the present excepted." [59] "In regard to all the cases of αἰώνιος which have a relation to future time, it is quite plain and certain that they designate an endless period, an unlimited duration" (the cases referring to future punishment being excepted). [60] He examines the Hebrew *olam*, and the Greek words αἰών and αἰώνιος in the LXX, with the same result.

With this general preparation he comes to consider those cases, already quoted in the investigation, in which these words are applied to future punishment. He finds these parallel in all philological respects to the cases in which the future blessedness of the righteous is stated, and he sums up his conclusion in the following words:

It does most plainly and indubitably follow that, if the Scriptures have not asserted the endless punishment of the wicked, neither have they asserted the endless happiness of the righteous, nor the endless glory and existence of the Godhead. The one is equally certain with the other. Both are laid in the same balance. They must be tried by the same tests. And if we give up the one, we must, in order to be consistent, give up the other also. [61]

The bearing of this will be seen when we recall that Stuart rested all these truths on revelation alone, since the powers

[59] *Op. cit.*, p. 37.   [60] *Ibid.*, p. 46.
[61] *Ibid.*, p. 57.

of our reason had never discovered them to heathen nations, nor ever could. He adds farther on: "I have long searched with anxious solicitude for a text in the Bible which should even seem to favor the idea of a future probation. I cannot find it." [62]

This part of the discussion ended, Stuart goes over to the consideration of Sheol, Hades, Tartarus, and Gehenna. The exposition is temperate and fair. He acknowledges all that Balfour says (though not mentioning him by name) in respect to the meaning of "Sheol" in many passages. He then introduces [63] a discussion of the figurative use of language, which sets forth the fundamental principles upon which such a word is to be interpreted, in any kind of literature. The figurative use of every word representing intangible and invisible objects must be derived from the literal uses by which it was originally restricted to objects accessible to the observation of the senses. Paradise was a pleasure garden literally; but figuratively it is the state of the blessed in the eternal world. Hence the question as to the meaning of "Sheol" and like words is not to be determined by their literal uses (as Balfour had sought to do); but the question still remains: Are they "ever employed in the figurative or secondary sense in the Old Testament?" [64] The determination of this question, Stuart confesses, "depends perhaps in great measure on the state of knowledge among the Hebrews with regard to future rewards and punishments." That they were entirely ignorant of such things, the acknowledged belief of the Egyptians as to the

[62] *Loc. cit.*, p. 60. On pp. 72 ff. Stuart notices the supposition that the meaning of αἰώνιος is "spiritual." This was a phase of the meaning suggested by Winchester in his "aionian," and resembles the modern notion that the word is "qualitative" rather than quantitative.

[63] *Ibid.*, p. 94.

[64] *Ibid.*, p. 98.

future forbids us to suppose. Many texts are evacuated of their meaning on such a supposition.[65]

The sum of the evidence from the Old Testament in regard to Sheol is that the Hebrews did probably in some cases connect with the use of this word the idea of misery subsequent to the death of the body. It seems to me that we can safely believe this; and to aver more than this would be somewhat hazardous, when all the examples of the word are duly considered.[66]

A like discussion of Hades follows. The Hades of Luke 16:23, he says, has the significance of Tartarus, the place of future and endless punishment. As to Gehenna, the discussion is shorter, but equally explicit. Of Balfour's notion that its punishment meant the destruction of Jerusalem, Stuart does not think it worth while to take notice.

This treatise practically closed the controversy on the side of the New England divines.[67] The dogmatic answer to Universalism was already made, and the exegetical answer, which only remained in some little doubt after the appearance of Balfour, was now in.[68] It is a curious illustration of the relentlessness of the logic of facts, and of the

---

[65] Such are Prov. 5:5; 9:18; Heb. 21:13; Ps. 9:17; Prov. 7:27; 15:24; Num. 16:30, 33; Deut. 32:22; I Kings 2:6, 9; Ps. 49:14, 15; Isa. 5:14.

[66] *Ibid.*, p. 114.

[67] Space forbids us to notice at length the admirable volume of Parsons Cooke, of Ware, Mass., *Modern Universalism Exposed: In an Examination of the Writings of the Rev. Walter Balfour.* (Lowell, 1834; 8vo, 248 pages.) The several chapters were originally parish sermons designed to counteract the efforts of the Universalists among his own flock, and were accompanied with success. The work rests largely upon Stuart, but has an independent value of its own, and is another proof of the well-known clearness of mind and cogency of reasoning of its writer. It is marked by the spice of wit and often sarcasm. His exposure of the "credulity" of the followers of Balfour is keen and not without apologetic value. In the same way there grew up a little book by Andrew Royce, of Wilmington, Vt., *Universalism a Modern Invention, and Not according to Godliness.* (Windsor, Vt., 1839; 12mo, 207 pages.) A. W. McClure (*Lectures on Ultra-Universalism* [Boston, 1838; 12mo, 126 pages]) fairly laughed Universalism down—a style of argument not always and everywhere fitted for success, but appropriate to the Balfourean type of doctrine.

[68] Public discussion between orthodox ministers and Universalists continued to form a feature of the times. See the "Danvers Discussion" between Braman and Thomas Whittemore, which lasted an entire day, an account of which was published by Whittemore in a pamphlet (1833).

impotence of the opinions of men to withstand their progress, that Balfour, whose theology and influence, both among the general body of the New England churches and even among his own denomination, had been annihilated by Stuart's *Essays,* had not the slightest thought that such a fate had befallen him.   He published a *Reply,* in 1831, which was full of personalities, but contained no substantial addition to the discussion.[69]   In the following year he published the third (largely rewritten) edition of his *Inquiry.*   In the Introduction he uses the following language.   After having denominated Professor Stuart's *Essays* an attempt to refute the *Inquiry,* he says:

We have too high an opinion of Mr. Stuart's understanding to think that he considers his essays deserving the name of an answer to the Inquiry. We have never heard of a single intelligent man, orthodox or otherwise, who thinks his essays a reply to it. But we have heard several express a contrary opinion. If the book [viz., the *Inquiry*] then is not unanswerable, we may say, it yet remains unanswered. . . . . Without these attacks, I might have gone down to my grave doubting whether I might not after all be mistaken in my views. It would be almost sinful in me now to doubt their correctness, considering the character, talents, and standing of the men, who have tried but failed to point out my error.[70]

And yet in 1840 Thomas Whittemore, who had been a Balfourean, issued his *Plain Guide to Universalism*—a kind of Universalist dogmatics—which leaned decidedly toward Restorationism; in 1841 the Universalists as a whole had become so favorable to restoration that the Restorationist Association could dissolve; and in 1878 the Universalist ministers of Boston and vicinity, by a vote of thirty-three to two, adopted a statement of belief which, while strongly Unitarian, and so far in accord with Ballou's theology, was

[69] *Reply to Prof. Stuart's Exegetical Essays on Several Words Relating to Future Punishment.* (Boston, 1831; 8vo, 238 pages.)

[70] *Inquiry,* pp. ix, x. Paul Dean was preaching in the same year a *Course of Lectures in Defence of the Final Restoration* (1832, large 8vo, 190 pages), which was much more in the line of the future than Balfour would have supposed.

decidedly restorationist, and marked the complete downfall of Balfour's system.[71]

[71] Eddy, *op. cit.*, Vol. II, pp. 339 ff. Discussion upon the topic was continued with intermissions and sudden resumptions for many years after this. A
pretty full bibliography may be found in Dexter's *Congregationalism*. Dexter
himself took frequent part in the controversy. Later, particularly in connection
with C. F. Hudson, the question of annihilation was broached and had a long
discussion. Nothing very substantial was added to the case, however, by the
later writers.

CHAPTER XII

THE SYSTEMS OF THEOLOGY, 1800-1840

The attention of the student of New England theology, though it is occupied again and again with the strife of public controversy, is ever recalled from the noise of debate and the glare of publicity to the quiet of some retired study in which an obscure minister, a laborious professor, or a peaceful thinker is doing the real work of promoting the progress of the school. We must now retrace our steps, go back again to about the beginning of the century into whose struggles we have so far penetrated, and study the quiet labor which was embodied in the systems of theology which were created in those early years, and which may be called the second generation of such creations in New England. They were systems, or the products of consistent and comprehensive thought; they were remarkably independent in their character; but they were prepared in full knowledge of what men were disputing upon, and register the matured conclusions of their authors upon the controverted topics. They are in this sense conditioned upon the controversies, even where they give little definite evidence of such a connection. They could not well be understood at an earlier point, but they must now be introduced, for without them the later controversies will also be unintelligible.

The first of these systems in the historical order of its origination is that of Nathaniel Emmons.[1] It was not put forth by its author; it was never written in the literary form of a treatise, and has been given to us in the original sermons preached by its author in his ordinary labors as a

[1] The best edition of Emmons' *Works* is that of the year 1860 (Boston), with a "Memoir" by Professor E. A. Park.

340

parish minister; it has thus the defects of repetition, of incomplete statement at many points, of limitation to the
necessities of popular address, incident to the sermonic
form. But it is, nevertheless, sufficiently complete; and so
far as specimens of logical and powerful reasoning are concerned it could not be improved if it had been prepared in
a more ideal way. As it appears, it is a system almost entirely rationalistic in its tone and method, though in his
own mind it was a biblical system. But little reading of it
is required to show that a true inductive method of exegesis
was unknown to Emmons, and that, when he had got
clearly in his mind what he thought to be the meaning of
the Bible in general, and had adjusted it to other truths
in a way that seemed reasonable, no single text had any
chance for an objective interpretation from him. The general effect of his style of presenting truth is to make
the hearer boldly and exclusively rationalistic.

One marked defect of the system as a system might have
been remedied if Emmons had written a systematic treatise,
though this is perhaps doubtful. This is the absence of a clear
statement of his philosophic position. On some points he
seems to have had no philosophy, for he evidently had a
profound horror of ontology, in this respect quite antici-
pating the attitude characteristic of the last half of the last
century. Did he believe in a substantial soul? His language is here and there against it. Did he even believe
in the reality of the external world, or was he a thoroughgoing Berkeleian? A clear word upon such points would
scarcely have failed us, had he been writing for more than
the exigency of a present moment. Now and then the suspicion assails us that he had really resolved all things into
the present thought of the divine Being. He has not said.

Professor Park, in the remarkable "Memoir" which he
prefixed to the last edition of Emmons' works, in which he

writes as a friend, admirer, and defender, but not as a blind partisan, has done much to clear up these questions. He recognizes the phenomenological dress in which the theology appears, when he vindicates Emmons from the charge of having taught the mode in which God secures the fulfilment of his decrees.[2]   Dr. Jacob Ide, the original editor of Emmons' works, and his son-in-law, quoting from Rev. Thomas Williams, long and intimate friend of Emmons, says that Williams said "he conversed with the doctor particularly on this subject [Berkeleianism] and was told by him that he read the work of Berkeley and was at first much perplexed with it, but when he read it a second time, he saw its fallacy and thought he could answer it." [3] He thus broke away from the Berkeleianism which had hitherto characterized the New England school, and we should scarcely suppose that he could hold the idea that the soul is a mere series of exercises.   The truth seems to be that his forms of expression are designed to emphasize the spirituality of the soul, its activity as essential to its nature, and the fact that moral character consists in activity and voluntariness.   On the other hand, there are not lacking passages which speak of the soul distinctly as an agent, possessing powers, and itself a substance.[4]   Upon the whole, we are justified in assuming that Emmons held the philosophy of the unsophisticated man upon such points, and the more because we know him to have been familiar with the early leaders of the Scotch school—Reid, Stewart, and Brown.[5]   The time had not come, however, for the distinct transfer of our theology to the new philosophical basis.[6]

Emmons regarded himself as a Hopkinsian; and with

[2] *Op. cit.*, p. 417.   [3] *Ibid.*, p. 414.
[4] *Ibid.*, p. 412.   [5] *Ibid.*, p. 70.
[6] Professor H. B. Smith (*Faith and Philosophy*, pp. 239 ff.) maintains that Professor Park's interpretation is apologetic and false; and that Emmons was a Berkeleian of an advanced type, and denied the substantial soul.

this statement we may dismiss the consideration of a considerable portion of his system. The leading idea is the sole
causality of God, which is pushed to such an extreme that,
though room is made for freedom by a bold adherence to
it as a fact of consciousness, consistency would lead rather
to a denial of all freedom. A very prominent topic is
"moral agency," in which agency is made to consist in
"exercises," and this point of view, with the divine causality
kept constantly in mind, determines most that is striking in
the system. Like Hopkins, he maintains the historic faith
of the church in the divine Trinity; in the two natures of
Christ, human and divine; in the inspiration of the Scriptures; in human depravity; in atonement, justification, sanctification; and in the future punishment of the wicked. Fur-
thermore, as to the leading explanatory, systematizing positions and theories of Hopkins, he demonstrably is, or may
safely be assumed to be, in accord with his predecessor. He
himself regarded the peculiarities of his system as *"evolved
from* Hopkins' system rather than as *added to* it." [7] Yet he
is individual where he agrees, and cannot always be dispatched with a mere reference to his master.

Emmons did much service in the earlier stages of many
of the great controversies which have already passed under
our review. Settled in the ministry in the year 1773, he
was in the full height of his power when the infidel tendencies which originated with the influence of the French in
the War of the Revolution became evident in the last decade of the eighteenth century. In 1793 he was printing
against Hume. The Antinomianism of an earlier period
had also attracted his attention and roused his efforts. In
1789 he had published against the antagonism to creeds already manifesting itself, and had tersely said: Men do not
"object against creeds because they do *not* understand

[7] Article "Emmons" in Schaff-Herzog, by Professor Park.

them, but because they *do*." And two years before West, Edwards, and Smalley had published against Universalism, Emmons had issued his first sermon (1783) against that error.[8]

Nevertheless, we must keep distinctly in mind that in respect to the Trinity and Christology Emmons belongs entirely to the generation which preceded the formal Unitarian controversy, and contributed nothing to its settlement. He was already seventy years of age when the controversy openly broke out in 1815. We may, indeed, say that his modes of representation of the Trinity had had something to do with provoking the controversy, as elsewhere shown. He belonged to that class of theologians who put the mystery of the Trinity, not in the threeness, but in the oneness. This, as Professor Park was in the habit of saying, is a legitimate form of the doctrine; but it generally leads to the charge of tritheism. His Christology was equally incapable of preventing such a movement as the Unitarian from arising, and of meeting it when it had arisen; for it had no helpful word to justify the doctrine of the personal union of the two natures. In fact, he gives it utterly up.

The question still recurs, what is meant by Christ's being one person in two natures? I answer, *the man Jesus,* who had a true body and a reasonable soul, was united with the second person in the Trinity, in such a manner as laid a foundation for him to say with propriety that he was man, that he was God, and that he was both God and man; and as laid a foundation also to ascribe what he did as God and suffered as man, to one and the selfsame person. If any should here ask, how could his two natures be thus personally united? We can only say, it is a mystery. And there is no avoiding a mystery with respect to Christ. His conception was a mystery. And if we admit the mystery of his conception, why should we hesitate to admit the mystery of the personal union between his two natures? If we only admit this, all Christ said concerning himself is easy and intelligible. Being a man, he might with propriety make himself God.[9]

[8] Park's *Memoir*, pp. 362 ff.   [9] *Works* (1860), Vol. II, p. 745.

The italicized words show how essentially Nestorian Emmons' doctrine was.

The doctrine of inspiration advocated is that of suggestion. "God . . . . not only directed them to write, but at the same time suggested what to write; so that according to the literal sense of the text, they wrote exactly as they were moved by the Holy Ghost." The argumentation in support of this position is exclusively rational and *a priori*. Not a particle of attention seems to have been paid to the facts pertaining to the theme.

Passing, now, to the distinctive tenets of Emmons, we have the great advantage of possessing an enumeration of them by Emmons himself,[10] which we shall follow in the ensuing pages. They are eight in number.

1. "Holiness and sin consist in free voluntary exercises." We have already seen that Emmons belonged to the tendency in our theology which emphasized the sole agency of God till it had excluded any proper agency in man. True, Emmons affirmed a real agency in man, and said that it was as real and perfect as if the agency of God had nothing to do with it; but he really removed it when he spoke of God's "creating" our volitions. Be that, however, as it may, we are to note now that he made holiness and sin to consist in "exercises." Hence he consistently rejected the doctrine of a sinful nature, for "there is no morally corrupt nature distinct from free, voluntary, sinful exercises;"[11] as well as the doctrine of our union with Adam in his sin, and every imputation of his guilt to us. "Adam

---

[10] In Park's Schaff-Herzog article on Emmons.

[11] *Works,* Vol. II, p. 592. Professor Park, *Memoir of Hopkins,* p. 200, traces this position to a "germ" found in Hopkins' *Two Discourses* of the year 1768. Hopkins wrote: "It is difficult, and perhaps impossible, to form any distinct and clear idea of that in the mind or heart, which is antecedent to all thought, and exercise of the will, or action, which we call principle, taste, temper, disposition, habit, etc., by which we mean nothing properly active . . . . ;" and suggests that possibly it "is wholly to be resolved into *divine constitution* or law of nature."

was the only person who committed and who was guilty of original sin." [12]   In all this he was only somewhat more clear and positive in his statements than other New England divines.[13]

With the word "exercises," however, is connected a controversy which this is the most convenient place to notice, that about the "exercise" and the "taste" schemes.

The process of regeneration will be understood differently according to the different theories which are held as to the nature of mind and of moral action.   The exercise controversy arose from these differences; but, strange as it may seem, both parties agreed for a considerable time in respect to the element of the controversy which was more important than those upon which they differed, and which had to be modified before a conclusion could be reached; viz., as to the agency of God.   Both held that this was immediate, and an act of his almighty power.

Hopkins himself, in accordance with the somewhat undefined theory of the will which he held, distinguished between regeneration and conversion, as between the divine and the human action.[14]   The Holy Spirit puts forth a causative activity, the effect of which is the "exercises of the regenerate in which they are active and agents."   The Spirit works immediately upon the heart, without means, and produces an instantaneous change in it.   The word "heart" here is used in the sense of will.   The understanding, considered as distinct from the will, is not the seat of this operation, because it is not disordered, or only so as the disorder of the will is the cause of the disorder in it.   Regeneration is not by light or truth, but the light appears

[12] *Loc. cit.*, p. 596.

[13] Henry B. Smith (*Faith and Philosophy*, p. 225) says: "The divine efficiency is the constructive idea, and the theory of exercises is the regulative factor, of the distinctive theology of Emmons."

[14] *Works*, Vol. I, pp. 367 ff.

and the truth is perceived by the mind after regeneration. It is a change in which the subject is not conscious of the divine operation; and it is perfectly consistent with human liberty, "leaving men in the exercise of all desirable or possible freedom." "The right exercises of the new heart . . . . are as much their own and as free as if they had taken place without any divine influences, were this possible." Upon regeneration conversion follows. It is "turning from sin to God . . . . holy exercise which is true love to God . . . . which implies sight and belief of the truth, repentance, faith in Christ, and submission to him."

The meaning of Hopkins is sufficiently clear in the main, but it was not stated with that crystalline clearness and positiveness with which Emmons loved to see every theological proposition enunciated. Hopkins had implied there was a holy act of the will before repentance. He proceeded therefore to "evolve" Hopkins' true meaning. There is, according to Emmons, no true difference between regeneration, conversion, and sanctification.[15] They are all the production of holy exercises in the hearts of sinners in the same way. This God does by an immediate act of power.[16] Sometimes he strives with sinners, and produces conviction, etc., uses means.[17] But all this does not effect regeneration. In this God produces holy love. He makes the heart willing.[18] This is the first act of the regenerated will. It is repentance, not some mysterious thing on which repentance follows. Emmons also combats the idea that there is planted in the heart a new taste, disposition, or principle which is prior to all holy exercises and the foundation of them. The heart that is renovated is the will. Hence the sinner is not passive in regeneration at all. He

---

[15] *Works* (ed. 1860), Vol. III, p. 96. [16] *Ibid.*, p. 79.
[17] *Ibid.*, p. 131. [18] *Ibid.*, pp. 91, 92.

is indeed as active in this as in any other exercise, for God "always works in [men] both to will and to do in all their free voluntary exercises," [19] religion constituting no special sphere by itself in this matter, since men's "activity in all cases is owing to a divine operation upon their minds." Thus he follows out logically the division of the mind into two faculties, intellect and will, and the doctrine of the sole divine causality. His answer to the supposition that the taste is affected before conversion, and that the latter is caused thereby, is, in fact, that there is no such taste, independent of the will, to be thus affected.[20]

Such a view of regeneration was as certain to be opposed as the theory, or lack of theory, of the will upon which it was based. The "taste scheme" received a powerful reinforcement when Asa Burton came on with those improvements in the classification of the faculties of the mind which were ultimately to work so great a revolution in the theory of the will. In his twenty-ninth *Essay*, "On Regeneration," [21] he dwells first upon the necessity of regeneration. This he derives from the fact that unregenerated men are not *fit* for heaven, having no relish for its delights. Christians must have benevolent love as God has it, and, since it is no mere exercise in him, but a principle, so men must have a principle, appetite, relish, or disposition for happiness as an absolute good. Burton then passes on to the *nature* of regeneration. "It is a new creation." [22] That which is created is the "appetite, relish, or disposition to be pleased with divine objects." This work is effected by the

---

[19] *Loc. cit.*, p. 110.

[20] He thus explains the necessity of Hopkins' "divine illumination:" "It is not possible, perhaps, in the nature of things, that the love of complacence should take place in the heart of any man before the love of benevolence; because he cannot see the divine beauty and excellence of benevolence before he has felt it in his own breast." Hence God first produces benevolence in man, and this is regeneration. But it is, of course, not followed by conversion: it *is* conversion.

[21] *Essays*, etc. (1824), pp. 314 ff.   [22] *Ibid.*, p. 317.

Holy Spirit instantaneously. It is immediately wrought in the "taste" or sensibility alone, and affects the other faculties mediately. From the new appetites proceeds a new train of volitions according to the necessary connection of the volitions with the taste. It would seem as if Burton agreed with the rest of his cotemporaries in teaching that God wrought this change by an exercise of his divine power. It should be added that he does not lay much stress upon the volitions, but speaks at considerable length of the effect of renewal upon the heart or taste itself. This is the more natural because he makes the taste the "spring of action" and the "principle of virtue." [23] He thus presents apparently a polar opposition to Emmons.

According to Smalley,[24] regeneration is not necessary to confer new faculties upon men or to restore old ones, to confer the power of will, or to produce a sufficient conscience; but it is necessary to give a good disposition. It is immediate and supernatural. Like Hopkins, he rejected the idea of a special illumination which should lead to regeneration.

Emmons made what he deemed a conclusive reply to these considerations.[25] The relish for good, he said to his opponents, which you demand as a condition of repentance is a feeling of complacence in holiness. But a being cannot "see the divine beauty and excellence of benevolence before he has felt it in his own breast." "Hence benevolence will produce complacence, but complacence will not produce benevolence." He elsewhere says: Sin is hating God. Can a man have a relish for the holiness of God while he hates him? The hate must first be put away, and then the relish will follow; or the change in the will must precede

[23] Emmons: "Such a principle appears to be a mere creature of the imagination."—*Works*, Vol. III, pp. 105, 122.

[24] *Sermons* (Hartford, 1803), pp. 282 ff.

[25] *Works*, Vol. III, p. 93.

a change in the affections. He also objects to the scheme that it makes a man unable to repent until this new taste be given him, which relieves him of moral obligation till that time.[26] And he adds that the law does not require this change in the taste, though it does require that change which shall make us holy.[27]

The time was not come for the conclusion of this controversy; and we dismiss it for the present. Enough has now been said to show what Emmons meant by "free voluntary exercises."

2. "Men act freely under the divine agency." What Emmons meant by "freely" we have now seen. He devoted considerable attention to the discussion of the reconciliation of divine agency with human freedom, and an entire division of his theology was allotted by the editor to this theme.[28] His doctrine may be condensed in his own forms of speech by saying that men both act and are acted upon by a divine operation, in all their voluntary exercises of whatsoever kind. Man cannot act without the divine agency, any more than a stone can move of itself. Hence in the acting of man God also acts. Second causes have no true causality. It is impossible that God should sustain moral agents in the possession of their active powers so that they should act themselves without him.

The meaning of this proposition will be clearer as we proceed. But meantime it may be observed that Emmons did not hold a very complimentary opinion of the treatment of this topic by theologians in general. "The fatalists give up activity for the sake of dependence."

The Arminians, on the other hand, give up dependence for the sake of activity. . . . . Many of the Calvinists endeavor to steer a middle course between these two extremes, and first give up activity and then dependence, in order to maintain both.[29]

---

[26] *Loc. cit.*, p. 136.

[27] *Ibid.*, p. 182.

[28] *Ibid.*, Vol. II, pp. 403 ff.

[29] *Ibid.*, p. 410.

He was thus led to inquire why activity and dependence are so generally thought inconsistent. It is not because of experience.

To believers we make the appeal. Did you ever feel the least inconsistency between activity and dependence? Did you ever perceive the divine agency to obstruct your own? Did you ever find your moral powers suspended in regeneration, in love to God, in repentance, in faith, or in any other holy affection? Were you ever conscious of being less able to grow in grace and to work out your own salvation with fear and trembling because God wrought in you both to will and to do of his good pleasure? Should you all speak the language of your own experience upon this subject, we presume you would with one voice declare that the Spirit of the Lord never destroyed, nor even obstructed, your liberty.[30]

It may be said that he does not attempt to reconcile the two elements, the reality of which he is maintaining; but he gives some suggestive hints, if not more than these, in his discussion of the relation of consciousness to the question.

Some may suppose that dependence cannot be reconciled with activity because they are conscious of being active, but not of being dependent. . . . . They appeal to common sense as an infallible proof that men act freely and voluntarily, without feeling the least compulsion or influence from the hand of God. . . . . But to what does this dictate of common sense amount? Does it prove that we are not dependent upon the Supreme Being for all our moral exercises? For supposing that God does really work in us both to will and to do, we cannot be conscious of his agency, but only of our own, in willing and doing.

Though activity and dependence are perfectly consistent, yet they are totally distinct; and of course fall under the notice of distinct faculties of the mind. Dependence falls under the cognizance of reason; but activity falls under the cognizance of common sense.[31] It is the part of reason to demonstrate our dependence upon God, in whom we live and move and have our being. But it is the part of common sense to afford us an intuitive knowledge of our activity and moral freedom. We must therefore consult both reason and common sense in order to discover the consistency between activity and dependence. Nor is this a singular case. There are many other ob-

[30] *Ibid.,* p. 412.

[31] By "common sense" he means consciousness, as is evident from the next sentences.

jects upon which we can form no proper judgment without the united
aid of reason and common sense. . . . .

If all this is true, you must acknowledge that you have the evidence of reason that you act dependently, that you have the evidence
of common sense that you act freely, and that you have the evidence
of constant experience that your activity and dependence are entirely
consistent. You are therefore as certain of the truth and consistency
of your activity and dependence as you can be of any other truth,
whose evidence depends upon the united testimony of reason and
common sense.[32]

Having thus taught the coexistence of the divine and
human agency, it was only necessary for Emmons to add
that it extended to *every* action of man to complete his
doctrine. This he does, among other passages, in the following:

If God always works in men both to will and to do, then they
are as able to work out their own salvation as to perform the common actions of life. The only reason why sinners suppose they are
less able to work out their own salvation than to do the common
actions of life is because they imagine that they need more divine
assistance in working out their own salvation than in anything
else. . . . . But there is no just ground for this conclusion. They
never do act of themselves. They live and move and have their being
in God, who constantly works in them both to will and to do in every
instance of their conduct. They are as able, therefore, to do right as
to do wrong; and to do their duty as to neglect their duty; to love
God as to hate God; to choose life as to choose death; to walk in the
narrow way to heaven as to walk in the broad way to hell; and to
turn from sin to holiness as to perfect holiness in the fear of the
Lord.[33]

Yet, after all has been said, the divine causality so over-
shadows the human as to absorb it. There is no true efficient agency in man. God determines what man shall do,
presents motives to him, and excites him to act in view of
them. Man's freedom must therefore consist in something
different from God's, since God originates and man does
not. No amount of assertion and no appeals to conscious-

[32] *Loc. cit.*, p. 413.
[33] *Ibid.*, p. 426.

ness can break the force of these assertions, which are Emmons' own.

It would be a curious investigation to inquire whether determinist views of the action of the will are ever consistent with clear and correct views of what guilt is, as personal responsibility for broken law to God, and repentance, as the confession of guilt. Usually determinists make guilt consist in liability to punishment, and do not distinguish between it and moral deformity. By the same process of depotentiation and obscuration of moral ideas they make repentance nothing more than self-loathing. A deformed person may loathe himself for his ugliness; but when a man who has sinfully incurred his deformity, like an abandoned drunkard, loathes himself, he adds an element which the innocent cripple could not—the element of self-condemnation, of the acknowledgment of guilt, which is compressed into the phrase: *"I* did it, *I* brought it upon *myself."* Perhaps nothing can more clearly reveal the true nature of a man's ethical theories than this question: Does he distinguish between deformity and guilt? When tried by this test Emmons fails. In spite of all his claim, he does not rise to the height of a true "free, voluntary, moral agency;" for guilt, as he describes it,[34] is nothing but disorder or deformity, and repentance nothing but self-loathing. He expressly claims to be loyal to the facts upon both sides of this subject; but he unconsciously abridges the freedom of man.

3. "The least transgression of the divine law deserves eternal punishment."

We have already seen the part our divines took in the discussion of future punishment in connection with the introduction of Universalism into New England. Emmons regarded this element of the argument as his own special

[34] *Works* (Ide's ed.), Vol. IV, pp. 325, 375; cf. pp. 343, 344.

contribution. What he meant may be seen by the following extract:

Many imagine that no transient, momentary act of a finite creature can contain such malignity and guilt as to deserve an eternal punishment. . . . . Sin and guilt are inseparably connected. Guilt can no more be separated from sin than criminality. There is no sin without criminality, and no criminality without guilt or -desert of punishment. Therefore both the criminality and guilt of a crime must continue as long as the crime continues, or till it ceases to be a crime and becomes an innocent action. But can murder, for instance, which is a crime in the very nature of things, ever become a virtue? Can time, or obedience, or sufferings, or even a divine declaration, alter its nature, and render it an innocent action? Virtue and vice, sin and holiness, are founded in the nature of things, and so must forever remain immutable. Hence that which was once virtuous will forever be virtuous; that which was once vicious, will forever be vicious; that which was once praiseworthy, will forever be praiseworthy; that which was once blameworthy, will forever be blameworthy; and that which once deserved punishment, will forever deserve punishment. Now, if neither the nature of sin can be changed, nor the guilt of it taken away, then the damned, who have once deserved punishment, will forever deserve it, and consequently God may, in point of justice, punish them to all eternity.[35]

4. "Right and wrong are founded in the nature of things." Emmons was here only restoring the position of Edwards in his *Nature of Virtue*, which Hopkins had in a measure obscured by his more practical method of treatment, but which he had not forsaken. Edwards founded everything in the ultimate idea of the harmony of the universe; and Hopkins had asserted the agreement of the law of holiness with the highest reason. Calvinism had often developed its idea of the sovereignty of God by applying that sovereignty even to right and wrong, and made these to depend upon the will of God, sometimes upon his "arbitrary"—that is, his sovereign—will uncontrolled from without himself. Emmons said: They do not depend upon his will at all, but are what they are in the nature of things.[36]

[35] *Works* (Boston ed.), Vol. III, p. 766.   [36] *Works*, Vol. II, pp. 176 ff.

God cannot destroy this difference without destroying the nature of things. If he should make a law on purpose to destroy the distinction between virtue and vice, it would have no tendency to destroy it. Or if he should make a law which should forbid us to love him with all our hearts, and our neighbors as ourselves, it would not destroy the obligation of his first and great command.

To support this position, he evidently appeals immediately to the moral intuitions of his hearers, for he says:

No possible alteration in the nature of things can make it our duty to lie, or steal, or murder, or exercise the least malevolence towards our fellow-creatures. This must always be sinful in our world, and in any other world of moral agents.

The importance which he attaches to this principle may be seen from his inferences. The right of private judgment, the possibility of arriving at absolute certainty in morals, the impossibility of thorough skepticism, the importance of correct sentiments, the propriety of a day of judgment, and "that all who go to Heaven will go there by the *unanimous voice of the whole universe*," are certainly most great and important deductions.

5. "God exercises mere grace in pardoning or justifying penitent believers through the atonement of Christ, and mere goodness in rewarding them for their good works." Hopkins had not fully brought out this idea because his presentation of the atonement, while fully identifying him with the Grotian school, had been incomplete, and his application of it to the system partial. In contemporaries of Emmons we read repeatedly that the atonement makes forgiveness "consistent" with the honor of God, etc. Emmons put it:

If the sole design of Christ's atonement was to satisfy the justice of God toward himself, then he exercises the same free grace in pardoning sinners through the atonement as if no atonement had been made. It has been considered as a great difficulty to reconcile free pardon with full satisfaction to divine justice. The difficulty has arisen from a supposition that the atonement of Christ was designed to pay the debt of sufferings which sinners owed to God. If this were

the design of the atonement, it would be difficult to see the grace of
God in pardoning sinners on that account. For there is no grace in
forgiving a debtor after his debt is paid, whether by himself or by
another. But sin is not a debt and cannot be paid by suffering.
Christ's suffering in the room of sinners did not alter the nature of
their sin nor take away their just deserts of punishment. . . . . None
will deny that it was grace in God to send Christ into the world to
make atonement for sin, or that it was grace in Christ to come into
the world and suffer and die to make atonement for sin; and it is
certain that the atonement he made did not lay God under obligation, in point of justice, to pardon sinners on account of his atonement; it therefore plainly follows that God exercises as real grace
in pardoning sinners through the atonement of Christ, as in sending
him to make atonement. Free pardon therefore is perfectly consistent
with free grace.

6. "Notwithstanding the total depravity of sinners, God
has a right to require them to turn from sin to holiness."
Emmons here touches upon the subject with which the
two remaining peculiarities are connected, the practical
matter of conversion and the labors of the evangelist. We
must, therefore, add these at once.

7. "Preachers of the gospel ought to exhort sinners to
love God, repent of sin, and believe in Christ immediately."

8. "Men are active, not passive, in regeneration."

Emmons' meaning is that the depravity of sinners is a
depravity of act, and, since it is moral, lies wholly in the
act. Hence, if God can ever require any act of them, he
can require their turning from sin to holiness, which consists simply in beginning holy acts. Hence preachers ought
to require the same, and nothing else—nothing which is in
any way substituted for the one essential and primal act
of repentance. And since regeneration does not take place
till men act, and consists in creating their holy acts, they,
when they are regenerated, act, and only act. He is here
but uttering concisely the contention which he had made in
opposing the "taste scheme."

Such were the leading positions of Emmons, and these

the claims which he would himself have made to the gratitude of posterity. To have sharpened somewhat the statement of important truths, to have brought them thus into
clearer light, to have made more consistent and effective
the practical labors of ministers in converting men, was
to him a source of satisfaction as an adequate aim in life
and a sufficient performance.

The "Theological Lectures" of Leonard Woods,[37] first
professor of systematic theology at Andover, are remarkable as being the first example of strictly academic lectures in theology issued by the New England divines. Andover Seminary was formed in 1808 by the union of two
parties in the evangelical wing of Congregationalism—the
"old" or "moderate" Calvinists, and the Hopkinsians, of
whom Dr. Emmons was the most eminent representative,
and the efficient leader. In deference to the first party, the
Westminster Confession was made the credal foundation
of the school, and the second party, not for the sake of
weakening the authority of the Confession, but to secure
its permanent interpretation in a truly orthodox and evangelical sense, added a special creed of their own. To both
of these creeds the professor of systematic theology was
bound; and the success of the new institution depended
upon finding a man for the first professor who could suppose himself to be true to the original creed of the Puritans, while a member of a school of thinkers who had
essentially modified it in the process of defending and improving it. Such a man was found in Leonard Woods,
who was one of the chief agents in bringing about the
establishment of the seminary, and served it with great ap-
plause and success till 1846. His position was essentially
self-contradictory. He held the main doctrines of Westminster, while rejecting the underlying philosophy of that

[37] Included in his *Works* (5 vols., Andover, 1851).

Confession; and the change in philosophy brought about many a change in details, and many a one which uncompromising supporters of Westminster, like the school at Princeton, must regard as destructive of the system. But this ambiguous position, which perhaps itself rose from the nature of the man—for he created it for himself— made him what Professor H. B. Smith called "emphatically the 'judicious' divine of the later New England theology."[38] His "Lectures" are marked by comprehensiveness, discussing the whole round of theology, and by a successful avoidance of extremes. They are discursive and explanatory rather than strongly argumentative, and confine themselves to the facts of doctrine, often to the exclusion of explanation. They avoid ontology. In the sense in which Hegel sought to ground theology in the profound truths of spirit and the world, they know nothing of speculation. They are Hopkinsian, and show strong marks of the influence of Emmons; but they do not follow this master into all his peculiarities. They give no evidence of any powerful original thinking, and if they contain new matter, it originated in every case with others. They instructed young men well and prepared them to meet the questions of the day and do their evangelical work with success. Thus they rendered good service in their generation. But they contributed nothing to the progress of theology, and have therefore a very small place in this history.

In respect to the great principles of his system, Woods built it upon the foundation of the Scriptures, which were given by inspiration.[39] Inspiration so operated as to make the Bible a book free from all error. Thus his doctrine of inspiration is "plenary." The argument is wholly from the claims of the Bible itself, and this never seems to Woods to be, what it is, a begging of the whole question.

[38] *Faith and Philosophy*, p. 258.   [39] *Works*, Vol. I, pp. 95 ff.

In fact, his argument is substantially this, that the proposed theory is necessary to justify *our idea* of the Bible. But is that idea correct? Woods neither answers nor considers this question.[40] The placing of the Bible at the head of the system would have enabled him to draw out a more complete doctrine of God, one more permeated with the biblical spirit than was becoming customary in the school; but this advantage he does not utilize. In the Trinity he agrees with his school, laying an Emmonian emphasis upon the separateness of the persons,[41] thus departing from Stuart, whose favorite word "distinction" he rejects as inadequate. He agrees with Stuart in the rejection of "eternal generation." [42] The doctrine of decrees—or, as he prefers to call it, God's purposes—is treated with constant reference to methods of popular presentation of it as an obnoxious doctrine. The characteristic of the school to give a large place to the topic of anthropology reappears here, the theory of the will being Burtonian, or a modified Edwardean theory.[43] The atonement is squarely governmental in its statement and theoretical basis,[44] the theory of virtue.[45] But it is stated in the terminology of the older theory, by the device of giving the terms surreptitiously a new meaning. Thus justice is by no means to Woods what it was to Princeton; but this fact must be inferred, for Woods does not frankly state it.[46] The system is brought to its close by discussions of regeneration, justification, eschatology, etc., as to some of which his positions will come up better in other connections.

As Woods may be called the immediate official successor of Emmons as a theologian and theological teacher—for Andover was the outcome of an endeavor to perpetuate the

[40] *Ibid.*, pp. 157 ff. [41] *Ibid.*, p. 431.

[42] *Ibid.*, p. 393. [43] *Ibid.*, Vol. II, p. 95.

[44] *Ibid.*, p. 468. [45] *Ibid.*, Vol. III, p. 56.

[46] *Ibid.*, Vol. II, p. 469.

influence of Emmons in a Hopkinsian theological school—
it will be well to compare his positions explicitly with Emmons' own statement of his distinctive principles given
above. As to the first ("holiness and sin consist in free,
voluntary exercises") Woods demurred.

Holiness or unholiness belong primarily and essentially to *man
himself,* as an intelligent, moral being, and to his *actions* secondarily
and consequentially. You may ask whether there is anything *back*
of right moral action, that is *prior* to it. I answer, yes; there is an
agent, endued with all necessary moral powers and faculties. And
there is something more than an agent, and something more than a
moral agent. If the actions are holy, there is a *holy* moral agent,
and if the actions are unholy, there is an *unholy* agent. It is in reference to this subject that Christ says, "The tree is known by its fruit."
. . . . The connection between the character of the actions and the
character of the agent is invariable. Take an unrenewed sinner, who,
according to Scripture, is an enemy to God. What now is necessary
in order that he may love God? It is necessary that he should be
born again. *He,* the *man,* must be created anew; and if he is created
anew, it will be *unto good works:*—not that *good works* must be
created, he himself remaining unchanged; but that *he* must be created
anew, and then, as a matter of course, good works will be performed.
If a man is regenerated, or made holy, holy affections and acts will
follow—he will love and obey God. . . . . To say that regeneration
consists in good moral exercises, that is, in loving God and obeying
his commands, seems to me to be an abuse of language. It is as unphilosophical and strange as to say that the birth of a child consists
in his breathing, or that the creation of the sun consists in his shin-
ing.[47]

Thus he went wholly over to the Burtonian scheme, the
"taste" scheme, and taught that God immediately creates
in the sinner a new taste for holy things, consequent upon
which he wills to do them.

As to the second ("men act freely under the divine
agency"), Woods, while necessarily differing, in consequence of his position as to the taste, in the definition of
the divine agency in relation to ours, on the whole adopted
a decidedly Emmonian way of defending this position,

[47] *Loc. cit.,* pp. 537 f.

proving the divine agency from the divine attributes,
works, and word, and human freedom from consciousness.[48] As to the third ("the least transgression of the
divine law deserves eternal punishment"), Woods, in reply
to John Foster, lays emphasis upon our inability to determine what is a just punishment for sin, thus substantially
rejecting Emmons' position; while he makes the chief force
of his own reply, outside of the scriptural argument (his
ultimate proof), to consist in the affirmation that sin will
be eternal, and consequently eternal punishment is appropriate.[49] As to the remaining positions, Woods was in
substantial agreement with Emmons, the differences only
excepted which follow immediately from the difference as
to the will already developed.

Chronologically the remaining system, that of Timothy
Dwight,[50] president of Yale College, preceded that of
Woods, and the latter writer frequently quotes from
Dwight. It was presented to the public in the form in
which it was delivered, viz., that of sermons, which were
preached before the college audience each Sunday of the
college year, the complete course occupying four years in
delivery. It was therefore begun about the year 1795, was
committed to writing in 1809, and published in 1818.[51]
But in a peculiar degree it represented no special school in
the New England divinity, and did not lie in the line, pro-

[48] *Ibid.*, Vol. I, pp. 514, 518.

[49] *Ibid.*, Vol. III, pp. 285 ff.

[50] Timothy Dwight, born at Northampton, Mass., May 14, 1752; died at New
Haven, Conn., January 11, 1817; graduated from Yale in 1769, at a little more
than seventeen years of age; tutor there, 1771, etc.; joined the army at West
Point as chaplain, 1777; served in the Massachusetts legislature for Northampton in 1781 and 1782; settled in Greenfield, Conn., in the ministry, in 1783;
D.D. from Princeton in 1787; president of Yale College, 1795–1817. He was a
grandson of Jonathan Edwards, and his own grandson, Timothy Dwight, was
president of Yale 1886–98.

[51] *Theology Explained and Defended in a Series of Sermons* (Middletown,
1818), and many times thereafter, the last current editions being from the press
of Harper Brothers.

ceeding through Hopkins and Emmons, in which we are to place Woods. It stands largely by itself, and may be appropriately considered by itself, at the close of this collection of early systems.

The position of the author, at the head of the strongest religious institution of the country, in which he had the opportunity of presenting his system to successive generations of students who furnished the most numerous single group of Congregational ministers, gave him a very wide influence as a theologian. The lectures deserved their reputation and their influence, for their learning was ample, their grace of manner considerable, their practical character marked, and their chiefest characteristic their strong common-sense. Free from vagaries of every sort, they often stopped to rebuke vagaries with emphasis. They held strongly to their course, reviewed the great doctrines with comprehensiveness and completeness, and, without the intermixture of much metaphysics, defended the standard positions of Calvinistic orthodoxy as it had been developed in New England by the year 1800. If they contributed little to the further development of the system of New England theology, they did much to hold that development to sound lines; and it was from the sermons of Dwight that Lyman Beecher obtained his theology, as well as one still greater, not only as a defender of the past but as an original mind—N. W. Taylor.

Lacking the creative element, these sermons do not claim a large place in a genetic history of New England theology. They are strongly argumentative so far as the discussion of single doctrines is concerned, but they do not build the whole system from its beginnings, step by step, till all is erected one substantial and linked structure. They begin, it is true, with the existence of God, and go back to the ultimate principle of causality as the foundaton of the proof; but though they employed the Scriptures both in this argument and later as the source of much proof, and in fact of the principal, and at times of the exclusive proof of doctrines of the first importance, the Scriptures are themselves nowhere *proved*—that is, their inspiration and authority established by appropriate and cogent argumentation. This topic was probably remanded to the author's lectures upon the evidences of Christianity, which have never been published.

Dwight's general conformity to the New England school might be shown by illustrating his adherence to the elder Edwards in the outlines of the theory of the will and of the nature of virtue, by showing that he held the governmental theory of the atonement with the younger Edwards, and by exhibiting his tendency to reject the more marked excrescences of the Calvinistic scholasticism, like imputation. It will be enough here to mention these facts.

One of the chief services rendered by this work was its steady and broad antagonism to that tendency in our theology which seemed at one time about to triumph, and to put all agency in God, to the real destruction of human agency. The predecessor and teacher of Taylor, who was to vindicate a true place for man as an agent, ranged himself with Burton and other advocates of the "taste scheme," and rejected both of Emmons' main points, his "exercises" and his exclusive divine agency. He has hardly got fairly into the swing of his discourse before he stops to put in the caveat that "God cannot be proved to be the efficient cause of sin," [52] and in the first volume has a sermon on "exercises." [53] He argues vigorously that the soul is not a "mere succession, or chain, of ideas and exercises." This view is contrary to those natural conceptions of mankind by which every man regards himself as "a being, a sub-

[52] Sermon VIII.   [53] Sermon XXIV.

stance, an agent, immediately the subject of his own
thoughts, and the cause and author of his volitions and
actions." "Attributes cannot be conceived to exist independently of substances, or of something in which they in-
here." He objects to the view as "destroying personal
identity."

An idea is a mere event, having a momentary existence and then
perishing forever. Should another idea afterwards exist, exactly
resembling it in everything but the period in which it exists, it would
not and could not be the same. . . . . On this plan, therefore, the
soul of man has no continued existence, except for an indivisible
moment, and is not the same thing which it was the preceding hour,
day, or year, but has varied and become an absolutely new soul
through every moment which has passed since it was created, and
will continue to be a new thing every moment throughout eternity.

There is, then, nothing which can be rewarded or punished
by God. Neither guilt nor virtue can exist. The influence
of motives is forever gone, being replaced by the "immediate creation" of every volition. And it is rendered impossible for one human being to receive impressions from
any other, since to give an impression is to act, and an
idea, "a thing, merely passive," cannot act.[54] Regeneration therefore consisted to Dwight in a change of heart
which "consists in a relish for spiritual objects communicated to it by the power of the Holy Ghost." This is like
Burton; but, whereas Burton was perfectly sure about the
connection of this change with the new volitions, Dwight
said: "Of the metaphysical nature of this cause [of voli-
tions] I am ignorant." But virtuous volitions as truly and
certainly followed this communication of relish as if they
were created. Then follow new views of truth, or Hopkins' "illumination."

[54] Professor H. B. Smith (*Faith and Philosophy*, p. 241) suggests that this
sermon was not directed against Emmons, but against Jonathan Edwards the
Younger. This is very doubtful, for Edwards had no influence in New Haven,
having in fact died at Schenectady in 1801, while the sermons were not put in
writing till 1809. Emmons was, however, still living in the full tide of his influence.

But there was a new element in this system which demands more careful attention, in the presentation of which Dwight had been anticipated by none of his New England predecessors. He added to the "system of doctrines" a "system of duties" which occupies seventy-two out of the one hundred and seventy-three sermons of the series. It is a complete system of practical ethics.

The general outline of the system of duties is simple. It begins with referring all virtue to the two great commandments upon which all others are dependent, the commandments to love God with all the soul, and one's neighbor as oneself. The Ten Commandments of the Decalogue are next taken up, and all the various Christian virtues derived from these by a process of inference or of logical extension of the literal meaning of the specific commands. Thus, in discussing the "first great commandment," the duties of reverence for God, humility, and resignation are added to the literal obligation to "love" God. The second great commandment leads him to treat of the effects of benevolence upon personal happiness and on public happiness. He then inserts the somewhat remarkable proposition: "that Virtue is founded in Utility." [55] No wonder that he was called a Utilitarian, since he took the name himself, and that the charge of Utilitarianism long attached to the New Haven school. But in the sense in which he used the term he was entirely right when judged by the principles of the "Rightarians," as they have sometimes been called. He meant, in his own words, that "a tendency to produce happiness constitutes the excellence and value of virtue." There was to Dwight, as well as to the other New England theologians, an ultimate good which it was the intuitive obligation of every man to seek to attain. That good he made "happiness." This was the only "ultimate

[55] Sermon XCIX.

good;" and the only "original cause" of happiness was virtue. Had he defined happiness as the full and normal exercise of all our powers, he would have seen that holiness, as
the exercise of the moral powers, was itself happiness; and
as the exercise of the noblest of those powers, the highest form of happiness. But he never would have admitted
for an instant that any result of malevolence, arising from
any new perversity of things, whereby it produced happiness, could justify hating any creature, or constitute such a
hate into virtue!

So general is the acceptance with which Dwight's views
on practical subjects have met that it is not necessary to
follow his discussions into their details. We may therefore leave this majestic figure in our middle history, who
was all the greater because he left so little that was peculiar
to himself. He powerfully sustained the general work of
our theology, and transmitted it buttressed and defended
at essential points. That he did this so well as to relieve
his successors of the necessity of doing it again gave them
the opportunity, which he scarcely had, of exercising the
critical and originating faculty and of asking what further
errors might be corrected and what further truths introduced.

THE RIPENED PRODUCT

CHAPTER XIII

NATHANIEL W. TAYLOR

This great thinker has already been brought before the reader in connection with the discussions upon the will and with the Unitarian controversy. It may be said that the latter controversy determined his whole theological career for it was his purpose to refute the Unitarian reasoning thoroughly, and for this end to explore completely the whole subject of anthropology, that led him to the theological positions which he took and which have received the name of Taylorism. Yet it was his fate to wage his controversies with his brethren rather than with the common adversary; for he assumed the aspect to many of them of the theological innovator, and they felt called upon to oppose him in the interests of the very orthodoxy which he was trying to defend in a more fundamental and conclusive way. It is not the first example in the history of theology of men's confounding defending a doctrine in a new way with subverting that doctrine.

What has been already said of Taylor's doctrine of the will must therefore be constantly kept in mind in our further studies. And it must also be noticed that the full measure of his departure from Edwards remained concealed from Taylor himself. Neither his opponents nor he had a fine historical sense, nor perceived that they were in the midst of a great theological development, and themselves the actors in it. To agree with Edwards was still the high ambition of them all; and when they consciously disagreed, as did Taylor, they thought they were only expressing better Edwards' true meaning.

The great controversies of Taylor began with a sermon

delivered in New Haven, in 1828, upon moral depravity, the famous *Concio ad Clerum*. The proposition maintained in this sermon was "that the entire moral depravity of mankind is by nature." In it Taylor successively maintained, among others, the positions that moral depravity is sinfulness; that this is not created in man, nor does it consist in acting Adam's act; that it is not a disposition or tendency to sin which is the cause of all sin; that it is "man's own act, consisting in a free choice of some object rather than God, as his chief good;—or a free preference of the world and of worldly good, to the will and glory of God." [1] He then advances to the proposition that this depravity is by nature. He defines it: "that such is their [men's] nature that they will sin and only sin in all the appropriate circumstances of their being." [2] Men's nature is not itself sinful, nor is it the physical or efficient cause of their sinning, but it is the occasion of their sinning. In the applicatory "remarks" of the sermon he said again that "guilt pertains exclusively to voluntary action." [3]

In these positions, while supposing himself to hold the essence of the doctrine of his predecessors, Taylor had consciously modified its form. He had, in fact, only brought out more clearly than they the positions toward which Hopkins, Emmons, and Dwight were historically tending. But the full meaning of his teaching depended upon his new conception of the will, upon the new and real freedom which he had at last succeeded in giving it. This constituted the strange element, and was the true occasion of the opposition which he aroused.

This opposition was, however, more directly excited by a position taken in the sermon quite incidentally to its main purpose. Taylor suggested a new idea upon the prevention

---

[1] *Concio*, p. 8.   [2] *Ibid.*, p. 13.
[3] *Ibid.*, p. 25.

of sin. In defending the proposition that universal moral depravity was not inconsistent with the moral perfections of God (thus intentionally meeting the grand objection of Channing and other Unitarians), he opposed the doctrine which, under the influence of Bellamy, had been prevalent in New England, that sin was the necessary means of the greatest good, and sought to substitute for it the supposition (for it was not presented as a matter susceptible of exact proof) that, owing to the nature of moral agency, God *could not prevent sin,* or at least the present degree of sin, in a moral system.

It is exceedingly important for a comprehension of the following discussions that Taylor's meaning be fully understood. He took the words of the old proposition in their obvious meaning. By "necessary" he understood indispensable; and by "means," that directly employed to effect a given purpose. The only means of good to Taylor was good itself; and since the greatest good, which is the permanent prevalence of the highest holiness, might be procured by the unvarying holy choices of all moral agents, if they only would thus choose, he could not call evil "necessary" to that good. He believed that God gave man free agency because he could thereby make him a being capable of holiness, which consists in free choices. He gave it to him for this positive purpose only. Incidentally, it involved the possibility of sin, which actually followed in the history of the human race. *Perhaps* God, having given, and maintaining free agency among men, could not prevent all sin. But he chose, not the sin, in any sense, but holiness, and free agency as the condition thereof; neither did he prefer sin even, in the words of some, "all things considered," or that degree of sin actually existing, but always holiness. He did prefer moral agency, though it would involve sin; and hence he never preferred or decreed sin directly. It is involved in his decrees, but not as itself a thing decreed.

To let Taylor speak for himself:

> Is it more honorable to God to suppose that such is the nature of *sin* that he could not accomplish the highest good without it, than to suppose that such is the nature of *free agency* that God could not wholly prevent its perversion? . . . . The prevention of sin by any influence that destroys the *power to sin* destroys moral agency. Moral agents must then possess the power to sin. Who then can prove *a priori*, or from the nature of the subject, *that a being who can sin will not sin?* How can it be proved *a priori*, or from the nature of the subject, that a thing will not be, when for aught that appears it may be? [4]

It will be noted here that the fundamental thought underlying all the discussion is the new idea of freedom. God has given man the power of acting as a true first cause, and has thus placed him beyond the reach of true power, even the divine power, as a determining cause of his volitions.

Three controversies followed the appearance of this sermon, of which two sprang directly and solely from it, the third partially.

I. THE CONTROVERSY WITH HARVEY

The year following (1829), Joseph Harvey, pastor of the church at Westchester, Conn., reviewed Taylor's sermon in a pamphlet of forty pages. The review begins with discussing the proposition that moral depravity is man's own act. As soon as he has finished his review of Taylor's citations of authorities, he affirms that the theory is "irrational and unbiblical. It alleges an effect without a cause." [5] He thus shows at the outset that he has not followed Taylor in the adoption of the new position as to the will, and cannot conceive of the cause of any volition lying entirely in the causing agent. He is still upon the

[4] *Loc. cit.,* p. 32.

[5] *A Review of a Sermon,* etc. (Hartford, 1829), p. 14.

old Edwardean basis. Such criticism is not likely to help.
Hence he goes on to maintain, by a variety of arguments,
that the corrupt nature of man is itself sinful, though even
Edwards had taught that all sin was voluntary. The great
proof is that God regards and treats infants as sinners.
The fundamental objection to Taylor he states in these
words:

> If then Dr. Taylor means, as he says he does, that nature is not
> the efficient cause of sin, but the occasion or reason of it, he relin-
> quishes the certainty of effect and admits that its actual occurrence
> depends upon circumstances. And this, according to his own defini-
> tion, is Arminianism.[6]

In other words, Harvey cannot understand the new
theory of the will.

The last division of the criticism considers Taylor's
views upon the permission of sin. Harvey begins with a
complete misunderstanding of Taylor. He summarizes his
opponent thus: "Sin is on the whole an evil in the government of God which he did not choose to permit, but which
he could not prevent." Nothing is clearer than that Taylor taught that God did, on the whole, "choose to permit"
sin. He said in the *Concio* "that the providential purposes
or decrees of God extend to all actual events, sin not excepted."[7] God ordained "the system" with a full knowledge of what it involved, and therefore he, on the whole,
chose to permit what was involved. Harvey, in reply to
what he has stated as Taylor's position, maintains that
God can prevent sin, and cites the angels as a proof of this
fact; but he does not touch Taylor's argument by this
objection, since Taylor would include the angels in the system in which we are, would also cite the fallen angels, and
even now had in mind a thought, which he brought out
more clearly later, that God was limited by the best good

[6] *Ibid.,* p. 28.
[7] *Concio,* p. 34.

of all considered, or could not *consistently* prevent sin in a moral system. So completely had he failed to understand Taylor. The idea of any self-limitation upon the part of the Deity was thoroughly abhorrent to his thinking.

The following June (1829) both these pamphlets, the *Concio* and Harvey's *Review,* were discussed in the *Quarterly Christian Spectator,* published in New Haven, and serving as the medium for the extension of the influence of the Divinity School and its leading professor. The position of Mr. Harvey, as lingering upon the untenable ground of Edwards, where he had remained after rejecting imputation, by an "utter confusion of personal identity," [8] is exhibited, and it is declared necessary either to go back to imputation or forward to the position that all sin is actual. Harvey's argument from sin to a sinful cause is shown to rest upon the groundless supposition that "the cause of a given effort must have the same properties or attributes as the effect itself." [9] The defects of his theory of the will are reduced to his failure to distinguish between the three faculties of the mind.[10] A discussion of efficient and occasional causes is added, in which the former kind of cause is reserved for the acting agent. Pains are also taken in this review to present again Dr. Taylor's theories as to the prevention of sin, and to show how the theory that sin is the necessary means of the greatest good was, in Taylor's mind, an excess of speculation from which he desired to recall theology. The reviewer strikes again the keynote of the discussion in the following words:

The moral government of God, in distinction from his providential dominion, has been a subject of but little discussion. The views of men concerning it are apt to be loose and indefinite. Almost everything pertaining to the government of God has been referred to his physical agency. Hence it has been inferred from his omnipotence,

[8] *Spectator, loc. cit.,* p. 349.
[9] *Ibid.,* p. 352.
[10] *Ibid.,* p. 362.

as a kind of axiom, that God could, in a moral system, have prevented all sin. This has been supposed to result so directly from his power that a doubt respecting it has seemed to involve a question respecting his perfection. Yet it is not a limitation of his power to say that what in the nature of the case is impossible, could not have been done. And do we know that, in the nature of the case, all sin, or the present amount of sin, could have been prevented and yet a moral government have existed at all? Plain it is that, if sin be prevented, this must be done not by force alone but by a moral influence exerted upon created minds. Moral beings are voluntary beings. They act under the influence of motives. If they are kept from sinning, it is not because they cannot sin, but because obedience is their choice.[11]

Mr. Harvey himself (it would seem) replied to this review in an *Examination* (1829).[12] He tries, with little success, to turn the objections which had been made to his positions. For instance, he tries to modify the position that a cause must have the attributes and properties of the effect; but he ends by saying that "in the case supposed . . . . they are in respect to each other invariably the same, like a stream to a fountain."[13] He puts the question in dispute in this form: "Are men sinners from their birth?"[14] Harvey answers this question in the affirmative because he does not acknowledge that the knowledge of law is necessary to sin.[15] He thinks that there may be moral action, which is sinful, from birth, even before knowledge of law can be had, and this condition of sinful moral action is what he means by nature when he says that man is a sinner by nature.

Ineffective as all this was, Harvey nevertheless rendered some service in the dispute by pressing Taylor upon points which he had scarcely considered sufficiently. Thus he demands to know how Dr. Taylor accounts for the certainty of sin and for its certain universality upon his theory

[11] *Ibid.*, pp. 379 f.

[12] Published at Hartford; 8vo, 53 pages. In Oberlin College Library, No. 204 R 2721.   [13] *Examination*, p. 10.

[14] *Ibid.*, p. 13.   [15] *Ibid.*, p. 30.

of freedom.[16]   Taylor had been quite indistinct as to this crucial point, and needed to be sharply called to a definite answer.   But no such answer was forthcoming.   And then Taylor had propounded an explanation of the way that sin rises historically in the developing life of an infant.   He had said:

A child enters the world with a variety of appetites and desires which are generally acknowledged to be neither sinful nor holy. Committed in a state of utter helplessness to the assiduity of parental fondness, it commences existence the object of unceasing care, watchfulness, and concession, to those around it.   Under such circumstances it is that the natural appetites are first developed; and each advancing month brings them new objects of gratification.   The obvious consequence is that self-indulgence becomes the master principle in the soul of every child long before it can understand that this self-indulgence will ever interfere with the rights, or entrench on the happiness, of others.   Thus by repetition is the force of constitutional propensities accumulating a bias towards self-gratification, which becomes incredibly strong before a knowledge of duty or a sense of right and wrong can possibly have entered the mind.   That moment— the commencement of moral agency, at length arrives.   Does the child now come in a state of perfect neutrality to the question whether it will obey or disobey the command which cuts it off from some favorite gratification?   If the temptation presented to constitutional propensities could be so strong in the case of Adam, as to overpower the force of established habits of virtue in the maturity of his reason, how absolute is the certainty that every child will yield to the urgency of those propensities under the redoubled impulse of long cherished self-gratification and in the dawn of intellectual existence!   Could the uniform certainty of this event be greater if the hand of Omnipotence were laid upon the child to secure the result? [17]

Evidently, this is an explanation of the case by "circumstances," as Harvey points out, and by circumstances which differ greatly in different cases.   And though Harvey does not avoid forms of expression that lay him open to a sharp verbal reply, he is right in urging the necessity of explaining how universal sin results from such a condition of

[16] *Loc. cit.,* p. 36.

[17] *Spectator,* June, 1829, p. 366.   This suggestion had been considered by Edwards in his *Original Sin;* cf. above p. 86.

things as is here presented. "The consent or choice of the will is, then, after all, the turning point in the existence of sin. The reviewers have told us how the natural propensities are excited and increased, but they have not told us how they result in choice." [18] In pressing Taylor so hard at this point, Harvey pointed the way to a necessary further advance. But Taylor was not able to make it.

Taylor, however, replied to Harvey in an *Inquiry*,[19] in which he first defended himself from the charge of departure from Dr. Dwight, and then discussed the points brought forward in the *Examination*. He thought the prospect "fair" "of a speedy and an almost exact agreement" between the contestants. He recalls Harvey from the point which that gentleman had stated as the true issue (whether men are sinners from their birth), to the true point as he conceives it, the nature of sin. He drives Harvey into the corner as to the possibility of a sin before conscious voluntary transgression; but he does not answer the difficulty about the previous certainty of sin upon the basis of a doctrine of freedom.

One or two more tracts followed in this controversy; but they added nothing to the presentation of the issue. Taylor's views were still too new to be properly understood by the churches.

II. THE CONTROVERSY WITH WOODS

We have already followed Dr. Leonard Woods, of Andover, in his controversy with the Unitarians, and have seen the immovable conservatism of his position, which prevented him from attempting any constructive work upon the doctrines involved, by which work alone a helpful reply could have been given and the state of theology really advanced. The same conservatism, joined with

---

[18] *Examination*, p. 38.　　　　[19] New Haven, 1829; 43 pages.

some inability to put himself at another man's point of view, led him to form an unfavorable estimate of the tendencies of Taylor's suggestions in the *Concio,* and, with a good deal of solemn and misplaced unction, to reply to them at considerable length.[20]

The reply is principally confined to Taylor's suggestions as to the prevention of sin. But no sooner does Woods strike the subject than it is evident that he is incapable of understanding Taylor. Whereas Taylor's idea was that it was impossible for God to prevent sin while maintaining the moral system in which agents are inalienably able to sin, Woods infers that he meant that God had no power to prevent it "in the literal and proper sense."[21] As soon as the discussion of the subject fairly begins, Woods presents his own theory,[22] which may be concisely stated thus: The existence of sin is a mystery. "The incomprehensible God, for reasons which lie beyond human intelligence, taking a perfect view of his own attributes and of the whole system of created beings, saw it to be best not to prevent the existence of moral evil" and "chose to admit it into the universe," and "will make it a means of glory to his name and of good to his kingdom." Thus he takes a position midway between the plain, unvarnished Hopkinsian "means of the greatest good" and Taylor's ascription of the difficulty to the will of man. He later argues powerfully in support of Hopkins' view[23] and is, on the whole, inclined to it. But he is always prepared to deny stoutly the supposition that God could not prevent sin.

The root of his opposition to the idea that God could not prevent sin while maintaining moral agency is exhibited as soon as he touches upon the subject of the will. He does not believe in "power to the contrary," thus occu-

[20] *Letters to Rev. Nathaniel W. Taylor, D.D.* (Andover, 1830; 114 pages).
[21] *Op. cit.,* p. 27.   [22] *Ibid.,* p. 37.   [23] *Ibid.,* pp. 70 f.

pying the Burtonian position.[24]   Taylor's theory, he says,
"seems to imply that moral agents as such, that is, moral
agents in the exercise of their moral agency, are not dependent upon God;" and dependence upon God he defines
thus: "That it depends upon God's will whether their
moral agency shall be exerted in one way or another." [25]
That is strict Edwardean determinism.   He was thus led
to believe that Taylor's scheme would tend "towards a
denial of all divine power and divine influence in the conversion of sinners except merely such a kind of power and
influence as we have over the minds of our fellow men." [26]
He himself later recurs to the old theory of the arbitrary
will of God, for he proves that God has power to convert
men by several arguments, among which are, "God is
omnipotent," [27] and makes an antithesis between the "will,
counsel, or pleasure of God" and his "power" to convert.[28]

Thus it is evident that Woods could not understand
Taylor, and that his part in the controversy was not calculated to throw any more light upon the subject than Harvey's had been.   Both of these writers were, in fact, outside the current of the New England development, and,
while loyal to such predecessors as Hopkins, failed entirely to comprehend Hopkins or his great constructive associates in the true significance of their labors.   This was
the less astonishing in Wood's case, for it was a fundamental idea in the constitution of Andover Seminary, for
which he was more responsible than any other person,
that a man could be both a Hopkinsian and a true follower
of Westminster.   The theological struggle to unite these
irreconcilable positions is the tragedy of that institution.

[24] *Ibid.*, p. 40.

[26] *Ibid.*, p. 47.

[28] *Ibid.*, p. 65.

[25] *Ibid.*

[27] *Ibid.*, p. 61.

As usual, the New Haven writers replied in the *Spectator*.[29] The reply is exceedingly sharp when compared with the labored and cumbrous style of Dr. Woods. After showing that Woods has erected Taylor's hypothesis into a theory, thus improperly changing the point at issue, the reviewer goes on to prove that Woods "conceded the great principle maintained by Dr. Taylor . . . . by affirming that *all* that the nature of the case admits of our saying is this: that God for wise and good reasons decided to permit the existence of sin." [30]

Now if these things are so—if the reasons for God's permission of sin are known only to his own infinite mind, if we are incapable of discovering the reasons—if the case does not admit of assigning a reason, then to assign the reason in question, viz., "that sin is the necessary means of the greatest good," is wholly unwarranted. Has not Dr. Woods, then, most abundantly conceded all that Dr. Taylor asserts on this point? The whole includes the parts; and if *no* reason can properly be assigned in the case, then, this particular reason, Dr. Woods himself being judge, cannot be assigned. What concession could be more ample or complete? If God *"only"* knows the reasons for the entrance of sin into the universe, then Dr. Woods does not know them; and, as Dr. Taylor says, "ignorance is incompetent to make an objection."

But ample as these general concessions are, Dr. Woods has been more specific. He has actually adopted the very statements of those whom he has come forward to arraign before the public. Dr. Taylor asks in substance, may not God have chosen his present "method of administration" not *because* (as any part of the reason) it embraced moral evil, "but *though* or notwithstanding it would not entirely exclude (such) evil." Now this is the identical statement made by Dr. Woods in the following passage. *May* not this have been the case, says Dr. Taylor. *Might* not this be the case, says Dr. Woods; this is the sole difference.—"Might not God see that the particular mode of proceeding which he actually adopted, was better than any other, ... and *though* it would not entirely exclude evil, would ultimately raise his kingdom to a higher degree of holiness and happiness than any other? [31]

Aggravating as this mode of turning the controversy

29 Volume for 1830, pp. 540 ff.   30 *Ibid.*, p. 542.
31 *Ibid.*, p. 543.

must have been, it did in fact exhibit the entire consistency
of Taylor's new explanations with the fundamental positions of his predecessors and contemporaries, and thus legi-
timatize his speculations in the system of New England
thought. The remaining portions of the reply, while
equally effective as an answer to Woods, did nothing to
further the controversy. Others joined in the discussion,
as, for example, Rev. E. R. Tyler in a sermon with the
illuminating title, *Holiness Preferable to Sin* (1829); but
the controversy was soon lost in the stir occasioned by a
still greater one, viz.:

III. THE CONTROVERSY WITH TYLER

The roots of this controversy lie far back in the New
England history. We have seen the great interest which
was displayed from the time of Edwards himself in all the
philosophy of revivals. The discussions of methods of ex-
horting sinners, and of the proper use of the "means" of regeneration, had been frequent; and the appearance of a
new work upon this subject at any time would have been
always regarded as entirely appropriate—indeed as a favorable indication as to the piety and earnestness of the
churches.

It was therefore quite in the order of things when
Gardner Spring, pastor of the Brick Church, New York,
published in 1827 *A Dissertation on the Means of Regeneration.* He defines the means as "whatever is adapted to
arrest the attention of men to moral and spiritual objects,"
including the Bible, ministry, word of God, sabbath, sanctuary, etc. God seems uniformly to connect the operation
of his Spirit with these means,[32] and in the offers of the
gospel he is entirely sincere. Now, unregenerate men make
only an insincere and wrong use of the means,[33] and the

[32] *Op. cit.*, pp. 6, 7.   [33] *Ibid.*, p. 13.

question hence arises how such a use of means is connected with regeneration.[34]   Such a use is not acceptable
to God; there is no promise made to such a use of means;
they do not bring man to holiness; they do not always terminate in regeneration; they do not change the heart,
which is the result of the immediate exercise of the divine
power.   Spring speaks of this as the "production" of holiness.[35]   He thus uses the phrase of Emmons, and his doctrine is that of Emmons, its metaphysical elements being
omitted.   He says:

> The principal reason why this influence is necessary is that un-
> regenerated men are enemies to God and holiness, and their hostility
> is so unyielding that no light communicated to their understanding,
> no obligations addressed to their conscience, no motives presented to
> their hopes or their fears, can produce holy love.[36]

Thus they are substantially put out of the entire reach of
the moral government of God and reduced under a government of force.

It can be of little interest to know that Spring found
under these circumstances some use for "means."   They
enlighten the understanding, impress the conscience, illustrate the obduracy of the heart, exhibit the powerlessness
of men.[37]   Hence the only true exhortation to be addressed
to men when unrepentant is to repent, not to use the means
of regeneration.

Taylor, who was a great preacher and evangelist, could
not rest easy under the publication of such doctrines, after
he had once got clear ideas upon the nature of the sensibility and the will, and had begun to understand the moral
government of God.   Accordingly, he reviewed Spring in
the several numbers of the *Spectator* for 1829 at great
length.   Spring left the question why the sinner should do
anything preparatory to conversion substantially unan-

[34] *Loc. cit.*, p. 16.   [35] *Ibid.*, pp. 17–24.
[36] *Ibid.*, p. 25.   [37] *Ibid.*, pp. 26–32.

swered. He did not show a way to the heart whereby it might be influenced to repent, nor justify his doctrine that the sinner should be exhorted to nothing but immediate repentance. The pulpit, unless sustained by reasons drawn from other regions, was prostrated by his argument. It was to raise it again, to perform the task left unperformed by Spring, to find a neutral point in the mind to which the motives of the gospel could be addressed and the pulpit make its appeal, that Taylor wrote.

He begins by denying that acts which are themselves sinful can be in any proper sense of the words called "using the means of regeneration." [38] He lays down the great principle that "the mode of divine influence is consistent with the moral nature of this change as a voluntary act of man; and also that it is through the truth, and implies attention to truth on the part of man." [39] Thus he rescues freedom and the divine government at the outset. For the purposes of the discussion he takes the liberty which every writer has, of defining his terms according to the way in which he proposes to use them, and confines the term "regeneration" to "that act of the will, or heart, which consists in a preference of God to every other object." [40] He thus differs from Hopkins, but differs explicitly and consistently.

The process of regeneration (or, as the Hopkinsians would have said, conversion) Taylor describes as follows:

There is in man a capacity of feeling, which responds to appropriate motives, even those which exhibit the glory and excellence of God. This he sometimes terms a "desire for happiness," which is constitutional in man, and hence unalienated by the course of sin in which the unrepentant man has lived. His usual designation for this was "self-

[39] *Ibid.*, p. 17.　　　　　　[38] *Ibid.*, p. 16.
[40] *Ibid.*, p. 19.

love," which gave rise to a great amount of misunderstanding, and may have been the reason why he did not gain even a hearing from his opponents for the important suggestions which he had to make in human psychology. Hopkins had used the term synonymously with "selfishness," and so it was often interpreted in Taylor's use. In a reply to Dr. Tyler,[41] Taylor subseqently said that the distinction between "self-love" and "selfishness" was the turning-point of the whole discussion; and so it was, for by propounding the idea of "self-love" he had made a most important addition to theory of the will. He added:

> On the authority of Dugald Stewart, we use the term self-love to denote the simple desire of happiness. In this sense it is employed by Dr. Griffin and many other divines. "Mere self-love is only the love of happiness and aversion to misery; and so far from being sinful, is an essential attribute of a rational and even a sensitive nature" (Park-street Lecture, 3d ed., p. 74).[42]

Such being the meaning of "self-love," the sinner acting upon this desire, has chosen the immediate gratification of his passions and appetites in preference to all other things, or has made his happiness to consist in self. He is supremely selfish. Let, now, God and duty, in contrast with the world and self, be presented to the mind, and let there be an "intellectual perception of their adaptedness to the nature of man as sources or means of happiness," and they will appeal to this desire of happiness. If, now, under the influence of the Holy Spirit, the sinner ceases to perform acts under the governing influence of his former selfish choice and stops to deliberate, and if thus "the selfish principle is suspended," and the man considers these ob-

[41] Review of the *Strictures*, *Spectator*, March, 1830, and separately printed, p. 15.

[42] He might have cited Hopkins himself, "Nature of Holiness" (*Works*, Vol. III, p. 22). So in the controversy with Mills (*ibid.*, pp. 293 and 424):—"Self love . . . . the principle of all exercises and actions, both good and bad."

jects as fitted to gratify his constitutional desire and if then, under the view of them as the greatest good, he actually chooses them, thus taking God as his portion, he is regenerated; and these motives which have appealed to his desire of happiness are the means of regeneration, and in yielding to them he "uses" them. The agent of regeneration is thus the Holy Spirit, who acts as such *in presenting these motives*. Here then is freedom, the neutral ground to which appeal can be made in the sensibility, and the divine government, preserved by the theory of the divine action through motives.

The following single and unbroken paragraph summarizes the whole position. Speaking of "self-love":

Nor ought it to be overlooked that this part of our nature is always with us, be our moral character what it may. It always longs for happiness, without including in itself the act of the will or heart fixed on any given source of object, whence we resolve to seek our happiness: for whether by an act of the will or heart we resolve to seek our chief happiness from one object or another, we still desire to be happy. Whenever we do fix upon the object, self-love primarily prompts to the choice (not determines it); and therefore exists prior to the act of will by which we fix our affections on any object as our chief good. To self-love the appeal may always be made, and feelingly made, even in the lowest stages of moral degeneracy, to produce both the conviction and impression that there is greater good in God than in the world. To this part of our nature all motives designed to change tbe governing purpose or supreme affection of the heart must always be primarily addressed. They cannot be addressed to a holy heart, already existing in sinful man. Nor will it be pretended that God proffers gratification to the selfish principle in man as the means of winning him to holiness, since this would have no other tendency than to prevent the change. The motives fitted to destroy the selfish principle (and such must be all the motives addressed to man to restore him to holiness) can find nothing in that principle but resistance. If therefore there be not in man a constitutional capacity of happiness from some other source than the world; if man cannot be made to *see* and *feel* that there is to him greater good in God than in any other object, the motives of holiness might as well be addressed to the trees of the forest as to men. So certain as man is a moral agent and is properly addressed by motives to holiness, so certain is it that he has constitutional susceptibilities to that good which these motives proffer; and that, if he is led at all to prefer this good to every other, he is primarily prompted to the choice by the desire of happiness or self-love.[43]

Taylor then takes up the issue more sharply with Spring and maintains that "no acts of the sinner while the selfish principle remains active in the heart constitute using the means of regeneration." And before he closes the series of articles he enters upon the nature of moral government at large, and upon the agency of the Holy Spirit through motives, rejecting with great emphasis the idea that the change in regeneration must be in the "very substance of the soul." [44]

To these articles Bennet Tyler,[45] then minister in Portland, Me., replied in *Strictures* (1829). He was most unfortunate in having written his pamphlet before the articles in the *Spectator* were completed, although he supposed that they were complete. He had to adjust his discussion to the last article of the series by an appendix, in which he was rather unsuccessful. He had, in fact, thoroughly misunderstood Taylor, having failed to get the initial proposal of a neutral point in the soul, to which the preaching of the gospel could appeal, at all into his mind. Thus he thought that Taylor was already substantially gone over to Arminianism, and he scrutinized every word under this false light. He misstates the question to begin with. He says: The question is "whether any *acts* performed by the sinner antecedent to a change of heart are *means* of effecting this change." [45] Taylor never confused acts with means. The motives were the means, and motives are not

---

[43] Reprint, p. 22.   [44] *Spectator,* p. 504.

[45] Born at Middlebury, Conn., July 10, 1783; died at East Windsor, Conn., May 14, 1858; president of Dartmouth College, 1822–28; pastor at Portland, Me., 1828–33; president of the Theological Institute of Connecticut, at East Windsor, 1833–57. For the later quotation in the text see *op. cit.,* p. 8.

acts. Then Tyler makes a sharp, though totally incorrect, analysis of the mental operations. He says: "To my mind it is plain that if sinners use the means of regeneration, they must use them with a holy heart, or an unholy heart, or no heart at all; that is with right motives, or wrong motives, or no motive at all." [46] He thus denies that there can be any volition (such, for example, as fixing the attention, which Taylor mentions) of a morally neutral character.

A passage will illustrate Tyler's difficulties:

But what is the moral character of the man after the suspension of the selfish principle and previous to regeneration? Is he holy? No. Is he sinful? No. Then he cannot be a moral agent. And how has his moral agency ceased? Has he lost his reason? No. Has he ceased to act? No. He is *using the means of regeneration*. But to use means for the accomplishment of an end is to act with some intention; and it must be either a good or bad intention. Consequently the act must be either sinful or holy. But what does he do? He "determines to direct his thoughts to the objects" of choice, viz., God and the world, "for the sake of considering their relative value, of forming a judgment respecting it, and of choosing one or the other as his chief good." He takes into solemn consideration the question whether the highest happiness is to be found in God or the world;— he pursues this enquiry, if need be, till it results in the conviction that such happiness is to be found in God only;—he follows up this conviction with that intent and engrossing contemplation of the realities which truth discloses, and with that stirring up of his sensibilities in view of them which shall invest the world, when considered as his only portion, with an aspect of insignificance, of gloom, and even of terror; he perseveres in this contemplation, till he discovers a reality and an excellence in the objects of holy affection, which shall put him on direct and desperate efforts to fix his heart upon them; and he enters upon this process of thought, of effort, and of action, as one which is never to be abandoned until the end proposed by it is accomplished. All this, it must be recollected, he does without either holiness or sin, and consequently without performing a single moral act. Believe this who can! [47]

The reader, if entirely dependent upon the present history for his knowledge of this controversy, will be aston-

---

[46] *Ibid.* [47] *Strictures*, p. 17.

ished at this extract and will be inclined to wonder how Tyler could ever have supposed that he was correctly representing Taylor's position. But a reference to the page in the *Spectator* to which Tyler refers (32) will show that nearly all these phrases, describing processes and acts of choice, are Taylor's own! The passage, however, was not designed as a careful view of Taylor's understanding of regeneration, but was designed to illustrate how a sinner might be regenerated in a totally different way from that which Spring had described. Natural as the misunderstanding was, especially when Tyler had not put himself at Taylor's central point of view, it might have been entirely avoided if Tyler had seen the following passage, from the article still unprinted when he was writing his *Strictures*.

The question arises . . . . where do *we* place the using of the means of regeneration? We answer, under regeneration itself, in the comprehensive sense of that term—in those acts of contemplating divine truth which we have spoken of as necessarily co-existing with the act of choice or love, denominated regeneration in the restricted, theological meaning of the word. Up to that moment the selfish principle had predominated in the soul, and no acts performed under its influence could be a using of the means of grace. But at this moment, by the influence of the divine Spirit, the selfish principle ceases to predominate in the heart. At that moment, God and divine things stand before the soul, no longer pre-occupied by supreme selfishness and love of the world. At that moment this view of God and divine things becomes *the means of regeneration.* A mind thus detached from the world as its supreme good, instantly chooses God for its portion, under the impulse of that inherent desire for happiness without which no object could ever be regarded *good*—as either desirable or lovely. . . . . In that moment—which is properly esteemed *an indivisible moment*—and in that only, does the sinner so use the truth of God that it can according to the laws of mental action become the means of a right act of the will or affection of the heart. All his previous perceptions of divine objects were so obscure and inadequate, his sensibilities were so far from the requisite excitement and direction, through the counteracting influence of the selfish principle—this principle itself, in the form of earthly affection, was so far from relinquishing its final hold of its object (though it may have ceased actively to pursue it), that with-

out a farther change in these respects, the heart will never yield. This
farther advance in respect to the suspension of the selfish principle—
in respect to the vividness of the intellectual perception—and in respect to the degree of excitement in the susceptibilities of the mind,
must take place in every instance of regeneration.[48]

To resume the argument of the *Strictures*: Tyler advances to charge Taylor with denying total depravity, because, if the means are used without motive, the heart is
then not under the dominion of depravity, which is therefore not "total." And, finally, Tyler says: "The question is reduced to this single point, whether unrenewed men
perform any acts in consideration of which God grants
his renewing grace,"[49] as if the divine presentation of motives, which attract the attention of the sinner and cause
him to suspend his wicked course to consider them, was
made in consequence of anything which the man does!
We may have more sympathy with the difficulty which the
word "self-love" caused Tyler, when he said that the
theory destroyed the radical difference between sin and
holiness, since sin was seeking one's own happiness by
choosing the world as his chief portion, and holiness seeking one's own happiness by choosing God.[50] Yet he himself
teaches that holiness is choosing God, and sin choosing self.
Sometimes he identifies self-love, which Taylor made entirely non-voluntary, with a choice. In short, he stands
substantially upon the ground of Hopkins and Spring,
has no thought of any advance in the theory, and hence,
especially after he has once classified Taylor under Arminians and Socinians, is unable to understand him.

The *Strictures* close with seven questions addressed to
Dr. Taylor, which exhibit compendiously Dr. Tyler's opinion of the new proposals. They are: (1) Whether regeneration is not (to Dr. Taylor) a gradual and progressive

---

[48] *Spectator* for 1829, p. 694.   [49] *Strictures*, p. 12.
[50] *Ibid.*, p. 20.

work? (2) Whether the theory does not involve the inconsistency of supposing that the heart is changed antecedent to regeneration? (3) What becomes of the sinner's conviction of sin while using the means of regeneration? (4) Whether the theory does not dispense with the necessity of divine influence in regeneration? (5) Whether Dr. Taylor does not represent the sinner as laboring under a natural inability to do his duty? (6) Whether he does not, in effect, deny the doctrine of sovereign and distinguishing grace? (7) Whether this theory, if drawn out in detail, and inculcated by the teachers of religion, has not a direct tendency to stifle conviction of sin, and produce spurious conversions?

The *Strictures* were reviewed in the *Spectator* for 1830, probably by Taylor himself. The review is keen and meets Tyler's sharp distinctions with others equally sharp. The reviewer shows abundantly that Dr. Tyler himself differed from many of his predecessors, as indeed he must, since they differed among themselves. His orthodoxy was, therefore, not that of the universal consent of New England thinkers. There was no such consent. Taylor soon strikes the main question, viz.: What is a free moral agent?[51] He rescues neutrality of voluntary action, states the question as "not whether regeneration includes the act of God, but whether it excludes the act of man,"[52] vindicates his use of the term "self-love,"[53] points out that Tyler's theory makes natural depravity physical[54] and regeneration a physical change,[55] that he robs the nature of man of any neutral point to which the gospel can appeal and thus denies that the gospel presents "motives to sinners,"[56] and so further clears up his theory—in which we have anticipated him in the first statement of it.

[51] *Spectator*, 1830, p. 150.   [52] *Ibid.*, p. 155.   [53] *Ibid.*, p. 159.
[54] *Ibid.*, p. 163.   [55] *Ibid.*, p. 198.   [56] *Ibid.*, pp. 164, 165.

This controversy was well-nigh interminable, for it lasted eight years longer, and was carried on by means of a multitude of articles in the much-suffering *Spectator*, pamphlets, etc. We need, however, note but few of these, for the main points of proposition and of opposition are now before us, and the further discussion led to no essential modification on either side. In 1833 the Theological Institute at East Windsor was formed to resist the influence of New Haven in Connecticut, and Dr. Tyler was made its president. From this time, of course, there was no hope of an accommodation. We shall therefore dismiss the subject after noting a few incidental features of the debate.

Dr. Tyler replied to the review last mentioned by a *Vindication* (1830). A number of other writers came to Taylor's defense, such as Rev. Hubbard Winslow [57] and Rev. Samuel Rogers.[58] Dr. Hawes joined in the controversy by requesting from Dr. Taylor a fresh statement of his views, which was given in the *Connecticut Observer*, and was followed by a little interchange of articles in the *Spirit of the Pilgrims*. Dr. Taylor took occasion to affirm explicitly his belief in election, in total depravity, in the necessity of the atonement, in the moral character of the change called conversion and in its production by the Holy Spirit through the truth, in special grace, and in the perseverance of the saints. The most interesting of these later papers is the one in which Dr. Taylor followed the practice which he had introduced with the former disputants, and wrote an elaborate letter to show that, "on the basis of Dr. Tyler's last statements and explanations, all controversy between us may be terminated in an entire agreement on the chief points at issue." [59] He abundantly shows in this

[57] *An Evangelical View of the Nature and Means of Regeneration*, etc., and *An Examination of Dr. Tyler's "Vindication,"* etc., both of 1830.

[58] *What Is the Real Difference Between the N. H. Divines and Those Who Oppose Them?* (1833.)

[59] *Spectator*, September, 1833, and reprinted.

article that Dr. Tyler had the same objections to certain implications of various terms (necessary means, etc.) which Dr. Taylor thought natural or inevitable implications, as he himself had. He also shows that their differences were not in the great facts of Christian doctrine, but in theories. Dr. Tyler identified his own theories, as many another theologian has done, with doctrine; and accordingly, no doubt somewhat incensed by the turn given to the discussion, he replied in a pamphlet,[60] which may be regarded as closing this controversy, in which he reiterated most of his original objections and misunderstandings.[61] As late as 1837, in a little book entitled *Letters on the Origin and Progress of the New Haven Theology*, an exceedingly interesting collection of the small personal gossip of the controversy in connection with a summary of the principal positions taken by both sides, Dr. Tyler is "of the same opinion still." [62]

It would be gratifying to be able to state that Dr. Tyler finally, if slowly, came to understand the new positions better and to accept them. This is, however, impossible. He had still twenty years to labor and study, but his theological lectures, as published in their final form, the year after his death, reproduce unchanged the propositions and arguments of the controversy. His theory of the will remains the strict Edwardean theory,[63] and hence he continues to ascribe moral character to the affections,[64] although he distinguished between affections and volitions sufficiently to recognize the fact that Edwards united both under the

[60] *Letter to the Editor of the Spirit of the Pilgrims* (1833).

[61] Tyler Thacher published in 1834 his *Taylorism Examined*, a vigorous book against Taylor.

[62] Cf. a review of Taylor's theology by Professor George P. Fisher in the *New Englander* for April, 1868—one of the finest monographs in the department of the history of doctrine ever written.

[63] *Lectures on Theology*, etc.(Boston, 1859), pp. 255 ff.

[64] *Ibid.*, pp. 155, 190, 196, 296, 357.

will.[65] Hence native depravity is put in the emotions; right and wrong in conduct depend upon these affections, which are the "motives;" and hence regeneration is a change by the immediate power of God in the "relish," that is, the affections. All the old misunderstandings and misrepresentations of Taylor are repeated without even essential modification of their verbal expression.[66] He refused to permit posterity to write him down among them who either assisted or understood the progressive movements of his day.[67]

With Taylor the case was far different. He remained a student to the end of his days, and was always hoping to add to his knowledge and his teaching. As in Tyler's case, his theological lectures as published cover but a portion of the system of theology; but they make a marked advance upon the positions in which he was at the time at which we have left him. These volumes will therefore reward our careful examination.

It is significant that the first two volumes are entitled *Moral Government*. This subject had been a favorite one since the time of Bellamy. Hopkins, particularly, had distinguished between the providence of God, which operated through "power," and his moral government, which was conducted by "law." Emmons does not, in the fragmentary form in which his system has come down to us, treat specifically of moral government. All the writers upon the atonement were full of the subject; for the very idea upon which their theory was founded was that of a preservation, by means of the vicarious sacrifice, of the divine government. Dwight defines moral government with great accuracy as "a government of rules and motives;" and con-

[65] *Ibid.*, pp. 255 ff.

[66] For example, *op. cit.*, pp. 158, 218 ff., 370.

[67] His little work on *The Sufferings of Christ* (1847) shows him to have held the governmental theory of the Atonement.

tinues: "A government of *mere power* may be upheld in its full strength by the exercise of power only. But a moral government cannot be thus preserved, unless the motives to obedience are continued, to the view of its subjects, in their full force." [68]   But all these writers had failed to set forth the central element of divine moral government, because they had none of them arrived at a correct understanding of the freedom of the will. It remained for Taylor to clear the subject of many errors and infelicities. This he did with a very large degree of success, and may be said to have first formulated a correct theory of moral government.

His definition of moral government does not, at first sight, seem to differ from that common to his predecessors. It is a system of influences on moral beings, implying a moral governor, designed to control the action of moral beings, and possessing the character of authority.[69]   All this has been said as well before. But the word "influences" and the word "control" have a new meaning; for, while the idea of causation from without had always entered into their connotation heretofore, that idea was entirely eliminated by Taylor, who distinguished sharply between influence and causation. All the causation of volitional action resided in the agent putting forth the volition.

But this point has been abundantly illustrated before. We need only call attention to it now. With equal brevity may we dispatch the fact that Taylor founds the divine government upon the Edwardean theory of virtue,[70] and that he follows Hopkins in reducing all sin to selfishness. A large portion of the treatment is devoted to the discussion of the sanctions of the divine law, where the principle is clearly brought out that the true punishment of sin

---

[68] *Theology*, Vol. II, p. 196.   [69] *Moral Government*, Vol. I, p. 1.
[70] *Ibid.*, p. 471.

is the suffering of the eternal world, and that all the sufferings which men undergo in this world, including death itself, are of the nature of correctives, and should receive the name of chastisements.[71] An important turn to apologetic, adopted by Park, was the introduction of the doctrine of the immortality of the soul in the discussion of the divine benevolence to remove objections to the equity of the divine government as displayed in this world.[72] The element of grace in the government, which effects its ends through revelation and atonement, is also newly emphasized. In all this we see the vigor and scope of the new and great suggestion of freedom which Taylor was thus working out.

One more of these details we must note, and this time at length, for it marks the point where Taylor became conscious of his fundamental difference from Edwards. He says:

The Edwardian theory of inability, what is it? The inability to love God, which it maintains, is the inability to love and hate the same object at the same time, or the inability to will opposites at the same time. The ability which this scheme affirms, to soften it may be the revolting aspect of the inability which it maintains, is the wonderful power of man not to will, or to avoid willing opposites at the same time, or power to will without willing against his will. Now as to this inability, it is an absolutely fatal possession, for God can never remove it, i. e., he can never impart power to man to will opposites at the same time, any more than he can impart power to a body to move in opposite directions at the same time. And then again, as to the ability, or natural ability of this scheme, there is the same difficulty; for the mind neither has nor can have in the nature of things, the power or ability specified. It doubtless has power to will, but has not power in willing to avoid willing against its will, any more than a part has power to be less than the whole, or than two and two not to be four. . . . . A part is less than the whole in the nature of things, and not as the result of power. . . . . The natural ability of man to obey God, as defined by Edwards and others, has no existence and can have none. It is an essential nothing. Thus,

[71] Ibid., pp. 82 ff; cf. Vol. II, pp. 224, 367 ff.
[72] Ibid., pp. 230 ff.

according to this Edwardian theory, while there is not a shadow of
ability or power on the part of man to obey God, the moral inability
of the theory, the inability to love and hate the same object at the
same time, though undeniable, is unchangeable either by man or his
Maker.[73]

In one department of the system these final lectures of
Taylor present an essential advance. This is in the treatment of the subject of the prevention of sin.

The topic was introduced in connection with questions
relating to the government of God.[74] The subject of the
divine benevolence must necessarily arise in connection
with the divine government, and did thus arise. Taylor
found all the arguments for the divine benevolence before
his own time defective. Particularly, he rejects the argument which would prove benevolence from the Scriptures,
since it begs the question. To credit revelation, we must
assume at least the divine veracity, which is but one form of
benevolence, "which is the very thing to be proved." We
must therefore prove the divine benevolence from the light
of nature before we are capable of presenting a proof of
revelation; but when the latter has once been done, we
may, of course, gather additional evidence from revelation
for our thesis. Here again Taylor laid down the method
which New England theology was thenceforward to follow.

Considering the supposition of the divine benevolence
in the light of nature, Taylor comes to the fact of the existence of sin in the world, which seems to impugn benevolence. He meets this objection in the following way:

The divine benevolence is the disposition to produce the
greatest good, or the highest happiness which it is possible
to produce. This requires that there should be not merely
more happiness than misery in the world, but that God

[73] *Moral Government*, Vol. II, pp. 133 f.
[74] *Ibid.*, Vol. I, pp. 276 ff.

should adopt the best possible system in creating the world. That is, God could not have made a better world than this is in its stead. By this is meant that the present world contains the greatest good *possible to God*. There might be more good through the combined action of God and his creatures. If men and angels had voluntarily chosen holiness invariably, with the system of the universe otherwise unchanged, more good would thus have resulted than will now be attained. But sin has actually entered by the free act of moral agents. If, on the contrary, we should suppose that there is in the world the greatest good possible on the whole, or under any condition, then we should be driven to suppose that sin is the necessary means of the greatest good, because it actually exists. This is to say that the worst action is the best action, which is absurd. Hence what we mean when we say that the world is the best possible world, even though sin is found in it, is that it is the best possible *to God*. And if this is so, then the fact of sin is no detraction from his benevolence.

Taylor seeks therefore to prove that this is the best possible world by the following arguments:

1. If this system, containing evil, *may be* the best possible to the Creator, then the presence of evil in it is no impeachment upon his benevolence. Under this head he considers, first, natural evil, or pain, and, after several ingenious remarks, advances to the subject of moral evil, or sin. Now, it may be an impossibility in the nature of things that God should prevent the present degree of moral evil under the best moral system, and therefore moral evil may exist because, in respect to divine prevention, it is incidental to a moral system which is not only better than no system, but the best possible to the Creator.

In answering an objection to this line of argument, that it is better to leave the great question of the mystery of evil alone, as one that has baffled the minds of the best thinkers of all generations, Taylor cites the parable of the tares as containing the same solution which he has offered, thus meeting this objection, if it proceeds from Christians, who must allow any explanation given by our Lord. In this parable, he says, we are taught (*a*) that the kingdom of heaven is perfectly fitted to its great design of reforming and saving men; (*b*) that the existence in it of moral evil is in direct contravention of this great design of its divine author; (*c*) that the reason that moral evil exists is that there is an impossibility, in the nature of the case, that God should prevent it under the system which exempts him from all responsibility in respect to its existence. And hence (*d*) the interposition requisite to remove the evil would do more hurt than good by modifying the freedom of the will and thus diminishing the amount of holiness under the system.

2. Taylor now advances two points:

a) There may be an impossibility that God should prevent all sin under a moral system. Here he stands exactly upon the ground of the *Concio,* and sustains the position in exactly the old language. He repeats that this supposition does not derogate from the divine omnipotence because the creatures who have this power have it as a gift, and God is limited in the involved limitation only as he has limited himself. But he advances upon the doctrine of the *Concio* when he adds:

b) If it be conceded that God may prevent all sin in *a* moral system, it may still be impossible that he should prevent all moral evil, or even the present degree of moral evil, under the *best* moral system. That is, it may be better to suffer such an amount of sin as does actually enter into this system without taking those means which would prevent it, than thus to cause the degree of moral weakness, or that diminution in happiness, which might result. Against this supposition Taylor declares there are no valid objections. For himself, however, he still stands upon the ground of his former contention.

In a word, as the sum-total of results in this long discussion: The freedom necessary to a moral system, unchecked by influences which may be inconsistent with the highest perfection of that system, may lead to that degree of sin which we actually find in the world.

Now, says Taylor, if this hypothesis is a rational hypothesis, it completely removes the objections to God's goodness derived from moral evil. We are now prepared for the positive proofs of God's goodness, and these are so great that the argument is soon complete.

Thus we close our review of the work of this great thinker. It must have become already manifest to every discerning reader that we have been following the thoughts of a bold and innovating, but logical and essentially conservative, mind. Radical as Taylor was in his determination to get at the root of every matter he handled, and unflinching in his loyalty to the logical outcome of new positions in respect to fundamental truths, he was thoroughly convinced of the divine truth and authority of the historic faith of Christendom, and sought only to defend it better and set it forth with greater power. And when we consider the topics upon which he made original contributions of the first importance, and the breadth of the theological field which he cultivated with distinguished success, his true greatness appears in the most striking light. Finding a fruitful suggestion as to the nature of the will and its relation to the other faculties in Burton, but lost there in a tangle of inconsistencies created by the effort to buttress again the fabric of necessitarianism, he first affirmed and vindicated the freedom of the will, and made this to reside in a true power of original causation. In pursuance of this idea, he threw some light upon every topic of anthropology, upon original sin, human ability, prevenient grace, the means of regeneration, the process of conversion, the psychology of childhood, the processes of divine election and providence. His discussions of the prevention of sin surpass in depth and comprehensiveness those of any other theological writer, whether in New England or out of it. He saw more deeply into the Unitarian contention than any of his contemporaries, and formulated an answer more thorough; as well as defining the Trinity so as to escape the various evils of tritheism, subordinationism, modalism, and substantial unitarianism, as successfully as had ever been done, or more successfully. Besides these, he illuminated in passing a multitude of minor topics in theology. He contributed to Christian apologetics a better stating of its problems, and a more logical, and thus more successful, method of approaching them. In most of these suggestions, while not independent of his predecessors, he went largely his own way and was substantially original. While his acuteness was not inferior to Edwards', his originality in both substance and manner was far greater. He appears in the review of his work which we have now completed as the greatest mind which New England had produced for penetration and originality, and for that constructive force which carries a man on to great intellectual achievement.[75]

[75] A comprehensive and strong review of Taylor (though his name is not mentioned), from the standpoint of a deterministic theory of the will, is given by Henry B. Smith in *Faith and Philosophy*, pp. 152 ff. He regards Taylor's great error as setting up an (incorrect) ethical theory, and then bringing every Christian doctrine forcibly into conformity to it.

CHAPTER XIV

THE LATER NEW HAVEN THEOLOGY

Under this head we may most conveniently subsume certain writers who, without belonging to the creative forces of New England theology, have either served to sustain it, or have modified it greatly while remaining in substance loyal to it, or have opened new vistas before it while standing in its succession, and all in connection with the Divinity School of Yale College, or under the influences which emanated from Dwight and Taylor. Of these the first in importance was Horace Bushnell.

The theological labors of Bushnell will never be understood and appreciated till his distinctive position is clearly conceived and carefully kept in mind. He was pre-eminently a preacher, and his work as a theologian was such as a preacher is qualified and naturally led to perform. He never held academic position after his life-work was fairly begun, and never engaged in the instruction of candidates for the ministry. There were great advantages in this position, and decisive influences proceeding from it to determine the lines and character of his work. The academic teacher is to a degree imprisoned in routine. He must pay attention to every department of his subject, for he has to teach them all. He may be thus diverted at important moments from studies which might otherwise prove largely fruitful. He gains in comprehensiveness and critical quality, for he must know and judge many opinions, and must be a man of books; but he loses in originality, spontaneity, and freshness. The preacher, on the contrary, need pay no attention to routine. He will best serve his people when he is most fully himself. He is regularly engaged in work

which is largely creative, and thus his originality is receiving constant stimulus and training. And, above all, he is
constantly brought into direct contact with men, with life,
with the pressing problems of the living present, with the
needs which the day and hour have created, and which the
theology of the day needs to meet. Hence, if the preacher
becomes a theologian, the theology is likely to become one
of life and of power. This effect Bushnell amply illustrates.

At the same time there are disadvantages in this position,
from which have flowed most of Bushnell's defects. As we
are to be occupied with the positive estimate of his services, we shall best prepare ourselves, as well as relieve the
discussion of a certain burden, if we briefly note some of
these disadvantages at this preliminary stage of our theme.

His lack of historical knowledge was one disadvantage.
After he had written his chief contribution to the discussion of the doctrine of the Trinity, he reviewed the matter
in another work, in which he wrote: "On a careful study
of the creed prepared by this [the Nicene] council, as interpreted by the writings of Athanasius in defense of it, I
feel obliged to confess that I had not sufficiently conceived
its import, or the title it has to respect as a Christian document." [1] He might have gone farther and said that he
had not *even then* "sufficiently conceived the import" of
that creed, or of the New England divines whose writings
he was criticizing with a vigor which sometimes bordered
on acerbity, and demanded some "charity" of his readers,
as Dr. Munger suggests.[2] If he has himself not received a
due share of that comprehension which a more historical
study of his writings would have produced, he has certainly
failed in comprehending the full scope of those forms of
stating Christian doctrine against which he protests.

Then the preaching habit led him into another error,

---

[1] *Christ in Theology*, p. 177.   [2] *Bushnell*, p. 190.

which for a constructive theologian, such as Bushnell as-
pired to be, was a very serious one—that of premature publication. "He not only wrote, but published first, and read
later." [3] The three discourses which form his first principal
work, *God in Christ,* were all prepared and delivered in
one half-year, and published almost immediately. Thus his
thought was not only not finished—which he would esteem
no great reproach—but it was not even matured—which
every reader has a right to demand of a writer who aspires
to large and permanent influence.

We need note but one more of these preliminary and
cautionary criticisms, before plunging into the main work
before us—that as a preacher he was naturally inclined to
the method which he employed, the method of intuition.
He *saw* truth; he did not laboriously reason it out. It
was the precipitate in his mind resulting from long processes of solution and digestion. It finally was its own
chief evidence. Hence he neither carefully criticized the
positions of his opponents, scrupulously refuted them, nor
elaborately defended his own. He thus brought life into
the discussion of great themes—and this was an advantage; he forged his way into new regions and made "discoveries," which can scarcely ever come except as the inexplicable findings of great and independent minds; but he
failed to do what is specially incumbent on those who have
the faculty of "insight," and which the methods of natural
science have increasingly emphasized as essential—he
failed to treat his discoveries as mere hypotheses and to
subject them to verification before he announced them as
truths. In no other respect, possibly, has he had more influence on later thinkers than in promoting the intuitive
habit of thought; but his imitators have generally been
more able to follow him in his neglect of the sober and

[3] *Ibid.,* p. 155.

prosaic labors of necessary verification and self-criticism than in his brilliant and often profound intuitions.

Bushnell's first and greatest contribution to the world of thought was himself. When he began his theological life, he found New England theology somewhat sharply formulated under the direct influence of a controversy which had been going on for nearly a century, but was just about coming to a close. It began with Edwards' books against Arminianism and closed with Stuart's against Unitarianism. Bushnell found great difficulty in adjusting himself to prevailing forms of statement among orthodox teachers and preachers. The many controversies, with their subtle and often mutually contradictory distinctions and definitions, seemed to him more like an impassable jungle than a well-ordered garden. He felt himself compelled to reconsider every doctrine from its foundation—and it is his title to enduring fame, and the condition of his highest service, that he followed this inward compulsion. He thought his way through the difficulties for himself, and the result was that he had something to say which was often vivifying and permanently instructive.

The gain made by this history of struggle in the department of theological method was gathered up in the essay on language. He says:

Words are the *signs* of thought to be expressed. They do not literally convey or pass over a thought out of one mind into another, as we commonly speak of doing. They are only hints or images held up before the mind of another, to put *him* on generating or reproducing the same thought; which we can only do as he has the same personal contents, or the generative power out of which to bring the thought required.[4]

In other words, there can be no thinking in theology but what is *original thinking,* the production of the thought by the student's own mind, assisted by others, but not receiv-

4 *God in Christ,* p. 46.

ing doctrine in a state of passivity. If it is *supposed* to be
thus received, there is and must be even then individual
thinking—only in this case it is hasty, careless, and mostly
worthless. Hence the true method of theological teaching
is that of suggestion. It seeks to kindle thought, to provoke to originality. It employs the indirect path to its
end, if this is more suggestive; it brings up diverse forms
of statement.

Thus, as form battles form, and one form neutralizes another,
all the insufficiencies of words are filled out, the contrarieties liquidated,
and the mind settles into a full and just apprehension of the pure
spiritual truth. Accordingly, we never come so near to a truly well-
rounded view of any truth as when it is offered *paradoxically,* that
is, under contradictions, that is, under two or more dictions, which,
taken as dictions, are contrary, one to the other. [5]

How profound and important is the principle embodied
in this emphasis of the necessity of re-creating truth for
one's self by the originative processes of the mind, everyone who has watched the growth of his own knowledge
of truth or engaged in the education of others will appreciate. It is so very easy to accept doctrines from others
without understanding either their grounds or their meaning, and so easy to settle down upon beliefs which gradually acquire the seeming character of self-evident truths,
when we have even forgotten the reasons originally urged
for them and are totally incapable of defending them from
any earnest attack! New England was, no doubt, as free
from this paralysis of the faculties of theological discussion
and digestion in Bushnell's day as any portion of the Christian world; but some trace of it will be found wherever
the indolence which is a part of humanity's inheritance of
original sin is to be found. His services in banishing it
and awakening the unparalleled activity of Congregationalism in leading the efforts of later days to discover and

[5] *Ibid.,* p. 55.

appropriate the new thoughts of the age, can scarcely be too highly appraised.

Bushnell had also discovered, and he now opposed with biting severity, some of the perennial fallacies of theologians. Nothing is more common among orthodox theologians, and among their heterodox critics, than the fallacy of merely verbal reasoning—the using, that is, of words as counters of a logical process forgetful of their meaning—as we employ the symbols *a, b, c,* in algebra, and carry them through long operations without ever pausing to question what they may mean. Nothing, also, is more fatal than this. He employed his own methods of "suggestion" and "paradox" with great effectiveness to expose this error. "A writer without either truth or genius, *a mere estimating, inferring machine,* is just the man to live in definitions." [6] "That deductive, proving, *spinning* method of practical investigation, commonly denoted by the term *logical,*" was held up to pitiless derision. He pushed his affirmations to the extreme, as when he suggested "the very great difficulty, if not the impossibility" of theology and of psychology as well. "Poets," he says, "are the true metaphysicians, and if there be any complete science of man to come, they must bring it." The impression which most sympathetic readers would carry away from these pages would be that of the worthlessness of systematic theology. It has become the fashion in certain quarters to sneer at the very effort to obtain exact conceptions of great religious truths and to put them in accurate form, and this tendency has derived a powerful impulse from Bushnell's pages. He has thus assisted the tendency to loose thinking, and to the abandonment of *all* thinking, and has helped in the process of emasculating the church and bringing it into contempt with earnest men, trained and exercised in the strenuous

[6] *Loc. cit.,* p. 57.

methods by which truth is advanced in our day. But this has been, after all, a *misuse* of Bushnell. It has been because men have not used *his* words suggestively and themselves burrowed down by original thinking into his true meaning. No man was ever more anxious to promote correct thinking and clear views than Bushnell. It was *because* he was so earnest for the *substance* of thought that he exposed and ridiculed the abuse of its *form* as though that were substance. Listen then with discriminating attention to his summary of this whole question in the words:

Considering the infirmities of language, therefore, all formulas of doctrine should be held in a certain spirit of accommodation. They cannot be pressed to the letter, for the very sufficient reason that the letter is never true. They can never be regarded as *proximate* representations, and should therefore be accepted not as *laws over belief* or opinion, but more as badges of consent and good understanding. The moment we begin to speak of them as guards and tests of purity, we confess that we have lost the sense of purity, and, with about equal certainty, the virtue itself.[7]

But, while Bushnell did not justify the excesses of some of his followers in abuse of creeds and systems, it is undoubtedly true that he failed to give creeds their true place. We are never to forget Bushnell's great idea, that systems are to be revivified and in a sense re-*made* by every generation for itself. But it is not true that there are no such things as best forms of stating truths and best methods of their presentation and defense. Bushnell did not see this because he did not study the past sympathetically. He did not let it work "suggestively" on his own mind. He was too eager in discovery, he had too much of the independence of a strong spirit, and perhaps something of its conceit. The great dogmatic systems of the past have actually done just what he says they cannot, they have conveyed the *same* system of thought to countless minds, and been

[7] *Ibid.*, p. 81.

sources of instruction and of strength to religious opinion and life without which the church would have been impoverished indeed; and they have done this for two reasons: because they worked "suggestively," originating re-creative processes in multitudes of minds, and because they were admirable formulations of the truth as their authors conceived it. Theological progress will never be gained except by building on their foundations, correcting their errors, and supplying their defects. The original genius who begins everything from the foundation and presents a system of doctrine of which the church has never heard before, erects a castle of mist on a rock of cloud. And Bushnell would have been the last man to attempt such a chimerical task.

The preacher appeared again in Bushnell's second contribution to the world of thought, in his quite original and characteristic emphasis on *the religious life* as the source and guiding principle in theology. As a preacher he was daily engaged in the task of developing the religious life of his people. He needed truth for this work, and needed to find those elements in it, and those forms of expressing it, which were best adapted to promote the religious life, and therefore he was compelled in his thinking to approach theology on the experiential side. He seems to have gone a step farther and to have said to himself, not only that truth must contribute to life, but also that nothing was truth which did not thus contribute—a step leading easily to the further and quite false position that the theologian's personal view of the religious life, limited though it may be by his defects of temperament and character, is to be made the measure of universal truth. Thus this movement of Bushnell's mind had elements of danger in it from the beginning; but also contained the promise of fresh and valuable results.

The theological situation in New England, where there had been a division among the churches, and where Unitarians were an exceedingly influential portion of the religious community, comprising the chief personages of influence socially and politically in the greatest of the New England states, and holding the control in the oldest and greatest of our universities, led Bushnell naturally to reflection on the doctrine of the Trinity; and here the application of his new principle began. His thought moved between two poles—the incomprehensibility of the Absolute, and the necessary accommodation of any revelation of God to our human capacities. Hence he found a trinity of *revelation,* an *"instrumental trinity,"* as he called it, by which "we are elevated to proximity and virtual converse with him who is above our finite conditions," and by which "the Absolute Jehovah, whose nature we before could nowise comprehend, but dimly know and yet more dimly feel, has waked up within us all living images of his love and power and presence, and set the whole world in a glow." [8] This was, of course, a "modal" Trinity; but Bushnell would not affirm that it was "modal only." "I will only say," he puts it, "that the trinity, or the three persons, are given to me *for the sake of their external expression, not for the internal investigation of their contents.* If I use them rationally or wisely, then, I shall use them according to their object. *I must not intrude upon their interior nature,* either by assertion or denial." [9] He is equally reticent as to the nature of the divinity in Christ. He affirms his true divinity, and puts the personific element of his nature in the divine—and this with abundant citation of Scripture proof. But the Nestorianizing forms of statement about the two natures common to all Re-

[8] *Loc. cit.,* pp. 173, 174.   [9] *Ibid.,* p. 175.

formed theology, and never more offensive than in some
expressions current then in New England, he repudiates.

This theory of two distinct subsistences, *still maintaining their
several kinds of action in Christ*,—one growing, learning, obeying,
suffering; the other infinite and impassible,—only creates difficulties a
hundred-fold greater than any that it solves. It virtually denies any
real unity between the human and the divine and substitutes colloca
tion or copartnership for unity. If the divine part were residing in
Saturn, he would be as truly united with the human race [under this
theory] as now.[10]

It was, thus, not the human soul of Christ, and not the two
natures, but the "*distinct* subsistence [of the soul] so as to
live, think, learn, worship, suffer by itself," [11] that he
denied. Thus it was Bushnell's purpose in his discussions
of this theme to secure a real revelation of God to man in
Christ, a real condescension of God to our estate, a real
entrance of divinity into humanity, so that God could sympathetically know our lot, suffer like us, "be tempted in all
points as we are," "learn obedience," and bring to us the
help and consolation which only a true incarnation of God
can procure. He saved for orthodoxy, which in reaction
from Unitarian humanitarianism was about to believe
nothing but the deity of Christ and so lose his humanity
and lose Christ, Christ's true, *consubstantial* humanity; and
this was an immense and priceless service. We need the
divine Christ to bear our sins and uphold us by his almighty
power; but we need fully as much the condescension, pity-
ing sympathy and fraternal love of our Elder Brother, the
human Christ. We owe our present realization of this side
of Christ very largely to Horace Bushnell.

But Bushnell did not by any means state the whole truth
as to the Trinity—he did something, indeed, to obscure it.
He was so impressed with the danger of tritheism that he
could not do the Scripture representations as to the rela-

[10] Note the likeness of this term to the Nestorian συνάφεια.

[11] *God in Christ*, p. 154.

tions of Father, Son, and Spirit justice, nor appreciate the
great current of church expression on this theme in creed,
psalm, and system. The distinction of the three personific
factors in God is undeniably emphasized in these representations and expressions. The many prayers of Christ all
emphasize it, and none more so than his last, in the seventeenth chapter of John. The *Te Deum* rings with the worship of "the Father, of an infinite majesty; Thine adorable,
true, and only Son; also the Holy Ghost, the Comforter."
It is strange that Bushnell, with his doctrine of expression
through paradox, did not value more highly these individ-
ualizing, anthropomorphic forms of speech. Why should
not he, of all men, have said what Professor Park, in the
large-minded comprehensiveness of his truly catholic intellect said, that "one might either lay the emphasis in the
trinity upon the *unity* of God, and find the mystery in the
threeness, or lay it on the *threeness* and find the mystery
in the oneness?" Professor Park, like Bushnell, occupied
for himself the former position; but he defended the legit-
imacy of the latter position.

In truth, Bushnell was at this point a substantial rationalist. To apply his own remark about New England in
general to himself—"without being at all aware of the
fact as it would seem, *his* theologic method was essentially
rationalistic; though not exactly in the German sense." [12]
He never gives evidence of careful exegetical study of the
Bible—had, in fact, never had any competent training in
its methods. He *saw;* but his vision was not always produced by the light that streams from the pages of the
Bible. And hence, in the left wing of his followers (if I
may import a German designation into American theology)
there has been a neglect of Scripture in theorizing which

[12] *God in Christ*, p. 92.

has wrought sad results, some of which, as we shall later see, were anticipated in Bushnell's own labors.

Those who are acquainted with the writings of Albrecht Ritschl will be struck no doubt with the resemblance, both in point of departure and in detailed results, between this great German leader, so prominent in the world of English and American thought, and Bushnell.[13] The resemblance is indeed striking, and it is not merely superficial likeness, but fundamentally the product of like histories. While Ritschl was a purely academic character, and proceeded by the methods of the scholar, and Bushnell was a pastor whose vital atmosphere was that of the poet, both had been trained in an orthodoxy which was uncongenial to their minds; both had been taught by gifted professors of that orthodoxy who only repelled them; both, in deep personal throes of intellectual and spiritual labor, had given birth to a new theology, which started with the Christian life as source and norm, both hated metaphysics (except their own); both concentrated their chief attention on the atonement of Christ; both arrived at substantially the results above sketched as to the Trinity and the person of Christ; both had their long period of suffering under suspicion and ostracism; and both lived long enough to emerge from this and to begin to see the fruits of their labors, but neither of them long enough to know on earth the full power of the influence that they were to exert. Of the two, Bushnell was the greater man—greater in vivacity (*Geist,* in German phrase), in prophetic vision, in range of thought and depth of religious experience, and greater in his appreciation and retention of most of the chief elements of the historic theology. It is a sad commentary on the superficiality of much of what styles itself "thought" that in Bush-

[13] A considerable number of the similarities have been drawn out by Professor George B. Stevens, in an article on Bushnell and Ritschl, in the *American Journal of Theology* for January, 1902.

nell's own land he has been so ignored and the inferior
Ritschl so much quoted—and that often by men who owe,
historically, every valuable thought they have to the great
American. But *omne remotum* (*et novum*) *pro mirifico!*

Bushnell's deeper religious life led him into one practical discussion, which demands a brief notice as we prose-
cute our theme—that upon *Christian Nurture*. Ritschl
could never have undertaken this because of his lack of
pastoral experience; and still more for the reason that he
had no adequate doctrine of the new birth. Bushnell had.
He lived in a time when certain forms of religious conversion were greatly emphasized, and when the conscious conversion of adults was aimed at with an intensity of purpose
which obscured other forms of entrance on the religious
life which he felt were even more normal and worthy of
direct effort. Hence he brought out his new idea with
great power—which was *"that the child is to grow up a
Christian and never know himself as being otherwise."*

The work was received with much sharp criticism, most
of which arose from misunderstanding. New England had
never wholly forgotten the duty of Christian nurture or denied the possibility of child piety. But the overemphasis
of covenant relations and of the importance of baptism in
the period before Edwards had led him and his followers,
as we have seen, to correct certain disastrous results by
a corresponding overemphasis on conversion as an epoch
in the conscious experience of the believer. And the
development of the theory of the will at New Haven had led
to a great revival epoch in which the elder Beecher, Taylor,
Nettleton, and others were the chief leaders. At times it
seemed as if "nurture" had been forgotten. Yet many a
church, like the First of Springfield, had always been receiving children into full membership. Bushnell's book was
a protest against the excesses of revivals and an arraign-

ment of a system which depended on them well-nigh exclusively as the times of conquest and victorious advance upon a hostile world. As we review it now, it seems an exceedingly well-balanced and careful statement of the truth. Bushnell did not neglect the doctrine of innate depravity —which, indeed, he knew how to set forth with unsurpassed power—nor deny the necessity of regeneration and conversion. He did not even depreciate revivals as such. He said:

We have been expecting to thrive too much by conquest and too little by growth. I desire to speak with all caution of what are very unfortunately called revivals of religion; for, apart from the name, which is modern, and from certain crudities and excesses that go with it—*which name, crudities, and excesses are wholly adventitious as regards the substantial merits of such scenes,*—apart from them, I say, there is abundant reason to believe that God's spiritual economy includes varieties of exercise, answering in all important respects to these visitations of mercy, so much coveted in our churches. *They are needed.* A perfectly uniform demonstration in religion is not possible or desirable. *Nothing is thus uniform but death.*

Nor did he teach baptismal regeneration, nor any other departure from a sound evangelical theology. He simply emphasized anew the possibility of child piety, the organic character of the family, the normal results of Christian training, the duty of expecting early conversion and of laboring directly for it. And if he had done nothing else, the one scorching epithet by which he designated parental neglect of the religious life of children as "ostrich nurture" would have been worth all the labor expended.

Hence, though sharp controversy arose, Bushnell's book, plus the wholesome tendencies which were both latent and active in the churches, brought back a better balance of the methods of nurture and of conscious conversion in the churches. The last thirty years of the nineteenth century were the period of the greatest revivals, and of the development of the greatest society for nurture, the Christian

Endeavor, and its daughter-societies in various denominations. If certain extremists have hailed the "passing" of
the revival and have credited Bushnell with the "honor" of
destroying it, they have ascribed to him a work which he
repudiated, and have run into the danger of having prophe-
sied according to their own limited acquaintance and sympathy with evangelical history and principles.

Of Bushnell as an apologist of the Christian religion
there could be said very much. His principal work in this
department is *Nature and the Supernatural*. He distinguishes nature as the realm of *force,* and the supernatural
world as the realm of *freewill*. He has made here a profound distinction which has prepared the way for the modern apologetics, in which the teachings of natural science
as to evolution and law—which Bushnell lived too early
to appropriate—are gradually approaching an adjustment
with the Christian ideas of personality and freedom. He
also put the defense of Christianity upon its modern
ground, upon its own distinctive religious character, as he
had sought to place the whole edifice of doctrine upon
its true foundation in the Christian life. The proof of
miracles he rested on the specific Christian truths. Here
again is a point of contact with Ritschl, but here also a
point of superiority, for he never occupies the ambiguous
and evasive attitude as to the reality of biblical miracles
above which Ritschl never rose. But all this work was
only preparatory. The new epoch of apologetics could
not come in until evolution was cordially accepted by
Christian theologians and the task of adjustment to it sympathetically undertaken. Bushnell had not time enough
to undertake this task before he was called away from
earth. He anticipated it at many points, as in the new
emphasis he lays on heredity. A fully modern atmosphere
breathes through his pages. We fail to realize it, possi-

bly, if we have not been compelled by professional study to go back and live for a time in some theologian who calls himself modern, and writes the date eighteen hundred and something on his title-page, but does nothing except reproduce Turretin and the English theologians of the seventeenth century. But Bushnell's work will be so modified by his successor, even in order to gain the full force of what he actually did, that it will be his no more. To save his life, he, like many another, will have to lose it.

The third and greatest contribution made by Bushnell to theology was the enrichment bestowed by him upon the doctrine of the atonement. I am aware that some will say that he *impoverished* the doctrine—and so, in a sense, he did. But, I believe when thought has finally adjusted itself again in respect to this theme, and the defects of Bushnell's theory have been supplied by the restoration of elements which he neglected or denied, it will be found that the church is richer in thought and in experience for the labors of the great Hartford preacher.

When Bushnell began his career, the doctrine of the atonement was still incumbered with many artificial and erroneous elements. The prevailing theology was still forensic, artificial, external. Ethical relations were feebly perceived and little emphasized. True, New England theology had introduced that revolutionary theory of virtue which was eventually to remodel the entire system in the direction of ethical demands. But as yet, it had accomplished little. The old theology still reigned among the people and in a majority of the pulpits, the new belonging, as a kind of privileged private possession, to the comparatively few "Edwardeans," of whom Professor Park, then just beginning his labors at Andover (1836), was easily chief, and was destined to give it a passing supremacy in Congregationalism. Bushnell did not fully understand this new school, and in his arguments attacked chiefly the old. Perhaps he was not so culpable for his failure to understand it, for its new theory of the atonement was professedly only a better form of stating the old, and was couched like that in forensic formulas, and expounded in the terms of human law and government, with little reference to the ideal basis of the whole in the nature of virtue, and with the retention of many of the forms which had been employed in stating the older ideas now to be abandoned.   Hence, as a general average of the New England situation, Bushnell's conception that the prevailing theory of the atonement involved immoral ideas, was derogatory of the justice and goodness of God, and needed to be replaced by something *real* and true, was correct.

His earlier objections, as expressed in the Cambridge address,[14] did not lack piquancy of expression. He objects to the lack of "real economy" in the older view, its double ignominy, first of letting the guilty go, and, secondly, of accepting the sufferings of innocence."   And of the later view he says that

no governmental reasons can justify even the admission of innocence into a participation of frowns and penal distributions. If consenting innocence says, "Let the blow fall on me," precisely then is it for a government to prove its justice, even to the point of sublimity; to reveal the essential, eternal, unmitigable distinction it holds between innocence and sin by declaring that, as under law and its distributions, it is even impossible to suffer any commutation, any the least confusion of places.

In the later volume on *The Vicarious Sacrifice* [15] he dismisses the later view as having "no base of reality even to those who resort to it, save as it reverts to the older scheme, and resumes all the methods of that scheme."   He therefore concentrates his attack on the earlier view, and his objection in a word is that, while professedly satisfying justice, it really travesties and offends justice.

[14] *God in Christ*, pp. 194 ff.   [15] Pp. 364 ff.

Bushnell here fell into two of those errors incidental to his method to which reference has already been made. He failed to do justice to the biblical statements as to the atonement because he had no sufficient and correct methods of exegesis; and he rejected the "later," or New England, view because he did not study it carefully enough to understand it. We may make this charge of failure to understand, because Bushnell himself presents, as an integral element of his own theory, the precise idea which underlay the New England view. That view was much obscured by poor forms of statement, and he might well claim that, if he misunderstood, the friends of the theory and not he must bear the blame; but misunderstand he did. For, as just remarked, he affirms the same things. He says:

It is even a fundamental condition, as regards moral effect upon our character, that, while courage and hope are given us, we should be made at the same time to feel the intensest possible sense of the sanctity of the law and the inflexible righteousness of God. What we need, in this view, is some new expression of God, which, taken as addressed *to us,* will keep alive the impression in us that God suffers no laxity. In a word, we must be made to feel, *in the very article of forgiveness,* when it is offered, *the essential and eternal sanctity of God's law*—his own immovable adherence to it, as the only basis of order and well-being in the universe. . . . . In order *to make men penitent,* and so to want forgiveness,—that is, to keep the world alive to the eternal integrity, verity, and sanctity of God's law,—that is, to keep us apprised of sin, and deny us any power of rest while we continue under sin, it was needful that Christ, in his life and sufferings, should consecrate or reconsecrate the desecrated law of God, and give it more exact and imminent authority than it had before.[16]

Could Bushnell have united these ideas with the biblical statements as to the death of Christ, under the influence of the new and correct discriminations which he introduced, he would now be known, not as the antagonist of the "gov-

[16] There are many such passages, for which see *God in Christ,* pp. 234, 272; *Vicarious Sacrifice,* p. 298.

ernmental theory," but as its chief advocate, as the one who had converted it into a truly "ethico-juridical" theory.

For what he positively *did* was to put the divine relation to the work of atonement in a truly ethical light, and emphasize with new power the fundamental doctrine of the Edwardean school, that God in all his activities, and especially in his work of atonement, was actuated by the great motive of *love*. Man was lost and miserable in his sin. God went forth in Christ to effect his salvation. He performed, as one of Bushnell's followers phrases it, the *direct* work of saving men. He came into the world to lead men to repentance and thus to reconcile them to God. They needed to know God, and God himself needed to gain a new moral power over them whereby he could lead them to turn away from sin and to him. Hence God came and did on the earth, out of the supreme motive of love, in obedience to its inner obligation in his own heart, just what every man has to do when he tries to save his fellowmen. He entered sympathetically as well as actually into the lot of men, bore with them, suffered under their opposition and sin, served them in every way, healing their bodies as well as their souls, subjecting himself to the same law which laid its commands on them, and finally made perfectly clear what God was, in all his holiness and suffering love, and broke their opposition thereby. He pre-engaged their feelings so that they "liked the friend before they loved the Saviour;" he awakened their conscience; he stood the exemplar of God's perfections and holiness; and thus he *gained* them. This was the atonement.

This was all good, because all true. It opened to the apprehension of the theological world a new view of one side of Christ's work, and greatly enriched the humanity of Christ, which Bushnell had already done so much to save to the apprehension of the times. This enrichment of the doctrine will never be lost. Particularly was it valuable as bringing out the fact that the ethical principles underlying Christ's action and that of all good men in doing good are the same. The work of Christ is imitable and *demands* imitation. To see this is well. But it is also *in*imitable and surpasses—defies—imitation. This Bushnell did not see so clearly and rather obscured than set forth. Could he have seen that the law of God which Christ honored included the penal law, and that the obedience which he rendered included obedience "unto death," and that there was a real sense in which God "laid on him the iniquities of us all," then he would not have run in danger of being charged with impoverishing the biblical doctrine of atonement.

To a degree, he did see all these things. While persistently maintaining that his "subjective" view of the atonement was the whole of the doctrine, he was constantly endeavoring to gain an "objective" view. His first effort was by laying emphasis on the "altar form," by which he supposed certain correct impressions to be conveyed to the minds of Israel and the church which were really indispensable. The trouble with these explanations was that they did not go far enough to accomplish their object. They sought to make *objective* what was to be unswervingly maintained as *solely subjective*. It was to be objective and not objective in the same breath! Surely, this was a free use of the principle of paradox! But this earlier attempt did not satisfy Bushnell. He increasingly felt that he had not done justice to such terms as "propitiation" found in Scripture. Hence, on the "arrival of fresh light," he finally propounded the astonishing principle that *neither God or man can forgive a sinner* until he has sought to do him good and suffered under his repulses, and thus so identified himself with him as *to have*

*burned up in this flame of suffering sympathy all his
"disgusts."* This is a true propitiation—a self-propitia-
tion, which God laid upon himself and performed ere he
was able to forgive men! Bushnell did not see that he
had thus made God inferior to what good men are commanded to be and *are*.

We accept, then, with gratitude from Bushnell's hands
the enlargement and clarification of our views of the atonement which he has given us, regretting his failure more
perfectly to adjust himself to the best thinking of his own
time. The failure is the more regrettable because the influence of this theory of the atonement has actually been
to lower the plane of theological thought and to lead to denials of the positive statements of the Bible. Everybody,
it is sometimes said, now teaches the moral view of the
atonement; and that is generally interpreted as this, that
Christ makes so complete and affecting a display of the
love of God for sinners by his death that he wins men to
God. Even his sanctifying the law by his obedience is
let drop out of sight, and as for future punishment—upon
which Bushnell depended to maintain the authority of
God's law—he is a bold man who is willing to be known
as believing in it. The profound view of Bushnell, that
God himself gained moral power over men by the humiliation of Christ, is too strong meat for many of his professed
followers.

To this theological decline Bushnell undoubtedly contributed, and for it he is to be held in part responsible.
But it is to be hoped that his deeper meaning will yet have
a new influence, that the passionate devotion to truth
which kept him ever alert and pressing forward, and the
great loyalty to the personal Christ which inspired him,
and to the Bible in the atmosphere of which he lived, however defective his methods of its study may have been,

will yet produce, under the original and creative action of
the awakened mind of the age, a broader, deeper, and more
ethical understanding, first of law and penalty, and then of
the relation of the sacrifice of Calvary to both.

The work upon the atonement closed Bushnell's theological labors, and here our review of his theological career must close. As a man amid the practical affairs of
life too much cannot be said in praise of him. But men are
too apt to overlook the element of heroic manliness dis-
closed in the story of his theological work—the heroism
of the lonely and retired student. For twenty-six years
he was a pastor, in the full light of publicity and the gla-
mor of evident success. Then came seventeen years of
retirement and comparative obscurity. A lesser man
would have consumed this time in self-indulgence under
the plea of ill-health. This man girded his loins for the
hardest and most persistent labor of his life. He gathered
together all he had seen and thought, and put it forth for
the benefit of the world. He regarded himself responsible
to God for the full use of his remaining powers and the
delivery of his message. For this self-neglecting and constant loyalty to opportunity, to his vision of truth, and to
his Master, those who believe in Christian theology will
join in honoring Bushnell, theologian and hero, man of insight and man of faith.

The coming of George P. Fisher to the chair of ecclesiastical history in Yale Divinity School in 1861 was in many
respects the beginning of a new era. For the first time
there was a man in the chair of history in an American
theological seminary who had an adequate preparation for
his task. Professor Fisher's great services to the department of history it does not fall within the scope of this
work to review. They have been epoch-making. But he
also rendered high service to the department of theology by

his writings in one branch of the systematic disciplines, viz., apologetics. A thoroughly loyal and appreciative son of New England, he more than maintained her repute in the philosophical defense of the doctrinês of religion, while he pushed the historical defense into regions into which our fathers never could have penetrated. A master in German theology, he confuted its errorists with a power equal to the best among German apologists, and with a sanity and cogency which they have sometimes seemed to lack. The latest edition of his *Grounds of Theistic and Christian Belief* (1902) shows him still true to the great positions of New England orthodoxy. But his discussions are for the new time. If he maintains the position won by Taylor, that the will is free with the power of originative causation, it is not to discuss Edwards, but Spinoza, Hume, Mill, Spencer, etc. He defends the reality of the evangelical miracles, and the Johannine authorship of the Fourth Gospel, and the integrity and trustworthiness of the Book of Acts, as his predecessors would have done; but it is with reference to new difficulties and to meet objectors of whom they had never heard. Apologetics are not systematic theology; but Professor Fisher has made it evident, that, however he might feel himself in accord with the writers with whom this history has been engaged in the results of their labors, the time had come when he could no longer avail himself of their work, and when the questions which must be met lay far beyond their horizon and had entered regions in which they were strangers.

The addition to the Yale faculty in 1871 of Samuel Harris [17] in the chair of systematic theology gave to that institution one of the clearest and fullest minds which have labored in this department in our theological seminaries.

---

[17] Born, June 14, 1814; professor of systematic theology, Bangor, 1855-67; president of Bowdoin College, 1867-71; Yale, 1871 till his death in 1899.

After nearly thirty years of service he retired, having published in three separate works, the *Philosophical Basis of Theism* (1883), the *Self-Revelation of God* (1887), and *God, the Creator and Lord of All* (1896), the principal elements of his system.

Harris stood squarely upon the general ground of New England theology, and may be regarded in this respect a member of the school. He teaches the Trinity, the deity of Christ (but not as meagerly as Stuart and Park had), defines original sin as native corruption, thus making all "sin to consist in sinning," thoroughly adopts Edwards' doctrine of the nature of virtue as benevolence, teaches a true freedom with even more clearness and cogency than Taylor did (as already shown), emphasizes the moral government of God, and accordingly affirms the governmental theory of the atonement, rejects imputation, and teaches regeneration by the use of means.

For all these statements, proofs are now about to be offered—not so much for the sake of proof as of another thing which will become evident as the passages are perused, a fact of the greatest importance in its bearing upon the history of New England theology after Harris' day. Let us note it as it appears.

In respect to the less meager treatment of the Trinity and Christology:

God is numerically and indivisibly one in his substance or essential being. This is the common doctrine of our evangelical Protestant creeds; as the Westminster Confession. . . . . The same has been the teaching of the great Protestant theologians. Turretin affirms that God, in his essential being, is indivisbly and numerically one. . . . . It is sometimes said that God as absolute transcends all number. "To apply arithmetical notions to him may be as unphilosophical as it is profane" (Cardinal Newman). But this position is as fatal to monotheism as it is to tritheism and polytheism. If God transcends all forms of number, it is as profane to say there is one only God as to say there are three, or a thousand. It is argued that, in order to count things together, there must be some point of likeness among them so that they can be designated by a common name. But Dr. Newman says, God "has not even such relation to his creatures as to allow, philosophically speaking, of our contrasting him with them." Here, then, is a complete sundering of God from all likeness to his creatures and from all relation to them. Man is no longer in the image of God nor capable of coming into any communion with him or of having any knowledge of him. This speculation is founded on some false idea of the absolute which necessarily issues in pantheism, epicureanism, or agnosticism. . . . . The doctrine is not that the Father is God the absolute being, the Son God in his personality. The one only God is the absolute personal God, and it is this absolute personal God who exists in each of the three, Father, Son, and Holy Spirit. The distinction is not a quantitative distinction, a part of God in the Father, a part in the Son, and a part in the Holy Spirit, and the whole God only in the unity of the three. The one God is indivisible. It is not that the Father is God, and the Son and the Spirit attributes, faculties, or powers of God. The one personal God is undivided and eternal in each of the three; yet in each mode of being he is distinguished by some peculiar *proprietas,* or property, and so by a peculiar relation of each to the other. Hence the personal God cannot be fully known in all his manifoldness till we know him in all three of his modes of being,—as Father, Son and Holy Spirit. . . . . The Father is the original fountain and source of light and life and energy; in the Son he goes forth in creating the universe and energizing in it, and in the Spirit he abides in the universe, and especially in the spiritual system, quickening spiritual life and carrying forward the great designs of his wisdom and love. And yet in all conditions and modes of manifestation it is one and the same God. . . . . In Hegel's trinity the absolute being is conceived as evolving itself into the universe and returning into itself enriched with the consciousness of itself as revealed to itself in the universe. Here the Spirit, the third in the trinity, is conceived as God thus returning into himself conscious of himself in his oneness in this threefold form. But because Hegel's conception is pantheistic it loses all real significance. . . . . The Hegelian trinity suggests truth, but gropes in vain for its real significance and its adequate expression. These are found only in the Christian trinity.[18]

That "fact of the greatest importance" has, no doubt, already made itself manifest to the attentive reader. It is the new tone which breathes through the discussion. Here is no provincial theologian, under the influence of one re-

[18] *God, Creator,* etc., Vol. I, pp. 322–53.

stricted current of theological thought. The variety of quotation illustrates his range of search for material. In the chapter from which these extracts have been principally taken, Harris cites Neander, Doederlein, Robert South, Gebhardt, Reuss, Ritschl, Baur, Strauss, Pliny, Ewald, Tiele, Hodge, Rothe, Edersheim, Gess, Luther, Goltz, Orr, Calvin, Augustine, Gieseler, Tertullian, Newman, Dorner, Turretin, Stuart, Athanasius, and many more like. Kant was one of his chief favorites. You have here a theologian drawing his material from the whole world. But that is not all the fact. We shall see more yet.

As to the nature of sin:

Sin is the choice of self as the supreme object of trust and service. This is sinful character in its primary and essential significance. It is this which distinctively characterizes an act or character as sinful. It is the sinful character which manifests itself or finds expression in every sinful act. Because it is the choice of self as the supreme object of trust and service, it must present itself in two forms: self-trusting and self-serving. Each of these, again, will present itself in two forms: the former as self-sufficiency and self-glorifying, the latter as self-will and self-seeking. The supreme choice of self acts in these four forms in every sinful character.[19]

We may note as we pass that Harris has here taken up the doctrine of Hopkins that all sin is selfishness, but has given it a much deeper grounding and sharper analysis. But to go on—as to the nature of virtue:

The knowledge of existence in a moral system being presupposed, the knowledge of the real principle of the law is immediate and self-evident in rational intuition. This intuition, that the law requires love to God and our neighbor, arises, like all others, on some particular occasion in experience and is practically operative before it is recognized and formulated in thought. When a man finds his own action affecting the interests of another person, and recognizes the fact that he and the other exist together in a rational system, he knows intuitively that he ought to respect the rights of the other equally with his own. . . . . This intuition is germinal in the

[19] *Loc. cit.*, Vol. II, p. 193.

virtual consciousness before it is recognized and formulated in thought.[20]

It will be necessary to add but one more quotation—one pertaining to the theory of the atonement:

The only conception which admits the rightfulness and the ethical obligation of punishment, or of atonement in order to the justification of sinners, is that which recognizes the law of love as eternal in God the absolute reason, which he cannot rescind without annulling his own rationality; and also recognizes God, by his eternal free choice, acting in obedience to that law in all its righteousness and benevolence, constituting and evolving the universe in accordance with it; and Christ, the exponent to us, under human limitations and conditions, of God's love in the redemption of men from sin, obeying the law of love even unto death. Thus God reveals the inviolable authority, the universality and immutability of that law, the inevitableness of the persistent punishment of the persistent transgressor, and the impossibility of redeeming the sinner from sin to God, except in such way as asserts, maintains, and vindicates the supremacy of the law of love as effectually as does the punishment of the sinner persisting in sin,—and thus makes atonement for sin. If God in the exercise of his benevolence in the redemption of sinners is not himself obeying the law of love, then he is not asserting and maintaining it, and therefore is not making atonement for sinners; and he needs to make none, because, being above law in his benevolence, he can, at his mere lawless will, remit the penalty which the law imposes on transgressors. David sank the judge in the father. Brutus sank the father in the judge. God is both father and judge in every act, alike when commanding, condemning, redeeming, or justifying.[21]

This is New England theology, but it is that theology from a new point of approach. The materials are brought from new regions, but the starting-point is new, and the methods, and the principles, in very many respects. How significant this is, and how far-reaching, will be evident at once if we but glance at a number of the topics discussed, and the terms employed, say, in the *Philosophical Basis of Theism*.

This work begins with a discussion of knowledge and agnosticism. This leads to the topic of the reality of

[20] *Philosophical Basis of Theism*, p. 209.

[21] *God, Creator*, etc., Vol. II, p. 486.

knowledge, and the criteria of primitive knowledge. The "Acts and Processes of Knowing" are then introduced, including an elaborate consideration of the inductive and the Newtonian methods of investigation. The fourth chapter is upon "What Is Known through Presentative Intuition." In it is a section of ten pages upon "Kant's Thing in Itself." Then comes "rational intuition," with thorough examinations of Mill, Clifford, Hamilton, Mansel, Kant, Spencer, Diderot, etc. Then the ultimate realities of knowledge are taken up—Being, the True, the Right, the Perfect, the Good, the Absolute. Under the Right the ultimate principles of ethics are discussed. Chapters on the Sensibilities, the Will, Personality, etc., follow; and under the head of "Materialistic Objections to the Existence of Personal Beings" is to be found one of the earliest (1883) and best discussions of the ultimate meaning for ethics and theology of the theory of evolution.

We have, then, here the Sir William Hamilton of the New England theology. Sir William was a loyal member of the Scotch school, but he enriched it with a learning which none of his predecessors had had, defended it more ably against wider, if not subtler, antagonism, and sunk for it deeper foundations in his "philosophy of the conditioned." Such was Harris' relation to the New England school. And, as Sir William was more than a member of his school, being in fact that thinker who formed the transition to later and different modes of thought, so Harris formed the transition from the New England to later theologies, now, perhaps, only in course of formation among Congregationalists—or rather, among Americans; for the theological process has become a common labor shared fully, under the new conditions of the modern learning, by the representatives of many different communions. He built the New England edifice of doctrine, but he built it upon other foundations, or foundations laid much deeper, and with other methods. It remained to be seen whether the new would really assimilate with the old, or whether the new methods and new problems of the new time would lead to the substantial abandonment of the old theology.

CHAPTER XV

THE NEW SCHOOL IN PRESBYTERIANISM

It was inevitable that the theological movement which has been traced should have a great influence upon the Presbyterian church. It had become dominant in Congregationalism, and whatever was dominant there must command the attention of the leaders of a church which from the beginning had been inextricably involved with Congregationalism. Some of the early Congregational churches had been Presbyterian in their internal government rather than democratic. The great churches of Long Island, and particularly New Jersey (Newark, Elizabeth, etc.), which had become the main support of early Presbyterianism, were of New England origin, and originally Congregational. The most numerous and strongest religious element in the emigration which began to build up the West, even before the Revolution, came from New England, and carried an attachment to Congregationalism into the new home. In 1801 an agreement, called the "Plan of Union," was entered into between the General Association of Connecticut and the General Assembly of the Presbyterian church, whereby Congregational churches might form relations with presbyteries, and Congregational ministers might serve Presbyterian churches and have a connection with presbytery. When Lane Seminary was founded, Lyman Beecher, one of the most prominent Congregational ministers of Boston and a strong representative of the new school, was called to the professorship of theology (1832). Union Theological Seminary in New York was a union of Presbyterians and Congregationalists (1836), and was supplied with professors principally from

New England.   The number of members and ministers
who have passed from Congregationalism to Presbyterianism in the settlement of the western states from the beginning till now has been very large.

From an early point this intermingling of Congregationalists with Presbyterians, and the consequent influence
of the new school upon the theology of the Presbyterian
church, was looked upon with suspicion.   Edwards was
called to be president of Princeton College, and his son of
Union College.   But as the theology of Hopkins and particularly Taylor, began to be understood (or, rather, misunderstood), antagonism to Congregationalism began to
develop, till in 1837 it culminated in the abrogation of the
"Plan of Union," to be followed in 1838 by the separation
of the new-school element, and the formation of the New
School Presbyterian Church.   This result was brought
about by the old-school and high-ecclesiastical element in
the church, aided by the southern element and their north-
ern, pro-slavery friends.   Congregationalism was distrusted
and disliked for its theology, for its democratic influence in
church polity, and for its anti-slavery attitude.   It might
be supposed that the old-school element would now regard
itself as done with Congregationalism, and let it alone.
But this was impossible, for Congregationalism still continued to exert a most powerful influence throughout the
entire West in every Presbyterian church and ecclesiastical
gathering.   Princeton specially recognized in everything
New England a permanent enemy, and Professor Charles
Hodge set himself so determinedly to oppose all its emanations, whether in the theological or in the ecclesiastical
sphere, that he occupied a large portion of his time in this
work, and had, in particular, an epoch-making controversy
with Professor Park.   His standard charge against Taylorism was Pelagianism.   "There is no ghost which so

greatly disturbs Dr. Hodge," said Professor Park on one occasion, "as that of Pelagius,—unless it be that of *Semi-Pelagius!*" In fact, Dr. Hodge showed no ability, and but little desire, to understand the New England men. He so constantly misinterpreted them that he soon lost all influence in opposing their speculations among thinking men, and may be entirely neglected in a history of the school. He may be safely left by the historian of a progressive school of theology to the natural consequence of his own remark that during the many years of his predominance at Princeton that institution had never brought forward a single original thought.

In the New School Church the new-school theology was, of course, dominant. Yet, as that church continued to pledge her ministers to the Westminster Confession, it was not to be expected that she would develop enough of the spirit of freedom to prove theologically productive. She was, in fact, remarkably sterile. She received her ideas from the New England thinkers, and spent her own theological strength in the effort to adjust them to the Confession. She did not produce in all the thirty-one years of her separate existence one single great theologian. Hence her ecclesiastical individuality may be left out of the account in the following pages. Her writers will be treated simply as members of the New England school. Of these the greatest was Henry B. Smith.

We begin, however, with an earlier teacher—the famous Lyman Beecher.[1] Born in Connecticut, and a pupil of Dwight at New Haven, he became famous in connection with the Unitarian controversy in Massachusetts, and became a Presbyterian upon going to Lane. He joined the

---

[1] Born at New Haven, Conn., October 12, 1775; died in Brooklyn, N. Y., January 10, 1863; graduated at Yale College, 1797; pastor at Easthampton, L. I., 1799; at Litchfield, Conn., 1810; called to the Hanover Street Church, Boston, 1826; president of Lane Seminary, Cincinnati, O., 1832-51.

New School church at the time of the division, and thus became one of its most important leaders. His *Views in Theology*,[2] issued in connection with his trial before the Synod of Cincinnati for departure from the Westminster Confession, are the most valuable source of knowledge as to his special theology.

Were we engaged in the external history of the churches, or of our theology, we should therefore have much to say as to Lyman Beecher. His *Bible a Code of Laws* at Park Street Church, Boston (1818), his Worcester sermon at the ordination of Mr. Hoadley (1823), and his *Rights of the Congregational Churches of Massachusetts* (1826), were all powerful blows against the rising Unitarianism of the day, and clear theological defenses of the New England theology at the points in dispute.[3] But in all these he was on the defense, and they contribute nothing to the further exemplification of the doctrines of the school or of his own thinking. The *Views* suffers under the same limitation, since it was his defense before the Synod of Cincinnati against charges of heresy. It is engaged in exhibiting his agreement in doctrine with the Westminster Confession, and carefully avoids theoretical statements which might bring him into conflict with either the philosophy underlying that Confession, or even its phraseology. Had he ever published his theological lectures, they would probably have been found to suffer under the same unfortunate necessity of considering a document beyond which he had actually passed in his theologizing. We know from his biography [4] that he was a warm friend and ardent admirer of Taylor, and agreed substantially with him in his

---

[2] Cincinnati, 1836.

[3] His *Works* were published in three volumes in Boston, 1852–53, but are incomplete. See Dexter's Bibliography in "Congregationalism," Nos. 4241, 4463, 4530, 4580, 4774, 4899, 4924, 4975, 4996, 5017, 5118, 5353, 6140.

[4] New York, 1864–65; two volumes.

theology. At one point this fact appears even under the restrictions of a defense, for he adopts Taylor's phrase "power to the contrary." "Choice," he says, "without the possibility of other *or contrary* choice, is the immemorial doctrine of fatalism." Again: "Their [the early Fathers'] doctrine of free will is . . . . the antifatalism doctrine of mind free as uncoerced in choice, and with the power always of contrary choice." And still again: "The Confession of Faith teaches plainly and unanswerably the free agency and natural ability of man, as capable of choice, with the power of contrary election." [5] But in general we only see what he might have done, had he only been himself as free as the will was whose freedom he was advocating. He is strong in the advocacy of a real power of choice, a real natural ability to choose. To the proof of the proposition that ability and obligation are commensurate he devotes many pages. The following passage deserves quotation as being one of the best interpretations of Augustine which have ever been given:

Down to his time, the free will and natural ability of man were held by the whole church, against the heretical notions of a blind fate, of material depravity, and of depravity created in the substratum of the soul. The great effort, hitherto, had been to maintain the liberty or uncoerced action of the mind in choice, with the power of contrary choice. But now Pelagius arose and denied the doctrine of the fall; and from this spot it became necessary, not so much to prove *natural ability* which Pelagius admitted, as to prove *moral inability,* which was as much opposed to the Pelagian heresy as natural ability was to that of the Pagan philosophers, the Gnostics and the Manichaeans. The church had now to enter upon a new controversy, and to fix her eye upon the question. what were the consequences of the fall? The question of free agency was no longer to be argued, for that was not now controverted. Both Augustine and Pelagius admitted it. . . . . The question indeed turned upon the same words, viz., free will; but it did not mean the same thing. The question between them was, is the will unbiased? Is it in equilibrio? It was not whether it was free from the necessity of fate, or the coercion

[5] *Views,* pp. 35, 48, 101.

of matter, or of created depravity; but the question was, has the fall given it a bias? has it struck it out of equilibrio? and struck the balance wrong? Pelagius said, no. Augustine said, yes; and while in opposition to Pelagius he denied free will, meaning unbiased will; he was as strong in favor of free will in the other sense as any of the fathers before him; as strong as I am: so that if I am a Pelagian, Augustine was a Pelagian; although his whole strength was exerted against Pelagius. If what I teach is Pelagianism, then Augustine, and Calvin, and Luther, and all the best writers of the church in this age have been Pelagians, except the few who deny natural ability.[6]

In the last sentences Beecher voices the answer of the whole New England school to the standing charge made against it by Princeton.

But, strange to say, though familiar with Taylorism, Beecher fell into confusion as to the nature of the moral government of God, and repeatedly refers regeneration to the "almighty power" of God, "as really so as the creation of worlds or the resurrection of the dead!"[7]   It would seem as if Taylor had forever established the doctrine that the *moral* government of God was not conducted by *force*. But, alas, no!

Henry B. Smith[8] received his theological instruction from Leonard Woods, of Andover, and at greater length from Enoch Pond,[9] of Bangor. Woods, we have seen, was

[6] *Ibid.*, pp. 56, 57.

[7] *Ibid.*, p. 202.

[8] Born at Portland, Me., November 21, 1815; died at New York, February 7, 1877; graduated at Bowdoin, 1834; studied at Andover "for a few months" in 1834; resumed his studies at Bangor in 1835, and left the seminary in the summer of 1836 for a year as tutor in Bowdoin College, at the close of which he went to Europe (1837–40). Here he had some contact with the intellectual world of France in Paris; spent the year 1838–39 in Halle, where he had the inestimable advantage of a close intimacy with Tholuck, and 1839–40 in Berlin, where he came in contact with Hengstenberg, Neander, Trendelenburg, and Twesten. He was pastor at West Amesbury, Mass., 1842–47; professor of mental and moral philosophy at Amherst, 1847–50; of church history in Union Theological Seminary, New York, 1850–55; and of systematic theology in the same seminary, 1855–77.

[9] Born at Wrentham, Mass., July 29, 1791; died at Bangor, Me., January 21, 1882; graduated at Brown University, 1813; studied under Dr. Emmons, pastor of the church at Auburn (Ward), Mass., 1815–28; editor of the *Spirit of the Pilgrims*, 1828–32; professor in Bangor Theological Seminary, 1832–82.

a moderate follower of Hopkins, and as an adherent of the "taste scheme" would be called a member of the "old school" in New England theology.   He exercised a large influence over Smith, short as was the period of their connection.   Pond was a pupil of Emmons, and the marks of Emmons' influence are very clearly traceable in the *Lectures* [10] which he published at the close of his theological career; but what had survived at that distant date were chiefly the analytical method of discourse, the simplicity and clearness of thought, the emphasis upon plain common-sense, and the general agreement with the New England thinkers upon the great doctrines of the evangelical system.   The tone of the whole is far more biblical than that of Emmons' *Sermons* had been.

To note a few features of Pond's system:

His treatment of the divine authority of the Bible closes with the argument from the witness of the Spirit, to which he gives one of the best statements ever made. He says:

I have but another argument to urge in favor of the divine authority of the Bible,—the same which was urged in support of its truth: it is that which the Christian finds in his own soul. "If any man," saith Christ, "will do his will, he shall know of the doctrine *whether it be of God.*" True Christians have fulfilled the condition here proposed, and they realize the truth of the promise. They do know of the doctrine that *it is of God.* They find such a blessed agreement between the representations of Scripture and the feelings of their own hearts that they cannot doubt as to the divine origin of the Bible. It must have proceeded from the same Being who knows the hearts of his children perfectly. . . . . This argument has more weight, probably, than every other, with Christians in common life, to remove their doubts and give them a settled, unwavering faith in the truth and divine authority of the sacred word.[11]

That is, as we trace certain of our own experiences to the agency of God, so we trace the book which records the

[10] *Lectures on Christian Theology* (Boston, 1867).
[11] *Lectures*, p. 120.

same experiences to the same hand. Like effects, the same cause.[12]

As to the Trinity, Pond shows the effects of Stuart's work in modifying the sharp and gross distinction of persons between the members of the Trinity which Emmons had made.

The distinctions in the Godhead are commonly called *persons;* and if this word is understood with some necessary qualifications, there is no objection to it. When used in relation to this subject, it cannot mean (what it commonly does) that those to whom it is applied are *entirely separate beings,* like three human persons; for this would be inconsistent with their essential unity. But in *some* sense, and to *some extent,* the divine persons are distinct. They are *so far* distinct that they may properly speak, or be spoken of, in the plural number. They may use the personal pronouns, *I, thou,* and *he,* in reference to each other. They are represented as entering into a covenant, and as holding an infinitely blessed intercourse and communion, one with another. They are said also to discharge different offices and works. . . . .

Neither is the doctrine thus stated self-contradictory. To say that God is one and three in *the same sense,* would be a contradiction. But to say that God is in *some* sense one, and in some *other* sense three, is no contradiction.[13]

As to the will, his doctrine is entirely the Edwardean determinism. His formulation of its law is in simpler language, but less felicitous than Edwards' own: *"The will is always as the strongest motive."* [14] The "power of contrary choice" he regards as an Arminian position.[15] His definition of freedom may be added to the museum of psychological curiosities which the readers of this history cannot have failed of accumulating. It is this: "It consists in voluntarily yielding to the strongest motives.[16]

On the foundation of obligation and the nature of virtue

---

[12] The same argument is more fully stated in the monumental work of a successor of Pond in the chair of theology at Bangor, Lewis F. Stearns, *Evidence of Christian Experience,* pp. 303, 304; and by F. H. Foster in *Christian Life and Theology,* pp. 104 f.

[13] *Lectures,* pp. 172, 173, 176.   [14] *Ibid.,* p. 294.

[15] *Ibid.,* p. 297.   [16] *Ibid.,* p. 304.

Pond is entirely Edwardean. He did not follow Taylor in his endeavors to improve theodicy, maintaining stoutly that God could prevent all sin without impairing free will. He regards it as a strong argument for this position that God can convert sinners,[17] not perceiving that restoring from *some* sin is quite a different thing from preventing *all* sin. In regeneration, he follows Emmons in identifying regeneration, conversion, and sanctification, as in nature the same, and in making the Spirit of God "the *efficient* cause of all holy affections," though he makes man himself the "agent" or "active cause." [18]

It is evident from Smith's later work that he carefully studied Emmons,[19] and that he fundamentally rejected his peculiarities, as both Woods and Pond led him to do. But when he had arrived at the point of constructing a theological system for the instruction of his pupils, he had received, first of all the theologians whose work has passed under our eye, the full influence of a wide acquaintance with the theologians of Germany, and through them with those of all Christian history. Owing to the character of his published works upon theology, which are mere fragments, and those, fragments of lectures designed to introduce the student to theology rather than to set forth a complete system, it will ever remain doubtful to the historian whether he had a truly originative and creative capacity. He was certainly a great historian. The tradition handed down by his friends is that he was a great theologian. But that tradition remains unverified by his actual productions. Whether it be true or not, he was certainly a very receptive mind. His works are full of citations from a wide range of read-

[17] *Loc. cit.*, p. 345.

[18] *Ibid.*, pp. 462, 463.

[19] See "The Theological System of Emmons," in the volume *Faith and Philosophy*, pp. 215 ff.

ing, and are equally full of criticism of the most trenchant and suggestive sort. He brought into our theology for the first time the influence of the entire Christian world of thought. In this historical review we have had occasion to observe the effect upon our theology of the importation of influences from abroad of an essentially hostile character. That effect may be concisely stated as the creation of the Universalist-Unitarian theology, on the one hand, and of the formation of the theology represented best by Professor Park, on the other. We have now to see what will be the effect upon it of the reflections of a mind so widely informed and variously disciplined as was Henry B. Smith.

First, was his theology New England theology? Was the effect of his wider introduction to the field of Christian thought obtained at the best universities of Europe to exhibit the thought of his native New England in so unfavorable a light as to lead him to turn aside from it as inadequate and to build upon other foundations and after a different plan? Or could he retain the chief results of the dogmatical development here and build on after the same general plan, and in the same spirit, as his predecessors? The return to America and the call to theological thinking of so great a mind as Smith's was a critical moment for our theology. What would a gifted son who had gone out into the wider world think of his home?

It is distinctly and decidedly to be answered that Smith remained a member of the New England school. He found, as others have after him, that Germany had much to teach him, especially in enlarging his conceptions of what theology was, in opening new problems, in giving depth and breadth to his thinking. It was here that he got a profounder view of the relation of "faith and philosophy." [20] Here he came to see the lack in many of the

[20] See book of same title, pp. 35 f.

forms of New England theology of a "principle," as the
Germans call it, a starting-point, a norm by which all the
thinking of the theologian is to be guided, and a germ
which shall contain the secret of the whole system. But
he found that no thinking has been more thorough than
that of the New Englanders upon many of the themes
of the discipline, and that at many a point New England
had advanced far beyond Germany. Not to discard, nor to
uproot and destroy, did he return and take his place among
teachers and laborers in his native province, but to honor
the past, to conserve the valuable, to advance as he should
be able, and everywhere to deepen and enlarge. To note
certain particulars:

He taught that benevolence is the one comprehensive
moral attribute of God.[21]   In accordance with this, justice
is finally public justice,[22] and "punishment is needful to express the displeasure of a holy God against sin as ill-deserving, and also to preserve the love of holiness and hatred of
sin in others."[23]   Human virtue is determined by this idea.
It is "love to God as being in effect all being;"[24] or, otherwise stated, it is the "love of all intelligent and sentient
beings, according to their respective capacities for good,
with chief and ultimate respect to the highest good, or holiness." This is strictly Edwardean. Edwardean also was
the theory of the will. To be sure, Smith did not follow
Edwards in all the minor points of his theory. Thus he
adopted the threefold division of the faculties of the soul
in place of the twofold, and was much clearer as to causation. "Man," he says, "acting as will, choosing, is an efficient cause; among second causes in this world, the chief;
a dependent, but real cause. There is proper causal efficiency in every act of choice. Power is an attribute of

[21] *System*, pp. 34 f.   [22] *Ibid.*, p. 45.
[23] *Ibid*, p. 47.   [24] *Ibid.*, pp. 142, 223.

cause: it is the distinctive attribute of an efficient cause: it is that in the cause which gives it its efficiency in respect to any particular end or object." [25]   He expands the terminology of the subject to follow Dr. Richards in distinguishing between the executive and immanent volitions,[26] defining the latter as Taylor had defined "primary, predominant choice."   Germany is drawn upon for the distinction between formal and real freedom,[27] as had been done by Park.   He does much to relieve the Edwardean theory of misunderstandings, and of unnecessary complications.   But he finally comes fully to the Edwardean position that "the will always acts according to the strongest motive," [28] or, as he elsewhere phrases it, more in accordance with Edwards, "always choosing that which in the view of the mind is most desirable." [29]   And in the theory of the atonement he is one with the New England school in rejecting the theory of a satisfaction to distributive justice, and in making the service of the sacrifice of Christ to consist in "satisfying the demands of Public Justice, meaning . . . . what the divine holiness sets before itself as the chief end of the universe, or that which is the end of the requirement of the law." [30]

These positions, which are the cardinal positions of the New England school, fully identify Smith with that school.

At the same time he did not go to the lengths of single teachers in respect to extreme positions.   The phrase, "All sin consists in sinning," which was characteristic of the Emmonian strain, and which Professor Park fully accepted as a most valuable and illuminating suggestion, Smith contrasted with the other phrase, "All men sinned and fell in Adam," and said: "Each of these plants itself on one side

[25] *Ibid.*, p. 238.
[27] *Ibid.*, p. 243.
[29] *Ibid.*, p. 245.

[26] *Ibid.*, p. 240.
[28] *Ibid.*, p. 247.
[30] *Ibid.*, p. 470.

of the dilemma, as containing the whole truth; and each of these taken strictly by itself, is about as true, for the solution of the problem, as the other; for each neglects the other, and leaves unaccounted for about half of the difficulty." [31] Hence, while rejecting "immediate imputation," he finally adopts a position of "mediate" imputation.[32] One cannot but feel that here is a trace of the undue influence of the Westminster Confession upon a New Englander who had consented to accept this yoke; for, after all, Smith found "neither immediate nor mediate imputation fully satisfactory."[33] He refers the corrupt nature of men to heredity.

On account of this innate depravity, all men, mankind as such, are exposed to evils. . . . . For this native corruption before act, we need not say that the person who is the subject of it will receive, or deserves everlasting death. It is a liability, exposure,—justly such; but not personal desert. The desert of eternal death is a judgment in respect to individuals for their personal acts and preferences. Until such choice there cannot be, metaphysically or ethically, such a judgment.[34]

He goes back with some satisfaction to Edwards' treatment of imputation.[35] But, in fact, with his view of moral action, he is only entangling himself in phraseology which was formed under the influence of another philosophy, and which only impedes him in the expression of his thought.

An interesting incidental topic is his treatment of the governmental theory of the atonement which he, in general, espoused.[36] He divides this theory into two forms, of which the first is the form which views the atonement as "having reference to happiness or expediency, in maintaining the divine government." The two representatives chosen for this form are Grotius and N. W. Taylor. It is quite evident that Smith had no adequate idea of Grotius.

[31] *Loc. cit.*, p. 304.   [32] *Ibid.*, pp. 314 ff.
[33] *Ibid.*, p. 314.   [34] *Ibid.*, pp. 315 ff.
[35] *Ibid.*, p. 317.   [36] *Ibid.*, pp. 469 ff.

He refers to Baur and is open at least to the suspicion of
not having read Grotius himself. Baur did not understand
Grotius.[37] Smith accordingly fails to note the great point
of the Grotian theory, that it changes the idea of God
from that of offended party to that of ruler; to give a true
estimate of its office of law and punishment; or to show
that Grotius thought the atonement to maintain the authority of the law by effecting *the same thing* that the punishment of men under the law would have done, viz., the
prevention of sin among the subjects of the law. Law
certainly was no more "individual, personal . . . . exclusively" to Grotius than it was to Smith when he wrote, upon
the following pages: "Moral law has two main ends, to
secure the supremacy of holiness in the universe, to furnish the rule for individuals." Grotius' "consulting for the
order of things and for the authority of [God's] own
law" [38] does not differ essentially from Smith's "maintenance of the supremacy of holiness." Nor is Smith's
treatment of Taylor much more successful. He understands Taylor, when including holiness in happiness, to
mean the same thing as he does himself, when *distinguishing between* holiness and happiness. Unsatisfactory in
some respects as the statements of the New Haven theologians had been from Dwight down, they did not mean substantially anything different from Smith whose statement
was so much better.

The second form of the theory is that which makes the
atonement to have reference to holiness as the end of all
moral government. He identifies government and law, since
government is *by* law; and the atonement is that sacrifice
of Christ which answers the end of public justice—that is,
substantially effects, by the substitution of Christ for the

[37] Baur's errors are somewhat fully exhibited in the notes to the present
writer's edition of the *Defence* (Andover, 1889). See Index for the passages.

[38] *Defence* (Andover ed.), p. 137.

sinner, just what would have been effected under the law by the punishment of the sinner. "It secures the highest good of the universe, viewed as true happiness as well as holiness." [39]   This is the form which Smith adopts.

Returning for a moment to the name of Nathaniel W. Taylor, one of the interesting inquiries as to Smith's theology is upon its relation to Taylorism. It might be anticipated that he would find little in the special work of Taylor to commend, rejecting as he did the fundamental proposition which Taylor made as to the will. Taylor taught "power to the contrary," or a real prime causality in man; while Smith remained upon the platform of the Edwardean determinism. He therefore rejects Taylor's positions in respect to the prevention of sin.[40]   With Park, he maintains that God *can* prevent sin in a moral system, thus rejecting the positive form of Taylor's favorite hypothesis. Its hypothetical form does not diminish its offense in his eyes very much. "On this basis, sin could never be certain in the system." He thus held up before Taylor his great failure in this topic, either to combine freedom and certainty by a rational explanation, or to drop the idea of certainty in its strict Calvinistic, mathematical application. He himself refers God's ability to prevent sin to his omnipotence, as he may upon the Edwardean basis, thus exhibiting how completely he failed to accept the new proposals as to moral government, and furnishing a new proof, if one was needed, that the Edwardean "moral" government did not differ essentially from the government of external nature, both being by force. He finally says:

The only question which can be proposed in respect to vindicating the divine government, and the point to which any theory that attempts to solve the question must come, is this: To show why a holy and benevolent God chose a system in which sin *was to be a matter of fact,*

[39] *System*, p. 477.
[40] *Ibid.*, pp. 149 ff.

and why the existence of sin in that system was a condition of its being the best system. Understanding that to be the question, it may be said that the theory that sin is the necessary means of the greatest good fairly undertakes to meet the question, though it does not answer it. But the other theory does not *meet* the question. It merely says that in the best system free agency involves the possibility of sin, and that there cannot be a moral system without free agents. The theory thus leaves the question and problem wholly undecided. No relief can be found in a scheme which limits divine omnipotence.[41]

Smith has here entirely forgotten the place of Taylor's argument in his system, which was to remove an objection to the benevolence of God by introducing a hypothesis which should evacuate the objection; not to solve the question of the permission of sin.

The same attitude is held in reference to other points in the system. The efforts of Taylor to establish the existence of a neutral point in the soul to which preaching could appeal, receive no proper attention, but the unfortunate phraseology which he adopted as to "self-love" is made the ground of a definition of his position which admits of an easy refutation, viz.: "My happiness in the general happiness is the spring *and sum* of virtue." [42] The position that "all that is moral is in voluntary action" is said to resolve all original sin into physical depravity.[43] Taylor's neutral state, which was introduced according to him by the Holy Spirit, "suspending the selfish principle," is characterized as "neutral, yet always producing sin" [44]—a characterization of which Taylor would have said that it had no correspondence to his meaning. And so forth.

Smith thus joined Park in rejecting the advanced positions of Taylorism. In one theological center alone did they receive full recognition—in Oberlin. The foremost representatives of the school thus united in saying, at the

41 *Ibid.*, p. 152.   42 *Ibid.*, p. 206.
43 *Ibid.*, p. 310.   44 *Ibid.*, p. 312.

end of the development, that Calvinism could not be maintained upon a theory of freedom.

What, now, did Smith do in the way of advancing the New England problems? The answer cannot be a very satisfactory one. He had early seen the necessity of a better "principle" in our theology, and a great vision of what it ought to be had risen before him. He formulated it as "Incarnation in order to Redemption," which ought to be the principle "which gives the true center of unity to the whole theological system, ... that in which the whole system hangs together and moves together, ... the principle in the sense that all the parts can be best arranged in relation to it." [45] If his thought can be reconstructed from his various expressions of it in abstract form, it would seem to have involved a new point of approach to the system; for example, man as a sinner and needing *something,* which something should be defined from his needs as redemption, which redemption should be developed as involving incarnation, and this the Trinity, etc. This would have involved a new use of Christian experience, such as that made by Stearns and Foster in connection with the German, Frank,[46] and it would have effectually disposed of the Calvinism of the system, when due attention had been given to all its implications. But no such new approach was adopted by Smith. His system moves along the old paths, and his division into "antecedents of redemption," "the redemption itself," and "the kingdom of redemption" is scarcely more than a verbal suggestion of his principle. He himself recognized this failure to realize his early visions and aspirations.[47] Whatever the explanation of it may be, the fact remains that he did not introduce his principle into the development of the system.

[45] *Introduction to Christian Theology,* p. 58.
[46] *System der Christlichen Gewissheit.*
[47] *Introduction,* p. iv.

Nor did he contribute much to carry the system farther on at points where it sadly needed it. The Unitarian challenge to exhibit the possibility of the old Chalcedon formula, one person in two natures, had never been met. Germany was doing something really to meet it. Smith knew this. He presented clearly the central importance of the unity of the person to Christology, and he put the personal center, the Ego, unmistakably in the divine element. But, though he knew Dorner's suggestions as to the gradual development of the incarnation, and the kenotic suggestion as to the divine self-limitation in the incarnation,[48] he adopted neither for himself, nor brought them forward in such a way as to furnish any appreciable help.

As an apologist,[49] Smith appears at greater advantage. His *Introduction* to theology is full of valuable generalizations, gives evidence of the widest reading and fullest knowledge, and is illuminating and stimulating in a high degree. The *Apologetics* proper give a great outline of a learned and cogent argument, and cause the greater regret for their incompleteness by the greater evidence which they give of the entire competence of their author. And yet, nothing can be more plain to the reader of today than that both of these works belong to a bygone age. How completely this is so one may judge from the simple fact that the plan for the "Ely Lectures" upon evolution which Smith had been appointed to give in the year 1877, regards the evolution which began with the work of Darwin as a member of the long series of speculations which have gathered about this word. "The history of evolution," he says,[50] "is as old as human thought. Its materialistic forms were advanced and rejected in the dawn of philosophy.

[48] *System*, pp. 422 ff.

[49] *Introduction to Christian Theology. Apologetics.* Two volumes in one (New York, 1891).

[50] *Apologetics*, p. 170.

It is now newly formulated (by Spencer more ably than any other)." Thus the vital consideration that an age of *exact observation of facts,* such as had never been known, had been ushered in, and that all reasoning was to take on new forms in consequence, had entirely escaped him. As a representative of the old apology, Smith had had no predecessor in America; as an apologist for the new age, he was incapacitated by the fact that he did not live in it. Evolution can never be rightly appraised nor its relation to Christian theology set forth by one who begins with the idea that ancient philosophy stands upon a level with the inductive science of the present day. The historic spirit, so strong in Smith, blinded him to the fact that a right method of investigation had made the nineteenth century absolutely revolutionary in human thinking.[51]

Smith's immediate successor at Union Seminary was William G. T. Shedd.[52] He was a son of New England, and graduated in theology at Andover while Woods was in the chair of theology and Park in that of homiletics. But while a student in Vermont University he came in contact with Coleridge's philosophy, under the influence of President Marsh, and thus received a philosophic tendency which led him far away from the positions of the New England divines. Of Edwards' doctrines as to the will he retained only the idea of determinism, which was, however, more of a Burtonian position with Shedd than an Edwardean.[53]

[51] The completest examples of Smith's apologetic work are to be found in the volume, *Faith and Philosophy,* essays upon "The New Latitudinarians of England," "Sir William Hamilton's Theory of Knowledge," "Draper's Intellectual Development of Europe," "Renan's Life of Jesus," "The New Faith of Strauss."

[52] Born at Acton, Mass., June 21, 1820; died in New York, November 17, 1894; graduated from the University of Vermont, 1839; Andover Seminary, 1843; pastor at Brandon, Vt., 1844–45; professor of English literature in the University of Vermont, 1845–52; of sacred rhetoric at Auburn, 1852–53; of ecclesiastical history at Andover, 1853–62; of biblical literature in Union seminary, 1863–74; and of systematic theology, 1874–90.

[53] He rejected the threefold division of the mind in favor of the twofold (*Dogmatic Theology,* Vol. II, p. 118). He made a distinction between the "in-

The Nature of Virtue he entirely abandoned, denying that
benevolence was the single moral attribute of God,[54] and
refusing to accept "public justice" as being justice at all.[55]
The proposition that obligation is commensurate with ability he acknowledged,[56] but he put the ability in Adam, not
in us.[57]   He taught that all sin is voluntary, but made
original sin the voluntary sin of every individual man *in
Adam*.[58] He totally rejected the New England doctrine
of ability to repent, and declared its preaching injurious
to sinners,[59] thus reacting to the paralyzing position of the
Puritan epoch.   He rejected the governmental theory of
the atonement.[60]   And he was so far opposed to Taylorism that he did not think it worthy of mention, and the
name of N. W. Taylor does not even get into the index of
the work.   In his own words, the "general type of doctrine is the Augustino-Calvinistic: upon a few points, the
elder Calvinism has been followed in preference to the
later."   He well says:

> It will be objected by some to this dogmatic system that it has
> been too much influenced by the patristic, mediaeval, and reformation
> periods, and too little by the so-called "progress" of modern theology.
> The charge of scholasticism, and perhaps of speculativeness, will be
> made.   The author has no disposition to repel the charge.   While

clination," and the volition, closely corresponding to that between "primary predominant choice" in Taylor and individual volitions. "Inclination" was fixed upon
evil at the moment of the fall, by what seems to be an act of primal causality,
and so of true freedom.   But it is the only such act.   The Burtonian turn of
the thought consists in the fact that in regeneration the "holy inclination is re-
originated in the sinful will of the individual men by the Holy Ghost," and that
individual volitions then follow of necessity this bent of the will. (*Theology*,
Vol. II, pp. 144, 165, 171, 178, 250.)

[54] *Theology*, Vol. I, pp. 369 ff.; cf. Vol. II, p. 434.

[55] *Ibid.*, p. 383.   [56] *Ibid.*, Vol. II, p. 241.

[57] *Ibid.*, pp. 168 ff.   [58] *Ibid.*, p. 181.

[59] *Ibid.*, p. 255.

[60] He quite misunderstands Grotius as to the meaning of the "relaxation"
of the law, and to the necessity of satisfaction (Vol. I, p. 383; cf. Vol. II, p. 453).
He himself takes God in the matter of forgiveness as acting as the offended
party (Vol. II, pp. 384, 447); and other positions of his render the governmental
theory an impossibility (Vol. II, pp. 435, 437, etc.).

acknowledging the excellences of the present period in respect to the
practical application and spread of religion, he cannot regard it as
pre-eminent above all others in scientific theology.[61]

Hence he shows himself even more impervious to the
fact of the revolution in methods of thought wrought by
scientific evolution than Smith, and continues to quote
Aristotle and the Fathers, with a very large addition of
material from a quarter where Smith had not anticipated
him—from the scholastics of the Middle Ages. This he
does as if their utterly *a priori* and altogether ungrounded
and groundless speculations were quite on a level, if not
above, the best results of modern inductive thinking. With
great, though somewhat inaccurate, learning he has, therefore, presented a system of theology which might equally
well have been written before Edwards wrote his first work,
and which represents the extreme of recoil from everything that New England had done.

Shedd was the last of the incumbents of the Roosevelt
chair in Union Seminary who could be reckoned to the
New England school. This position of his is, therefore,
of the nature of a judgment of New England theology,
and a condemnation of it. Smith had declared, in harmony with Edwards, that Calvinism could not be maintained except upon the basis of determinism, and had thus
rejected the crowning work of Taylor, while otherwise
acknowledging his connection with the school. But Shedd
said in substance that the whole effort of the school, from
the beginning in Edwards to the summit reached in Taylor, was a mistaken one and had ended in failure. To
him the alternative was between Calvinism of the unmodified type and not-Calvinism; and he was a Calvinist.

Of other thinkers in the New School Presbyterian church
it is not necessary to speak at length. Albert Barnes was

[61] *Theology*, Vol. I, pp. v, vi.

a singularly beautiful and religious nature who early in his ministry adopted the chief distinguishing doctrines of New England. His sermon on *The Way of Salvation*,[62] delivered to his own people in the midst of a revival of religion "to bring together in a single discourse the leading doctrines of the Bible respecting God's way of saving men," was in effect a kind of creed, and was made the basis of his trial before the Second Presbytery of Philadelphia for heresy. The following extracts will show his agreement with New England:

God's plan of saving men is based on the fact that the race is destitute of holiness. . . . . Christianity does not charge on men crimes of which they are not guilty. It does not say, as I suppose, that the sinner is held to be personally answerable for the transgressions of Adam, or of any other man; or that God has given a law which man has no power to obey. . . . . The violation of this pure law is held to be the first act of the child when he becomes a moral agent; and continued act of his life unless he is renewed; and the last act on his dying pillow. . . . . The Son of God died in the place of sinners. He did not, indeed, endure the penalty of the law—for his sufferings were not eternal, nor did he endure remorse of conscience; but he endured so much suffering, bore so much agony, that the Father was pleased to accept of it in the place of the eternal torments of all that should by him be saved. "The atonement of itself, secured the salvation of no one." It made it consistent for God to offer pardon to rebels. It so evinced the hatred of God against sin—so vindicated his justice—so asserted the honor of his law, that all his perfections would shine forth illustriously, if sinners through this work should be saved. . . . . This atonement was for all men. . . . I assume the free and full offer of the gospel to all men to be one of those cardinal points of the system by which I *gauge* all my other views of truth. It is, in my view, a corner-stone of the whole edifice; that which makes it so glorious to God, and so full of good will to men. . . . . While God thus sincerely offers the gospel to men, all mankind, while left to themselves, as sincerely and cordially reject it. . . . . Those who are saved will be saved because God does it by the renewing of the Holy Ghost. . . . . There is here supposed to be no violation of freedom. In all this the sinner chooses freely. The Spirit compels no one: he shuts out no one. . . . . It is no part of this

[62] Edition before me, the seventh, with Barnes's defense before synod and presbytery (New York, 1836).

scheme, as you will see, that God made men on purpose to damn them. . . . . This is done by a change in the affections and life of man. . . . . It is not merely a love of happiness in a new form, it is a love of God and divine things because they are good and amiable in themselves.

These are the leading positions of the New England theology, and Barnes continued to teach them to the end. But his theological activity was largely consumed and his creative faculties permanently lamed by the necessity under which he lay of reconciling all this with the Westminster Confession.

We therefore close this chapter of our history with the remark that the verdict of the history justifies the contention of Princeton in its chief objection to the New England theology, however little justification there may be for the details of the Princeton warfare against everything which New England proposed. The new theology, if consistently carried out, must in the end disrupt the system of Calvinism, and in this sense it was irreconcilable with the Confession. The influence of the Confession, whenever it began really to be felt by a New England thinker, was always for reaction and ultimately for stagnation. Princeton might well say to New Haven what Luther said to Zwingli: *Ihr habt einen anderen Geist denn wir.*

CHAPTER XVI

THE OBERLIN THEOLOGY

The greatest mind and the regulating force in the development of Oberlin theology was Charles G. Finney. Converted under remarkable experiences in the comparative solitude of a New York village, in his early manhood, and after he had already begun the practice of law, he formed his theology in connection with his early labors as a preacher with but little assistance from human teachers.[1] His thinking was marked from the beginning by strong originality; but he was not so completely independent as he was sometimes thought to be. Various underground currents set from New Haven westward, and some of them bore theological ideas into the region where Finney was. Subsequently he had personal association with the great New Haven theologian.[2] Influenced by legal analogies, and early adopting the doctrine of the freedom of the will, he had struck into the path which all New England theology was following, and had arrived at its main results before he left the seclusion of his home and became the most famous revivalist of his time. It is not strange, therefore, that he ultimately adopted most of Taylor's positions, and was, among the great leaders of New England, Taylor's true successor.

Finney's earliest studies had given him the governmental theory of the atonement, and the doctrine of general atonement; had taught him the freedom of the will, true human ability, that man is active in regeneration, and

[1] *Memoirs of Rev. Charles G. Finney* (autobiographic; New York, 1876), pp. 42 ff.

[2] Professor G. Frederick Wright, *Charles Grandison Finney* (New York, 1891), pp. 177 ff. A very valuable and discriminating chapter on Finney's theology.

that he is converted by the influence of the truth; and had led him to reject imputation, and by implication the remaining artificial elements of the Westminster system. It is an interesting detail that it was the presentation of the old Rellyan arguments for universalism by a traveling Universalist minister that led him, as it had the younger Edwards and his associates, to the formulation of the governmental theory of the atonement.[3]

When he arrived at Oberlin, he found there three other powerful men—Mahan, Morgan, and Cowles. These four leaders had all been engaged in the remarkable revival movements of those days, and had almost come to feel that the earnestness and warmth of the revival were the proper characteristics of any normal Christian experience. The Oberlin colony was a collection of men and women intensely in earnest in the Christian life, and dissatisfied with anything which fell short of the highest attainable degree of perfection.[4] The preaching was pungent and searching. There soon arose the inquiry whether complete victory over temptation, by the help of the almighty Savior, was not possible to true Christian believers.

This question took the strongest hold upon the interest of Mahan, who had been made president of the college. He had been originally educated in the old Calvinism, which had been, with few real improvements in his estimation, taught by Leonard Woods when he was a student at Andover.[5] Under the influences emanating from New Haven, he had later adopted the doctrine of the true freedom of the will, and was thereby prepared for further changes.[6] One thing he had long desired, and that was

[3] *Memoirs*, pp. 49 f.

[4] The theology of Oberlin can scarcely be understood without a view of the "Colony," for which see President Fairchild's *Oberlin, the Colony and the College*.

[5] *Autobiography* (London, 1882), pp. 140 ff.   [6] *Ibid.*, pp. 203 ff.

deliverance from the power of sin. When the inquiry was solemnly put, in one of the Oberlin meetings, by a young man, whether he could hope to gain a complete victory over temptation, or must expect to go on stumbling as he had done before; and when at another time a third of the professing Christians present [7] rose to signify that they saw that their hopes were not well founded, he felt that he had come to a crisis when he *must* know the secret of such a Christian life as the apostle Paul lived, hid with Christ in God and filled with triumphant power. A remarkable experience of the love of Christ gave him the answer, and from this event he dated a new period in his Christian life.[8]

This answer was expressed by him in a sermon immediately preached, in the following form:

Speaking of his former preaching, he said, "When a sinner had inquired of me what he should do to be saved, I had known perfectly what was needed to be done in his case. . . . . But when a believer had come to me and confessed that he was not living as God requires, and asked me how he should escape the "bondage of corruption," and attain to "the liberty of the sons of God," I had instructed him to confess his sins, put them away, renew his purpose of obedience, and go forward with a fixed resolution to do the entire will of God. Now, here was a fundamental mistake. We are not only to be "justified by the faith of Christ," but to be sanctified also by the faith that is in him. . . . . If you desire a victory over your tempers, your appetites, and all your propensities, take them to Christ, just as you take your sins to him, and he will give you the victory over the former, just as he gives you pardon for the latter. . . . It is not he that resolves, but "he that abideth in Christ and Christ in him, that bringeth forth much fruit." (1836.)[9]

A little after this (1839) Mahan, in his *Scripture Doctrine of Christian Perfection,* defined this perfection as follows:

It is the consecration of our whole being to Christ, and the perpetual employment of all our powers in his service. It is the perfect

[7] *Out of Darkness into Light* (London, 1875), p. 133.
[8] *Ibid.,* p. 135. [9] *Ibid.,* pp. 140 f.

assimilation of our entire character to that of Christ, having at all times, and under all circumstances, the "same mind that was also in Christ Jesus." It is, in the language of Mr. Wesley, "In one view, purity of intention, dedicating all the life to God. It is the giving God all the heart; it is one desire and design ruling all our tempers. It is devoting, not a part, but all our soul, body and substance to God. In another view, it is all the mind that was in Christ Jesus, enabling us to walk as he walked. It is the circumcision of the heart from all filthiness, from all inward as well as outward pollution. It is the renewal of the heart in the whole image of God, the full likeness of him that created it. In yet another, it is loving God with all our heart, and our neighbor as ourselves." [10]

The distinctive thought of this little treatise is that such perfection is attainable, and is to be sought for by prayer and by the exercise of faith in Jesus Christ who, taking up his dwelling in the soul by his Spirit, will bring it into perfect sympathy with himself, stilling its passions and destroying the power of its temptations.

Professor Morgan somewhat later (1845) published in the *Oberlin Quarterly* an article upon "The Gift of the Holy Ghost." He maintained that this gift, spoken of in the Book of Acts so continually, was not designed for that age alone, was not the gift of working miracles, nor in any other way exceptional, but was designed for all Christians to fit them for the development of holy character and the performance of effective Christian service. He summarizes his view:

The baptism of the Holy Ghost, then, in its Pentecostal fullness was not to be confined to the primitive church; but it is the common privilege of all believers—of believers even of this generation, and of every generation to come. It was at first indispensable to the appropriate happiness and befitting characteristics of the children of God and brethren of Jesus Christ—a happiness and dignity impossible except by becoming one with him, not by an external bond . . . . but an internal union through the indwelling of the same Spirit. We say it was at first indispensable for these ends; and it has not ceased to be indispensable for the same ends by the lapse of time. It was necessary to make Apostles, and Prophets, and Saints, able efficient ministers of

[10] *Op. cit.*, p. 13.

the New Testament. Till endued by this baptism with power from on high, they were not prepared to convert the nations to God. The same necessity exists at the present day, and will continue to exist till the last sinner is converted through the gospel preached with the Holy Ghost sent down from heaven. Who without the Holy Ghost is sufficient for these things? And of what other sufficiency from God does the inspired word make mention? Nor will a less effusion of the Spirit, a less degree of the Spirit and power of sonship, answer now, than was found necessary in the apostolic age.[11]

With these presentations of the matter both Finney and Cowles agreed, though themselves employing somewhat different terms.

The idea was much the same under these varying forms of expression, namely, that there is an experience attainable in the Christian life, subsequent in general to conversion, in which the believer rises to a higher plane, secures new views of Christ and his salvation, obtains victory over weaknesses which had before marred his character, and attains a stability to which he was before a stranger.[12]

Mahan insisted upon a sanctification of the sensibility, and claimed that he had experienced a stilling of passions before which he had previously been impotent, so as to be delivered from their bondage. It sometimes seemed as if he viewed this as essentially mechanical. Finney spoke more of the moral power of the truth upon the heart. None of them noted, so far as I have observed, an interesting point of contact of the new view with President Edwards' view of original sin. Our corruption was traced by him, not to some positive taint implanted in our nature, but to the withdrawal of the Holy Spirit upon the sin of Adam. We were intended to live in communion with the Spirit, and without him we are, of course, unfitted for our environment, and hence liable to sin. If now the Holy Spirit is bestowed upon all believers who will receive him, then the

[11] Reprint of 1875, pp. 70 ff.

[12] See the very interesting and valuable article by President J. H. Fairchild in the *Congregational Quarterly*, Vol. VIII (1876), pp. 237 ff. It is itself an original source of high rank.

defect which we call original sin is repaired, and sinners are restored to the original elevation of unfallen human nature. That such a consummation has been a dim but ever present ideal of the church's, the Roman doctrine of the removal of all guilt of original sin by baptism may serve as a proof. Here at last the way was opened for a spiritual development of the same idea; but it was never followed out.

The emphasis laid at Oberlin upon the peculiar character of the experience of sanctification gradually disappeared.[13] It was gradually felt that it did not differ so much as had been thought from the experience of ordinary Christians. In the realm of doctrine the movement resulted in the proposal of a new psychological principle, that of the "simplicity of moral action."

This doctrine was first propounded in public by William Cochran, a graduate in the year 1839, in an address before the Society of Inquiry, and subsequently the Alumni, in 1841. It "was very generally accepted," says President Fairchild, "as conclusive on the subject." The position it presented was adopted by all the leading teachers in Oberlin,[14] except Professor Cowles, though with different degrees of earnestness and different success in applying it in the development of other doctrines. It became, however, especially by the consistent and unvarying advocacy of Pres-

[13] The literature of this phase of Oberlin theology is large. The *Oberlin Evangelist* (1839–62) was established in the interest of Christian perfection. It had five thousand subscribers for many years. It is a mine of information as to all the higher Oberlin affairs. Morgan published an essay on *The Holiness Acceptable to God*, which was incorporated in the first (Oberlin) edition of Finney's *Systematic Theology*, and reprinted in 1875 at Oberlin. Cowles wrote for the *Evangelist* articles reprinted as a small book at Oberlin (1840) on *Holiness of Christians in the Present Life*. Finney reprinted from the *Evangelist*, *Views of Sanctification* (1840), and from his *Theology*, *Guide to the Saviour, or Conditions of Attaining to and Abiding in Entire Holiness of Heart and Life* (1848).

[14] See the original address in the *Oberlin Evangelist*, 1842, pp. 33 ff., and 41 ff.

ident Fairchild, a characteristic portion of the Oberlin theology.[15]

Cochran begins his discussion by defining moral action as "the coincidence or disagreement of the free will with the law of right which Reason reveals and imposes;" or again, as "choosing good for its own sake, and of course as the ultimate end of effort, or, when good is apprehended, refusing thus to choose." Two ideas underlie the discussion which are not definitely mentioned. It could hardly have been thought at that time necessary to mention them, so fully were they presupposed by all the philosophy of the day as self-evident truth. These were that the action of the will was single, making but one volition, or choosing but one object at a time; and that it was entirely a phenomenon of consciousness, for philosophy was confined then to the conscious mind, the main, if not the sole, implement of investigation being introspection. These suppositions are, therefore, passed over without specific mention, but it is thought important to specify, as conditions of this conception of moral action, responsibility and its presupposition, freedom, the latter understood in the Oberlin sense. Cochran also lays down the principles that "intentions or choices alone are moral actions," and that "it is often in choices or intentions alone that there is any essential difference between men who, nevertheless, are in character as opposite as the poles." After a few other preliminary remarks he is ready for his thesis, which he defends in the following words:

The question whether a moral action may be of a mixed character can now be easily answered. From what has been said, the question is simply this: can the will at the same time be coincident with *impartial reason and self-centering inclination?* Or thus: can a moral agent choose the general good as the *ultimate* end of his exertions,

[15] Cf. President Finney's discussion in his *Theology* (original Oberlin ed., Vol. I, pp. 150 ff.), which adds nothing essential.

and at the same instant choose his individual good as the *ultimate* end of his exertions? Or, less abstractly still: can one *supremely* prefer the good of being in general, and at the same point of time *supremely* prefer his own to the general good? If I were to reply affirmatively to the question as at first put, I should say that one could choose *partially* and *impartially;* that is, do and not do the same thing at the same time. If to the second form of the question an affirmative answer were given, it would involve the absurdity of saying that at the same time we may have *two ultimate ends.* To answer the question as last put in the affirmative would be to say that at the same time by the same will *two preferences may be supreme.* That is, to affirm and deny of each that it is supreme—a contradiction as palpable as saying that a thing may be and not be at the same time. Tertullian, whose rule of faith was, *it is absurd, and therefore I believe it,* might have answered either of these questions in the affirmative and believed what he said. But I should be loath to expect as much of any man living.

The chief objection which would naturally strike every reader of this address would be that the theory destroys character. Every choice is either wholly sinful or entirely holy, and hence, since all admit that the Christian falls into sin, when he sins he is entirely a sinner and not a Christian at all. Thus there is no abiding or permanent thing about him which can be called character, and what he is at any moment, saint or sinner, no observer can tell. Cochran saw this objection, and in the following paragraph he meets it after the following manner:

There are not wanting those, however, who believe (whether from a thorough investigation or not it is not mine to decide) that our ultimate design to serve God may permanently remain and yet specific volitions from time to time be contrary to it. Let us examine this theory, for it can claim in its support high authority and many great names. When it is said that specific volitions are contrary to the generic purpose, or ultimate design, it must be meant, either that self-gratification is their end, or that it is not. If it is not, as there is no third end, they must be classed among instinctive or irresponsible actions, and moral character must be denied of them. Of course, if this be done, they can with no more propriety be said to be inconsistent with the ultimate end than the beating of the heart. If self-gratification is their ultimate end—that to which they sustain the relation of means, then either the ultimate end of serving God is not existing—and this contradicts the hypothesis; or there are two ultimate ends co-existing, which we have just shown to be absurd. If, notwithstanding this absurdity, the co-existence with wrong volitions of a generic purpose to secure universal good be still contended for, it must at least be conceded that during their existence *it retires to the dormitory of the soul* and takes on a sleep which is the exact image of death. How this can be conceived of as an existing choice, may well excite our wonder. A choice which chooses nothing! A purpose to promote the general good which results in nothing! Nay, which, somehow or other, results in volitions to promote the opposite! . . . . The doctrine, I apprehend, originates in the mistaken notion that the choice of self-gratification as an ultimate end, is a deliberate determination never again to serve God. Nothing in most cases is farther from the truth. For the present, and it may be for some time to come, the sinner chooses his own gratification, promising himself and others that he will repent before he dies. This he expects to do in his sense of repentance. That there is no virtue in this expectation is true, that it is real is equally true.

The words italicized above contained a suggestion which would have brought Cochran to the contemplation of the sub-conscious mind, if it had been followed out; but the presupposition upon which he was proceeding, that all the acts of the mind take place in consciousness, combined with the further error that all sin is the deliberate choice of self-gratification and involves a perception of the irreconcilability of this with the choice of the general good, shut his eyes to this fruitful suggestion. Upon his psychological basis he was right and his reasoning conclusive; but the basis was not right.

The remaining portion of the address dealt with various objections. The subject was handled in an exceedingly thorough manner. The fact that a single volition may be the product of many motives does not give it a mixed character—partly good and partly bad—since it is the subjective motive that determines the character of a choice, and this must be either a supreme choice of good, or of self-gratification. Lack of intensity of choice does not make it partly good and partly evil; for if this is lack of choosing less than the good we ought, it is not choosing that good *at all* in any proper sense; and if it is merely a failure of the natural powers, it does not involve culpability.

While still answering objections, Cochran advances to positions which constitute the true contribution of this discussion to New England theology. To gain a biblical proof for his proposition, he argues that "the indispensable condition of reconciliation to God is the abandonment of all sin." The act of self-surrender to God must be a perfectly holy act, since it must consist in a choice of the will of God as our supreme good. "Entire conformity to the law of God is a condition indispensable to continuance in his favor." The effect of these positions upon the theory of sanctification, of a "second blessing," and of a peculiar sanctification attained by some Christians and not by others, is at once evident. President Fairchild summed up this result of the theory of the simplicity of moral action in the following form:

One of the most obvious consequences of the doctrine is that conversion is entire consecration; that the earliest obedience of the converted sinner is entire obedience, and that his moral state is entirely approved by God. The very first exercise of faith involves all the faith that under the circumstances is possible, and therefore all that is obligatory. There is no partial faith, in the sense in which faith is a duty, nor, in the same sense, any imperfect love. The sinner in giving his heart to God gives it all,—makes no reservation; any holding back corrupts the whole action. . . . . The idea, then, of rising from a partial to a complete obedience, from imperfect to perfect faith and love, in the sense in which these are voluntary and responsible acts or states to be required of men, is incompatible with the idea of simplicity of moral action. . . . . The work required in Christian progress is growth in grace, enlargement of views, experience of Christ's power and of one's own weakness,—all resulting in establishment of Christian character and more and more complete deliverance from these interruptions of obedience,—an obedience more and more constant until it becomes permanent and suffers no interruption. In this view every believer is sanctified, in the sense that he has utterly renounced sin in his acceptance of Christ, and given him his whole heart. This is sanctification in the Scripture sense, and all believers are called saints in the Bible, that is, sanctified ones. We hear nothing in the Bible of justified people that are not sanctified. . . . . The work of edification which follows conversion is of vast consequence; it is growth from infancy to manhood. But it can be accomplished by no one act of the will, no immediate exercise of faith. There is no promise in God's Word upon which a believer can plant himself in present faith and secure his stability in faith and obedience for all the future, so that we can say of him that he is perfectly sanctified. We can say of one that he has grown in the grace of Christ, that he has made attainments in knowledge and experience and stability. We may judge at length that he is perfectly sanctified; but God alone can know. It is not a question of his own consciousness. Consciousness can give the fact of entire consecration, which is the essence of conversion; it cannot give the fact of permanent sanctification; that is in the history of the future, not in present consciousness. . . . . We find, then, no line of division, upon this view of Christian character, between sanctified and unsanctified Christians. All Christians while in the exercise of faith are sanctified, nor is there any clear line between the simply sanctified and the permanently sanctified.[16]

Cochran seemed in this discussion to be the originator of a new doctrine, which was soon accepted by the eager laborers in the field of theology at Oberlin as of the highest value. But, in fact, the same position had been presented still earlier by Emmons.[17] In his sermons upon "The True Character of Good Men Delineated" he has the following passages:

Let us inquire whether [the saints'] imperfection can arise from their moral affections being partly holy and partly sinful. If their affections were of such a mixed nature, they certainly would be criminally imperfect. For, if each of their moral affections could be partly holy and partly sinful, then each would have something in it of moral perfection and of moral imperfection. But can we conceive of such a mixture of moral good and evil, in one and the same exercise of heart? Let us pursue the inquiry. Can the affection of love be partly

[16] *Congregational Quarterly, loc. cit.,* pp. 248 ff.

[17] Professor Wright, in his *Finney,* says that "he had adopted the view of Emmons," making no reference to Cochran as contributing to the discussion (p. 209). In fact, it goes back beyond Emmons, for Hopkins dropped a hint of it when he said (*System,* Vol. I, pp. 29): "Every moral action is either perfectly holy or perfectly sinful."

love and partly hatred to God? Can the exercise of repentance be partly love and partly hatred to sin? . . . . It is absolutely absurd to suppose that any voluntary exercise should be partly holy and partly sinful. . . . . The notion that the imperfection of saints arises from their moral affections being all partly holy and partly sinful, is contrary to reason, Scripture, and their own experience.[18]

Emmons further taught that "saints do have some *perfectly* good affections," and insisted upon their "duty to become absolutely perfect." His greatest difference from Oberlin arose from his theory of human dependence, which was much more strongly accentuated by him than by the later teachers, in accordance with which he taught that gracious exercises are not necessarily and inseparably connected with each other; and, of consequence, they may at any time be interrupted by totally sinful affections. They have no permanent source or fountain of holiness within themselves, from which a constant stream of holy affections will naturally and necessarily flow. As one holy affection will not produce another, so they are immediately dependent upon God for every holy affection. The moment he withdraws his gracious influence, their gracious exercises cease, and sinful exercises instantly succeed. And in this case they are no more able to renew the train of holy affections than they were to begin it at first. Their sanctification, therefore, is precisely the same as continued regeneration.[19]

Finney began the publication of his theology in the form of skeletons of lectures in 1840.[20] But one volume of these appeared, for, six years after, he began the publication of more finished lectures, of which two volumes were issued. These later volumes began with the subject of moral government, and had been in part anticipated by the first. It was his intention to prefix a first volume which should

---

[18] *Works* (Boston, 1860), Vol. III, pp. 290 ff.

[19] Emmons was commonly understood to hold that the soul consisted merely in a series of exercises, which view is most consistent with the doctrine of the simplicity of moral action. It is scarcely necessary to observe that the Oberlin theologians did not follow him into this peculiarity.

[20] *Skeletons of a Course of Theological Lectures.* By Rev. C. G. Finney, Professor of Didactic, Polemic, and Pastoral Theology, in the Oberlin Collegiate Institute. Vol. I. Oberlin. Printed and published by James Steele, 1840. 8vo, 248 pages. (Olivet College Library.)

begin, as the skeletons had, with the first principles of the science, but this intention was never carried out. The imperfect *Skeletons* therefore remains our chief source of information as to his views upon natural theology, the Scriptures, the Trinity, and Christology; and deserves, therefore, our first attention in a review of his theology.

The topic may, however, be dispatched very briefly. The existence of God is argued from moral obligation, from design, from the dependent form of man's existence, and from the necessity of a first cause. The divine authority and inspiration of the Bible are then argued from the need and the possibility of a further revelation and from the correspondence of the Bible to the revelation required (as authentic, genuine, and credible). Thus the basis is obtained for the development of the attributes of God, including his moral attributes, and for the proof of such doctrines as the Trinity, the divinity of Christ, etc. The treatment is everywhere strong, logical, rational, and biblical. The inspiration of the Bible implies that the writers were "infallibly secured from all error," and that "they communicated authoritatively the mind and will of God." The argument is from miracle, prophecy, the assertions of the writers and their credibility; and makes no mention of the witness of the Spirit. On the other points mentioned there is no disagreement with the general trend of new school divinity at the time. The same meagerness and defects which we have found elsewhere in the treatment of the Trinity and Christology reoccur here.

As already remarked, the fuller edition of 1846–47 in part repeated the discussions of the earlier. It begins with the moral government of God, nothing being written upon natural theology, or the revealed doctrines of the Trinity and Christology, except what is incidentally brought in in discussing later portions of the system. It was republished in England with some modifications by the author in 1851, and from this edition an abridgment was prepared by President Fairchild and published in Oberlin (1878).

Finney begins with a remark which exhibits the foundation and indicates the trend and probable value of his work:

The truths of the blessed gospel have been hidden under a false philosophy. Of this I have long been convinced. Nearly all the practical doctrines of Christianity have been embarrassed and perverted by assuming as true the dogma of a Necessitated Will. This has been a leaven of error that, as we shall see, has 'leavened nearly the whole lump' of gospel truth. In the present work I have attempted to prove, and have every where assumed the freedom of the will.[21]

A little below he adds: "What I have said on the Foundation of Moral Obligation is the key to the whole subject." He might have added that his whole theology was controlled by two fundamental purposes—to make men Christians and to keep them so—and was hence a theology of conversion and sanctification.

The first volume (second of the proposed complete system, which was never finished) is entitled "Moral Government," as was the main portion of N. W. Taylor's. Moral law is defined as "a rule of moral action with sanctions." [22] It is the "law of liberty, as opposed to the law of necessity—of motive and free choice, as opposed to force of every kind that renders action necessary or unavoidable." His conception of freedom, and his argument from consciousness, already developed, need not be repeated.

Finney's position as to moral obligation has often been thought to be original; but it does not seem to differ in any degree from Edwards'. He differs only in his conception of freedom, which affects the moral action of men, but not the specific point of the foundation of moral action. The

[21] Oberlin ed., p. iii.   [22] Ibid., p. 2.

whole matter is comprehended in his statement: "It is a first truth of reason that we ought to will the valuable for its own sake." [23] This is the same as Edwards' "love to being in general," being simply considered, viewed as possessing worth. Historically the formulation of the principle originated in Oberlin in a discussion of the year 1839, as Professor W. E. C. Wright has shown.[24] Mahan had advocated intuitive rightarianism, and Cowles a rational utilitarianism. Finney presided at the discussion, and finally summed up the truth of the two conflicting views in the statement that "I ought to love my neighbor because his welfare is valuable." The Oberlin audience saw in this result, which was generally accepted, and became the foundation of the Oberlin theology in this division, a new illustration of the genius of their great leader, and a new point of progress made then and there; but the historian will refer it to the Taylorism into which Finney had long before been initiated. In his *Theology* he later put it: "The well-being of God and the Universe is the absolute and ultimate good, and therefore it should be chosen by every moral agent."

It will be the less important for us to dwell further upon Finney's system because it may be dismissed in the one word "Taylorism," independent as it was, and vigorously as its author had impressed upon it the marks of his own pronounced individuality. As an illustration of the often minute correspondence between the two thinkers, the following explanation of the rise of moral depravity may be cited:

The impulses of the sensibility are developed at birth. The first acts of will are in obedience to these. Self-gratification is the rule of action previous to the development of reason. No resistance is offered

---

[23] *Ibid.*, p. 25.

[24] "Oberlin's Contribution to Ethics," an article in the *Bibliotheca Sacra*, July, 1900, pp. 429 ff.

to the will's indulging appetite until a habit of self-indulgence is formed. When reason affirms moral obligation, it finds the will in a state of habitual and constant committal to the impulses of the sensibility. The demands of the sensibility have become more and more despotic every hour of indulgence. In this state of things, unless the Holy Spirit interpose, the idea of moral obligation will be but dimly developed. The will, of course, rejects the bidding of reason and cleaves to self-indulgence. This is the settling of a fundamental question. It is deciding in favor of appetite against the claims of conscience and of God. Light once rejected can be thereafter more easily resisted. Selfishness confirms and strengthens and perpetuates itself by a natural process. It grows with the sinner's growth and strengthens with his strength, and will do so forever unless overcome by the Holy Spirit through the truth.

This connection with Taylor is fully recognized by Professor G. Frederick Wright in his *Finney* in many places.[25] At one point, in the very valuable and detailed review of Finney as a theologian and a philosopher, which constitutes the principal chapter of his book, he criticizes Taylor as maintaining that "all the goodness of an action pertains to its adaptation to produce results." He continues: "Finney clearly maintains that the obligation to use any particular means to do good must be conditioned upon the supposed 'tendency of those means to secure the end.' But this is the obligation to put forth a proximate rather than an ultimate choice. *Ultimate intention has no such condition.*" [26] But even here, however much disagreement there may be in forms of speech, the final meaning of the two thinkers seems to be the same. Taylor defines benevolence as "an elective preference of the highest well-being of all other sentient beings as *his supreme object.*" [27] That choice is founded upon the ultimate "worth" of such beings; and this worth is defined as consisting in the "capacity of happiness." [28] Such is the implication of the whole context. And that would seem to be Finney's doctrine precisely.

[25] Cf. pp. 25, 179, 181, 196, 200.   [26] *Ibid.*, pp. 214, 215.
[27] *Moral Government*, Vol. I, p. 19.   [28] *Ibid.*, p. 32.

Aside from this, however, so sharp-sighted a thinker as Professor Wright, and one so well acquainted with Finney's theology, with which he has been familiar from his youth, can find no substantial disagreement with Taylor upon the great doctrines of the system.

Finney's immediate successor in the teaching of theology at Oberlin was James Harris Fairchild,[29] whose *Elements of Theology, Natural and Revealed*,[30] continue the Oberlin tradition and brings its work in New England theology to a close. The connection of this work with the *Theology* of Finney is evident at once, but its differences are still more noticeable. It is less formal, seeks less constantly for cogent proof, treats each subject as largely independent rather than as dependent upon all that has preceded for its evidence, pursues the objector less uncompromisingly, and relies more upon general rationality and the utterances of simple common-sense, than had its predecessor. But it maintains the same great principles with Finney—the freedom of the will and the simplicity of moral action, the foundation of moral obligation in the essential worth of sentient being; teaches the great central doctrines of the evangelical system in the sense in which Finney and other New England divines taught them, minimizes the Calvinistic element, though not eliminating it, and maintains the divinity of Christ, the atonement (governmental theory), and the endless future punishment of the incorrigibly wicked. In apologetics it shows a distinct tendency to waive the unimportant and to concentrate the argument upon the central and decisive elements of the

[29] Born in Stockbridge, Mass., November 25, 1817; removed to Ohio in 1818; graduated at Oberlin in 1838, and from the Theological Seminary in 1841; professor of Greek and Latin, and instructor in Hebrew, in 1842; professor of mathematics and natural philosophy in 1847; professor of theology in 1858; president in 1866; published his *Moral Philosophy* in 1869; his *Elements of Theology* in 1892; retired from the presidency in 1889, and from the professorship of theology in 1895; died in 1902.

[30] Published by Goodrich in Oberlin, 1892 (8vo, xvi+358 pages).

question in hand. Its strength lies in its adaptation to the
needs of plain men in search of a workable system of
thought, in the simplicity and clearness of its anthropology,
in the prominence with which the great essentials of
Christian doctrine stand out above the controverted and uncertain. Its defects are those of the school at this time:
its philosophical shallowness, its failure to supply the omis-
sions of its predecessors in the treatment of such themes as
the unity of the person of Christ, the two natures, human
and divine, and in unfolding the meaning and application
of the doctrine of the Trinity in the system. It was not
fertilized by the new thought of its day, and had little to
say to the times in which it was finally published; but its
place as a plain and untechnical statement, in a moderate
and sensible way, of the general results at which New England theology had arrived, will never be challenged.

CHAPTER XVII

EDWARDS A. PARK

We have now arrived in the progress of our history at the close of the New England development, having considered all the great productive minds which contributed to the erection of this system of thought. The impression made upon the mind of the reader must still be somewhat discordant, for the history has been one of many differing tendencies, which have as yet been brought into complete and comprehensive expression by no one theologian. If the history had to close here, it would appear like a broken column in the great edifice of human thought. So far as it is a history of printed systems, it must close here; but there is a system which, though it does not exist yet in printed form, and may never do so, is still in existence in so many students' notebooks, and in so complete and careful reports, that it may be included among the materials of this history, and will serve the essential purpose of representing New England theology in its most perfect systematic form. Professor Edwards Amasa Park, of Andover,[1] was himself the ripest fruit of New England, and was one of her most loyal sons. His theology summed up in the most perfect form the long line of her theological

[1] Born at Providence, R. I., December 29, 1808; died at Andover, Mass., June 4, 1900; graduated at Brown University, Providence, 1826, and at Andover 1831; pastor at Braintree, Mass., 1831–33; professor of intellectual philosophy at Amherst, 1835–36; professor of sacred rhetoric at Andover, 1836–47; professor of systematic theology there, 1847–81; professor emeritus till his death. He was one of the founders of the *Bibliotheca Sacra* in 1844, which he continued to edit till its transfer to Oberlin in 1883; published largely in this and other periodical issues; wrote a number of valuable memoirs, of which the most important theologically are those of Hopkins and Emmons, and one still (1906) expected from the press, of Jonathan Edwards; conducted a most trenchant controversy with Professor Charles Hodge (*The Theology of the Intellect and That of the Feelings*, 1850, etc.); issued a volume of *Discourses;* and this list has been increased by a posthumous *Memorial Collection of Sermons.*

discoveries and ratiocinations. He himself was contemporary with some of her greatest and her latest theological
innovators. He continued to lecture till all the original
contributions of the last explorers had been brought in, and
while he lectured he thought critically upon all that was proposed, and incorporated what seemed good into his instruction and his system. Thus closing his lectures in 1881,
he was among the last, though not the very last, representative of New England theology; and he might thus, for
this reason alone, be placed at the end of the historical
account of the school. But the relation of the material
contents of his system to that of his predecessors makes
such an arrangement imperative upon the historian. Even
the results of that theologian who taught and published
after the close of Park's public labors, President Fairchild,
had been weighed and discussed before 1881; and these two
may certainly be said to have been the last of our public
teachers of theology who were controlled by the unmodified tradition of New England alone.

It is important to note, first, that Park had come squarely
upon the ground of the Scotch school of philosophy. We
have already noted this in part in the chapter upon the
will. There his adoption of the threefold division of the
faculties of the mind was shown to have modified his
theory of the will. But he adopts quite as earnestly the
intuitive element of that philosophy and its realism of "common-sense." The Berkeleian sublimation of the material
world into one merely ideal received no countenance with
him. His sarcastic wit delighted in the practical answer
of the philosopher who kicked a stone to prove its objective existence. Both the beginning of his reasoning and its
entire method rested upon the Scotch principles and pre-
cedents. The names of Reid and Stewart were often upon
his lips; and, if he did not give so large a place to Ham-

ilton, it was because he regarded him as having passed off somewhat from the sound basis of the school upon questionable ground. To this result both Woods and Taylor had contributed; for Park had heard both, Woods in the regular progress of an Andover education, and Taylor upon a special residence in New Haven for the purpose. Park was a pupil of Taylor more than of Woods, to whom he seldom referred and whom he probably did not fully appreciate. Taylor captivated his imagination by boldness of speculation and led his judgment into substantial agreement with himself. He even accepted the "power to the contrary," while remaining much more completely upon Edwards' ground as to the will than Taylor did. This complete adoption of the late change of philosophical base in the school becomes, therefore, both decided and of large influence upon the whole structure of his system.

Professor Park's theology was, first of all, *a system*. He began with a principle—"Every event has a cause"—but this was not assumed till it was shown to be a fundamental postulate of thought, and involved in all our thinking. When he had thus *proved* his principle, so far as it admits of proof, he proceeded to build up his system upon it step by step, proof by proof, proof resting in every case on what had been proved before. Thus his system was not a system in the sense of a mere orderly arrangement of parts, each, however, standing by itself, in no inner and vital connection with the rest; but it was a system in the sense that it was one linked process of proof, every step preparing for, and not depending on, the following, every step adequately prepared for by, and naturally flowing out of, all the preceding. It was like the wall of the cathedral, resting on footing-stones laid deep in the earth, course rising on course, each depending on what was beneath it and capable of bearing all that was to be above it, till the last pinnacle stood in its place perfect, secure in the security of the whole wall. In this respect Professor Park's system presented a great contrast to that of his contemporary and friend, Henry B. Smith, who wrote, in his *Faith and Philosophy:*

> Systematic Theology is not a mere arrangement of the facts and doctrines of the Bible in a lucid order; it is not a series of unconnected doctrines, with the definitions of them, it is the combining of doctrines into a system: its parts should not only be co-ordinate, they should be regularly developed. It should give the whole substance of the Christian faith, starting with its central principle, around which all the members are to be grouped. It must defend the faith and its separate parts against objections, and show that it is congruous with well-established truths in ethical and metaphysical science.[2]

Park said all that, but much more. Hence his system was always the system of a progress from the known to the unknown by rational examination and logical proof. If he failed at any point, it was not for lack of effort or for forgetfulness of the necessities of such a method of procedure.

The method of proof was the inductive, or the *a posteriori*. Park always proceeded from the known to the unknown, from the facts to the principles involved in them, from elementary principles to those pertaining to detail. Hence his theology was always subject to revision. Give him a new fact, and you have made necessary a new induction, and perhaps a new conclusion. Hence he was always open to new light, and manifested the most remarkable hospitality for new ideas. "Take them in," he said once, "and entertain them as you would guests at your table, until you know them; and then you can estimate their worth and their bearing on the truth." Textual criticism never disturbed him. If a text had to go, he looked to see if anything had been built on it alone, and to cast out such an element of his thought; for error eliminated he thought

[2] P. 27.

to be truth gained. The new theory of evolution did not trouble him. It had not "come to itself" during Park's day, and neither friends nor foes understood it. But while Professor Hodge, in his little book, was styling it bluntly "Atheism," Professor Park observed a scarcely interrupted silence upon it, except as he was ready now and then to ask what effect it *would* have on theology *if* it were to be found true. The present writer remembers very well asking him one day, on one of those walks and talks which he delighted to take with inquiring students, what the bearing of the doctrine of the origination of man by evolution would be on the doctrine of original sin. "What do we need," I asked, "to maintain universal depravity? If the race originated at several independent points, do we need to suppose anything more than an early sin, at one or more of these points, and the involvement of all mankind, by whatever process, in this early sin, to have all the elements now given in the common idea of the fall of Adam, and all the consequences that can legitimately be drawn from it?" His answer was, "No!" And the discussion, as it went on, showed how deeply interested he was in the adjustment of theology and evolution, though not yet ready to adopt either evolution or any such adjustment.

The treatment of the propositions discussed was predominantly rationalistic. True, the starting-point was the biblical; but the method was rational, and the cogent elements of the proof, exciting the greatest interest of both teacher and pupils, were the rational. Not that the doctrines were formulated with little reference to the Bible, or that the Bible was belittled whether by the formal treatment it received or by implication. Professor Park's exegesis was always accurate, and quite in accord with the best of the exegetical departments under his younger colleagues, Professors Mead and Thayer. But theology in his conception was the *philosophy* of Christian truth.   The Bible gave that truth, but why it was so, and how it could be defended, and what, precisely, it meant to the modern mind, were all rational questions, and constituted the burden of theology.   The biblical argument hence sometimes tended toward the dry and formal.   Sometimes its force had been so anticipated that it seemed almost superfluous.   Even before the days of modern criticism, it had lost something of its power.   The system must, therefore, be weighed rather as a rational creation than as a biblical elaboration.   Nor did the historical argument, either the critical or the positive, receive due attention from Professor Park.   It was sometimes appealed to in a general way, as when "the general opinions of men," or "the voice of Christian experience," were alluded to.   But such a thing as the "verdict" of the scientific history of Christian doctrine for or against any position was never heard of in the lecture-room in systematic theology.   Professor Park's education had, in fact, scarcely fitted him for such an appeal to history.   He knew the history of New England theology intimately and well, and understood its current of progress and the intellectual forces that bore it on.   But the appeals of Anglicans and Catholics to the church "fathers," by their specious adulation and irreverent reverence for mere men, and often for men of little training and feeble intellectual grasp at that, awoke a scorn in the mind of the practical American theologian, who was as strong in the element of common-sense as he was in intellectual acumen.   "Fathers!" said he once, with a flash of his sarcastic wit, "They would better be called the church *babies!*"   The elaborate efforts of the brilliant Professor Shedd at Andover to bring history, in a totally unhistorical and really a crypto-dogmatical method, to the defense of an exceedingly "old" form of Calvinism, had not tended to help Professor Park to a bet-

ter understanding or use of history. To its formal and
real disadvantage his system was essentially unbiblical and
unhistorical in style, and occasionally in substance.

The simplest method of gaining a clear conception of
Park's theology would be to set forth the great determining principles which made it what it was, and then trace
their influence upon the several doctrines, passing over
those in which he did not differ from his predecessors and
other evangelical theologians. With the advantage of simplicity would, however, be combined the disadvantage of
losing some of the most important lessons which he has to
teach us, particularly in the department of theological
method, where he was an unsurpassed master. We shall
therefore follow his lectures in the order of their delivery,
and this, in the early part of the system, quite strictly.

Professor Park adopted and employed the distinction
which had been handed down from the days of the deistic
controversy, and had been so ably used by Paley, between
natural and revealed theology. His object, as already
said, was proof. He desired to put the biblical doctrines
upon a sure basis of irrefragable proof. This, and this only,
would lift them from the rank of mere pleasing opinions,
of more or less value, of that of the *truth,* upon which men
might venture their immortal destinies; and *truth* was alone
a worthy object of consideration to a Christian theologian.

Now, to the proof of the Christian doctrines, the proof of
the Bible, from which they are derived, is essential. If
the Bible is such an authority as the church has always
said, it is a revelation from God. To prove the Bible, you
must therefore first prove the being and benevolence of
God; and you must do it without the Bible, since you are
not permitted to commit any circle in your reasoning.
Hence natural theology must precede revealed. Professor
Park therefore begins here, and lays down as his first prop-

osition that every event has a cause. But here he meets at once with a principal difficulty of theology. To prove the Bible he has to prove a benevolent God, because a God not benevolent could never be relied upon to give a revelation to man, however great man's need. But the benevolence of God is not a doctrine of pure natural theology, which can never either originate or prove it, and has never done so; but it is historically and logically itself a doctrine of the Bible. Hence, if you need a doctrine of the divine benevolence to prove the Bible, you need a Bible to prove the divine benevolence. How shall this circle be escaped? Ritschl recognized this peculiarity of the argument, and stated it better than any recent theologian, but Park also fully perceived it, and sought to do full justice to it. In fact, its necessities determined the entire course of the argument of the natural theology.

Park, therefore, began by giving "some elemental idea of God, not the whole being." He defines God as "the Mind which other minds are obligated to worship, because they are ultimately dependent upon it." The existence of such a being can be proved by logical arguments from nature proceeding on the basis of the principle of causation; and to establish this is, for the time, Park's sole effort. He takes up successively the arguments for a creator, a preserver, a contriver, a natural governor, and a moral governor. In the discussion of these, however acute, comprehensive, and profound it was, there was nothing which differed essentially from the general positions of natural theology as developed by his predecessors. Yet one innovation had already been made, and this was the introduction of a "biblical argument" on point after point. He expressly says that he takes the Bible for these arguments only "as a book written by sages," or as "containing the wisdom of the world." But when the argument is completed, he devotes more careful attention to this biblical argument. He remarks that "some men believe that all truths in natural theology are derived from the Bible: others believe that the Bible is drawn from natural theology." His own position is that the Bible is "a part of natural theology." Just as we infer a God from the solar system considered as a fact, so we infer God from the perfectness of the biblical description of Christ. The Bible, as a record of assertions, rests upon natural theology, and it proves the existence of God, not by the assertion that there is a God, *as an assertion,* but by the fact that it *makes* such an assertion, by this *act;* just as Webster proved he was alive, not by the *assertion* "I still live," but by the *act* of speaking.[3] The Bible as it is, with all its contents of natural theology, demands a cause, and that cause must be God.

How happens it that we may find in the writings of Peter a system of Natural Theology more in accordance with later times than in Aristotle or all the ancients? Philosophers grasped only by piecemeal that which fishermen have given in fullness and perfection. All the results of modern investigation can detect no fallacy in the statements of these fishermen who purport to have been divinely inspired.

The accord of the Bible with natural theology is also seen in the fact that the Bible is explained, in passages otherwise dark, by natural theology; and this, as a fact, demands an explanation, which it finds only in the existence of God.

This is the first stage of Professor Park's answer to the problem of getting a true order, which shall avoid the fallacy of circle, into the argument. He has incidentally

[3] As an illustration of Park's close dependence upon his predecessors it may be said that this striking argument is to be found in Hopkins (*Works,* Vol. I, p. 35): "The being of God is made evident by the Holy Scriptures; not merely by being there abundantly asserted *but by the existence of such a book as the Bible.* It is as much impossible there should be such a book, were there no God, as that there should be such a world as we see, without an invisible cause. For it is as much beyond the power and skill of man, or any number of men, to form such a book as it is to make the world. . . . The character of God there given is far above and beside the thought of man, and could no more be drawn by man, were there no such God, than the world can be made by him."

brought out the fact that the Bible, as a textbook of natural theology, precedes the modern treatises. He now takes up successively the "natural attributes" of God—his self-existence, omnipotence, omniscience, omnipresence, eternity, immutability, and unity—in treating all of which he introduces, on the same basis as above, the "biblical argument." He is thus brought finally to the benevolence of God. How does he prove this attribute, to the proof of which the Bible is essential?

It is characteristic of the method of Professor Park that he often makes an objection against one point of his argument the gateway through which he introduces the following point. Thus each argument, like the pinnacle of the flying buttress, solidifies and strengthens by its weight that which goes before, while itself dependent upon it. From the proof of the omnipotence of God arises the question: How can he then be benevolent, when he has not prevented sin? He could but would not, or else he did not because he could not. The last alternative being excluded by the argument for God's omnipotence, is not his benevolence impugned by his permission of sin? Before he advances to the positive argument for the divine benevolence, Park therefore discusses the prevention of sin, and as a preparatory argument to this, a *lemma,* if I may so say, he discusses the immortality of the soul.[4]

The argument for immortality is relatively weak and somewhat inconclusive. Park was accustomed to acknowledge this; but he added immediately: "We do not need much proof of such a proposition." He "took" it (lemma), in part, as a hypothesis, more or less reasonable, and helpful for his argument even in this hypothetical form. But

[4] He thus adopts the brilliant suggestion of N. W. Taylor (see p. 395 above). These two thinkers were, in fact, bent on the same thing—*proof*—and it may quite possibly be that we owe this great excellence of Park's to Taylor's example and influence.

he felt, no doubt, also that there was little real disposition or ground for denying it. He practically rolled the burden of cogent proof upon the shoulders of the deniers. Yet he presented such an argument as his inability to use at this point the testimony of Jesus, who "brought immortality to light," left to him. There is nothing decisive (in the phenomena of death, etc.) against the supposition that the soul is immortal. The fact that the soul exists up to the moment of death, and our belief that nothing that has once existed has ever been annihilated, point to the probability of immortality. Then, man is fitted for immortal existence by the scope and character of his powers which find only a partial employment here upon the earth. In fact, he has generally to die just as he is on the brink of some discovery or achievement greater than any he has been able to make; and, so far as we can see, he might go on developing greater powers of acquisition and labor forever. He is made for eternity, and he ought to have eternity in which to realize the idea implanted in his very being. This argument is confirmed by the character of God, who, whether benevolent or not (the point under argumentation), is certainly *skilful* and cannot be believed to have done so unskilful a thing as to make such a creature as man, for a brief space of an existence of seventy years! Man, if destined to extinction at death, is out of place, and constitutes the greatest riddle of the universe, and cannot be so explained as to leave the universe of which he is so important a part, rational. This preparatory, and chiefly negative, argument is reinforced by the biblical statements, which are given in all their fulness; but the Bible is still "a collection of wise sayings," and not a source of decisive authority.

The idea of immortality partially answers those objections to the goodness of God which have been already summarized. All that is incidental—the pain in the world, the frustration of powers in the range of their expected and appropriate accomplishment by death, and all the other disorder of the world—presents no serious obstacle if it is understood that there remains another life in which inequalities shall be removed and mysteries resolved. But there still remains a fundamental difficulty. Pain may be disciplinary, and may lose its appearance as an evil in view of the greater good to come. But *sin* is different. It is rebellion against God; it is *moral* disorder of the soul; it introduces disharmony and disease into the very highest and most central that there is in man, into his conscience and all his moral faculties. It is structural evil. How can it be explained or palliated? And how can God be truly good, and have his highest choices fixed on holiness, if he permits it? These questions lead to the deeper problem, that of the permission of sin.

It will at once be recalled that this topic had engaged the attention of our divines from the beginning. The answer which Bellamy and Hopkins had substantially given to the question why God permitted sin, was that it is the necessary means of the greatest good. Taylor had been unable to accept this position, and had substituted for it the supposition that God could not prevent sin in a moral system. He had done this in consequence of the new position to which he had come upon the freedom of the will. He taught a "power to the contrary" which constituted a real freedom, and which placed man beyond the control even of motives, so that in a system in which free will was a component part, though this or that sin might be prevented, all sin could not be because prevention would make impossible that which was constitutionally and permanently possible. And yet, as heretofore pointed out, he held the further position, which was quite irreconcilable with this, that all moral events were previously certain.

Park took up the discussion where Taylor had left it. He did not meet Taylor squarely upon the doctrine of the will, in which he held a position more Edwardean than Taylor's; for to both of these theologians their disagreement was obscured by their supposed agreement with Edwards. Nor did he by any means oppose Taylor at every point. He says, on the contrary, that "the New Haven controversy has brought out the fact that sin is not the necessary means of the greatest good." With the hypothetical form in which Taylor stated his theory Park was satisfied, and indeed regarded it as a distinct advantage for the construction of the apologetic argument, for both Taylor and he were laboring to remove objections to God's benevolence, and "a reasonable hypothesis is as complete a refutation of an objection as a positive fact." *If* God cannot prevent sin, then he is benevolent, *although* sin exists. But the New Haven answer did not commend itself to Park in another aspect. It was "unphilosophical," because inventing one hypothesis to explain something that could better be explained by another hypothesis; and "too specific," because fixing the difficulty in the freedom of the will, whereas it might lie elsewhere. Indeed, Park said explicitly that it *did* lie elsewhere, for to him freedom—Edwards' freedom—was perfectly consistent with the control of all action through motives. Accordingly, to the question, *"Can* God prevent sin in a moral system (i. e., a system of agents possessing free will and governed in accordance with that fact)?" Park with Hopkins replied directly, "Yes." The argument for the answer is, in a word, that it involves no breach of a man's freedom to prevent him by persuasives from doing what he is still perfectly able to do; and the argument is reinforced by the example of the angels in heaven. He thus rejected the original and favorite solution which Taylor had given to this vexed question; but even here he was

not abandoning Taylor, for he did this only to bring forward with great power the alternate suggestion which Taylor
makes in his *Moral Government,* that *perhaps* God cannot prevent sin in the *best* moral system, or—what is the
same—*wisely* and *consistently* prevent sin in the best moral
system. Both of them thus held the Leibnitzian optimism
which was now the common possession of the New England school. This hypothesis Park adopts as his answer
to the question as to the divine permission of sin. The
leading thought under this department of the discussion
is that the prevention of all sin might require a degree of
direct oversight of the members of the system, a degree of
tutelage, and a consequent degree of dependence, inconsistent with their moral strength; and greater strength with
some sin (finally overruled) may be better than unbroken
holiness and the consequent weakness.

The force of this position, whether in Taylor's hands or
Park's, depends on the view held in respect to the nature of
the moral universe. Park regards it as constituted by God
as a system, or, to use modern phrase, under general laws.
Among the facts of the system are free will, and its correlate, that a free will is to be governed *only by persuasives*
and never by forces. These "persuasives" constitute the
great mass of things, principles, and events in the world.
Not independent of God, they proceed under his divine government; but they have been wisely established and are not
to be interfered with, even by God himself, except for great
and wise reasons. It is better that man should grow into
righteousness and true freedom under such system, than
that he should have righteousness thrust upon him, and be
maintained in it, even by persuasives alone, if for the
sake of these extraordinary persuasives, the constituted system
should be destroyed.

Although Park has thus varied somewhat from Taylor

in the interest of a stricter adherence to the standard of the school, the Edwardean theory of the will, he affords here an instance of that larger doctrine of the will which he really held, as has been brought out in the chapter dealing with that doctrine. There can be no more "weakness" under a providential course which excludes all sin, upon the strict Edwardean theory, than under one which permits sin; for motives are no more controlling, and no more of direct divine origin, in the one case than in the other. When Park uses the language he here does, he is giving a large play to the free will of man, is emphasizing the value set by God upon it, and the sacredness with which he has invested it.

Park's final answer, therefore, to the objection against the benevolence of God, derived from the existence of sin is this, that our limitations and our ignorance are such that we must acknowledge the possibility that sin was permitted for wise and good reasons. Thus he comes to the question of the benevolence of God unhampered by this objection, and can answer directly from the facts that God is good. The conduct of the argument is so characteristic of Park that we may profitably devote more attention to it than to any hitherto.

After calling the attention to the fact that the previous course of argument has now removed objections to the divine benevolence arising from the existence of sin, of the various other moral evils (such as indolence), and of pain, Park argues (1) from God's *natural* attributes to his benevolence. "Thus far we have found God absolutely perfect; therefore we anticipate the same in all his attributes." This form of argument, an application of the principle of the continuity of the universe, was a favorite one with him. "If a rope sustains a certain weight and gives no signs of breaking, we unhesitatingly intrust more weight to it. If it has borne so much, it will bear more." He then proceeds: "The natural attributes present him the strongest motives to be, and take from him all motives to be otherwise than, benevolent and good." Men are inclined to envy and other sins because they have so vague ideas of the real meanness of these sins, and so obscure ideas of the opposite virtues. But the omniscience of God lifts him above all such obscurity. He has no motive to be malevolent. Again (2) the natural emotion, the taste for the noble and beautiful, argues for benevolence; for sin is most ignoble, and virtue, benevolence, is most sublime. A being having infinite conceptions of the grandeur of virtue could not fall into sin. (3) The phenomena of the universe constitute another argument. Its *physical* phenomena, for "we might have been in such a state that every ray of light would pierce the eye as a dagger and every taste be acrid. But happiness is the law, misery the exception." "The vast preponderance of contrivances are for our good." The *moral* phenomena furnish a parallel argument.

We might have been constituted so as to feel joy at the sight of pain; but now, when we commit a vile act we are ashamed, and pain in others calls forth our pity. We must take the future life into account to get the full force of this argument. The *tendencies* here are towards good: they will have become prevailing and exclusive of all others there. Now, the fact that God has made us with these moral feelings, inclining us to the right, indicates that he is good, for *no Creator would render it necessary for his creatures to despise him.* But if he is not morally good, his creatures *must* feel that they occupy a higher moral level than he.

Professor Park was accustomed, like other great thinkers, to make sudden plunges to the very depths of thought. Such a plunge occurs at this point of his argument. He enters here, according to his custom, certain "objections." Among them is this, that "after all, God, to make us more miserable, may have deceived us, and made himself *appear* to us benevolent, while he actually is malevolent." Park shows that this objection involves the fundamental skepticism of doubting the trustworthiness of our faculties. Lotze says in his *Metaphysik,* when a man comes forward with this "groundless perhaps"—perhaps everything may be other than it necessarily seems—"I simply turn my back upon him and go my way." Park's answer was that such a position implied substantial falsehood.

Then (4) the moral instincts of men, (5) the accordance of the divine benevolence with the nature of things (contrivances for pain may be for our good), and (6) the general opinions of men, are urged.

Finally (7) the biblical argument, the Bible's direct assertions, its structure, and particular doctrines, like the atonement, is presented. The argument is still from the Bible as a wise book, and may be thus expressed: The greatest scheme of thought which the world has ever produced, the biblical, teaches the benevolence of God; therefore it is true.[5]

Now, this, we submit, is a great and a valid argument. It has committed no circles, but has marched straight from the first premises to the final conclusion. It makes the benevolence of God credible and reasonable—vastly more reasonable than the conception of his indifference to human needs or his malevolence. It gives a ground of belief, and of further argument. Nor can it be said that it draws its materials improperly from the Scriptures. Ritschl says that the idea of *order* is a biblical idea. This is true; but it is also a pre-biblical idea, for Plato has the idea of order and of justice, though not of the divine goodness, in its full Christian sense. Park rests heavily upon order and reason in the argument. But the argument may be criticized as not being complete. It does not give the *full* Christian idea of the divine benevolence. We do not see

[5] Compare Lotze's: "Es ist ja unmöglich, dass das grösste von allem denkbaren nicht wäre."

"the glory of God in the face of Jesus Christ." It is a
"benevolent" God, but not a "Father," and not *"the*
Father of our Lord Jesus Christ." Park would undoubtedly
have admitted this objection at once. He would have said:
"But I am not done yet." He has not got the full idea of
God now, any more than at the beginning; nor can he get
it till the entire dogmatic process is performed. But he
has enough even now to base his next argument upon,
enough to prove that we have a God who, in condescension to man's need, will make revelation of himself and
provide a Bible. And then, having at last a Bible, he can
use the biblical argument as sufficient and final, and present the benevolence of God in its full sweep as that love
of God by which he "sent his only Son."

But the treatment of the divine benevolence, even at
this stage, is not yet done. Great ideas are never satisfactorily disposed of in Park's view till they have been fully
defined and exhibited in their various relations; and this
labor he proceeds now to perform.

It is Park's position not merely that God is good, but
that the divine goodness comprehends his entire moral nature. God has but one, comprehensive moral attribute,
and that is benevolence. He here follows Edwards, in his
posthumous treatise on virtue. We enter into moral relations with all sentient being, and that which constitutes the
basis of these relations is the capacity of feeling itself.
Happiness, the gratification of the feeling, is the object
sought ultimately in all moral action, and when a sentient
being is perceived to be in want, conscience at once and imperatively enjoins upon us the *duty* of satisfying that want,
so far as possible. The active choice to do this is benevolence, and it is the primary and fundamental moral action.
Happiness is, of course, not to be taken in so restricted a
sense that it shall embrace nothing but physical gratifica-

tion. The highest happiness of the highest beings is derived from the approbation of conscience, and thus requires their holiness. The "sentient" being who is also a moral being, finds his happiness chiefly in this highest element of his nature. But, high or low, that which calls out moral choice in respect to him is his capacity of feeling, his value, his worth; and the benevolent choice of his worth, the choice to promote it—holiness first, but happiness finally—is virtue, and this alone is virtue.

These are, according to Edwards, the fundamental principles of human ethics; and both Edwards and Park apply them immediately to God. We know God by knowing ourselves. His "great, generic moral attribute" is love, and every other moral attribute is only a new application of this attribute according to the differing circumstances in which God is placed. He views men (and other beings) primarily as simply capable of happiness; and he then chooses their happiness. Viewed as having moral character, men are regarded by God with "complacential benevolence"—that is, either approved as holy or disapproved as sinful. God "loves all men" with *primary* benevolence, but "hates the wicked" with complacential benevolence—for benevolence can hate, *must* hate the wicked. But there is a "consequential benevolence," or justice, which Park defines as "the cherishing of the love to the right character of sentient beings followed by the cherishing of the desire to reward the character—or the reverse, a hatred of the wrong character and desire to punish it." This justice is of two sorts, "distributive" and "public." The former is "a choice to make such an expression of approval or disapproval to an obedient or disobedient agent as shall be to that agent a merited recompense to his act." The latter is "a choice of expressing complacency or displacency to an obedient or disobedient agent on the ground of, and in pro-

portion to, the usefulness of the expression." The latter
definition was not the one always given by Park, and the
idea may, perhaps, be better expressed for the present time
if public justice be defined as "such treatment of an agent in
view of his obedience or disobedience as shall most promote
his and all others' holiness and happiness." Consequential
benevolence is also "grace," which is "the choice of a ruler
to bestow favor upon a subject when the distributive justice
of the ruler prompts him to inflict evil on that subject," or
it is "a choice to favor the guilty."

As to justice, two things are to be noted as we pass on.
Park teaches distributive justice, but he does not teach that
there is an eternally fixed relation between offenses and
punishments, founded in exact and undeviating fitness, to
be inflexibly executed. He declares many times that "distributive justice may be forever unsatisfied"—in fact teaches
that it *is* unsatisfied and *must* be in regard to all those who
are forgiven. They are still guilty (in the sense of having
done the wickedness) and still deserve all the punishment
they ever did. Park's "justice" is always determined by the
relations of the act. The penalty justly due to any act is
determined by all the relations in which the act stands. If
"distributive justice" be defined so that these general relations be ignored, Park denies such justice. There is always
to him a view of the great universe of fact in determining
what a given choice shall be, and so the most distributive
of his distributive justice has an element of "public" justice
in it, or of regard to the public interests, the general whole
of things.

Then, again, the "public justice" is not to be distinguished from benevolence. It is "*consequential* benevolence," but the epithet might be suppressed. It is simply
"general love," a choice as to individual beings determined

by the interests of all beings, a choice of "the good of being in general," as Edwards would have phrased it.

Park's view of the love of God thus emerges from the profundities of careful definition and dogmatic discussion, and becomes visible and capable of estimation. God's love is his sole moral attribute. Every other attribute, apparently diverse though it may be, is resolved ultimately into love, since it is a form of love's manifestation, and has no virtue apart from the love that it expresses and conveys. *The love of God is thus the determining principle of Park's theology.* We have seen, under the subject of the Will, that it meets certain restrictions in its application. Nevertheless the statement made remains true.

But Love, according to Park is no mere ill-regulated emotion. It does not desire simply the sensuous gratification of God's creatures. It does not lead to making each individual "happy" considering each by himself alone. It regards principally that lofty happiness which consists in holiness. Hence it necessitates "hate"—indeed, includes it in itself. If God loves holiness, he must in the same act hate sin. Love of holiness and hate of sin are the same thing, the two sides of one choice, as the piece of paper has two inseparable sides. This is of the utmost importance in following out Park's theology. It is not like a low landscape, basking in a tropic sun, every hill crowded with monotonous vegetation. It is rather like the Sierras, rising here and there into sublime heights, crowned with the eternal purity of everlasting snows. Will Park, who teaches that God is love, interpret that love in a way to lead to Universalism? Not while he holds fast to the eternal "displacence" of God toward sin!

A brief quotation will illustrate the inclusiveness of Park's conception of love:

The comprehensive truth may be stated thus: Our benevolent

Father does not administer his moral government under the influence of a limited attribute alone; not under the influence of mercy or grace or distributive justice without any regard to the general welfare; not under the influence of a choice of the general welfare without any regard to the demands of retributive justice or the pleadings of mercy or grace; but he administers his moral government under the influence of a general attribute looking at sin and at pardon in all their relations, and providing for the greatest and highest welfare of the universe. Under the influence of this general attribute our benevolent Father resists the plea of mercy and of grace when the safety of the universe requires him to resist it; he yields to the demand of distributive justice when the general good requires him to comply with it; his distributive justice holds the scales and his general justice holds the sword; the former urges its claims and the latter complies with them on the ground of their rectitude and on the condition of their necessity for the general welfare. The punishment which our Father inflicts is useful, but its usefulness rests on the ground of its being deserved; the justice of it comes first, the usefulness comes afterwards; the punishment cannot be useful unless it be just, and it must be useful if it is just, unless an atonement intervene. The fact that punishment is deserved rests on the ground that sin is intrinsically evil; the intrinsic evil of sin consists in the fact that it is a preference for the inferior above the superior good,—it is a love of self or the world rather than of Him who comprehends in his own being the welfare, not of the world only, but of the universe also; it is opposition to general benevolence, to general justice, to Him of whom our text affirms, "God is love." [6]

In the development of the system the point has now been reached where the Bible must receive a more careful consideration. It has been found to exist in the world, and to demand, as a fact of natural theology, constant attention. But Christianity is peculiarly the religion of the Bible. The doctrine of God and of his goodness does not constitute the whole of Christianity, nor even its peculiar and distinctive portion. There are other doctrines which are not attested by nature; as, for example, the doctrine of atonement. If they are true, they must derive their proof from the Bible, for they must depend on a revelation, such as the Bible professes to be. Hence before we come to

[6] *Memorial Collection of Sermons*, pp. 319 f.

them, we must discuss the authority of the Bible. Men need these doctrines; we must look to God for the revelation of his will in respect to them; and we come to look for such a revelation with the antecedent probability that so great a God, infinite in his power and moved by love, will in some suitable way make revelation of himself. The proof of the Bible thus rests upon the proof of the benevolence of God. But we need further to examine the facts in order to ascertain whether God has carried out his benevolent purpose for men by giving them the particular book of revelation which we call the Bible.

The argument contains nothing particularly striking. The Westminster argument from the "witness of the Spirit" is not even mentioned—abandoned, apparently under the rationalizing influence of the Unitarian controversy. Park proceeds, according to the method of that day, from the genuineness of the books to their authenticity, and thence to their claims and their inspiration. He arrives at the same rejection of verbal inspiration and emphasis of the infallibility of the Bible as is to be found in all the preceding members of the school.

But a new era, the era of modern science had already arrived, although previous to the issue of the *Origin of Species,* in 1859, it had not exercised the modifying influence upon theology which it was destined to do thereafter. The question of miracles, as supposed violations of the constituent laws of the universe, was becoming a little more serious, though nothing had yet appeared more thoroughgoing than Hume's discussion in the eighteenth century. In 1866 Graf's epoch-making efforts in the higher criticism of the Old Testament appeared, and it was soon evident to Park that "the question of our day is not what the Bible means, but whether we have any Bible; and even whether we have any God." But the forces wrapped up in both

higher criticism and evolution, of which the one is merely
a form of the other, did not fully reveal themselves till just
about the time when Park's public labors ceased (1881).
He was therefore not prepared to say anything that he regarded as conclusive upon the great topics which he saw
rising into new prominence. The time for the work of the
dogmatician had not yet come. But the apologist already
had a task, and this was to prepare for the coming discussions. He did this by the simple process of scrutinizing the
traditional dogmatic positions very keenly for their content of exact truth. He redefined the inspiration which the
Bible possesses, and stripped the doctrine of much of the
exaggeration and detail with which Protestant scholasticism, in a false ambition for a perfect system, had incumbered it. Distinguishing between "revelation," as God's
action in unfolding his truth to men, and "inspiration" as
the method under which the Bible, as a collection of writings, has come into existence, he makes a number of valuable, and sometimes radical, modifications in the teachings
of our historical Calvinism. His inspiration is mostly a
divine "superintendency" so exercised over the writers that
the Bible is perfectly according to the divine will, and thus
perfect for the purpose for which it is intended. A mere
abstract and unrelated perfection is never claimed for it by
Park. Inspiration, also, pertains to the writers of the
Bible and not to their writings.

Before defining inspiration Park lays down certain preliminary cautions. We are *not* to say that the Bible is, or
is not, correct in mere matters of science. Again, we are
not to affirm or deny that the Bible is correct in mere history. Affirmation or denial here is aside from the dogmatic problem, because science and history are both aside
from the purpose of the Bible, which is, in a word, to *save
men*. Hence the definition of inspiration which he next

proceeds to give is: "The inspiration of the Bible denotes
such a divine influence upon the minds of the writers as
caused them to teach in the best possible manner, *whatever they intended to teach,* and especially to *communicate
religious truth without any error* either in religious doctrine or religious impression." What did they intend to
teach? The phenomena in any case must show. Where
is our emphasis to be laid, and as to what may we be sure
that they are right? Religious truth! With one stroke
of definition Park has thus rendered unnecessary volumes
of current discussion and irrelevant pages of denunciation
of critics and scholars. He has done what Ritschl had in
mind as his own chief service to theology; but, as we shall
see, he did not later follow Ritschl into his many denials
of elements of positive truth.

Incidentally to this larger discussion the subject of the
biblical miracles received a careful review. The treatment
given them does not meet the modern objection to them derived from an evolutionary revival and reinstatement of
Strauss's mythical theory of their origin. That theory was
supposed by Park to have been forever discredited. But the
main philosophical considerations which connect the possibility of miracles with the personality of God, so that one
cannot deny them without impairing that, are fully brought
out; and, accordingly, discussion will always have to come
back to the principles laid down by Park. He begins, as
always, with careful definition. Four definitions are re-
hearsed. A miracle is (1) "that work which is produced
immediately by such an interposition of God's bare volition
as constitutes a phenomenon which without that interposition could not have taken place." Or (2) "a miracle is a
work wrought by the interposition of God producing what
otherwise the laws of created nature must have prevented,
or preventing what the laws of created nature must other-

wise have produced." Or (3) it is "a work wrought by the immediate volition of God interposing and violating the laws of created nature in their established method of operation." Under this definition he discusses Hume, who, he says, committed a sophism in his definition, for "he defined a miracle as a 'violation of the laws of nature.' He objects to the existence of God, being a skeptic, and hence in a miracle has an event without a cause. But when we admit the being of God, a miracle is no violation of the laws of nature, for *it is a law of nature that matter obey its Creator.*" And (4) he defines: "A miracle is an event which occurs without a cause in created nature, without regularity in the times and places of its occurrence, and in manifest opposition to all those natural laws which have been observed in other events."

Thus *possible,* miracles need a sufficient *occasion* for their occurrence, which Park finds in the necessity of making a revelation to man. Miracles attest the divine commission of the bearers of this revelation, and were necessary to convince men of their commission. He recognizes also the fact that at this point of time miracles themselves need proof, and so proceeds to ask whether they were actually wrought in attestation of the Bible. By a characteristic turn of the argument, he first establishes their antecedent probability, and then, remarking that they *need very little evidence* to prove their reality, cites their unequivocal character and the repute, concurrence, and devotion of the witnesses, as sufficient proof of their actuality.

From this point on, the argument of Park's system rests upon the sure foundation of the Scriptures. He begins this portion of his discipline, which he was accustomed to call "revealed" theology, with the doctrine of the Trinity.

Park's treatment of this theme is determined by his historical situation. New England was not yet out of the period of the Unitarian controversy when he began his professional work, and the antithesis to Unitarianism remained throughout his entire career more distinctive of the theological condition of things than any other element. Hence Park devoted an unusual amount of space to the doctrine of the Trinity. But this did not lead him to go into such discussions as fill Augustine's treatise, or make up what Dr. Hodge would call the "protestant doctrine." The great portion of this unusual space was devoted to the central part of the Unitarian denial—to the divinity of Christ. As to the rest, Park followed historically, and for substance of teaching, Moses Stuart, who, it will be remembered, had abandoned the word "person" as descriptive of the three elements of the Trinity, substituting for it the less definite word "distinction." With this had gone the "eternal generation" of the Son, and the "procession" of the Spirit. And, in general, Stuart had confined himself to the simple results of Nice and Chalcedon—one God in three ontological and eternal distinctions, one Christ in two natures, human and divine. Park also refused to advance beyond this point, affirming our ignorance of many things. "On this doctrine," he says, "we must be careful not to know too much." "The profit of the doctrine of the Trinity is derived in some degree from the fact of its mysteriousness."

The path of approach to the subject was determined by the inductive method of investigation, which Park had adopted, and of which many an example has already been given in the discussions of the order of his arguments. He begins the Trinity with the doctrine which historically led to it, the nature of Christ; and this he begins at the point nearest to the investigator, the humanity.

As to this, comparatively little is said. The ordinary and simple New Testament evidence of a genuine human body and soul are presented, and the conclusion of true humanity drawn without great elaboration. No special controversy existed in New England over this point. Simple facts, like Christ's ignorance of the condition of the fig tree and the time of the destruction of Jerusalem, are noted without further comment. They serve to help prove that Christ was truly man.

When the argument passes to the divinity of Christ, however, the combatant has evidently come forth in his full armor. The sole question is: "What is the *fact?*" and that fact is the biblical fact. Consequently the whole argument consists in a biblico-theological discussion of the New Testament; but it is conducted in the most elaborate manner, with the marshaling of innumerable texts, and under eleven general heads. Christ is God because (1) he is *called* so; (2) is said to be equal with God in *condition;* (3) does the *works,* and (4) has the *attributes* of the Supreme Being; (5) receives divine *honors;* (6) has applied to him in the New Testament the *same* passages elsewhere applied to the supreme God; (7) left the *impression* on his contemporaries that he was God; (8) the Scriptures make this *impression* on the masses of men; (9) Christ's divinity commends itself to the *moral nature* of man; (10) the *concurrence* of these proofs is itself a distinct proof; (11) *no other supposition* will reconcile the Scriptures and consciousness.

As one re-reads the argument today, he is struck with its scrupulous accuracy in the use and interpretation of the texts. Under the first head, I Tim. 3:16 is not cited, because "the external [MS] evidence is against the reading 'God,' although the internal is for it." Nor is Acts 20:28 adduced, because "God" is also disputed here. In treating Rom. 9:5 the argument is contextual, and the sense is relied on to show that the Christ is called "God blessed forever." The most impressive argument is drawn from

Christ's work—of creation, preservation, raising the dead, the judgment of the earth—which cannot run off into mere verbal discussion.

I have already said that Park did not advance in any respect beyond the Chalcedon positions as to the person of Christ—two natures, human and divine, each perfect and entire, in the unity of one person. He consented to follow his Calvinistic predecessors in the Nestorianizing distribution of ignorance to the humanity and omniscience to the divinity of respect to the same thing and at the same time. How ˙was any "unity of person" possible under such a view? Park does not seem to have really raised this question. He illustrates what he himself says of Julius Müller, whom he always styled (while he lived) "the greatest of living theologians," that "his greatness is nowhere better seen than in this monstrous blunder." The remark was made of Müller's efforts, by means of a doctrine of "kenosis," to solve the Chalcedon paradox. Park was therefore not ignorant of this most strenuous effort of German evangelical theology to solve the difficulties of the theme; but he rejected it. It is not plain that he fully understood it, for he says, in explanation of the remark, that the theory is "absurd." "A being who is weak cannot by his weakness turn himself into omnipotence." No kenotic ever thought he could. But one must make such a criticism of the acute and indefatigable Park with caution. If *he* did not understand the kenotics, it is perfectly certain that *they* did not understand one another. Like evolution, kenotism was long in "coming to itself;" if, indeed, it has yet done so.

The chief difficulty of the doctrine of the Trinity was met when the divinity of Christ was proved, for those who have accepted this element have never found special difficulty with the personality of the Holy Spirit. But Park gives an independent and thorough investigation to this remaining portion of the theme, that, when independently proved, it may lend corroboration, by its reflex influence, to the doctrine of the divinity of Christ. We need not follow him through this proof, which is exclusively biblical. At its close comes the summary of the whole doctrine in the form of definitions of the Trinity. The first and best of these is this: "The Father is God: the Son is God: the Holy Spirit is God. Neither is God without the others. Each has a property incommunicable to the others. There is only one God." There is no attempt at a rationale of the doctrine. Various objections are answered and misunderstandings cleared away; but the doctrine is confessedly a mystery resting on revelation, and only partially revealed. Although Park had studied Hegel under the guidance of no less a man than Kahnis, there is no trace of acceptance of Hegel's "construction," or of interest in it.

The treatment of the Trinity then closes with a couple of sections on the sonship of Christ and the procession of the Spirit. The term "Son" is applied in the New Testament to the historical Jesus Christ, and designates him as miraculously conceived and especially dear to the Father. Modern biblical theology has so generally followed this position that we need say nothing further on it here. But as this was the first distinctive point (formally) of the "new school," and was always introduced by Park as such, it is interesting to note his remarks made here on the characteristics of the school. "The New School," he says, "avoid those technical terms which will suggest a false idea, unless the terms are explained away (e. g., 'eternal generation'). They refuse to convert figurative, poetical phrases into metaphysical dogmas (e. g., the phrase 'This day have I begotten thee,' Ps. 2:7, into an assertion of 'eternal generation'). They refuse to substitute metaphysical theories for plain biblical teaching." In the first of these sentences speaks the dogmatician; in the second, the preacher of the sermon on "The Theology of the Intellect and That of the Feeling;" and in the last, the practical New England pastor.

Thus it appeared that New England theology as represented by Park no less than by Stuart was to fail to answer adequately the searching questions put it by the Unitarian leaders. The Trinity remained a doctrine reduced to its lowest terms—depotentiated—and having but one element of practical application to life, the true divinity of Christ. This element was in turn embarrassed with difficulties, for the Chalcedon specifications of supposed fact needed adjustment. What meaning had unity of person when the elements of the personality were things as diverse as divinity and humanity? All the old methods of bringing them into harmonious adjustment had proved failures. Was there still a method? Or was it to be confessed that the problem had been wrongly conceived, and that the two natures, or else the unity of person, must be surrendered? These questions are now thrust upon the modern public with terrific earnestness, and the old formulations of doctrine seem crumbling on every side. They were no less imperatively thrust upon the theology we are now reviewing. If to leave them unanswered then was not a confession of incompetence to meet the issues of the day, it was a certain and decisive disqualification for the more strenuous conflicts into which the American churches were soon to come.

The progress of our study is thus gradually, but only gradually, bringing us to a view of the distinctive theology of Professor Park. Most of his teaching was identical with that of all evangelical theologians. But one great distinctive position has been as yet noticed, and that only partially— his position on the nature of virtue as applied to the character of God. I do not include the so-called "first peculiarity of the New School," on "eternal generation," because, after all, that is not characteristic or determinative of his thought, however peculiar to the new school it may have been. We are to find our next distinctive position in his treatment of the will. It might conduce to clearness if we had placed that topic at this point. We actually encounter next, in the course of Professor Park's own development of his system, the subject of decrees; and faithfulness to him, as well as the necessity of letting him speak in his own way if we wish to gain the fullest knowledge of his innermost thought, compels us to attack decrees before the will. It was the *inductive* character of his system that prompted this order. The theory of the will is chiefly valuable as a means of explaining and defending decrees. The fact must come before the theory of the fact, and hence decrees before the will.

Whatever else Park was, he was a Calvinist. He used sometimes to say that Calvinism was the only "respectable" theology. This was a specimen of his playful sarcasm; but "many a truth is spoken in jest," and his sarcasm often covered his most profound convictions. He was also a High Calvinist. He was of the strain of Hopkins, in the New England theology. Other theologians might weakly leave something to the ungoverned freedom of man, as even Augustine seemed to leave the fall of Adam, but Hopkins, and Park after him, included the fall as fully in the decree of God as the sending of the Son or the election of an individual to salvation. And hence the subject of decrees was begun by Park with a definition: "The decrees of God are his plan so to constitute and circumstance the universe as to secure the *previous certainty of* ALL *events which actually occur.*"

Park derives his doctrine fundamentally from the sovereignty, or supreme causality, of God. His whole theology follows the Calvinistic tendency to exalt God. It is wise, best, desirable, and really accepted by all men (when in their right minds) that God should govern all things. Methodists and Calvinists really agree. If the latter say that God *intends* to do a thing, the former say he does it *intentionally!* And it is a fundamental idea that decrees are no greater, and no other thing in religion than in ordinary affairs. God "foreordains *whatsoever* comes to pass actually."

The development of the subject is therefore primarily apologetic. The word "decree" is a bad word. "Plan" would be much better. It pertains primarily to what *God himself* will do, and only secondarily to what his *creatures* are to do, as the *certain,* but *not* necessary, consequence of his action. The connection here is made under the Edwardean theory of the will, which Park maintained. God acts, and he knows exactly how men will act, and thus, by decreeing his own action, he plans, decrees, secures, but does not force or compel the action of man. No sooner does Park thus make a definition than he laments its terms; "predestination," "election," "reprobation" are all "unfortunate."

For the sake of illustrating both his doctrine and some of the elements of his method, I subjoin here, as I have hitherto refrained from doing, Park's treatment of one point of the subject of decrees. What follows are merely *heads:* the illuminating and enforcing discussion of the heads, their "development" in no ordinary sense of that word, we must dispense with. It was always extempore, and is gone into the great abyss of time, except as preserved in the memories of hearers. But something of the real Park will here be seen by all readers, and more will be recalled to some who were once hearers.

2. The doctrine of Reprobation is not inconsistent with benevolence.

a) It is for the best that God should not prevent sin, and he does not. It is best that he should leave some men to themselves, and he does leave some to themselves. The greater part he elects, the few he permits to perish. We have a right to make the supposition that the proportion of those lost to those saved, in this and other worlds, is as one grain of sand to the myriad grains of the seashore.

b) It is not unjust for God to leave the reprobate to themselves for they deserve nothing.

c) He does leave men to themselves; therefore it is right for him to *decree* to leave them to themselves.

d) God does place and constitute some men so that they will sin. Then it is right for him to do so.

e) All the arguments which prove that it is benevolent for God to permit sin, prove also that it is benevolent and just to decree to permit sin.

f) All the arguments which prove that it is best for God on the whole to permit sin, prove that it is for the best that he *decree* to permit sin.

Remark: All these objections to the doctrine of decrees lose their force when we consider that *men are free, notwithstanding the decrees.*[7]

We are now brought, in the regular progress of the system, to the subject of the will. For purpose of a more connected view of the New England speculations upon this important subject, a separate chapter has been assigned to this theme, and Park's work has been included there with the rest. Suffice it here to say that, while nominally holding to Edwards' determinism, Park had emphasized certain elements of Edwards and of consciousness, so as to modify greatly the substance of the Edwardean theory. In fact, a new thought, new for Calvinism, was struggling in Park's mind, as yet not quite able to come to the birth. It was the idea of freedom. Not of a "gracious freedom," such as Arminians had taught, but a new natural, consti-

[7] Here, as indicated by the notes, Professor Park introduced Lyman Beecher's famous comparison: Election is as if a man should go to a prison on fire, open all the doors, and loose every chain, and then call to the prisoners to come out! They will not. Then he rushes in, seizes as many as he can, and drags them out. These are the "elect." Those whom he is obliged to leave, all of whom have been set free, and invited to come out, and every one of whom *could*, but *does not, come,* are the "reprobates."

tutional, and inalienable attribute of man. On the side of
the theory of decrees and the will, it did not find consistent
expression; but in the doctrine of sin it did. It begat a new
bearing toward these doctrines, and toward all the remaining doctrines of theology; for it introduced into them,
for the first time with completeness and power, the ethical
conception. The mind of man is an ethical agent, possessed of freedom and influenced by motives. And all the
great processes of redemption—the atonement as well as
regeneration, conversion, and sanctification—are to be explained by this conception of his nature. We shall see how
thoroughly controlled Park is by this idea as we proceed;
and it needs no elaborate exhibition to show every theologian how great a modification in past theories, this fact
must produce. It was nothing less than an ethical revolution in the theological system which New England theology
in Park's hands now effected.

The next topic in the system is sin. As a follower of
Taylor and of Emmons—or, it might better be said, as
a follower of Edwards, whose the phrase is—Park had
already laid down the position that "all moral agency consists in choosing." Nothing which goes before the choice
is part of man's moral agency, and nothing that comes after
it. Hence, when he came to define sin, he put it tersely as
"the voluntary transgression of known law." He proves
his proposition from the testimony of conscience and the
common opinions of men, and from a long review of the
biblical use of the various words for sin.

This view would at once meet with opposition from
those who maintain that men are sinners by nature previously to any act on their own part. Many of their objections are met by a more delicate analysis than they had been
wont to apply. That "profound" objection that "men generally feel that sin lies deeper than action," is admitted;

but it is shown in reply that the chosen definition of sin does not mean that it is only the outward transgression. It is *chiefly* the ethical process, the act of *choosing.* When sin is said by Park briefly to be an act, he always means an act of the will, a volition. The objection, again, that "sin consists in something permanent, but actions are not permanent," is answered by showing that the sinner is "permanently choosing." Going still deeper, the reply uncovers the nature of character by showing that, even if moral action be interrupted, it always is sinful when resumed, for the sinner "sins whenever he can;" and even the citadel of his opponents is invaded by the further reply, that, "if a man's *nature* is such that he will sin whenever he can, then he may be called a sinner, even though he do not sometimes act it out."

Another definition of sin as "a preference of the less and lower above the greater and higher good," and of virtue as "a preference of the greater and higher above the less and lower good," and still another, "a preference of the world, or of self and the world, above God," bring Park to the question whether sin may be defined as consisting in selfishness, which he answers in the negative.

Such are Park's definitions of sin. As he defines virtue as consisting in love—love to God supremely and to our neighbor as ourself, or, more abstractly, love to being according to its worth—so he sometimes defines sin as any choice not consisting in such love or intended to carry it into execution. And it is in this sense particularly that the force of his doctrine of "depravity" appears. He makes this *universal* (all men sin) and *total* (none of the moral acts of the individual sinner are virtuous prior to regeneration). In a word, only the regenerate exercise Christian love. Stated thus, the principle seems axiomatic.

All this is simply the common result of the New England school. So far as it is speculative, it tarries wholly in the region of the appeal to consciousness and the common-sense of mankind. But church theology raises further questions, for so universal and so deep a fact as sin must have an adequate reason. Its cause, properly speaking, is the will of the sinner himself acting efficiently in producing it. But wills are led to choices by motives. Hence the question rises as to the motives leading to universal and total depravity or its *occasion*. Park specifies two occasions—the proximate and the remote. Of the former he says: "Total depravity may be referred to a disordered state of man's constitution, existing previously to man's voluntary moral acts and occasioning their uniform sinfulness." He further defines this "disordered state" as consisting in a disproportion in his sensibilities and moral powers. Since universal sin is a fact of man's active life, the cause must be found in his nature, and this cause is his disorder. He is not fitted, in the actual world into which he comes, to lead a perfectly holy life. This disorder of nature being antecedent to every moral act, and operative from the beginning, it is necessary to conclude that man begins to sin as early as he begins any moral action. Thus he never passes through a period of holiness before beginning to sin. But Park carefully avoids various unwarranted extremes into which theologians had sometimes fallen; such as, that infants begin to sin as soon as they are born.

We are thus brought to the doctrine commonly called "original sin." So far as it taught the corruption of human nature, Park thoroughly accepted it. But when corruption was denominated, in the language of Westminster, as "truly and properly sin," he recurred to his definition of sin as consisting in wrong choice, and denied the name sin to that which has come upon man without his own voluntary action. The central point and chief interest of original sin lay, however, in its connection with Adam. Park is thus brought, as well as by the course of his own argument, to the connection of Adam's sin (the fall) and our general depravity. He answered the question as to the *proximate* occasion of total depravity by saying it was the corruption of man's nature; he now asks the occasion of that corruption, or the *remote* occasion of depravity, and answers it by the fall of man in Eden.

The fall is thus defined: "That sin of Adam by which it was rendered certain that all the moral agents descended from him should be totally depraved, and necessary that all the members of the race (Christ only excepted) should suffer appropriate evil." The proof of such a connection between Adam's sin and ours is purely biblical, and does not differ from that employed by all other Calvinistic theologians.

What, now, is the link that connects Adam's sin and the disorder of nature in all his discendants? Edwards had made it all a "divine constitution," as he was most naturally led to do by his idealistic philosophy, which makes all connection of things a connection of ideas, and teaches that all ideas arise in us immediately by the operation of deity. It is remarkable that Park adopted the same view, so far as he adopted any. He does not seem to have relished the speculations into which some of his predecessors had gone. He follows neither the divine efficiency of Emmons, nor the theory of the prior preponderance of the sensual proposed by Taylor and adopted by Finney. As at many other points, he maintained great reticence. The relation was established by God. Why? We do not know. How? Here he is equally silent. A suggestion at one point that heredity *may* have had something to do with it, is the only hint pertinent to this question. Of one thing, however, Park is certain—that it was *not* by identification with Adam in his sin ("sinning *in* Adam"), nor by imputation of Adam's sin to us. We are better off today under the larger view of heredity given us by evolutionary studies. We now know how necessary it is, in accordance with the very principles which have brought the physical and even the mental nature of man to its present condition, that, when sin has once occurred, every descendant of the sinner should be profoundly affected by it; and how increasing sinning should enlarge the affected area of the soul; how individual sins should become first habitual, then automatic, and then hereditary; so that there should be finally racial tendencies to evil rendering, by the balance of the nature thereby created ("corruption"), actual sins by all the individuals of the race certain.

The treatment of these topics lacks a certain vigor because Park could never persuade himself to take sides clearly with either of the·parties to the old dispute between the "exercise" and the "taste" schemes. What was handed down by Adam to all his descendants? A nature. Was it sin? No! Was it sinful, so as to need a renewing by some divine change of its balance? Park was inclined to say "Yes." His treatment was not merely agnostic, where agnosticism becomes us; it was hesitating and not altogether consistent.

The defects of his positions in these portions of the system are nowhere better brought out than in his treatment of the salvation of infants dying in infancy. He should have said, in consistency with his fundamental principle that sin consists in the "*voluntary* transgression of *known* law," that infants dying before the age of moral consciousness and responsibility *have not sinned* and *do not need saving* in the sense in which we speak of saving sinners. Hence their salvation is as certain as that of *angels* who have never sinned. But he only ventures to say that infants *may* sin

from the first moment of their birth, and *probably* do sin
at an early period. They need regeneration because of their
participation in universal human corruption; and they are
saved by the atonement.

The whole impression of reason and of the Bible is that infants
begin to sin very early. We have an instinctive *hope* that infants are
saved. *We cannot perhaps prove it.* The true remark would be: I
have an instinctive hope that they will be saved. Yet I cannot prove
it, and am willing to leave them in the hands of God.

Yes! so must we all be! But, "shall not the Judge of all
the earth do right?" And can souls that have not sinned
be lost? Certainly Professor Park might have said more at
this point! His result falls far below the truth.

We are now brought to the subject of the atonement, in
reference to which Professor Park rendered, perhaps, his
largest service to theology. We have traced in a previous
chapter the progress of those modifications in the doctrine
of the atonement in New England which had brought its
theology in general to the acceptance of several positions:
that the atonement was meant for all men, consisted in the
sacrifice of the God-man by himself upon Calvary; that his
sufferings, while not satisfying distributive justice or paying the debt of the sinner, did render it consistent with
the interests of the divine government for God to forgive
repentant sinners; that the divine motive and regulating
principle in all this was love; and that both the imputation
of our sins to Christ and of Christ's righteousness to us
were artificial elements, which should be excluded from the
doctrine. The various writers on the subject did not, however, *explicitly* go back to the beginning of the theme and
take their start from a new principle, although they had
such a principle in the theory of virtue which Edwards had
left them, but were led by the particular circumstances of
the controversy to redefine the old terms and preserve, in
general, the tone and method of the older theology. At

many a point the influence of the new theory appeared, as when general justice was explicitly defined by some of them as benevolence. But they still employed chiefly the analogies of earthly governments in the formulation and defense of their positions. And their new theory received the name of "the governmental theory."

By the time that Park appeared upon the scene the theory of virtue was much better understood. Its application to the character of God, and the development of the system of Christian duties in accordance with it, had given it a new scope and importance. Professor Park had a larger comprehension of its meaning and of the range of its application than any of his predecessors had had. It might have been a question of great interest, when he first began the presentation of his views upon the atonement, what he would do; whether he would reject all idea of atonement in deference to the supposed requirements of the love of God which should need no propitiation; whether he would develop it afresh from the theory of virtue as a starting-point, exhibiting its ideal side and setting it free from a certain bondage to mechanical relations in which it had hitherto been confined; or whether he would let it stand substantially where his predecessors had left it. His historical sense, and his intense admiration of his predecessors and loyalty to them, finally cast the scale in the last direction. He continued to use the governmental analogies, which were rapidly becoming offensive to his times; and this fact, more than anything else perhaps, prevented him from coming to an understanding with the greatest thinker upon the atonement among his contemporaries, Horace Bushnell, or from doing much to prepare for the new epoch that was coming. There is something sad, if not tragic, about this, for Park studied every new writer upon this theme diligently, and has left incorporated in his lectures what he considered best and truest among their contributions to the theory.

As always, Park began with definition. The atonement is "that sacrifice of the God-man which is substituted for the punishment of men, and which therefore forms the sole ground on which God is justified and satisfied, and the chief motive by which he is influenced and by which he exerts an influence, in directly blessing men."

The definition is highly technical. By "directly blessing men" is meant converting and saving them. The "sole ground" is the last cause on which God directly depends for blessing men. The term "propitiation" is later defined in exactly the same words as atonement, except that the words "and by which he exerts an influence" are omitted. He hastens in this connection to guard against the idea that God antecedently to atonement was "too angry to favor sinners."

God is made propitious by the sacrifice of Christ in the sense that it is made consistent and justifiable for him now to bestow blessings which it was not antecedently consistent for him to do. Therefore it is figuratively that God is propitiated. He is propitiated in the sense that the atonement is a new motive for him to bestow blessings upon men. Also in the sense that he changes his outward conduct just as if he had changed his moral purpose.

The definitions also introduce a number of weighty modifications of old conceptions of the atonement. Park employed the word "satisfied" in his principal definition. But satisfaction was not the rendering of the strict equivalent in distributive justice. On the contrary, he defines "satisfaction" as "that sacrifice of Christ by which it is made consistent with God's blessedness that he waive the exercise of distributive justice." What he meant by distributive justice has been fully explained on a former page. He was thus gradually stripping off the artificial distinctions which had formerly incumbered the theory. He completed this process by his rejection of the application of the idea of imputation to the atonement. Christ's righteousness could no more be imputed to us than Adam's sin. In both cases the law holds that character is not transferable, since it is always produced by the individual choice. Something is done for us by the obedience of Christ, so that we receive the benefits of his death. But neither that obedience nor any other is imputed to us, for it is forever his obedience and not ours.

One other element which needs to be noted before we proceed to the more systematic development of Park's argument is the largeness of outlook given by his conception of the atonement as having relations to the entire universe. In this he was following his predecessors. The suffering of Calvary was not an event done upon a small planet in one corner of the stellar universe, without relation to other worlds and beyond the knowledge of other intelligent beings. Neither did it provide for the salvation of men alone nor, much less, for the salvation of some limited portion of the human race who might happen to hear of it. But it was the display, once for all, of the divine character, and it formed the ground of all forgiveness which should anywhere take place throughout all space and time. When God has once made himself fully known, then it is forever and everywhere consistent with his "justice" that he should be the "justifier of him that believeth."

The next step in the development of the atonement is its analysis, which was conducted under three heads: (1) the facts which are involved in it; (2) the facts which constitute it what it is; (3) the essential relations of it.

1. We have seen how Park guarded against the idea that God was an angry and implacable God without the atonement. He now again emphasizes the truth by placing at the very head of facts involved in the atonement the fact

(*a*) that the atonement has its origin in the grace of the Father. "God sent his Son," "God so loved the world," "I come to do thy will, O God," are the texts he cites. Christ is not more amiable than the Father, and it is infelicitous and injurious to give any such impression.

(*b*) The second of these involved facts is the divinity of Christ. In making the atonement he needs perfectly to represent the will of God; which is possible to God only. And then, all those expressions which represent the sacrifice of God in making the atonement require the Godhead of him who was thus sacrificed. The reverse of this idea was also in Park's thought; for if the one great work of atonement which required the divinity of Christ were denied, there would remain no necessity for any such divinity. Like Henry B. Smith, he adopted the thought expressed by the phrase "incarnation unto redemption." Remove the redemption, and you have removed the occasion for the incarnation. In this view of the essential connection of ideas, both these men showed their greatness. It is not a chance phenomenon of earlier times that the denial of an objective atonement has led to the denial of the divinity of Christ: the two doctrines are so connected by the internal necessities of thought that they stand in any system or fall together.

(*c*) The third involved fact is the humanity of Christ. He must be a man fully and genuinely to represent man. We see here the influence of Macleod Campbell upon Park's course of thought. His views were carefully and not unsympathetically reviewed in the *Bibliotheca Sacra* by Professor Park himself; but, long before, his great idea, that the atonement was the confession of humanity, had been fully incorporated in the theory. But while Campbell had rejected other elements in favor of his own newer light, Park, with his characteristic breadth, did not reject one truth because he had found another. The atonement makes forgiveness "consistent," and a profound confession of humanity's sin by the God-man adds another element to that consistency, but does not take away every other.

2. Passing now to the facts *constituting* the atonement, Park mentions (*a*) the sacrifice of the God-man. Sacrifice is so often conceived mechanically that Park's understanding of its meaning will have a permanent interest. Says he:

A sacrifice is a confession of the guilt of the person for whom it is offered. It is an expressive gesture, a symbol. It is thus an acknowledgment of the rectitude of the being to whom it is offered. It is an acknowledgment that the sin may be deservedly punished by the being to whom it is offered. It is an acknowledgment that the sin must be followed by some pain of the person by whom the sacrifice is offered. Thus the sacrifice of the lamb without blemish by the ancient Hebrews was not merely the loss of so much property, but was a crossing of the affections. It is also a prayer for the person in whose behalf the sacrifice is offered. It a public avowal of the offerer's intent to honor the being to whom the sacrifice is offered. And, finally, it is an avowal that the sufferings of one being are substituted for the punishment of another. The sufferings of the lamb are substituted for the punishment of the Jew: the sufferings of the Lamb of God are substituted for the punishment of the world.

(*b*) The second fact constituting the atonement was the death of Christ. Park conceived this in a large way. It was not the mere physical sufferings of the moment of death which constituted the atonement, but all Christ's sufferings, both physical and mental, culminating in Calvary. Park emphasized also the "public and judicial character of his sufferings;" and here he introduced—to the confusion of the argument, as it will seem to most—the attempt to connect the human government, cruel as it was upon the side of the Jews, weak and subservient upon the side of the Romans, with the divine government, so that the act of the one should be the act of the other. "He suffered at the hands of the rulers who are in this respect symbolical of the power of God." This element, it is true, plays no essential part in Park's theory, but it was introduced, apparently under the influence of the word "government" itself. It would much better have been omitted.

(c) "The atonement consisted in the sacrifice of the God-man substituted for the punishment of sinners." The proof of the substitution is derived from the use of the word ἀντί in Matt. 20:28 and parallel, from the word ὑπέρ which, while not so distinct, "in its connections denotes substitution," and from the other great cardinal passages of the New Testament, especially those which dwell upon the voluntary character of Christ's death. It is noticeable that Isa., chap 53, is not employed in this argument.

3. Park now passes to another grand division of the theme—to the essential relations of the atonement. These are relations to the created universe, to the sinner, and to God. He embraces them under the general word "appeal." The atonement is an appeal to the universe for God the Father. It expresses his love to his Son, to the universe, to the race of men; and it expresses his justice. It is an appeal for the God-man, who is an object of regard to angels, principalities, and powers. It is an appeal for the perfected race, since "the perfect representative man acknowledges by his sacrifice that God is right and man is wrong."

"Appeal" has therefore the meaning in this connection of a solemn setting-forth of the elements of the case and the demand for a proper attitude in reference to it. Park accordingly goes on to say that this appeal to the created universe exhibits and honors the justice and holiness of God as much as these attributes could have been exhibited and honored by the punishment of sinners; it exposes also the vileness of sin as much as this would or could have been exposed by the unconditional punishment of sinners. We begin, therefore, already to see what Park has not yet stated, that the atonement is intended to accomplish in one way exactly what the punishment of the sinner would accomplish in another way.

But the atonement has relation to the sinner. It is an appeal to the sinner to repent and be saved. God appeals: "Behold, how I love thee;" the God-man appeals: "I have come to suffer for thee;" and the perfected race appeals, because that race will universally desire the conversion of every sinner. And then there is the relation of the atonement to God. It takes away the motive for punishing the sinner, since the end of punishment has been perfectly gained; and it presents a positive motive for forgiveness. Park is aware that this last statement will meet with objection. God saves men to promote his own glory; but his greatest glory is the glory of his grace, and the atonement is the fundamental act of his grace. And then, the atonement is God in Christ; and to glorify the God-man expressing the desire of salvation is to glorify God himself.

With these many definitions and qualifications, suggesting repeatedly very broad conceptions of the atonement, Professor Park has now come to the "principle upon which the atonement operates." By this he means, of course, the theory of the atonement. We shall give the statement of this principle in his own words, but it is our purpose, in the further explanation of the theory to depart now from the exact reproduction of the form in which he expresses his thought and to strip it of the governmental analogies by which it was enveloped and possibly obscured. It is possible that thereby the suspicion may be aroused that a departure is being made from Park's real theology. But in fact an explicit reference might be given for every statement that is to be made. If there is any difference from Park's own statements, it is one merely of form, and scarcely of that.

1. First, then, for the formal statement of the principle. It is this:

> The atonement exhibits and honors the holiness, distributive justice, and law of God, and it promotes the holiness and happiness of the universe, so as to make the conduct of God in forgiving men consistent with the honor of his holiness, distributive justice, and law, and so as to satisfy his general justice in rescuing sinners from unconditional punishment, in adopting measures for inducing them to repent, and in eternally rewarding them if they do repent.

2. Second, for a running account of this theory:

The theory of the atonement begins in the theory of man. Park has given to men the attribute of freedom, and, whether successfully or not, has labored to establish the principle that all influence over their action, whether on the part of their fellow-men or of God, must be exerted by means of motives. We may speak of the divine "government;" or we may call God "Father," and seek to find the principles upon which he exercises his fatherly office in seeking and saving men; but, however we put it, men are controlled or led through motives.

As to these motives, Park has the further idea which exercises, as we have seen, a large influence at various points of his theology—the idea of "system," law, general methods; the same idea, in fact, which appears in the scientific emphasis of "natural law." God is not restricted to these methods so that he cannot follow anything else, but he proceeds upon great general principles from which he does not depart (as, for example, to perform a miracle) except for grave reasons.

God has, therefore, established a system of moral influences designed to lead men to salvation. One element of this system is the law, involving threat of punishment, and summarily comprehended in the verse: "The soul that sinneth, it shall die." This whole system, including the law, originates in the love of God. He is seeking the holiness of man, and he surrounds him with all appropriate influences which will tend to promote his holiness, exhibiting the attractiveness of holiness and the repulsiveness and danger of sin. All this is alike the outworking of the same love.

But if love originates such a system, then, while love prevails in the councils of God, the system must be maintained. This is true of the law. It was fully understood, its meaning carefully weighed, the possible results which might flow from its promulgation clearly foreseen, before it was ever proclaimed. When man has sinned, if he is to be saved, the penalty of the law must be waived, for to execute it would be to destroy the race; but, if it is waived, it must be so waived that the system of moral influences designed for man's good shall remain unimpaired. If man is not punished, then all that punishment would effect in the way of moral influence upon man must still be effected. His forgiveness must be made *consistent* with the maintenance of the moral system, with the undiminished total of moral influences tending to promote holiness and deter from vice, or else he cannot be forgiven: love forbids it.

It will be noted that this view of the case exalts the positive character of the law. God might have written his moral law in the nature of men as he has natural law upon the phenomena of nature, and left man to find it out in the same way. But that would have meant the destruction of men. He therefore adopted the method of revelation, of the communication of his law through chosen agents to men. He has declared his law and announced the penalty; and now he comes, and, with equally distinct objective declaration, he sets forth his Son as the sacrifice for sin, saying explicity that his sufferings are substituted for the punish-

ment of all who will accept of his salvation by believing on
him. Park did not suppose this declaration a matter of
necessity in the nature of things. If his Son had come and
quietly endured the sufferings which actually came to him
without any explanation, the mere fact that God so hated
sin, and had so involved all beings in its consequences that
not even his own Son could come into the world, sinless
though he was, without suffering, would declare his righteousness and the seriousness of the threat of the law, and
thus maintain its honor. But this is not God's method, because we are under a system of grace. God has declared
what Christ does by his death. He takes the place of sinners before the law.

What, when thus viewed, does the suffering of Christ
effect? Precisely that, all that, and even more than, the
punishment of guilty but repentant men could effect.

To understand this reply, we need to ask what, in Park's
thought, the punishment of men was designed to effect. It
must be designed to effect something good, for else it could
not be inflicted. Punishment, like every other act of God,
must be performed under the influence of love, or else his
act in this case is not holy. To ask what punishment effects
is therefore to ask what good it effects. Does it do any good
to the sinner? Park's answer is, "No." He thus rejects
the idea of the reformatory design of punishment. When
man is finally adjudged guilty before the bar of God, the
time for benefiting him through painful discipline is past.
Such discipline is properly called chastisement, not punishment. Punishment, when it is inflicted, is to the sinner
nothing but an unmitigated evil. Still it must do some
good somewhere; and this must be among the innumerable
intelligent spirits, men and angels, who may hear of this
punishment. With them it will effect two principal things:
it will vindicate the character of God as having no pleasure

in sin, but as eternally opposed to it; and it will powerfully deter them from sin, since it exhibits sin's true nature in the awful consequences which ultimately follow upon its commission.

All this, and more, the sufferings of Christ upon Calvary effect. They (a) vindicate the holy character of God. Did he really express his holy attitude and the profound truth of things when he promulgated the terrible threat of the law? Does he unspeakably hate sin? When he forgives it, is there no trace of carelessness in him, no complicity of heart with it, no relaxation of his moral earnestness, no giving of the lie to the solemn implications of the threat of death to the sinner? All these questions might be raised, if God forgave sin without an atonement.

What would it be to have such questions raised? Take the repentant sinner himself, what would it be to him? It would destroy his repentance; for why should he repent of that about which God cared so little? It would destroy his God; for he would find himself upon a higher level in repenting than that occupied by God in forgiving and thus reversing the law without a given reason, since he would exhibit a greater sense of the meaning of sin. What would it be to angels but to teach them that they might indulge in the pleasures of sin, if they seemed attractive, without much hesitation, since God thought far less of it than his law seemed to indicate, and the danger of transgression was small?

But the atonement forever shuts off such questions. God waives the punishment of the repentant sinner, but he does it for a great reason. His own dearly beloved Son comes and takes upon himself the suffering of the cross. This is the suffering of God. Man was to suffer to express the infinite ill-desert of sin, but now God suffers to bear testimony to the same thing. If man suffered, the suspicion might possibly arise in some mind that the suffering was inflicted in a mechanical manner or a routine spirit, and did not mean so much after all. But when God suffers, no such suspicion can arise. God is intensely opposed to sin, his law expresses the ultimate relations of things and his own most unchangeable attitude toward all sin, if, in order to waive the punishment of the law and relieve man from eternal suffering, God himself must first suffer. Such is the unavoidable impression of the beholder, be he angel or man.

But (b) the sufferings of Christ deter all intelligent beholders from the commission of sin as effectually as, and even more effectually than, the punishment of guilty men could. One might suspect that God had grown indifferent to men, and punished them without deep feeling; but no one can suspect this when he "sends his only-begotten Son." The threat of the law remains in all its terror. If God makes exception to its execution in the case of those who repent, what will he do to those who rush forward consciously into sin, are thus from the beginning unrepentant, and have no sort of warrant in themselves that they ever will repent? And to those souls to whom the thought of the vileness of sin is a greater deterrent than the thought of the danger involved, how much clearer is its essential odiousness in the sight of God, and of all holy beings like the Son, when God will not pass it over without so great a reason as the sacrifice of his Son, and that Son voluntarily takes the cross that sin may be condemned in the act of its forgiveness!

Thus, when Christ has suffered, the object of punishment in the case of the repentant man has been secured, and it is now consistent with God's honor and the honor of his law, and with the interests of all holy beings everywhere, that he should be forgiven. And, since he is now, by repentance and faith, brought into harmony with God, the love of God positively prompts him to receive into his fellowship one who is now fit for it. Thus love in all its aspects is fulfilled by the forgiveness of the sinner.

This is the form of the theory resulting from the introduction of positive law into the universe. Dropping this fact now from view, the atonement may be considered, in conformity to that ultimate principle already enunciated, as the means by which, when sin has once entered the world, man may be saved and still the "system of moral influences" originally inaugurated be preserved. Those moral influences are exerted substantially through the combined faculties of the intellect and the conscience. In the voice of conscience and in the teachings of history as interpreted by the faculty of the reason lie the great natural influences which are designed to restrain men from sin and lead them to holiness. If man repents of his sin, however blindly he may grope for the truth, and however little he may know of himself or of God, he is received by the forgiving act of God into the divine fellowship. It might be that, in a limited sense and for a time, a man ignorant of the atonement might find holy influences impaired by the very freeness of the divine approach to his soul. But the ultimate revelation of the atoning death which Heaven will make, the fact of the cost of sin, and hence the cost of forgiveness, to God, as shown in the sufferings of the Son of God, would so reinforce the voice of conscience and the lessons of history that the soul would ultimately rest in the eternal meaning and validity of its earliest impressions of righteousness. And thus God's intent in surrounding it and filling it with such moral influences in favor of righteousness would be both justified and maintained.

Into the remaining portions of Park's treatment of the atonement it is not necessary for us to enter. Enough to say that he thoroughly discussed, along lines which will be easily surmised by the trained reader, the old theories which the New England speculations were intended to replace. He then passed to the "fact" of the atonement, which he elaborately proved from the Scriptures. He derived its "relative necessity" from the principles we have already passed in review. And he taught that it was "general"— that is, made the salvation of all men possible. It is easy to see that if the atonement makes it "consistent" for God to forgive one sinner, it makes it equally consistent for him to forgive all. In these discussions Park displays all his characteristic acuteness and profundity.

For a time the theory of the New England theologians which Park presented received a very large acceptance among Congregationalists. It became the working theory of the great majority of practical ministers. But the original minds which were pressing on to new views of truth and felt most fully the influences of the new forms of thought which from time to time appeared, did not accept it. They did not even become acquainted with it. This was undoubtedly the effect of Park's error in following too loyally the modes of presentation of his great predecessors, as has already been suggested. It is quite possible that more attention may be paid to him in the near future, and that the main results of his studies may, under the interpretation of some appreciative student who possesses the necessary familiarity and sympathy with later speculations, supply the necessary corrective to too exclusively subjective theories. Almost all those who have recently gained the ear of the theological public have, more or less clearly, explicitly acknowledged the necessity of just that element which Park placed at the center of his theory, that men "must be made to feel, in the very article of forgiveness, when it is offered, the essential and eternal sanctity of

God's law." These are the words, not of Park, but of Bushnell, who was prevented from giving his adhesion to the
New England theory by confounding it with the older Calvinism, as I have elsewhere shown.[8] William N. Clarke,
who has removed most of the objective elements from Christian theology in favor of the subjective, lays great stress
upon the manifestation of God's righteousness in connection
with forgiveness. He says that Christ does not satisfy law
or punitive justice, but he has in mind here the elder ideas
of satisfaction which Park also rejects. He speaks of the
"gladly endured pain of saving love," and adds that it "is
a substitute for punishment which God is offering."
Again: "Whatever exhibits God's righteousness, or rightness of character and conduct respecting sin, has the character of a propitiation." He thus approaches very near to
Park.

One would suppose that in entering upon the topic of
regeneration, where so much of Dr. N. W. Taylor's strength
had been spent, Park would take the same position toward
his labors as he had done in the discussion of the prevention
of sin. But this was not so. On the one hand, he followed Taylor in the most important part of his labors: he
rejected, as Taylor did, Burton's change in the taste, leading by necessity to a change in the sensibilities; he rejected also Emmons' immediate creation of holy exercises;
he adopted the doctrine that the means of regeneration is
the truth; and he insisted that, whatever preparation for
regeneration there might be and however long this might
last, regeneration, as the last final presentation of truth by
the Holy Spirit and the consequent yielding of the soul to
it in conversion, was all one indivisible and instantaneous
event. But, on the other hand, he manifested no interest
in Taylor's eagerness to establish the existence in the soul

[8] See above, pp. 416 ff.

of a neutral point to which the truth could appeal; he did
not discuss the whole philosophy of the "selfish principle"
and its "suspension," nor adopt any of the phraseology by
which Taylor hoped permanently to advance the theme. In
fact, while he emphasized for the practical work of the pulpit the freedom of man, and thus followed Taylor, in his
theory he reacted fully to the Edwardean doctrine of the
will. He did not feel the need of Taylor's neutral point
because, whether there was a neutral point or not, motives
could be presented to the will in such a way that holiness
would appear the greatest good and would be chosen.
Thus, while preserving the most important of Taylor's results in his system, he was prevented from unreservedly
placing himself in the position which he really occupied
with reference to this great teacher by his remaining
amount of adhesion, real and imagined, to Edwards.

His definition was careful. Regeneration is "the change
from a state of entire sinfulness to a state of some degree
of holiness." As such, it was "the first change," differing
from all other, subsequent changes, such as the repentance
by which a Christian who has fallen into sin comes back
to his duty, both in its origin and in the fact that it is of a
fundamental character. It is also viewed by Park as the
whole of the complex change from sin to holiness, and not
merely, as some say, the divine side of the change. Regeneration thus embraces two elements, divine and human; but
they are not so separated by Park as to assign them two
separate terms, regeneration and conversion. Such a distinction had its advantages, but upon the whole Park preferred merely to say that "conversion was the most
important part of comprehensive regeneration."

Analyzing it more particularly, regeneration involves a
change of the primary, predominant choice. It may be
questioned whether there is any such fixed and conscious

choice before regeneration, but after it there is such a choice, which is recognized by the Christian as determinative of his whole life. It has "stopped the old habit of uninterrupted sin" and has "introduced the new habit of holiness." "It is not merely a holy choice, but the first one of a series; and not merely that, but an influential choice which stands so related to the former and subsequent states of the moral agent that it breaks up the continuity of the sinful habit and introduces a new habit." It also involves a change in the sensibilities and a change in the intellect, such that, in the order of nature, the change in these precedes that in the will; but in the order of time there is no priority of either over the other, for, as a whole, regeneration is instantaneous.

These preliminary and explanatory considerations are no sooner completed than the fact becomes clear that the treatment of the subject is to be determined by the philosophy of revivals which had grown up in the revival atmosphere of New England in the early half of the last century. Professor Park had himself been a revival preacher, and drew to the last some of his most illuminating illustrations from his experience with his parishioners in Braintree in revival times. The two perpetual tendencies of his system join here again in conflict: the Calvinistic tendency, to exalt God, which is brought out in his doctrine that God is "the sole author" of regeneration; and the practical interest of the pastor to clear away obstacles and stimulate activity on the part of sinners and so eventually to elicit the act of conversion. These chapters contain, therefore, a philosophy of revivals.

Thus, in the very "analysis," with the main points of which we were just now busy, he guards against the idea that the advocated "change in the intellectual view" of the man should necessarily involve new knowledge; for then

the unrepentant man would not be responsible for not having yielded to knowledge which he did not have. It may
be merely a new vividness of the old ideas. The emphasis
placed by the very term "regeneration" upon the agency
of the Holy Spirit is not to lead to inactivity, for man is not
responsible in any way for what God does; but he is responsible for repenting. This he can do, this he ought to
do, and this he is to be exhorted to do immediately. This
is the fulness of man's liberty.

The means of regeneration is the truth. By this Park
does not mean the Bible, but any truth; it may be simply
the truth of conscience. "God may regenerate little children by the truth which their own consciences give to them.
God may regenerate heathen by the truth which their consciences and the volume of nature give them." We are
thus incidentally brought to the fact that he followed the
tendency of our theologians to emphasize the freedom of
the working of the Spirit of God among all men, and the
consequent possibility of the salvation of the heathen. He
reduced the condition of salvation to its ultimate ethical element, the act of the will in view of truth. If a man knew of
Christ, he must believe in Christ, but the essential element
of this faith was the "affectionate *reliance*" on the atonement of Christ. This reliance was choice, and this choice,
when reduced to its elements, was Edwardean love. "There
is no holiness in religious faith or Christian faith unless
there be *love to being in general.*" Let any man anywhere
submit to the truth, more or less ample, which he understands; let him exercise a disinterested love toward such
being, and such a God as he knows about, or thinks he
knows about; and that man is *right,* because his will is
right, and will receive the forgiving grace of God. This
position, which was later designated as the holding of salvation by the *essential* Christ, rather than by the *historical*

Christ, was not the result of the rationalizing tendency of our theology, but was believed to be an interpretation of Scripture; for example, of such passages as Rom. 2 : 14, 15; 4 : 4.

And now, with his usual breadth, Park refuses to limit regeneration to any one fixed scheme. Some revivalists were always attempting, as some do still, to produce a single type of experience, their favorite type, which they understood most fully and could guide most easily to the best final result. Thus, while the "antecedents of regeneration" were defined as "increased thoughtfulness, fear and alarm, conviction of sin, endeavor to secure the favor of God, despair of securing this by works," he said most explicitly that "we must not insist upon these antecedents in the *order* specified above, nor in any uniform *degree*, nor must we insist upon them at all as the ultimate or chief *aim* of the sinner, nor regard them as *conditions* which ensure regeneration." Experience varies as the individuals which undergo it vary. There is one, and one only, condition of salvation, and that is repentance and faith. We are to insist upon this one thing only, and to admire the ways of God in what he otherwise gives and does.

And now there enters again, and for the last time in this review, that strange hesitation upon Park's part between freedom and determinism which characterizes his treatment of the will, to modify his treatment of regeneration. He is about to prove that God is the author of regeneration. By author, in this connection, he means the one who plans for a certain end, chooses it, adopts the means to bring it about, and actually employs these. God is the only one that thus has regeneration in mind, and thus effects it, and hence he is its only author. Park might have advanced here upon the straight road that lies before the determinist. He would then have said: God acts upon the sensibilities and the intellect directly and indirectly, and also sets in action trains of motives operating upon the will, and thus determines the whole man to the new act of repentance. God would thus have been made the author of conversion. But of this, because it is the act of the will, God could not be the author without becoming also the author of every other act of the will, and thus of sin. Hence man must be made the sole author of conversion, and God's authorship of regeneration must be proved by a method which shall leave out this element. But there is enough place, in the composite thing which regeneration had been defined to be, in the change of the intellect and the sensibility, for the action of God; and here it can be said to be a special, supernatural (in distinction from miraculous) exercise of his almighty power. Thus Park was landed in the strange position that God was the *sole* author of the whole comprehensive change called regeneration, while man was the equally *sole* author of the act of conversion, which is the central and vital thing about it all. He could have made a better distinction, and one which would have better conveyed, I am persuaded, his real thought, if he had asked the question: Who is the author of conversion? and had answered this question by saying that both God and man are its authors—God in the sphere of *influence*, as the source of that series of influences which in their combined working lead ultimately to repentance, so that without them the man never does repent; man in the sphere of *power*, because the final action which constitutes conversion, the choice, is entirely his, as the work of his free sovereignty.

Into the further definitions and distinctions of this subject we do not need here to enter, for it will be readily understood that Park would teach that the soul is both active and passive in regeneration, and that regeneration, while theoretically resistible, is practically unresisted. We pass, therefore, at once to the subject of sanctification.

This, according to Park, is the gradual development of holiness in the Christian under the guidance and by the agency of the Holy Spirit. The question is immediately suggested: What is holiness? And to the answer of this he turns first. One would think that it had already been abundantly answered in the discussions upon virtue which have been earlier reviewed. But Park now goes into the matter afresh, partly because he is considering it upon its human side, and partly because, since this is the place for the entrance of "ethics" into the system, it is the place to come to an understanding with divergent theories of morals, such as the utilitarian.

Virtue is therefore defined afresh, and this time as follows: "the preference of the greater and higher sentient being, on the ground of its value, above the less and lower sentient being." The definition does not differ in meaning from those already given, and we need spend no time now in elucidating that meaning.

The discussion of Utilitarianism is introduced under the head of an objection to Park's own theory, that it is in essence the utilitarian theory. The utilitarian theory, he says,

pronounces happiness and the means to happiness, the chief good and only good. This theory, on the contrary, makes happiness the lower good and holiness the higher. The utilitarian theory teaches that we have no idea of right apart from the tendency of an act to happiness. This theory asserts that right is a distinct idea. The utilitarian theory teaches that a thing is right because of its tendency, and hence that the love of the general happiness would be wrong if it did not promote the general happiness. This theory is that a thing has its tendency to happiness because it is right, and that right would be right whatever its tendency might be. In fact, there is a universally acknowledged distinction between the right and the useful.

Neither is a thing right because it is agreeable to the will of God. Benevolence, for example, is agreeable to the will

of God, but it would be right and possess the attribute of
imperative obligation if it were not agreeable to the will of
God. Nor is right right because it is agreeable to the fitness
of things. In opposition to all such theories Park taught
that

right is a simple term, which can only be defined by reference to
the occasions when the idea arises in the mind. Rightness, virtuous-
ness, is that quality of an act which conscience approves, obligates
us to practice, and feels complacence in; and which has a desert of
reward. In other words, right is the correlate of conscience which
perceives the right immediately and affirms our obligation to perform it.

And, again: "benevolence is right in itself, eternally and
immutably. It is right because it is right." Park sometimes called himself, in distinction from Utilitarians, a
Rightarian.

Sanctification is the production of this holiness more and
more in the heart and life of the Christian. The agent of
sanctification is the Holy Spirit. The means is the truth. It
differs in no essential respect in its nature from regeneration, except that that is the introduction of the holy life, and
is a fundamental reversal of what has gone before, while
this is the consistent development of what is already begun,
and the strengthening and deepening of holy habits, or distinct holy choices, in accordance with, and in consequence of,
that first "primary, predominant" choice. We need, therefore, spend no more time upon this topic. Of course, the
great historical controversies into which American theology
had fallen over these themes were sketched and illuminated;
Oberlin had its share of attention, with sharp criticism of
certain points, but in the most kindly spirit; but Park came
out in nothing peculiar or calling for especial attention
today.

Of justification it is also unnecessary to add more than
that he made it synonymous with forgiveness, stripping it

of the forensic elements of the older Calvinism; and that he grounded it wholly in the atonement of Christ.

We close our review of Park's system with an account of his eschatology. He brought the New England answer to the Universalists, which had occupied the school from the very beginning, to its conclusion, and thus completed the New England attempt to render a service at this important point to the general cause of Christian theology as well as to preserve its own borders from the intrusion of what was regarded as a dangerous error. For this reason alone it is important to know what Park had to say. But in a peculiar degree is it necessary that any history of New England theology should close with a statement of the positions upon eschatology at which it arrived, because it was at this point that the "new theology" which has succeeded it among the Congregational churches first manifested itself. In the theological seminaries, it was at Andover itself, and among former colleagues and pupils of Park's, that a proposition was made looking to a modification of the severity of the New England conception as to the condition of the heathen, which proved the entering wedge of a new eschatology and a new theology of atonement and incarnation. The new will not be understood except this New England background is clearly understood.

We may limit our discussion to the question of future punishment, for this was to Park, and is still in the thinking of the day, the crucial point of the whole theme. It has been already pointed out that Park did not suppose that the great majority of the race would be lost, but he did believe that those who were finally impenitent when overtaken by death would remain in sin and would be punished by God forever. It is his support of this doctrine to which our attention is now called.

The evils which come upon men in consequence of sin

and which possess the character of moral discipline are divided by Park into two classes, chastisement and punishment. Chastisements are all those pains inflicted upon a sentient being to prevent or correct sin, or to secure or increase the holiness of himself or other beings. All the evils coming upon us in consequence of sin in this life are of the nature of chastisement. They come under the head of grace, and are reformatory, corrective, and directly beneficial in their character. Punishment is, however, something radically different. "Real punishment is pain inflicted by the Lawgiver upon the transgressor for the purpose of satisfying the Lawgiver's distributive justice. The pain must be inflicted by the Lawgiver, upon the law-breaker, because it is deserved, and in order to satisfy distributive justice." The meaning of distributive justice as earlier brought out must be held constantly in mind. It is determined by benevolence; for, as Park adds immediately to the definitions just given, "the design of distributive justice is to promote the welfare of the universe."

With these distinctions as to discipline, Park now proceeds to a more careful explanation of the design of punishment. "What is the design of God in satisfying his distributive justice? Why can he not let it go unsatisfied, as men often do?" This question he answers:

1. Punishment is designed to vindicate the character of the law. The threats of the law are necessary to the very idea of law. The infliction of the penalty is necessary to the reality of the threats, and hence to the maintenance of the character of the law.

2. Hence punishment is designed to honor the character of the Lawgiver. It expresses his benevolence, because he thereby inflicts those evils which are necessary to the promotion of good. It honors his distributive justice, his holiness, and his veracity.

3. Hence the design of punishment is to prevent sin in the subjects of the law, and to promote their holiness.

Up to this point many of the advocates of final restoration would be willing to keep company with Park. He has put punishment directly upon the basis of the divine benevolence. But he next lays down the principle that "the punishment of the wicked will be eternal." In preparation for the proof of this principle, he lays down a number of preliminary propositions which contain substantially his apologetic for the doctrine. Thus he says:

God's government respects other worlds than this. The Universalist says that it is impossible to believe that God will make a race and punish the majority of that race. But he might punish all for the benefit of another race, or for many races, and still be benevolent. Positive benefits flow to others from condign punishment. One generation receives benefits from the summary visitation of the law upon a previous generation. Still we suppose that the majority of this race will be saved. Hell in the universe will occupy no greater place in comparison than the state's prison in the commonwealth. Again, man is free. He knows that if he sins he shall be punished, and he is free to sin or to refrain. It is the overlooking of this fact that gives so much difficulty with the subject of punishment.[9]

But Park went even farther than this in his apologetic. Universalism proceeds upon the supposition that wicked men will finally repent. Park meets this position by the proposition that "men may be punished even if they are penitent." He may have believed, upon the whole, that every penitent being would somehow be saved. He is reported to have once said that if the Devil would repent, God would find some way to save him. I myself never heard this remark, and have heard him say that "no atonement had been provided for the devils in hell"—which at least hints strongly at the impossibility of their salvation even if they should repent. All such questions, however, he regarded as belonging in the region of groundless and unprofitable speculations, for he believed firmly that men dying impenitent and the devils would continue obstinately in sin, and that eternally. Still he would invalidate the last

[9] It is worthy of remark that one of the latest forms of Universalism, that of Dr. G. A. Gordon, of Boston, involves a philosophy of determinism. God is finally to have his way; and man's freedom is enswathed in a divine determinism.

refuge of his opposers, and hence he maintained, whatever might be our speculations, that even repentance did not carry with it the certainty of forgiveness, for "even Christ, though he was holy, was not perfectly happy, but was the greatest of all sufferers." He even said: "The holier a man is, the greater his remorse for his past sins. How the redeemed spirits can be happy in spite of their past sins is the mystery of the atonement of Christ."

The last turn of thought suggested the further remark that

the distinctive punishment of hell is remorse and the other painful emotions of conscience. Punishment is rational, that is, it is produced according to the nature of the mind. If there be physical punishment, it is only to excite the action of conscience. If a man sin, he shall forever reflect upon his sin, and shall let conscience work according to its own laws. This is the doctrine of eternal punishment.

Park is now prepared to begin his proof of the doctrine. He sets the rational arguments in the front.

1. Sin deserves eternal punishment. Sin deserves remorse of conscience. This is an axiom. Now, remorse is perpetual. Guilt is personal and eternal. It is contrary to the first principles of the mind that punishment should diminish guilt. Once guilty, always guilty. This eternal remorse is eternal punishment. "The whole idea of hell is this: You have been free, you have chosen to pursue a certain course, you must reflect on it forever." Thus Park adopted what Emmons called his own special contribution to the subject of future punishment.

2. The nature of conscience proves eternal punishment. There is a presumption that the mind will always act in accordance with its present laws. It is a law of conscience to inflict pain for sin. Left to itself, conscience will always reprove men of sin. If this is not to be so, God must interfere to prevent the normal action of this power which he has given men. He is under no obligation to do this, there is no evidence that he will, and the very nobility of the faculty of conscience shows how irrational it is to suppose that he will interfere. Men will be left to themselves.

3. The fitness of eternal punishment to the nature and tendencies of sin. The tendencies of a single sin are to unending evil. Every sin adds to the facility of committing another, and the sin of one

man tempts another to sin. It is fit that the pain which thwarts these tendencies should be unending also.

4. Men may be punished as long as they sin, and they will sin forever. The mere possibility of eternal sin renders it impossible to prove universal salvation; for if men sin forever, they will be punished forever. But there is more than a probability here. There is evidence that the impenitent at death will sin forever. Their persistence in sin to the end of this life leads us to infer that they will sin forever, unless we have evidence to the contrary, and there is no such evidence. They have remained depraved in spite of good influences, and we infer that they will remain so forever. More, they grow worse and worse under good influences. Affliction and chastisement serve only to harden them, if they remain impenitent. And, then, the Bible represents the impenitent as continuing in sin, as long as it speaks of them at all, for they are sinners through life, at death, in the intermediate state, at the judgment. Now, after the judgment certain great advantages will be lost to them; "from him that hath not shall be taken away that which he hath." And there will be positive disadvantages: the power of habit, intensified and accumulated, the exasperating effects of unsuccessful punishment, etc. All these things will operate to perpetuate sin, just as similar things will operate to secure the eternal holiness of the repentant. In one passage eternal sin seems to be asserted of a certain class: "Whosoever shall blaspheme against the Holy Spirit . . . . is guilty of an eternal sin" (Mark 3:19).

5. The holiness and sincerity of God. God is infinitely holy. He must be sincere in expressing this feeling, and the sincere expression of God's abhorrence of sin is eternal punishment.

6. The benevolence of God. We have already touched upon this argument, and remarked that Park could not maintain eternal punishment upon his theory of the divine action, unless he could show how benevolence required it. This he now more fully undertakes. Avoiding the unfortunate expressions of Hopkins, he still follows the essential lines of his argument. His successive points are:

a) The eternal and deserved punishment of sin does good. It results in an increase of holiness in the universe, because men are deterred from sin by the fact of punishment. It thus promotes the general good.

b) As sin tends to work unending injury, benevolence requires that it have an unending connection with pain which will counteract the tendency of sin. This would not be so if men did not deserve to suffer, but they do deserve to suffer all that is useful in counteracting the evils which their sin has wrought.

c) Benevolence requires of God to hate sin more than any object in the universe, and particularly to hate sin far more than pain; and benevolence requires him to express this hatred, for otherwise it cannot enter into that system of moral influences by which he is guiding the world to its salvation. The only fit expression of this hatred is eternal punishment.

d) In the long run, benevolence requires what is fit and just; and eternal punishment fits eternal sin.

e) Facts confirm the supposition that benevolence requires eternal punishment. In proportion to men's conception of the evil of sin they are convinced of the eternity of punishment. Even men who doubt it are obliged to use the scriptural threatenings to the evil-doer. The tendency of men is to form low estimates of any punishment that will end; eternal punishment is adapted to this peculiarity of the human mind.

7. The veracity of God proves eternal punishment.

Up to this point we have been busy with the rational argument which Park brings in favor of the doctrine. With this head he passes to the biblical doctrine; for it is his position that the Bible, which is God's word, has plainly declared that there will be eternal punishment, and hence if God has told us the truth—that is, if he is Truth himself—punishment for some must be eternal. As this is, after all, his decisive argument, we shall trace it somewhat carefully.

a) Some sins are certainly threatened with eternal punishment, as the sin against the Holy Ghost (Matt. 12:31, 32), the sins "unto death" (I John 5:16, 17), and those who fall away into wilful sin (Heb. 6:4–8; 10:26, 27; II Peter 2:20–22).

b) Some sinners never will be saved, e. g., Judas (John 17:9–12; cf. Mark 14:21).

c) The Scriptures declare that some men receive their good things chiefly in this life (Luke 6:24; 16:25; Ps. 17:14).

d) The Scriptures declare that men of a certain character shall not be saved (John 3:36; Luke 14:24).

e) The Scriptures declare that some men shall perish, or be destroyed (II Thess. 1 : 9, etc.).

f) Some sinners shall be subjected to the action of instruments of punishment which shall be eternal (Matt. 3:12, etc.).

g) The circumstances under which sinners are said to be excluded from the kingdom of heaven imply the doctrine of eternal exclusion (Luke 13:23–28; Matt. 7:21–23; Luke 16:26. Note that there is no intimation in these passages of repentance upon the part of the excluded.).

h) The doctrine of election implies hopeless punishment of the non-elect.

i) The constant and great contrast between the state of the righteous and the wicked.

j) The express assertions that the punishment of the wicked shall be eternal. (1) The only works which writers of the New Testament had to express eternity (αἰών, αἰώνιος), they used. (2) The same words are used to express eternal misery as to express eternal happiness, or (3) to express the eternal attributes of God. (4) The same words are used to express the happiness of the righteous and the misery of the wicked in the same verse (Matt. 25:46). (5) As to the words αἰών and αἰώνιος the predominant usage is in favor of their meaning unlimited duration. When not so used, their signification is limited by the nature of the thing to which they are applied, or by positive announcements. There are no such limitations in respect to these words when used of future punishment. Our own use of the words "always" and "forever," "eternal" and "eternity," corresponds exactly to the biblical usage, and will suggest the modes in which they are used in the Bible.

k) The Bible has taught the doctrine of eternal punishment in every way consistent with its style. It never says "eternity in the strict sense of that word," but that is not the style of the Bible. It does, however, teach it by assertion and implication, in positive and negative forms, with all variety and great intensity. It could do no more.

Thus we close our review of the greatest of the New England systems. For logical concatenation and power, for argumentative force, for comprehensiveness, for genuine liberality in the treatment of principles and the emphasis placed upon the essentials, for clearness and luminousness of discussion, and for loyalty to the great doctrines of evangelical theology, it is unsurpassed, if not unequaled, in the history of Protestant dogmatics. It is a permanent loss to the cause that its author did not himself issue it in the form of a treatise. Its defect was its failure to compose the strife between the idea of liberty involved in its fundamental theory, that of the nature of virtue, and its theory of the will. Park did, as we may believe, the best that can be done with the elements which had been delivered to him. His failure at this point forces irresistibly upon us the question as to the possibility of success in the task which New England theology had set before it—to free Calvinism, while it still retained its characteristic features, from the paralyzing load of a doctrine of inability. Our task will therefore not be done till we have raised this question.

CONCLUSION

CONCLUSION

We have now traced the rise, course, and culmination of New England theology as a distinct school of thought. But nothing is more remarkable about it than its collapse. At the beginning of the year 1880 it was in control of all of the theological seminaries of the Congregational denomination, with possibly a single exception, and of some of the Presbyterian. At Andover the chair of theology was occupied by Park, at Yale by Harris, at Oberlin by Fairchild, at Chicago by Boardman. Fifteen years later these teachers had all been replaced, and in no case by a man who could be considered as belonging to the New England school. It had endured more than 150 years; it had become dominant in a great ecclesiastical denomination; it had founded every Congregational seminary; and, as it were, in a night, it perished from off the face of the earth. For this remarkable and almost unprecedented phenomenon there must be some instructive explanation.

In this concluding chapter, therefore, we retrace our steps from the beginning, in the effort to gain that wider understanding of our history which the multitude of details may have hindered us from gaining hitherto, and which shall disclose to us the secret of its fateful termination.

The history of Calvinism presents to the historical student, and presented to the slowly awakening consciousness of our fathers as they themselves lived through a portion of it, a mighty indictment against the system. It seemed in its beginning, when men felt themselves the elect of God and predestined to the pulling-down of strongholds, a powerful incentive to faith and activity. It hurled the scanty forces of a half-drowned Holland against the mightiest empire of the day in the Eighty Years' War, and gave them victory. It tore at the same time an empire from the grasp of Austria. It elevated England to the position of the leading European power. It created English freedom. This was all upon a great scale; but it could also fire the hearts of the humble and enable them to effect great things, and had forever laid its claim to the grateful appreciation of America when it created out of the peasants of Scrooby and Bawtry in Yorkshire a church which had the energy to face exile and the unknown dangers of a new continent for their faith's sake. Thus activity might seem to be of its very essence. But experience in the new land, as well as elsewhere, had shown that this was not so. It so conceived the sovereignty of God and so obscured human freedom that it exercised, when operating in any locality undisturbed for a long period, a paralyzing effect upon human initiative. Assisted, as this effect was in New England, by the influences of a frontier situation, it proved well-nigh fatal to the churches. Theology was gradually strangling life. This was the more so because, again, the system proved itself to be non-ethical, laying stress upon the external, and not encouraging—sometimes discouraging—attention to the inner meaning of spiritual processes, making holiness a state, entered into by justification consequent upon an experience essentially mysterious—faith—and consisting in an attitude of the soul and not in its activities. What was holiness in itself? The system had no answer. What were the virtues? Temperance, meekness, love, etc., said the system. Why was temperance a virtue, and by what law were its demands to be formulated and interpreted? There was no answer. How shall I live a holy life? Do this, that, and the other thing, replied the system. Thus all was external; not so much so as Rome had made it, for faith was still emphasized, and in some way souls

whom God had touched still found their way to personal,
face-to-face communion with him. The soul could not pass
from the cradle to the grave without an inquiry as to its
real possession of grace, as it could in the old church;
but under forensic justification and the "imputation" to a
man of both sin and righteousness which were not his, his
salvation was in great danger of being a thing in which,
however great his concern, his part was little or nothing.
The indictment was that the system was injurious to practical religion.

This indictment was reinforced by the tendencies of the
times. New forces were entering into the thought of the
world, and of the New World across the Atlantic, during
the century in which Calvinism was on its trial there, and
was getting its sentence. In 1637 Descartes had introduced
the appeal to consciousness into modern philosophy, and
under Locke (1632–1704) it had become domiciled in all
English thinking. Consciousness had given a new doctrine of freedom, as we have traced in the pages of Locke
himself, which was destined to become more and more
clamorous till it got a real recognition from leading thinkers. A new religious experience had come in, manifesting
itself in world-wide revivals beginning with Edwards in
America and with Wesley in England. Gradually a new
ethical sense, and a great vision of the true meaning of
virtue and holiness, had dawned upon the philosophic and
religious mind. And, above all, the new method of dealing
with the objects of thinking, introduced by the long neglected treatise of Francis Bacon (1620), the inductive, the
exact antithesis of the characteristic method of Calvinism,
had received a powerful impulse from the work of Sir Isaac
Newton (1672, etc.), and was soon (1778) to show its
importance in the epoch-making discoveries of Lavoisier.
All this ferment of thought meant much more for Cal-

vinism and for religion than the protest of Arminianism had meant, though at first it took the direction of assisting the Arminian movement onward. It meant in New England a thoroughgoing criticism of the system and its essential modification.

The study of the history just completed has shown us what New England attempted to do. Seizing upon these new instruments of thought, the Fathers sought to restate the old theology in such a way as to obviate objections and yet maintain it in all its great central positions. The correctness of Calvinism in general was not questioned. It seemed so clearly the meaning of the Scriptures, and their religious experience so thoroughly sustained its leading principles, especially its great determining principle, the sovereignty of God; it was, further, to so large an extent the common conviction of the Protestant theological world, that they did not suspect that perhaps these new principles of thinking might lead really away from Calvinism to something quite different. Radical as the positions of some of our divines were, they always seemed to themselves conservative. They were defending—in a new way, possibly, but still defending—the old system. Till near the last they all clung to Westminster as they clung to Edwards. To make the old armor still more impervious and still more efficient was their purpose and their hope.

Incidentally they effected some great things—to which it will be best that we turn before we pass to the greater question of their ultimate success. The conservative tendency led at first to the denial of the freedom of the will by Edwards. Still in him even the tendency of the day toward a real freedom was so strong that he gave man practically a much larger freedom than his theory allowed. The new principle of consciousness, the more it was consulted, spake the more clearly for freedom; and hence the school went on, by very gradual steps, and with many a digression, but steadily, toward a better doctrine, till it met with a certain check, upon which it paused, hesitated, and fell back into the old Edwardean determinism. They also ascribed a real character to God in teaching that his moral attributes were comprised in love, which was a choice, and a choice of something which we can understand, viz., the highest good of all sentient being. God was thus made an intelligible and imitable being, and taken at this vital point out of that realm of mystery which may favor a certain kind of rapture on the part of devotees, but is fatal to a rational and enduring piety. Probably no service that the school rendered surpassed this in importance. To uproot that whole view of God which spoke of his arbitrary will as if it might effect anything, and culminated in affirming that even the distinction of right and wrong depended upon the divine fiat, and to construct our idea of God from the nature of man whom God had made in his own image, was vital to the maintenance of religion. For religion is at bottom communion with God; and we cannot commune with a being totally unlike ourselves, and who might have made us the exact opposite of what we are. They thus ethicized theology, and threw a flood of light upon the nature of faith, regeneration, conversion, justification, prayer, the divine government, and the atonement. They necessarily broke down thereby the forensic system of Calvinism and introduced a new era of practical activity in the church. Thus Edwards was the greatest evangelist whom New England had ever known; Hopkins first suggested foreign missions, the direct result of his work being that current of interest which produced the hay-stack prayer-meetings and the American Board of Commissioners for Foreign Missions; Woods, a Hopkinsian, formed Andover Seminary; the New England ministers became the founders of that wonderful belt of colleges, Marietta, Oberlin, Olivet, Illinois, Beloit, Iowa, Tabor, etc., etc., and of that chain of churches of the Congregational order, which now extend from Albany to San Francisco. Whatever else the school did or failed to do, it made it necessary that the theology which should replace it should be primarily ethical, both in its doctrine of man and of God.

Another such service which the school rendered was in preparing the way for a comparatively peaceful and easy transition to the new order of things when new tendencies of thought came in to dominate the mind. Whether competent itself to serve the new age or not, it made the way open for some other one to serve it. It had familiarized the New England mind with the idea of theological modification; and men could hence believe that in the strange proposals of Darwinism there might, after all, be some germs of improvement. When the storms of biblical criticism burst upon the American world, there was genuine panic in denominations which had been trained under a less liberal system; but Congregationalism, especially when it had been taught by Park to lay stress upon the religious contents of the Bible in distinction from its outward form, could await with great patience for the outcome of the scholarly investigations of trusted leaders, and could even afford a refuge to scholars from its Presbyterian daughter-church, like H. P. Smith, till the stress of persecution should be overblown. With its elastic system of maintaining ortho-doxy, it could waive for a time insistence upon points of doctrine as to which there was actual question among competent thinkers, and emphasize essentials. While at the present writing (1906) the outcome is by no means clear, and the "new theology" of this day is still quite nebulous, it may fairly be said that Congregationalism is in a state of theological peace, and that its doctrinal discussions have not seriously affected its practical efficiency in the nation or in the world. The temper of mind which has produced this happy condition of affairs, and the denominational atmosphere which has rendered it possible, are the gifts to the new time of the school of thought which has now passed from view.

All these are wonderful achievements, upon which it would be a happy lot if one were permitted to expatiate. But the theme presses to the answer of the question: Was the school crowned with a real success upon the largest scale? Was its *theology*, were its distinctive *theories*, its systematizing *principles*, of permanent value? Or did its collapse, so sudden, and so complete, prove that it had failed, and was essentially incapable of propagating itself?

We m.st reply (1) that it failed when it sacrificed freedom to the Calvinism of the old system. Calvinism exalts the sole causality of God; and New England theology found a scheme of determinism essential to the maintenance of that causality. It felt the force of the argument from consciousness for freedom; and that argument almost carried the day. But to save the Calvinism, at last the word went forth for determinism; and when the new theology uttered this fiat, it pronounced at the same time its own judgment. Determinism belongs with materialism. The church was moving onward to a conflict such as it had never seen, with materialism in philosophy and with the materialistic spirit in practical life. On the one side stood the theory that the body is the man; that there is no soul, but all his thoughts and passions and purposes are the fruit of his brain; that, therefore, every human phenomenon stands under the strict law of cause and effect. Every deterministic theology is the unconscious ally of this theory. On the other side stood Christianity, teaching that man is an immortal and spiritual being, possessing a body as the organ of impressions and of activities, and possessed of personality and freedom as his inalienable characteristics. The Christian church knew it needed a philosophy which could sustain this position. It needed a clear doctrine of freedom, practical and theoretical. When New England theology refused to give it such a doctrine, the church turned away from it. The church also turned away from the other survivals of an *a priori* conception of God, from the contradiction with the theory of virtue and with the ethical conception of God which lay in the idea of God's unchangeableness, absolute foreknowledge and absolute decrees, etc. The drift of all the vital new thoughts was away from Calvinism; but New England theology still professed to be, and was, Calvinistic. This was its condemnation.

(2) This trouble lay in the *a priori* character of much of the reasoning with which the system was still defended. Never was a theologian more determined to pursue the *a posteriori* method than Park; but even he had *a priori* suppositions upon these topics which infected his system. The theology had not fully grasped the meaning of the inductive method, because it did not yet know what it means to obtain the facts upon which an induction can be based. It had no conception of such processes of research as those by which Darwin got at the facts upon which he founded his theory of evolution. Its failure to appreciate Darwinism largely flowed from its failure to understand how comprehensive and thorough his experiments had been. However hospitable some of the leaders, like Park, were to all new ideas, and however careful to clear the way for any future prevalence of Darwinism, still the system was too fully committed to a multitude of presuppositions, such as the special creation of each human soul, and the entire separation of humanity from the animal world in dignity and meaning, to be able to survive the triumph of evolution as

a philosophy of man and of life. It made its children able to sit down to the patient investigations that lay before them in sociology, psychology, and nature; this was its immortal service. But it had not itself entered into the new inheritance.

Neither did it succeed (3) in answering fully the questions put it within its own circle as to the central doctrines of the Christian system. The Unitarian questionings were not met, but the evangelical doctrines carried by a *tour de force,* by a mere appeal to authority; and at the same time they were depotentiated in the interest of a partial answer to these questionings. It was no wonder, then, that the "new theology" of 1880 on depotentiated the Trinity still further, inclined away from a true incarnation, and preserved only the shadow of an objective atonement. If these tendencies were to be made a cause of reproach to anybody, that reproach must fall primarily upon our elder new theology. Its failure to get any satisfactory answer to the objections to the doctrine of depravity, its reference of the corruption of human nature to a "divine constitution," its blindness to the help offered it in its last days by the Darwinian doctrine of heredity, further accelerated the day of its own rejection. A theology which resorted for the defense of the most important Christian doctrines to an *ipse dixit,* even if this self-contained and unanswering authority were that of the Bible, was thereby condemned—yes, self-condemned, since its great principle and the driving force of its long theological labors had been that whatever was biblical was therefore rational.

Hence there were three things in particular which it was a pressing necessity that New England theology should do:

1. Abandon the Calvinistic conception and use of the sovereignty of God in favor of a new recognition of the facts of human nature.

2. Readjust itself to an evolutionary view of revelation and of human history.

3. Introduce the new idea of a living, and not an abstract, God into its Christology.

As a practical fact, the leaders of this theology were unable to do these things. When their successors came into our theological chairs, they found they could not do their manifest professional duty and make use of their predecessors' labors. It was necessary to begin again. Just as the old exegesis was antiquated by a new point of view of all theological themes, the old theology was also antiquated. So far as the theology built upon the old at all, it was involved in vagueness and confusion. Even such leaders as Samuel Harris, who were themselves substantially upon the New England basis, felt compelled to build their identical theology upon other foundations and with other instruments. The pupils of Harris took the new foundations, and newer still, and built something which was also new. And thus New England theology perished from the earth.

Perished, at any rate, for the time. The questions of the present hour are still more fundamental than those with which New England theology or its immediate successors have had to concern themselves. A ringing call is sounding through the air[1] to face the true issue, the reality of God's supernatural interference in the history of man versus the universal reign of unmodified law. The question is not whether the old evangelical scheme needs some adjustments to adapt it to our present knowledge, but whether its most fundamental conception, the very idea of the gospel, is *true*. A religion founded upon God's self-revelation of himself, or a pure rationalism by which truth in religion is attained as it is in physics, or any other realm of knowledge—these are the antitheses. Before this all the half-way compro-

---

[1] For example, in George B. Foster's *Finality of the Christian Religion*.

mises of the present day must be given up. Men must take
sides. They must be for the gospel or against it. Evasions
as to the reality of the evangelical miracles must be abandoned. Criticism which renders every individual lineament
of the portrait of Christ uncertain must put an end to its
indefiniteness and either give us a Christ, or, confessing that
it knows nothing reliable about him, must attempt the
formulation of a theology which has no Christ except as
it has a Socrates and a Confucius, if it can.

What the future may hold, no eye of man can discern.
But if this great contest be decided in favor of the evangelical theology, then the fundamental distinctions by which
the New England Fathers sought to define the holiness of
God and bring the virtue of man into harmony and likeness
with it, their emphasis upon the work of Christ, their better
conception of the freedom and activity of man, will no doubt
receive renewed attention. If the interval shall have suf-
ficed to break certain illusions which they cherished, it will
not have occurred in vain. The future evangelical theology even of New England will not be "the New England
theology," but to it that theology will then be found to have
contributed some of its most important principles.

"Except a grain of wheat fall into the earth and die, it
abideth by itself alone; but if it die, it beareth much fruit."

INDEX

INDEX

(Figures starred indicate the principal reference, often containing the biography of an individual.)